The Poetic Logic of Administration

D0146099

This volume is an investigation of the most important organizational forms of our time, both theoretically as well as practically. Central to this investigation are four main trends: the rational bureaucracy, the human network, the harmonious system, and the strong culture.

The Poetic Logic of Administration provides a new and challenging picture of these organizational forms. Difficult to capture in common logical terms, they appear to follow a certain pattern – a "poetic logic". The forms are enacted in various ways and are marked by different conceptions of the world, such as the metaphorical and the ironical, and by different explanatory ideas.

In this way, Kaj Sköldberg's book contains a rhetorical analysis of the styles of modern administration and their changes. Interpretations and critical re-evaluations of individual approaches, including their "gurus" and current importance, are included in an overarching analysis.

Various forms of efficiency and effectiveness are discussed, and examples are given from both the private and public sectors.

Kaj Sköldberg is Professor in Business Administration at the School of Business, Stockholm University.

Management, organizations and society
Edited by Professor Barbara Czarniawska
Goteborg University, Sweden
and
Professor Martha Feldman
University of Michigan, USA

Management, organizations and society presents innovative work grounded in new realities, addressing issues crucial to an understanding of the contemporary world. This is the world of organized societies, where boundaries between formal and informal, public and private, local and global organizations have been displaced or have vanished, along with other nineteenth-century dichotomies and oppositions. Management, apart from becoming a specialized profession for a growing number of people, is an everyday activity for most members of modern societies.

Similarly, at the level of enquiry, culture and technology, and literature and economics, can no longer be conceived as isolated intellectual fields; conventional canons and established mainstreams are contested. Management, organizations and society will address these contemporary dynamics of transformation in a manner that transcends disciplinary boundaries, with work which will appeal to researchers, students and practitioners alike.

Contrasting Involvements
A study of management accounting practices in Britain and Germany
Thomas Ahrens

Turning Words, Spinning Worlds
Chapters in organizational ethnography
Michael Rosen

Breaking through the Glass Ceiling
Women, power and leadership in agricultural organizations
Margaret Alston

The Poetic Logic of Administration
Styles and changes of style in the art of organizing
Kaj Sköldberg

Forthcoming

Court and Spark
Deal-making on the borders of basic and applied research
William Kaghan

The Poetic Logic of Administration

Styles and changes of style in the art of organizing

Kaj Sköldberg

London and New York

Every effort has been made to contact copyright holders for their permission to reprint material in this book. The publishers would be grateful to hear from any copyright holder who is not here acknowledged and will undertake to rectify any errors or omissions in future editions of this book.

First published 2002
by Routledge
11 New Fetter Lane, London EC4P 4EE

Simultaneously published in the USA and Canada
by Routledge.
29 West 35th Street, New York, NY 10001

Routledge is an imprint of the Taylor & Francis Group

© 2002 Kaj Sköldberg

Typeset in Times New Roman by Exe Valley Dataset Ltd, Exeter
Printed and bound in Great Britain by TJ International Ltd,
Padstow, Cornwall

British Library Cataloguing in Publication Data
A catalogue record for this book is available
from the British Library

Library of Congress Cataloging in Publication Data

Sköldberg, Kaj, 1942–
    The poetic logic of administration: styles and changes of style in the art of organizing/
Kaj Sköldberg.
    p. cm. — (Management, organizations and society)
Includes bibliographical references and index.
ISBN 0–415–27002–2 (hardbound)
1. Management. I. Title. II. Series.

HD31 S5748 2002
658—dc21   2001040815

ISBN 0–415–27002–2

... scientists, too, produce works of art — the difference being that their material is thought, not paint, nor marble, nor metal, nor melodious sound.

— Paul Feyerabend

Contents

Figures

A note on footnotes

There are two basic systems for references and footnotes. One is the Harvard system, where name of author(s) and year of publication are placed in brackets within the text; there is no place for digressions or supplementary comments in this system. The other is the Oxford system, where both references and digressions/comments appear in footnotes (at the bottom of each page, or end of the chapter/book, as here).

The disadvantage of the Harvard system is that the text is weighed down by references to the literature. Moreover, information can be lost by excluding the opportunity for commentary. The disadvantage with the Oxford system, on the other hand, is that the reader is continually forced to jump between the text and the notes, as there is no way of telling whether they contain just a reference or a comment on the text.

In this book the Oxford system is used, but with a minor innovation of my own designed to avoid the inconvenience just referred to: notes containing only references are marked simply by a number; notes containing commentary are marked by a number followed by a close-parenthesis sign. This character is not added to notes beginning with expressions of the type "For instance", "E.g.", "Cf.", "See", "See also" etc., since these short introductory terms cannot be regarded as comments on the text.

Some brief remarks on the terminology of the footnote apparatus: "ibid". is an abbreviation of *ibidem*, the Latin for "in the same place". This means: "In the same place as in the immediately preceding footnote containing a reference." It usually refers to a place in a text (a page number) but may also refer to an entire book, or even to several books. For reference to a different page in the same book specified in the immediately preceding note, the term "op. cit.", short for *opere citato* and meaning "in the work cited", is employed. "Passim", used on only a few occasions, means "frequently"; it denotes that the word or expression has been used throughout the work in question. "f." means "and the following page"; "ff." means "and the following few pages". Thus "pp. 131 f." refers to pages 131–132, and "pp. 131 ff." refers to page 131 and the following few pages.

Finally, in notes and references to books written before 1900 I have added the original year of publication (e.g. "Vico, 1963/1744").

Preface

This book treats four main approaches to our way of viewing and designing organizations: as bureaucracies, human relations, systems, and cultures. A complementary discussion of organizational performance is also conducted. Examples are provided from the private and public sectors. These areas have been thoroughly researched, and one might ask what remains to be done, except for adjustments in detail. But a closer study indicates that things are not quite what they seem. . . . Thus, practically everything in this book is new, from re-evaluations of the particular approaches, including their "gurus" and their current importance, to the overall analysis. The fundamental idea is to investigate the *styles* of organizing and their changes.

A number of conventional truths, or received views, prevail about the four organizational approaches. To reach behind these myths, which in course of time have inevitably come to overlay the originals, it is necessary to go back to the primary sources: these should be studied on their own terms, with an analysis combining understanding from within with critique, familiarity with distanciation.[1]

The four approaches have each emerged as trends or fashions[2] during the twentieth century, and they are still very topical, both in theory and practice. But from where do these different fashions come? To give an answer to this question I shall conduct what might preliminarily be called an analysis of organizational style, or with the same words as in the title of the book, an investigation into the poetic logic of administration.

A fully rationalistic model of their development appears to be chimerical, yet the idea that the fashions would just appear quite inexplicably one after each other is also unsatisfactory. Here, inspiration can be drawn from the eighteenth century Neapolitan philosopher and social researcher Giambattista Vico. He investigated the transformations of human societal forms in general, and held the view that they could not be analyzed by means of traditional logic; nor, however, were they totally incomprehensible, but could be studied by employing a *poetic* logic.[3] In his *Metahistory*, Hayden White took up this thread, further developed the poetic logic, and used it on nineteenth-century historiography.[4] This book applies such a poetic logic to the field of organization theory and practice; it also develops the poetic logic – particularly the dramaturgical and narrative aspect of it – a bit further by making more extended use of some of the ideas of the literary theorist Northrop Frye.[5] As suggested earlier, this involves a kind of analysis of style, something which appears particularly well suited to investigating how fashions arise and develop.[6]

Chapter 1, the Introduction, provides a first outline of the framework of analysis, the poetic logic. Chapter 2 goes deeper into this and into the whole issue of the styles of organizing. Chapters 3–6 provide interpretations, critiques, and "poetical" analyses, of each of the four organizational approaches. Chapter 7 discusses the problematic of organizational performance, and is also a critical presentation combined with poetic analysis.

The book is aimed at three categories of readers (in no particular order): first, researchers; second, organizational practitioners and people with a general interest in organizations and management; third, university students in the fields of organization theory/business administration. It is written so as to be accessible to all three categories of readers.

Chapter 6 on organizational cultures is based largely on an article in the Danish management journal *Ledelse og Erhvervsøkonomi* (previously *Erhversøkonomisk Tidsskrift*). I thank the editorial board for permission to use this material.

My greatest thanks go to Martha Feldman, who as an editor of the book has been instrumental in bringing it to its present shape. Her never-failing help and encouragement have been invaluable to the process of carrying through this project.

Many people have taken the time to read parts or the whole of the book at various stages, from both a research and teaching perspective, and I wish to extend my thanks to them. Sven-Erik Sjöstrand had the kindness to invite me to a seminar at the Stockholm School of Economics, to lecture about the book. The seminar led to a considerable number of revisions and additions to the manuscript; it particularly inspired me to develop and deepen the analysis of organizational styles into dramatic genres – something which proved to be perhaps the most entertaining phase of the work. It also meant that I further developed and more precisely specified both the book's general purpose as well as its conceptual apparatus. Kristo Ivanov provided me with consistent moral support and encouragement. Barbara Czarniawska supplied written comments which hit the nail right on the head. Mats Alvesson both offered his overall opinions and made an in-depth study of the chapter on organizational cultures. Hans Stenlund, Department of Statistics, University of Umeå, specially reviewed the section on Joan Woodward. Lennart Rosenberg read through the entire manuscript and offered valuable and, as usual, deeply influential comments. Special thanks are due to my colleagues and students at Umeå and Stockholm universities, many of whom have commented on the text in its various versions.

Jon Kimber translated a first version of the book.

Kaj Sköldberg
Stockholm, November 2000

1 Introduction

In modern society, pervaded by organizations and organizational networks, powerful trends in administration and management will by necessity come to exert a crucial influence. Over time, a limited number of such "grand" organizational approaches have appeared, setting the tone for organizational theorists and organizational designers alike: the rational classics, Human Relations, the systems view, and the culture perspective. Later approaches have not replaced previous ones, but have rather been superimposed on them; as a consequence, all four are still very much with us today, both in theory and practice. Studying such important processes should be highly relevant, not only to organization and management theory but also to social science in general. How do these approaches emerge, and how do they take on their varying characteristics? Previous research has largely abstained from answering this question in an integrated way. The present book contends that the approaches emerge and take their shape, following a specific pattern – a *"poetic logic"*.[1] In other words, there is a logic to the processes; this logic, however, is not one of formal rationality, empty of meaning, but rather that encountered in poetics and dramaturgy.

Such an inquiry can be placed within a broader current of ideas. Poetics – i.e. literary theory or discourse on literature – as applied to texts other than those of fictional literature has drawn increasing interest during the last two decades.[2] Postmodernism and poststructuralism have drawn our attention to strongly textual and narrative aspects of seemingly rational conceptions and theories[3] (although at the price of often exaggerating these, even to the point of textual reductionism).[4] It is possible to make a rough distinction between the poetics of metaphor and the poetics of narrative, even though these two are often combined in practice.[5] In the study of organizations and management the poetics of metaphor saw a breakthrough in 1986, with Gareth Morgan's highly influential book, *Images of Organization*. Metaphors in organizational cultures have been a popular focus of interest, as have stories and narratives *in* organizations.[6] The poetics of organizations and organization theories *as* narratives has also evoked interest,[7] as has the aesthetics of organizations.[8]

The present work aims at integrating the poetics of rhetorical figures, or tropes (of which metaphor represents one), and the poetics of narrative, in discussing the various organizational vogues mentioned above. In what follows, not only the general characteristics, but also the inner structure of each of the four approaches – including its inner contradictions and incoherencies – is explained from the same poetic logic. Further, the texture of individual organization theories and practices *within* the particular approaches – including the tensions and inconsistencies of these theories and practices – are similarly explained from the influence of the overarching pattern of the poetic logic, together with their belonging to a certain approach. In addition, a discussion of organizational performance in the same 'poetic' mode serves to complement the investigation.

Organizational styles: a poetic logic

More particularly, this book purports to show that, rather than being the products of rational, scientific, or scholarly deliberations, the major organizational approaches constitute variants of different *organizational styles*. An organizational style consists of a particular *style of thought*, a corresponding *organizational drama*, and a corresponding *method* (see Figure 1.1). This triad is inspired by – and freely adapted from – Hayden White's book *Metahistory*, in which he traces the poetics of eighteenth-century historiography.

The style of thought is the dominating element in the triad; that is, it colours the method as well as the organizational drama. In the figure, this is symbolized by the top position in the triangle of the style of thought. This also provides an additional explanation of the term, style of thought. As to the two remaining elements of the triad, since they constitute aspects of organizational styles, we should, to be more exact, also have used the terms "style of organizational drama" and "style of method". For the sake of simplicity we speak instead of these as organizational drama and method.

The styles of thought can be identified as the *main rhetoric figures*, or *master tropes*. Research has shown that these are not mere superficial

Figure 1.1 Organizational styles: a poetic logic.

Figure 1.2 The order of the tropes for the organizational approaches.	*Figure 1.3* The general order of the poetic logic.

ornaments of language, but that they mould our very way of thinking. There are four master tropes, or styles of thought. *Metonymy* expresses the relation of contiguity between external elements. *Metaphor* is the trope of similarity between two items, and, since the similarity is essential rather than superficial, captures the inner meaning of things. *Synecdoche* focuses on the relation between whole and part. *Irony* expresses opposite meaning. The main organizational approaches are imbued by these styles of thought in turn (see Figure 1.2).

In course of time, the 'scientific' Metonymic style of thought becomes dissatisfying for those researchers or practitioners in the tradition of the rational classics, who have discovered that there is also an inner meaning; the Metaphoric approach is a natural result, in this case manifested in Human Relations. As the drawbacks with this individual-centred approach become apparent, a perspective with a more Synecdochic orientation towards the whole organization makes its appearance, as the systems view of organizations. Finally, there is a relativistically Ironic and anti-rationalistic backlash against all the earlier approaches – the culture perspective.

With one interesting difference, this process coincides with the general order of the poetic logic (Figure 1.3), which Vico – the eighteenth century Neapolitan philosopher – had proposed as the general, cyclical development of human societies. In our time, White discovered the same poetics both in nineteenth century historiography and in Foucault's theory of the transformations of the humanities.[9]

This general order is a natural consequence, as knowledge might reasonably be supposed to start with naive symbols based on similarity; move on via criticism to external differences; proceed through insight into the inadequacies of these to integrated wholes; and end up in scepticism towards previous phases. (Then it is time for a new cycle . . . .)

It is the contention of this book that external impulses, whether they be of ideational or material character, are not the prime movers behind the different organizational approaches. On the other hand, they may very well *overdetermine* them: i.e. have an impact on the form in which the tropes find concrete expression (see Figure 1.4). In this book I have concentrated on the deep structure – the tropes – rather than the overdetermining factors, since the former constitutes what is fundamental and primary. A discussion of the influence of the ideas of natural science has been the only extra element incorporated, for this explains not only the reversal of the tropological order relative to the normal sequence of poetic logic (see Chapter 2) but also certain other phenomena which are hard to understand *within* the various organizational approaches.

Now let us look a little closer at the other aspects of organizational styles – dramas and methods. The styles of thought (master tropes) constitute basic pictures of reality (ontological conceptions). A particular style of thought can find expression in two ways in an (organizational) text: both through *what* is said – i.e. the form of presentation, kind of story; and through *how* this is/should be arrived at – i.e. the working procedure. In the former case, we speak of organizational drama, in the latter of method. Thus, an organizational drama is a narrative about something. The organizational drama provides a characteristic course of events. The method is a way of investigating this "something". The method argues for a certain specific selection of facts and a certain way of interpreting these facts (a model of interpretation). Note in particular that both organizational drama and method are employed by *theorists and practitioners alike:* Whether they speak of, or act within, organizations, on the one hand they create narratives, in theory or in practice;[10] on the other, they select facts and interpret these in specific manners.

Our style of thought, our fundamental perspective on reality, sets its stamp on the way in which we present organizations, the drama within which

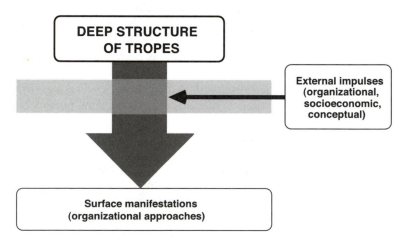

Figure 1.4 Deep structure, surface manifestations, and external over-determination.

we enact their world. If there is a story to be told, be it of organizations, personal computers, or the Court of King Arthur, it must be structured in some way. Over the ages, a number of fixed narrative structures have crystallized, and any potential narrators will have imbibed these since birth, in both writing and speech. When they then set about doing a presentation of their own, these structures will be used, either consciously or unconsciously. These are the ones that are readily at hand; and, above all, they are the ones that have proved to be effective. Even the teller of an organizational tale has to make use of them, and it is this that is captured by the term, organizational drama.

In the present text, we use four basic organizational dramas.[11] The first is *Tragedy*, which does not necessarily need to be sad, but which basically tells a story of the regulation of a rule-less state. The second is *Romance*, which revolves around the quest of the single hero. The third is *Comedy*, which – contrary to Tragedy – tells the story of the dissolution of a regulated state; a dissolution which expresses the happy end of this drama. The fourth is *Satire*, which obviously satirizes all the rest. As each organizational drama narrates a characteristic course of events, various *genres* can be discerned within the dramas, according to which phase in the process is most prominent – beginning, middle, or end.[12] These genres will not be presented here, but are described as they occur in the different approaches.

The method includes both the *interpretive model* used and the particular types of *facts* selected. These two elements are intimately related. The interpretive model always seeks to track down a special type of relation, which is regarded as essential. We call this *the basic relationship,* for two reasons. First, it is basic to the method in question. Second, it expresses a relation between, on the one hand, that which is studied (that which is to be grounded) and, on the other, the ground on which it is maintained that the phenomenon under study rests.[13] In other words, the interpretation in each model – e.g. causal explanation or understanding – is designed to reveal the ground sought behind the immediate object of study. In turn, the latter – the immediate object of study – determines which types of facts will be picked out. Positivists, for example, adhering to the Scientistic style described below, prefer to select quantifiable and analyzable facts; hermeneuticians, on the other hand, embracing an Idiographic style below, favour those that are qualitatively meaningful.

Among the four methods,[14] the first, *Idiographic*, typically deals with qualitative in-depth studies of single cases. It is often contrasted to the quantitative, measuring *Scientistic* style, which distills laws from isolated data. The third method is the *Functional*. It is finalist in nature, explaining a certain part from its function in relation to the whole, as a means to an end. The fourth method, the "*Contextualist*", is concerned with the general spirit or atmosphere pervading a certain community.[15]

Naturally, there are no water-tight bulkheads between story-telling and investigating, between organizational drama and method. The kinds of selections of facts and the model of interpretation we have available will, to a certain extent, affect the production of narratives at both ends. This is because the selection of facts makes up the raw material of the process, while the model of interpretation gives the final texture to the product. The semi-manufactured product, the organizational drama, which lies between them, must of course be governed by its raw material and its destination. And the other way round: if we subscribe to a certain kind of story in advance, "the semi-manufactured product", this tends to determine the kinds of facts we choose and the model of interpretation.[16] Thus, there are correspondences between different organizational dramas and methods, and these correspondences themselves correspond to different styles of thought.

Figure 1.5 provides a summary of the main tropological properties of the four dominant organizational approaches we study, in the order they occur.

The differences between the four organizational styles can also be illustrated by considering them on two dimensions: *focus* and *perspective* (see Figure 1.6). Behaviour focus and meaning focus refer to an orientation towards external behaviour and internal meanings/interpretations respectively. By a micro or macro perspective is meant a concentration on particular individuals or the organization as a whole. The separative organizational style concentrates on the individual – the micro perspective – and on external behaviour. The expressive also adopts a micro perspective, but focuses more on the inner meaning put into the plot. The integrative is oriented towards the organization as a whole – the macro perspective – but treats action from an external behavioural standpoint. The permeative takes the entire organization into consideration, and focuses on the inner, meaningful side of the plot.

The separative organizational style is characterized by Metonymy, Tragedy, and Scientism. The expressive organizational style features Metaphor, Romance, and Idiography. The third, comprising Synecdoche, Comedy, and a Functional method, was designated as integrative. The fourth and final organizational style, marked by Irony, Satire, and Contextuality, is termed permeative.

	STYLE OF THOUGHT	ORGANIZATIONAL DRAMA	METHOD
THE CLASSICS	Metonymy	Tragedy	Scientistic
HUMAN RELATIONS	Metaphor	Romance	Idiographic
THE SYSTEMS PERSPECTIVE	Synecdoche	Comedy	Functional
THE CULTURAL PERSPECTIVE	Irony	Satire	Contextualist

Figure 1.5 The poetics of the organizational approaches.

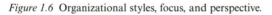

	Behaviour focus	Meaning focus
Micro perspective	SEPARATIVE	EXPRESSIVE
Macro perspective	INTEGRATIVE	PERMEATIVE

Figure 1.6 Organizational styles, focus, and perspective.

These different organizational styles have historically been incarnated as *variants*, in the form of four main organizational approaches: the rational classics, the Human Relations movement, the systems approach, and the cultural perspective.[17] These variants therefore express different, not mutually exclusive, sides of the whole of the organization. In individual theorists, and in individual organizations, the variants are mixed to a greater or lesser extent, but for reasons of stability one of them generally predominates. *Concrete organization theories* (for instance, Taylor's Scientific Management or Mintzberg's theory of management) and *concrete organizational designs* (such as Human Resource Management or cultural engineering) exemplify – more or less pure – forms of the variants in question.

Preview

Chapter 2 deals with the organizational poetics, the styles and the dialectics of the book. First we consider the choice of organizational approaches in this study, and argue for the importance of these, in both theory and practice. Next, the deep structure of poetic logic is presented; correspondences with and deviations from the actual development and formation of the organizational approaches are commented upon and discussed. After this, various alternative interpretive models are considered, and it is argued that these are less applicable than the poetics used in the present book. Following this, two separate sections are dedicated to the possible use of root metaphors and paradigms in the present context. It is contended that root metaphors can be seen as possible outflows of organizational styles, rather than the other way around; and that paradigms largely fail to capture the plurality of organizational approaches. Then we argue, instead, for the utilization of styles and stylistic analysis for the present purpose. The styles prefigure thinking before rational deliberation can even enter into the picture, and this – prefiguration – is the subject for the next section. Then issues of relativism and aspect-seeing are discussed, and, following this, social constructionism and textual reductionism. The tropes of organizational time are taken up after this, as a further support of the thesis in the present book. The penultimate section deals with dialectics, a subsidiary methodology used in the book. Finally, the relationship between dialectics and poetics is discussed. It is argued that there is an inner core of identity between these two, which also sheds new light over, and motivates, why the four rhetorical figures of the poetic logic have emerged as master tropes and been used in this inquiry.

Chapter 3 contains an analysis of the rational classics as a variant of the permeative style. Taylor's scientific management is discussed, as is Fayol's Principles of Administration, Weber's bureaucracy theory, and Simon's organization theory. It is argued that scientific management and the Principles of administration follow the separative organizational style rather closely, as this style has been described above. Each corner of the separative triad finds expression in these organization theories. The general style of thought is the Metonymic; things and people are conceived as isolated items with only external relationships between them, and as the raw material from which to extricate general, rational laws. Both scientific management and the Principles of administration are stamped by the Tragic drama, and both in the radical, utopian, genre which we shall term triumphant. Their method is Scientistic, based on collecting and measuring data, which are then used for explanatory purposes.

The case of Weber's bureaucracy theory is more complex, marked by inner tensions and contradictions. Here, the general style of thought is no longer Metonymic but Metaphoric, centring on the inner meanings of individual social actors. The organizational drama is Tragic, but in another genre than the previous ones. Rather than the radical utopias of (social) engineers, such as Taylor and Fayol, Weber's Tragedy was sombre and dystopic, yet at the same time even more characterized by iron necessity, determinism; the genre is the *fatalistic*. Often, though, the border is crossed to the *demonic genre*, in which latter human dignity is horribly tortured and mutilated by the bureaucratic machinery. The method is split between the Idiographic and the Scientistic, which are placed in an uneasy complementary relation to each other.

In Simon, the last of the classics, we encounter a Metonymic style of thought, where the organization operates as a "mechanism" – a word that recurs time and time again – for influencing the individual through decision premises, which are "injected" into her.[18] For Simon again, the individual is unfortunately equipped with "limited rationality"; an irrationality which the organization strives/should strive to place under "control" by influencing decision premises. Thus, Simon's organizational drama was primarily Tragic, albeit in softened form, and the laws of fate were revealed in the cleft between absolute and limited rationality. But in order to cement these laws, Simon was forced to labour with two organizational dramas: first the afore-mentioned Tragic decision-making machinery on which the bulk of the stage lighting falls, second a Comic shadow-play, namely the contribution-remuneration system, which, through its equilibrium, guarantees that the individuals remain in the organization, thus ensuring that they are able to take the decisions in question. This duality leads to discontinuities of style which express themselves as inconsistencies in the depths of his theoretical construction.

The law is brought to light through the method. In Taylor and Fayol this was Scientistic by nature. In Taylor it found expression in a pronounced interest in – almost an obsession with – the measurement of job movements, and the construction of the laws to accompany them; in Fayol, in traditional empirical induction, likewise leading to the formulation of laws. Weber combined what was principally an Idiographic method, comprising case studies and comparative procedures, with a Scientistic method, involving ideal type construction and statistical analysis. Simon's method, based on logical empiricism and operationalism, was thoroughly Scientistic.

Chapter 4 investigates the Human Relations movement, whose main organizational style is the *expressive*, but which went through three different phases. It was initially grounded in a Metonymic style of thought, taking its point of departure in scientific management's Tragic organizational drama and a Scientistic method manifested by measurements of physical relations in the Taylorian tradition.

However, their own research results forced the researchers into a Metaphorical style of thought, in which the meanings of the individual person are placed at the centre. This induced them to change method and adopt an Idiographic technique, involving interviews with individuals and interpretations of the meaning with which they charged their perceived reality. Human situations were assumed to be Romantically transformable by means of the changes it was possible to effect in the social attitudes of the individual.[19]

The theoretical message of the Human Relations movement culminated in a third phase combining Synecdoche and Metaphor, i.e. a form of systems thinking based on units imbued with meaning. However, the combination of the two styles of thought was incomplete, because of a deficient assimilation of the Synecdochic style of thought and its systems perspective. These Synecdochic deficiencies meant that the emphasis in Human Relations' style of thought was placed on the Metaphor. Moreover, as we shall see, the deficiencies in the Synecdoche created weaknesses in the Functional method with circular reasoning as a result.

In the organizational drama, this combination of styles of thought found expression in a Comic Romance – the so-called *social system*, a humane and meaning-laden organization, where everything in the long run promotes equilibrium and the best interests of all. The genre is, more specifically, dualistic. It describes two worlds. The one is temporary and unreal, marred unfortunately by a variety of flaws, such as misunderstanding and conflicts. These arise through the Comic blocking characters who succeed in forcing their compulsions on others; in this case management's excessively narrow demands for financial profitability which lead to meaningless, conflict-generating rules and decrees. The other is the real and Romantically idealized world, characterized by self-realization and harmony beyond all unnecessary misunderstanding – in the extreme case as mild and free of conflict as the idyllic world of bucolic poetry.

Chapter 5 looks at the the systems perspective, as a variant of the *integrative* organizational style. Its organizational drama is Comedy. Oppositions – "dysfunctions" – that culminate in an all-embracing and reconciling harmony are its central theme, but also the property for which the perspective has attracted the severest criticism.

The perspective is characterized by a Functional method and way of arguing; i.e. explanations relate particular phenomena to the overarching unity, and the interesting question for this method becomes which "function" the particularities have for the whole.

The trope which provides the ground for this is Synecdoche, whose style of thought relates the part to the whole. This, however, is only the general picture. In particular authors we find interesting tensions. Burns and Stalker are marked by a discrepancy between, on the one hand, an organizational drama enacted as comedy and, on the other, a Contextualist method. In Woodward we find a corresponding clash between a Comic organizational drama and a Scientistic method. In both, however, the genre is the dualistic comedy, with a clear presentation of the two different states of the drama – in this case the mechanistic and the organic. In both, contingency also serves as the *eiron* figure, which promotes a happy (i.e. successful) ending. In Burns and Stalker this role is played by environmental uncertainty, in Woodward by technology. By contrast with Woodward, Burns and Stalker also give significant scope to the opposite characters, the blocking characters who obstruct the path to the happy ending; they appear here as the power and the status system.

Lawrence and Lorsch generalized and codified the terminology of these classical works into a more sweeping systems conception – what they called contingency theory. Thereby, however, much of the richness of the classics was lost. The Aston school led the orientation in a more Scientistic direction through studies of organizational structure and its context. Child, with his concept of strategic choice, sharply criticized contingency theory from a Romantic perspective. On the other hand, a Romantic reform movement within the framework of Comedy was constituted by Weick's loosely coupled systems, Cyert and March's coalitions, and March *et al.*'s organized anarchies with the garbage can model of decision-making. Their genre was that of the disintegrating comedy, where the transition to Romance lies close at hand.

Mintzberg and his pupil Miller, in their metamorphosis theories, extended the range of possible system states beyond the two posited by the classical theorists (mechanistic or organic).[20] Mintzberg achieved a satisfactory balance between a Synecdochic style of thought, with a Comic organizational drama, and a Functional method. Miller subscribed to the same style of thought and organizational drama, but employed a Scientistic, mathematical/statistical method, something which lent a fruitful tension to his art of presentation without verging on discontinuity of style. The genre of both is picaresque – an uninterrupted and unprincipled, but never tragic and (because of its complications) never boring journey between different states. The genre pulls in certain respects towards Irony and Satire. In terms of method a question mark can be placed over a certain fragility in the factual bases employed by both Mintzberg and Miller.

Chapter 6 takes up the culture perspective as a variant of the *permeative* style. This is characterized by a Satiric mode of presentation, which demonstrates the intrinsic *irrationality* of organizations. More specifically, the genre is anti-intellectual, or quixotic Satire, which can also glide over into a more or less conservative, conventional Satire. The explanations are Contextualist, and investigate how the culture, a transparent and homogeneous medium, colours particular features of the organization. Irony, the underlying trope, expresses the illusory nature of our naive conceptions of reality (and thereby the naivety in the three other tropes): the world is the *opposite* of how it appears; there is another world of concealed meanings behind what we see, a kind of invisible atmosphere, which, as mild as it is unobtrusive, permeates every particularity in the environment and, with a sceptical smile, thwarts our most ambitious plans and calculations. Just as striking is the Ironic feature of sceptical *cultural relativism:* there are in principle however many cultures as you like, and one is worth as much as any other.

There is a built-in tension in the cultural perspective due to an underlying conflict between Irony as style of thought and the perspective's Contextualist method. Irony is the trope of dialectics above all others; it excels in paradoxes, as it already in itself expresses a contradiction. Contextuality, by contrast, requires an inner unity, where the opposition is focused instead on an external, naive conception (and all previous perspectives are naive). In the cultural perspective the harmonizing method of Irony has generally emerged victorious from the battle with its dialectical style of thought. The perspective has thereby come to overemphasize absence of conflict in and the unity of organizations, at the expense of what I have called the dialectics of symbolism. And this tendency is reinforced by the need of the Satirical organizational drama, as of all dramas, for at least some inner coherence of plot (albeit that the need here is less pronounced than in other cases). The result is that the quixotic Satirical genre's striving for renewal threatens to be outflanked by the conventional genre's ideal of stagnation.

Chapter 7 investigates, as a complement to, and an extension of the above, the concept of performance. Four main types of organizational performance are discerned: efficiency, human resource effectiveness, system effectiveness, and mission effectiveness. These have their counterparts in the four categories of poetics – as in the organizational approaches which make up the main theme of this book. In all cases, however, the method is Scientistic, for the underlying definition, "degree of goal achievement", is quantitative by nature. This preponderance of Scientism helps to explain the dominance of efficiency; since this is the type which is the easiest and most non-controversial to measure, and thus best compatible with its method.

- Efficiency
  Metonymy/Tragedy/Scientism
- Human resource effectiveness
  Metaphor/Romance/Scientism
- System effectiveness
  Synecdoche/Comedy/Scientism
- Mission effectiveness
  Irony/Satire/Scientism

The argument that different organizational styles are really no different from each other, since they are all basically out to improve performance, can therefore be countered with the question: "What kind of performance?"

2 Poetics

Styles of organizing

[W]hat we need, perhaps, as Nietzsche said, is a change of "style"; and if there is style, Nietzsche reminded us, it must be plural.

Derrida, *Of Grammatology*

This chapter first discusses the selection of organizational approaches – why precisely these four, rather than any others? Then we present the general matrix of the poetic logic and relate the development of the organizational approaches to this logic, including the deviations between the two – the underlying deep structure and the organizational reality. Next, other possible models of interpretation or explanation are looked at. Thereafter the question of paradigms is discussed. The following section treats the issue of root metaphors, and its place in the present problematic. Then the choice of styles and stylistic analysis is further explained. These styles prefigure our thinking, and the following section goes deeper into what such a "prefiguration" means. After this, since issues of relativism and aspect-seeing touch upon the present inquiry, these issues are critically discussed. The following section goes into the related subjects of textualism and social constructionism. Thereupon, further support for the present interpretation of organizational approaches is given, in the form of *time* and different times in organizations. Then the dialectic stance of this book – complementary to that of poetics – is considered, as well as the dialectical procedure of the study. Finally, dialectics and poetics are interrelated, and it emerges that they are converging lines of thought.

2.1 The choice of approaches

We are going to take a journey through approaches to organizations and organization theory. The overall aim is integration, and an attempt is made to find some sense in the development of the four organizational approaches. Various proposals for such a synthesis have already been presented.[1] By contrast with these, we shall only be concerned with what might generally be agreed to constitute the main trends in twentieth century organization theory. In textbooks, it is usual (with variations in detail) to present the development of organization theory in three phases: the rational classics, Human Relations, and systems.[2),3)] On the other hand, symbolically oriented researchers have described the stages of this journey in terms of "root metaphors", i.e. the basic images which are said to lie behind particular lines of thought: the machine for the rational classicists, the systems metaphor for the systems theorists, and the cultural metaphor for the cultural theorists.[4)]

Thus, there are two conflicting versions, which raises the question of which should apply. These are illustrated in Figure 2.1. On comparing the two, one important similarity emerges: both count the rational classical theories and the systems perspective as main themes in the development of organization theory. This correspondence is highlighted in the figure by putting a frame around the items in question. On the other hand, there are differences between the two accounts: the cultural perspective is lacking in the traditional textbook version, while Smircich ignores Human Relations. However, as this book will show, they have had a considerable influence, both theoretically and practically.[5)] Omitting either from a general account of the development of organization theory does not seem justified.

Thus, a complete picture of the dominating themes of organization theory can only be obtained if the two versions are combined. If we superimpose one on the other, we arrive at the development of organization theory as presented in this book, in terms of four lines of thought: classical theories,

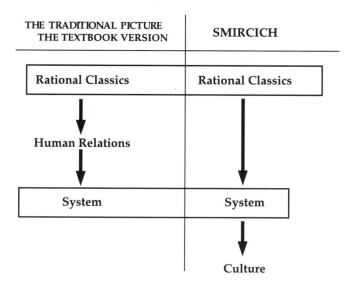

Figure 2.1 Main approaches to organization theory: the traditional textbook version and the Smircich version.

Human Relations, the systems perspective, and the cultural perspective. There may be some doubts whether Human Relations should be included, but a closer study of this provides evidence of its importance (see Chapter 4).

The location of Simon's decision-making school varies, in relation to both the classical theories and the systems approach. For instance, Dessler, 1986, regards it as a "nursery school" for the systems perspective; Scott, 1987, as a classic of our time. These differences can be clarified through the employment of our poetic logic. As we shall see in Chapter 3, the general style of thought and method adopted by Simon is closest at home among the classical theories in that its "organizational drama" is something of a hybrid – with the classical element predominant and the systems perspective subordinate.

It should be emphasized that no claim is made to provide an exhaustive presentation of organization theory. We are concerned with four main approaches to it. One criterion used in selecting these approaches is that they should have had *both a practical and theoretical impact* on the subject; synergy between theory and practice, through which forces of mutual reinforcement and development operate, has been assumed. This means that certain fields of study, which may well have importance in themselves, have been wholly or partially neglected, e.g. the currents of thought that have been influenced by Darwinian evolutionary theory and economic analysis (population ecology and transaction cost analysis).[6] Although both these approaches show promise, neither has been characterized within the literature as a main trend: they are not, for example, as prominent as the cultural approach, which may depend on their lack of practical impact and the accompanying stimulation to theory to which this gives rise. Postmodernism is certainly one of the trends in organization research, but it is not a dominant one.[7]

With respect to the rational classics, Human Relations and the systems approach, our attention has focused on the major figures of the past, those who cleared the way and created the patterns of thought. In these three cases, the research that followed may be far more finely chiselled, but it is still work conducted within an already prescribed framework. On the other hand, the cultural perspective is still too new for its main themes to have been crystallized in such a way; in other words, we do not yet know who the major figures are. (As Hegel used to say, the owl of history flies only at twilight.) This is why the chapter on organizational cultures has a different and more thematic form.

The organizational models and ideas of the rational classics and the Human Relations school are shown to be still topical, and they continue to be employed in practice within modern organizations. These are not just museum pieces – occasionally dusted off out of due respect for the historical background to modern and more relevant lines of thought.

Systems thinking, however, continues to possess so much force that the argument that it is applied in practice need scarcely be presented; one just has to refer to influential, widely used American textbooks (written by some of the most prominent authorities in the field),[8] which are entirely based on this approach. It has simply become the conventional wisdom. These textbooks and other kinds of literature have cemented in future American leaders (of both the private and public sector) the idea that organizations function as systems.[9]

Finally, the cultural perspective – which emerged as a real competitor to systems thinking in the 1980s. Glancing at the financial pages of a daily newspaper, a business magazine, or an academic journal is enough to confirm that the references made to "corporate culture" are legion – and these are made by executives, consultants and researchers alike.[10] Management courses, seminars and conferences on the theme are flourishing.[11] Again, no specific argument is necessary to demonstrate its topicality; the chapter on the cultural perspective is interspersed with illustrative examples of its application.

This book is not designed to present a complete history of the ideas that underlie these four main approaches; nor is there any intention to provide a review of the vast body of secondary literature that surrounds them. Rather, the aim is to employ rhetorical categories to analyze their basic structures, so that an overall pattern of explanation can be obtained. Furthermore, as referred to above, evidence is presented for the continued strength and vitality of the rational classics and the Human Relations approach. Naturally, the taking of a full inventory of the manifestations of these approaches within the modern organizational world is beyond the scope of this book.

2.2 The organizational approaches and the poetic logic

The four organizational approaches, in order of their appearance, can be designated as *variants of the four organizational styles* we introduced in Chapter 1; more specifically, the separative, the expressive, the integrative, and the permeative. The versions offered by the different authors whose works we have presented constitute *concrete organizational theories* within these variants. The order in which the variants occur over time (as represented by the arrow), and their inherent characteristics, is illustrated in Figure 2.2.

As can be seen in Figure 2.3, this historical development coincides rather well with the general matrix provided by the "poetic logic".

There is, however, one difference. The organizational approaches have the *same twelve terms* in the cells of the matrix, but in one case – between the two first phases – there is a *reversal of the sequence:* Metonymy → Metaphor for the development of approaches to organizations, but Metaphor → Metonymy in the matrix. (As the figures show, this reversal also applies to the corresponding organizational dramas and methods.) Can this modification be explained?

We find the key in the special metaphor which, to a not insubstantial extent, has stamped the first, Metonymic phase, namely the machine. The discrepancy can in fact be explained by reference to the external influence of the surrounding environment of thought. The machine metaphor was taken from

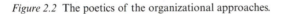

	STYLE OF THOUGHT	ORGANIZATIONAL DRAMA	METHOD
THE CLASSICS	Metonymy	Tragedy	Scientistic
HUMAN RELATIONS	Metaphor	Romance	Idiographic
THE SYSTEMS PERSPECTIVE	Synecdoche	Comedy	Functional
THE CULTURAL PERSPECTIVE	Irony	Satire	Contextualist

Figure 2.2 The poetics of the organizational approaches.

natural science, which had an exceptionally powerful influence at that time. More specifically, the model was that of physics, and in particular Newtonian mechanics with accompanying engineering applications within it. (Indeed, two of the classical writers, Taylor and Fayol, were engineers. The third – Weber – was, as we have seen, despite the basic Metaphorical nature of his thinking, torn between this and natural science's Metonymic style of thought.)[12]

A new branch of science might be supposed to be most sensitive to external influence during its initial phase. The strength of the impact of natural science on the style of thought means therefore that we do not obtain a first, Metaphorical stage, but that the process is initiated by Metonymy.

The continued powerful influence of natural science – even though its absolute prestige and iron grip over minds had to some extent been undermined by the dethroning of classical physics, especially Newtonian mechanics, by quantum physics and relativity theory – also explains the curious *instability* of Human Relations in comparison with the other movements. It flees from Metonymy via Metaphor to Synecdoche, and even touches upon Irony. The process of knowledge must pass the phase where inner meaning is discovered. But it does so at a time dominated by Metonymy,

STYLE OF THOUGHT	ORGANIZATIONAL DRAMA	METHOD
Metaphor	Romance	Idiographic
Metonymy	Tragedy	Scientistic
Synecdoche	Comedy	Functional
Irony	Satire	Contextual

Figure 2.3 The general matrix of the poetic logic.

and where the Synecdochic revolt has already begun. It is pulled between both these fields of force and becomes unstable as a result.

This provides an explanation of why we obtain a "delayed", but still major representative of Metonymy such as Simon. He carried out his work after Human Relations, and during the first flourishing of the Synecdochic phase. The impact of the latter is noticeable in the internal duality of organizational drama we will discuss in his theory.

The tensions in Woodward's work, discussed in Chapter 5, can in a corresponding manner be explained by the prolonged influence of Metonymy (via the Scientistic method) on the Synecdoche which then reigned supreme within the organizational arena.

To summarize: the poetic logic's matrix for the course of events shows a striking similarity to this as it was in fact played out. But there is a minor deviation. The influence of external ideas – the strength of the natural scientific model – does not only explain this minor permutation to which the matrix of poetic logic was subjected on "translation" into the reality of organization theory and practice; it also clarifies certain features *within* the different approaches (as in the cases of Human Relations, Simon and Woodward above). We are thus entitled to nominate the matrix in Figure 2.3 as the *deep structure* behind the development of organizational approaches. This claim will be substantiated in the following chapters.

2.3 Alternative interpretations

The growth of the main approaches to organization theory can be interpreted in many different ways. However, such interpretations are scarce in the literature. What is common, for example, is simply to present the various approaches in the form of a list, without making any attempt to explain its order. This is reminiscent of the chronicles of the Middle Ages, in which events are presented line-by-line in time sequence. Naturally, this is unsatisfactory from a scientific or generally more reflecting perspective. Alternatively, one or several rudimentary interpretive patterns can be presented. The more important conceivable or occurring possibilities are listed below. This is done in strictly ideal-typical form, without reviewing the literature; in reality, the types, to the extent that they appear at all, are presented as fragmented or intertwined with one another.

1 *Correspondence.* Organizations undergo basic changes, which are reflected in our ways of thinking.
2 *Base-superstructure.* Socioeconomic trends in society at large give rise to changes in perspective.
3 *Intra-disciplinary dynamics.* Dissatisfaction with prevailing orientations generates new approaches.
4 *History of ideas.* Ideas from external disciplines cause the changes in approach.

5   *Fashion*. The various trends in organization theory are just passing fads, which cannot be explained rationally.

The two first paths of interpretation can be designated as "materialistic", since they are based on material, economic factors; the latter three as "idealistic", since they are grounded in the development of ideas. They all make *some contributions* to our understanding; nevertheless, they are still unsatisfactory, both severally and jointly.

1   *Correspondence*. Change in the world of organizations over time cannot, for example, explain the emergence of the Human Relations approach in the 1920s, as this would presuppose differences of decisive importance between American companies then and those of the previous decade. Such differences (to judge from the Hawthorne study among others) do not appear to have existed.

2   *Base-superstructure*. A possible explanation for the varying prominence of the different perspectives might be in terms of the business cycle: a focus on the organization's hardware during periods of boom, and on its software during recession. This, however, is falsified by the continued flourishing of the cultural perspective under favourable business conditions. Other explanations couched predominantly in macroeconomic terms tend to incorporate such a wide range of factors that they can only be employed *ad hoc*; in any case, they cannot compete with the interpretation in the present book – in terms of either simplicity or explanatory power. Nevertheless, such factors may well have had a secondary influence. Thus, the interest in various kinds of Japanese corporate culture, which stimulated the culture approach, has quite definitely reflected the problems faced by Americans from competition with Japan.[13]

3   *Intra-disciplinary dynamics*. Naturally, dissatisfaction with a prevailing orientation is involved in some way with the emergence of a new one. But this is not a sufficient explanation in itself, for an endless number of alternatives are conceivable. The question is why a *specific approach* emerges as a reaction to the one that prevails. Why, for example, was it that the cultural perspective became generally accepted as the alternative to the systems approach, and not the "actors frame of reference", which had been proposed earlier?[14]

4   *History of ideas*. If external influences had been decisive, the Human Relations movement and the systems approach would never have emerged; rather, some kinds of positivist orientations would have prevailed. (For instance, at the time of the emergence of the systems approach, it was logical empiricism, a variant of positivism, that predominated.)

5   *Fashion*. Viewing organization theories as fashions[15] has certain similarities with Kuhnian paradigmatic theory – the associations with vicissitudes and irrationality. However, as we shall argue below, Kuhn's theory is not applicable in the field of organization theory, for while new

approaches might come to the surface quite suddenly, they do not replace the old; rather, the latter continue to exist. In other words, by contrast with fashions and paradigms, approaches to organization theory do not *succeed* one another.[16] The limit of the analogy is reached at this point. An interpretation in terms of the irrational emergence of fashionable modes of thought has a further disadvantage: fashions cannot be subjected to rational analysis.

2.4 Paradigms

Why are earlier trends important? Should not the spotlight be on more modern lines of thought? In other disciplines, does not discussion focus on the latest findings – past themes being left to the historian of ideas? Has not Kuhn shown that one scientific paradigm succeeds another, only one being dominant at any particular point in time?[17] Figure 2.4 illustrates Kuhn's thesis that the practice of "normal science" is always marked by the ascendancy of a single paradigm, which is then overlapped and finally replaced by another during a period of scientific revolution. P1 and P2 stand for two different paradigms.

This book, however, is not a treatise on historical doctrines; it is designed to illustrate styles that continue to be prevalent in organization theory. The latter – continued relevance – will be shown to apply for each of the organizational approaches that are discussed in the following chapters. In fact, the development of organization theory cannot be rendered compatible with Kuhn's picture of a single dominant paradigm. By contrast, Feyerabend's image of bodies of ideas in competition with one another seems more appropriate. Followers of Kuhn tend to explain such a state of affairs in terms of the discipline in question not having reached full (i.e.

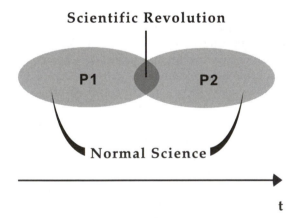

Figure 2.4 The Kuhnian paradigm. Monopoly of ideas for one line of thought within the scientific community.

Kuhnian) scientific maturity; instead, it is designated as "pre-paradigmatic", or even more amiably, as "pre-scientific".[18] Thus, a mature body of scientific thought is always to be characterized by a narrow-minded dogmatism with a monopoly of views favouring a single approach. But this picture is not reconcilable even with the state of theoretical physics in the nineteenth century – the heyday of Newtonian physics – which is otherwise referred to as a prime example.[19]

On a sliding scale of pluralism in ideas, Kuhn's normal science can be set at one extreme, where there is no pluralism at all; at the opposite extreme there is total chaos. Kuhn seems to think that his normal science is: (1) the normally occurring state of affairs; and (2) that which *should* occur.[20] The first thesis (as shown above) does not seem reconcilable with actual conditions; on the other hand, it is not easy to find the opposite, i.e. a state of chaos. It appears, therefore, that an intermediate state with a limited number of competing perspectives is the most common – although, of course, it is impossible to rule out *a priori* that any one perspective will gain a monopoly. The latter, normative thesis, which in Kuhn's work is consistently difficult to distinguish from the former (Feyerabend, 1985), can also be disputed; research is favoured by healthy pluralism – not by dogmatism (or chaos). Lysenko, who dictated the study of biology in the Soviet Union during the Stalinist period, thus managing to destroy for decades the subject of genetics as it was practised in his country, is hardly an ideal role model. This should not even need to be pointed out, but I have personally heard authoritarian researchers use Kuhn's thesis as an argument – how nice it would be to get rid of all uncertainties and contradictions!

On account of its Kuhnian associations, Feyerabend does not use the term "paradigm";[21] however, both for the sake of simplicity and for ease of comparison, we have used the denotations P1, P2, P3, and P4 in Figure 2.5. In accordance with the account we have presented above, these four (P1, P2, P3, and P4) can be identified as the rational classics, Human Relations, the systems perspective and the cultural perspective. Figuratively speaking, these are all flowers still in bloom; though their roots in the past are of different lengths. Earlier principal trends in organization theory, as has been shown, also constitute modern currents of thought. They remain in perfect health and have a major role to play, both in theory and in relation to practical private and public activities. Figure 2.4 requires modification to reflect this fact.

Thus, as is shown in Figure 2.5, Feyerabend's pluralistic picture more faithfully reflects the theory and practice of organization theory than does Kuhn's alternative image. Note that the new orientations occupy some of the space of the old, but the old are not entirely suppressed: at time point 1, for example, four principal current lines of thought coexist.

More generally, there are semantic problems relating to the concept of paradigm, which has been subjected to sharp criticism for ambiguity. A certain degree of ambiguity is acceptable and unavoidable, especially with new concepts. But in the case of paradigm, this is so extreme that the

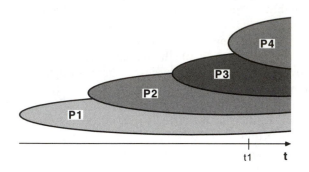

Figure 2.5 Organization theory. New themes take root, prosper, and coexist with others.

concept threatens to fall apart into its separate components, the more so since different aspects of its meaning seem partially inconsistent. In a study of the subject, Margaret Masterman distinguished 21 different meanings, which can be grouped into three mutually inconsistent main categories.[22] By virtue of the multiplicity of more or less conflicting images, such an intellectual hall of mirrors is confusing rather than rewarding.

Finally, it should also be taken into consideration that Kuhn, under the impact of criticism in the form of empirical counter-examples, has been driven step by step to dilute his thesis: from concerning actual revolutions, via "micro revolutions", to the point where "revolution" or "paradigm shift" has become synonymous with scientific change in general, and thereby lost their distinctive meaning.[23]

What remains of Kuhn's thesis, then, is that scientific theories often constitute relatively coherent systems possessing a certain inertia against change. But these general observations are too unspecific to be of practical use. An alternative might be Toulmin's theory of conceptual systems emerging through a process of natural selection.[24] Theories of natural selection, however, wrestle with unresolved fundamental problems – over what is meant by the "survival of the fittest" on which they are based; they run the risk of ending up as tautologies.

2.5 On metaphors

A description in terms of (root) metaphors might appear plausible at first sight, and has had great impact in organization research.[25] Nevertheless, it is not satisfactory in the present context. We can accept the machine metaphor of the classics – if we bear in mind that both Taylor and Fayol warned against using this in a blinkered manner.[26] Neither system nor culture, however, can be regarded as *metaphors* in any real sense; moreover, as concepts they are too abstract, non-visual. Rather, they are theoretical constructions, under which concrete organizations can be subsumed. As pointed out in Chapter 5, the systems perspective has two separate main sources: the biological concept of an organism and the theory of servo-mechanisms. Thus it cannot be captured with one root metaphor, since neither organism nor servo-mechanism will do *per se*. (But even were we to reduce the two sources to one, this would not do, because neither of these sources are metaphorical; rather, they are theories at a more abstract, non-sensuous level.)

It could be objected that all concepts *as such* are metaphors, since they are expressed with the aid of language and all language ultimately is metaphorical. Such a conception might seem reasonable, but its information value does not exceed that of the tautology, since all concepts then *by definition* = metaphors. Moreover, the definition makes two unjustified reductions: first, of concepts to language; and then, of language to metaphors. But concepts and language are not the same thing, which is demonstrated most simply by pointing to the fact that different languages have different words for the same concept; and, conversely, within the same language there can be the same word for different concepts. (Cf. also the well-known "conceptual triangle" of word-meaning-object, Ogden and Richards, 1956.) Nor can words "ultimately" be reduced to their meta-phorical origins, since their meaning content may have been completely transformed. A good example is "culture", which originally had to do with the cultivation of the earth; but this original meaning has long since disappeared when we talk of a national culture, organizational cultures, etc. As Hegel, 1952/1807, had already pointed out, we must distinguish between the sensuous-metaphorical and the abstract level of thinking.

The so-called root metaphors – which are rather close to an interpretation in terms of fashion – then appear merely as possible manifestations of our poetic matrix.[27] In the culture approach, for example, a great number of metaphors for culture are conceivable, and are found in the literature: exchange-regulator, compass, social glue, sacred cow, manager-controlled rites, affect-regulator, non-order, blinders, world-closure, dramaturgical domination, etc.[28] *Thus, although this is a common conception, it is not the metaphors that determine our thinking;*[29] *rather, the metaphors are themselves expressions of the underlying tropological categories.*

Moreover, in sociology in general, by contrast with the more limited field of organization theory, five root metaphors have been discerned:[30] mechanism, organism, play, language and drama. These, however, can be viewed as concrete illustrations of our tropes. The first two exemplify, or express, the tropes of Metonymy and Synecdoche. Play can express several different tropes, depending on the nature of the game, e.g. Metonymy (von Neumann and Morgenstern's game theory) or Irony (the later Wittgenstein's language games). Language is what poetics as such is concerned with. The dramatical form of presentation is a category of analysis for our poetics: Romance, Tragedy, Comedy or Satire.

2.6 Styles

Thus, we are seeking something that resembles fashion, but more than the latter is associated with the (prolonged) coexistence of emerging rivals, and also can be inquired into in a systematic way. The solution to the problem can be illustrated by looking at reliefs of the Arch of Constantine in Rome, from the years AD 313–15 (see Figure 2.6). The two roundels at the top – a wild boar hunt and a sacrifice to Apollo – are from an older epoch, dating from 117–38.

They constitute "elegantly suave examples of the Hellenized art favoured by the Emperor Hadrian, delicately cut, naturalistic, vivacious and graceful".[31] The frieze below, featuring the first Christian Emperor, Constantine, is in sharp contrast; its deliberate clumsiness and crudity, in particular the disproportionally large size of the heads of the figures, can be noticed immediately. For victorious Christendom, love of God was of greater importance than the Hellenic worship of worldly beauty; and a person's body less important than his or her immortal soul (as expressed by the size of the head). Nevertheless, these two styles could coexist on one and the same monument.

A further example: most readers will certainly remember Doric, Ionic and Corinthian columns from their history lessons at school. That these styles succeeded each other in time did not prevent them from being used conjointly later on – as, for example, in the best-known ancient building of all, the Colosseum, with "the ascending sequence established by the Romans for multi-storey buildings – Doric-Ionic-Corinthian".[32]

Thus, *styles* in the history of art, which appear after one another in time, are capable of coexistence. And here, referring back to our discussion in the Introduction, we have a striking parallel to the development of approaches to organization theory. Moreover, the emergence of these different approaches, if they are conceived as styles, need not be seen as something wholly irrational and inexplicable. On the contrary, it becomes relevant to employ an analysis of styles to attempt to find some "meaning in the madness". Use of our poetic logic involves just such an analysis of styles.

2.7 Prefiguration

As the basic conception of reality may be supposed to set its stamp on other parts of the thinking, it takes just a short step to interpret the figures of rhetoric, the tropes, or the styles of thought, as the primary category and the two others – the organizational dramas and the methods – as secondary. The tropes constitute "basic types" through which a field of research is "prefigured".[33] This prefiguring is pre-*critical,* pre-*cognitive* and pre-*analytical*, poetic by nature.[34] That is, before we even begin to conduct a rational analysis of a particular part of reality, we have already structured this within tropo-logical frames of reference by virtue of the style of thought we have adopted.

Figure 2.6 Reliefs from the Arch of Constantine in Rome, AD 313–315. (Photo: Alinari)
Reproduction by permission of Alinari Archives, Italy.

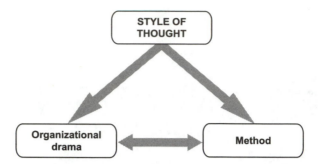

Figure 2.7 Style of thought, organizational drama, and method: dialectical relations.

Naturally, these frames influence our choice of method, just as they do our way of describing the particular part of reality with which we are concerned (in our case, organizational drama). The latter are therefore secondary. But they are not simply a mechanical reflection of the basic style of thought; rather, shifts, with dialectical tensions as a result, can take place between style of thought, on the one hand, and choice of method and, in our case, organizational drama on the other (and between the latter two as well). In Figure 2.7, the arrows have been drawn with discontinuous lines to symbolize the possibility of such shifts and tensions.

This then has the consequence that a given "discourse", in our case on organizations,

> should not be regarded as a mirror image of the set of events that it claims simply to describe. On the contrary, the . . . discourse should be viewed as a sign system which points in two directions simultaneously: first, toward the set of events it purports to describe and, second, toward the generic story form to which it tacitly likens the set in order to disclose its formal coherence considered as either a structure or a process.[35]

Thus, beyond a naive epistemological realism, our basic frames of reference also come into play. The reality is no longer "copied" onto a blank sheet of paper, a *tabula rasa,* but is always already structured, prefigured. And this prefiguring takes place through the four master tropes. But, from this perspective, by contrast with a current postmodernist conception – e.g. Derrida's – according to which there exists nothing but texts and the inter-play between these,[36] texts always refer to something external, in our case to the organizational reality. This referral, however, is never a simple mechanical reflection, but always constitutes a two-way play where language and reality meet each other in innumerable, ever more complex and varied *confrontations*: this is Vico's dialectic, which is not the dialectic of the syllogism (thesis, antithesis and synthesis) but rather the dialectic between language and the reality it seeks to contain.[37]

2.8 Relativism and beyond

Hayden White, whose work has been an important (if freely adopted) source of inspiration to the present book, takes the view that the four tropes are of equal value as representations of reality, and that we can choose whichever of them, according to inclination, taste and fashion.[38] This may seem plausible, and is also in line with a strong contemporary current against grand theories and absolutist solutions. At closer look, however, White seems to have ended up in Irony, one of the tropes he himself employs as analytical tool.

His conception certainly has the advantage of transcending the various dogmatic schools of thought which present their own tropological category as the one and only saving faith, while dismissing all others as unscientific, ideological etc. On the other hand, it expresses a cognitive relativism which ultimately results in irrationalism: one description of reality is no better than any other, and which we choose is simply a matter of taste.[39]

Here we return to the "aspect-seeing" which has become popular in the wake of the later Wittgenstein, Hanson and Kuhn.[40] Take, for example, the influential and well-known drawing that can be interpreted either as four elephants drinking out of a trough or as a four-leaved clover. Alternatively, there is Wittgenstein's "duck/rabbit", "the witch/the beauty" and a number of other familiar examples. What do these figures *really* represent? The conventional and unchallenged answer is that there is no such reality, just different aspects. Q.E.D. Thus, the moral is that of sceptical relativism: there is no truth, perhaps no reality, only different aspects which we lay on top of an intrinsically kaleidoscopic actuality.[41]

This line of thinking is based on regarding different aspects as mutually "inverted meanings" and is therefore, as argued in Chapter 1, an expression of the trope of Irony. These double-aspect figures *are* actually nothing else but visually represented, Ironic statements.

The reasoning is hypnotically convincing. Yet, a less conventional response might be that the figure "really" is an artefact, a puzzle picture which has been created for the specific purpose of presenting either a four-leaved clover or four elephants. But *reality* is no puzzle picture; in reality we always have the opportunity to transcend given boundaries by gathering further data on the object of study, on the spatial and temporal context, on relevant theories, etc.

The interest taken in elephants by aspect-seeing philosophers is also manifested in the Indian fable of "the five blind men and the elephant": five blind men are presented with an elephant and each of them touches a different part of its body. They draw quite different conclusions as to what kind of animal it is.

In the same way as with puzzle pictures, the analogy with human formation of knowledge is misleading, since we always have the chance to investigate further, i.e. to touch as many parts of the elephant as is necessary. Against the fable of the elephant, reference can be made to the *actual* fact that a person with a sight impairment, on whom no artificial restrictions are imposed, can find her orientation highly effectively in a dark room, and draw correct conclusions concerning the whole much more quickly than a person with normal sight.[42]

The thesis on aspect-seeing also functions as a boomerang: if it is true, then it is *itself* just one aspect from among many others that can be placed on reality. But if so, it is inconsistent to uphold it as true.[43]

And hereby we return to our organizational styles. These can be seen dialectically as complementary perspectives, which cover different parts of reality. The styles, therefore, do not exclude each other, as in relativistic "aspect-seeing". The truth is the whole, as Hegel pointed out. The separative organizational style concentrates on the individual – the micro perspective – and on external behaviour. The expressive also adopts a micro perspective, but focuses more on the inner meaning put into the plot. The integrative is oriented towards the organization as a whole – the macro perspective – but treats action from an external behavioural standpoint. The permeative takes the entire organization into consideration, and focuses on the inner, meaningful side of the plot. Behaviour focus and meaning focus refer to an orientation towards external behaviour and internal meanings/interpretations respectively. By a micro or macro perspective is meant a concentration on particular individuals or the organization as a whole.

These different organizational styles have in historical terms been manifested as variants, in the form of the classics, the Human Relations movement, the systems approach, and the cultural perspective.[44] These variants therefore express different, not mutually exclusive, sides of the whole of the organization. In individual theorists, and in individual organizations, the variants are mixed to a greater or lesser extent, but for reasons of stability one of them generally predominates. Concrete organization theories and concrete organizational designs exemplify (more or less pure) forms of the variants in question.

Thus, despite the claims for monopoly rights made by the different schools, they have all staked out only their own, restricted side of reality; *quite simply, they have each, in succession, focused on one aspect of organizations.* A comprehensive treatment would require that all sides are encompassed, at both a macro and a micro level, and with both a behaviour and a meaning focus.

Why then just these four aspects, and why have the schools emerged in precisely this time sequence? Well, because they tally with the four tropes: the substrata which ultimately make our reality comprehensible, and in this way create "different worlds". *Thus, rather than in real changes, the organizational approaches emanate from demands for stylistic variation.* Concrete circumstances – conceptual, ideological, socioeconomic, organizational – (over)determine the immediate design, but are secondary.

The classical writers were obsessed with finding methods which were correct under all conditions. (This is reflected, moreover, in the modern concept of "efficiency", see Chapter 7.) However, the methods cannot be seen in isolation from how people function within the organization; nor from

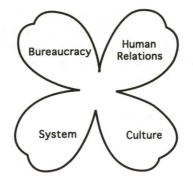

Figure 2.8 The organizational four-leaved clover.

the organization as an open system (comprising components) exposed to the environment; nor from the culture by which the organization is permeated.

Correspondingly, people in an organization cannot be studied separately from the methods which are employed, the open system and the organizational culture. Likewise, the open component-system is bound up with the methods employed, the individual persons and the culture. The culture, finally, interacts with, but is not reducible to, the conceptions of particular people; it affects and is affected by the methods which are employed; and it interacts with the organization in the latter's aspect as an open component-system.

In other words, the different organizational approaches can be jointly presented in the image of a clover, as in Figure 2.8, where each of the clover's four leaves is a part of the whole, rather than a puzzle picture which can only be looked at in just one way at any one time.

This is the first way in which we can avoid the trap which the tropes impose on our thinking; we do not need to confine ourselves to any particular one of the schools of thought.

Moreover, we should remember that each of these four organizational approaches is merely a variant of an underlying organizational style, and that other variants can be envisaged (examples of which, even though they do not constitute main currents of thought, are population ecology and transaction cost analysis, see note 6). We still remain, however, in the four tropes.

But, second, as I shall attempt to demonstrate, there are degrees of freedom *outside* the programme. As soon as we become conscious of the frames, we are in the fortunate position of being able to go outside them: the human being is never absolutely predictable. The critical discussion of the cultural perspective in Chapter 6 points to a way out of the tropological schema by adopting a more dialectical attitude to the interaction of symbols. Here we can link up with the earlier approaches. All four are based on the conception of a *uniform ground:* for the classics, frictionless bureaucracy; for Human Relations, conflict-free human relations; for the systems perspective, the harmonizing system; and for the cultural perspective, the homogeneous, transparent culture.

I shall argue that organizational symbolism is not characterized by unity and freedom from opposition, in other words by a predestined harmony; by contrast, it is fruitful to analyze this symbolism dialectically, through its own conflicts, tensions and changes. This, in turn, provides a way out of poetics' enticing but illusory net of categories.

2.9 Texts and social construction

In this book, I demonstrate how the emergence and shaping of the organizational approaches prevalent in theory and practice can be interpreted as stylistic processes, at the heart of which lie the classical rhetorical figures, or master tropes. So, does this not mean that there is no (organizational) reality "out there", that it is "nothing but" a text, and/or "nothing but" a social construction? This would seem a natural conclusion. However, such a textual or subjective reduction appears a bit over-simplified.

Of course, human activities can be *compared* to texts, and studied as such; yet this analogy should not let us lose sight of the fact that we are making an analogy, which like all analogies has its limits. Human beings and their interrelationships cannot be reduced to signs, and plays with signs, any more than signs can be reduced to people.[45] As to social construction: since it is imbued with social meaning, of course all social reality is socially constructed, but the buck doesn't stop there. As Bourdieu has pointed out, once we agree upon the rather trivial fact that social reality is socially constructed, this is where the really interesting questions begin, which social constructionism unfortunately falls short of.[46] First, how do the social constructions take place? What guiding principles lie behind the social constructions we make? Second, once a certain social construction is made, it eventually begins to live its own life.

The result of the process of autonomization is not necessarily a (pre–)postmodernist Frankensteinian one, of the created being turning against its creator, nor a Hegelian-Marxist one, of bleak alienation, nor a phenomenological one, of silent and towering, block-like restrictions; it may equally well prove to be invigorating, enhancing, or even liberating. The creations of the human mind are often ambiguous but not necessarily out-and-out bad. This is important to point out, not only as a rejoinder to simplistic interpretations of postmodernism, but also since advocators of a general reduction to the level of individuals in social science (e.g. social constructionists) have a tendency to depict patterns at higher levels as (1) something negative; (2) not really existing. The attitude is somehow like that of a parent explaining about ghosts and spooks to a frightened child: they are something bad, but they don't really exist, only in our imagination.

The opinion of the present author is that – in contrast to ectoplasms – organizational styles and the rhetorical figures at their core (a) have an existence of their own, at the supra-individual level, as figments of imagination turned real and (relatively) autonomous; (b) are not *ipso facto* something adverse, but something that we have to study to understand how it works, in order to learn how to be able make the best out of it – but also in order to gain knowledge for its own sake about an important part of the social world.

The recent marriage in some social sciences (including organization theory) between postmodern deconstructionism and social constructionism would be worth a book of its own. The alliance appears to be a rather shaky one, although the tensions have been temporarily glossed over by a mutual penchant for some degree of what a critic might term political correctness. For a true postmodernist, the subject–object dichotomy is dissolved into texts, to the extent that the world consists of texts, or more precisely: there is no world or "reality", only texts and intertextual relationships. For a social constructionist, on the other hand, the world is a construction by social subjects. Thus, in postmodernism texts, and interactions between these, are the ultimate units, whereas social constructionists have individual subjects and interactions between these as the basic elements. (In this respect social constructionism is inspired in the final analysis by phenomenology – a school of thought that has, interestingly enough, been severely criticized by post-modernism [Derrida].) But of course, a subject is not a text, and a text is not a subject, so there is a radical incompatibility between the basic tenets of postmodernism and social constructionism: an incompatibility which in my opinion merits more attention than it has so far received. From the point of view of poetics, this constitutes a clash between Metaphor and Irony, which has not yet succeeded in amalgamating into a really working Romantic Irony, a viable – albeit never easy or stable – fusion between idealism and scepticism.

Nor can this incompatibility be bridged by forging a genetic link between the two, claiming that the subjects are constructed by texts and that they – the subjects – in turn construct reality. Postmodernism has no room for a constructor (whether constructed or not), since the very idea of a stable constructor of a stable meaning turns out to be a chimera: "There is no constituting subjectivity. The very concept of constitution itself must be deconstructed."[47] The meaning of a text is disseminated as soon as it leaves the author. Even the very idea of an "author", or a subject, fails, for it attempts to make a self-identical, stable thing out of an ever-changing, free-playing process of differentiation. The intertextuality of postmodernism provides a shift to an entirely different terrain than that of the subject – and the latter also includes the inter-subjectivity of social constructionism. This is only natural, because the ultimate roots of social constructionism are found in Kant's philosophy of the transcendental ego, and those of postmodernism in Nietzsche's dissolution of the subject or ego.

2.10 Tropes and time

To shed further light on – and to obtain confirmation of – the four tropes of organization as analyzed above, we can refer to the American philosopher

Brumbaugh, who, without referring to poetics of any kind, has put forward a thesis of *four different conceptions of time*. These are:

1   Linear time, divided into discrete units.
2   Cyclical time, with its beginnings and ends of particular processes.
3   Evolutionary time, following an ongoing course of improvement and development.
4   Homogeneous continuous time, where events are regarded as taking place on an immutable continuum.[48]

In linear, discrete time we easily recognize a Metonymic style of thought. What is more, we can directly apply this to the conception of time in classical organization theory – Taylor's fixation with timing devices is the perfect example.[49]

Cyclical time finds its counterpart in a Metaphorical style of thought, focusing on particular phenomena's means of expression and the course of events, from beginning to end.[50] The Hawthorne interview programme and its interest in repetitive work as background to recurring grousing and squabbles is a good illustration. Even more striking is the cyclical concept of *"two equipments" as a "day's work"*[51] – the hub around which the entire investigation of the Bank Wiring Observation Room rotated.

To evolutionary time corresponds a Synecdochic style of thought.[52] The system perspective's image of systems in balanced development despite external disturbances – so-called homeostasis or dynamic equilibrium – is a good illustration of this in the organizational field.

Homogeneous continuous time corresponds to the Ironic style of thought (with its forms of expression), where reality is permeated by a subtle medium, one that stands in opposition to naive observation. The cultural perspective within organization theory is an idealist representative of this, so to say, gelatinous time, in which the world is encapsulated and where nothing really changes:[53] *plus ça change, plus c'est la même chose.*[54] That it is precisely the Ironic style of thought's concept of time which, paradoxically enough, appears as *timeless* is scarcely surprising.

In other words, the tropological categories also colour our fundamental conception of time, something which takes on concrete expression in our way of both assessing and designing organizations.

2.11 Dialectics

In addition to the poetics, this book is imbued with a further tradition of thought – dialectics.[55] Above all, the inspiration has come from Hegel,[56] but also from far earlier thinkers, as dialectics has an ancient tradition.[57] I intend, in another context, to provide a more extensive account. However, as it is not necessary for understanding the themes of this book, I shall refrain from making a detailed presentation here. The following résumé will suffice.

In a nutshell, dialectics is *the discovery and transcendence* of contradictions. In fact, the fundamental feature of dialectics is that it softens up and then crosses petrified limits of thought, even and particularly when these seem to involve radical incompatibilities. In our thinking we are continually compelled to draw boundaries around concepts and categories. Every definition already involves some kind of drawing of boundaries, which excludes more than it permits, according to the Spinozian principle (also adopted by Hegel), "Determination is negation".

What we tend to forget, however, is that the very boundaries of thought which originally helped us in our striving to orient ourselves in reality may be transformed into obstacles over time.[58] The basic idea therefore is to employ critical techniques to break down the partitions between artificially insulated concepts so that we arrive at a conceptual unit lying *behind* the apparent fragmentation. Thus, if we were to provide a succinct account of dialectics (not just Hegel's) it might be the following:

> The consciousness of the Conflict in Reason and the attempt to resolve it by rising to a plane higher than Reason is dialectic.[59]

In relation to the ideas of Derrida, it can be argued, that knowledge advances not only by tearing down systems (deconstruction) but also by building them up.[60] Against Hegel, the argument can be applied in reverse: the process of knowledge, viewed dialectically, cannot culminate in a closed system; rather, there must be a continual and permanent alternation between synthesis and the critical transcendence of boundaries. This position has found expression throughout this book. Nevertheless, Hegel remains the central figure that no modern discussion of dialectics can ignore, despite the fact that the system he constructed – indeed the very idea that such a final "totalization" of the world would even be possible – has crumbled to pieces. In this sense, any contemporary dialectician is by necessity post-Hegelian – not a wholly painless predicament, as is well described in the following elegy over a clarity lost:

> For what readers of Hegel, once they have been seduced by the power of Hegel's thought as I have, do not feel the abandoning of this philosophy as a wound, a wound that, unlike those that affect the absolute spirit, will not be healed? For such readers, if they are not to give in to the weaknesses of nostalgia, we must wish the courage of the work of mourning.[61]

A few words on the Marxist assimilation of dialectics, a full account of which would require several volumes of its own. Here the following résumé must suffice. During his lifetime (the first half of the nineteenth century), Hegel exerted an almost total influence on German philosophy. After his death, the Hegelian school rapidly fell apart into competing right and left factions, the right focusing their interest on his system, which seemed to serve, or at least could be employed for, the purpose of societal conservation.

The left by contrast, with Marx and Engels furthest out on this wing, sought to assimilate his critical, transcendent method into a means for changing the world, and it was within the Marxist left that Hegel's method has come to live the longest, in what might be called pupated form. It might even be said that the Marxist assimilation of dialectics ended up with a new system for the conservation of society, through the conception of historical materialism – but that is another story. It should, however, be firmly pointed out that there is nothing necessarily or intrinsically "Marxist" about dialectics, even though Marx made fruitful use of it, and his and Engels' method in catechetic form (as "dialectical materialism" or "diamat") became the national religion in some countries. But Marxism is just *one* (late) branch on the dialectical tree.[62],[63]

And its relationship to poetics? Here it may be enough to point out, with reference to White, that dialectics by its critically-transcendent nature, encompasses, among other things, the consciousness of plurality, and thereby also the *relativity*, of the categories of poetics.[64] That is, we do not subscribe to any particular one of these categories, but regard them all as possible. By contrast with White, however, we do not view them relativistically as so many aspects of an amorphous reality, but as perspectives which correspond to different sides of an already structured reality. There is also a deeper relationship between poetics and dialectics, as we shall see in the next section. But first a few words of the dialectics of the present investigation.

The remaining chapters of the book are based on a dialectic between understanding and criticism, inspired by Ricoeur's reasoning concerning the deep and surface hermeneutics of historiography – what he calls the "hermeneutic arc" between understanding and explanation.[65] Understanding of the texts "from within" is basic, and the first step. Critique of the texts is founded on this understanding. This is fundamental; a critique that does not treat texts in their own terms is bound to miss its target.[66] The criticism is then placed in a wider context of understanding, which concerns the *deep structure* of the theories studied. That is, contradictions, inadequacies and problems in the texts are explained by reference to an underlying structure. This makes it possible to take a more distanced, critical stance *vis-à-vis* this deep structure itself – to use it rather than be used by it (see Figure 2.9).

Thus, we have two levels of understanding: understanding of the particular texts, and understanding of the deep structures that underlie them. Correspondingly, the critique has two levels: text and deep structure. It is not just de(con)structive; rather, symptoms of the underlying structure manifest themselves as "cracks" in the text, which the structure generates. At the deep structural level critique acquires a *liberating* function: it unties the structural bonds in which we are entangled.

As Figure 2.9 illustrates, to start with, understanding of the individual texts is required. This has a value in itself: as became evident in the present

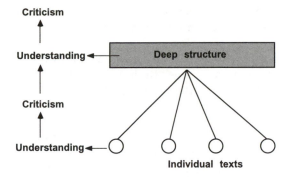

Figure 2.9 The dialectic between understanding and criticism. Individual texts and deep structure.

investigation, they have been subjected to many misrepresenting super-impositions which must be "washed away" for their real face to be revealed. Then we use this understanding of the texts both to critically examine them and to lay bare the underlying deep structure. Through understanding of the deep structure we can also place our critique of the texts in a wider and more fundamental context. Conversely, this structure finds expression, among other things, precisely through the defects in the texts that we find by criticism. In turn, understanding of the deep structure enables us to critically liberate ourselves from it. Thus we have a dialectical process of under-standing – criticism – understanding – criticism . . . .

2.12 Why (these) tropes? Poetics and dialectics

With respect to the path we have chosen, that of dialectical poetics, two critical questions call for resolution before can proceed to the actual investigation of organizational styles. First: Why just (these) four tropological categories? Where do they come from? Others are in fact conceivable.[67] Here, White provides no guidance.[68] Second: What is the *relation between* dialectics and poetics? Are they bound up with each other in some way? Or are they quite distinct models of thinking, baked together into an eclectic cake? Interestingly enough there does seem to be a connection, which goes to the very root of their traditions.

To find the answer to both these questions we undertake a deep dive into the history of ideas, to a dialectic far older than that of Hegel. More specifically, we go back 1,800 years in time to the Indian subcontinent and the dialectics of the *Madhyamika School*.[69] According to this, and its most outstanding proponent, Nagarjuna, there are *four and only four fundamental categories of thought,* of which two are primary and two secondary:

1 Affirmation – i.e. we assert "A".
2 Denial – thus "not A".

These are the two primary: they are based on the ultimate categories Being and Nothingness, existence and non-existence.

3   Affirmation of both 1 and 2, i.e. that phenomena both have and do not have a certain property – thus "Both A and not A".
4   Denial of both 1 and 2 – thus "Neither A nor not A".

These, i.e. 3 and 4, are the two secondary categories.[70] They are derived from the two primary, but cannot be reduced to them (see Figure 2.10).

According to Madhyamika, these four provide the ground for *all* the schools that have been and might conceivably be found within different fields of thought.[71]

Making a comparison with the tropological categories we find the following. According to the poetic logic there are four tropes, which usually emerge sequentially in the order Metaphor, Metonymy, Synecdoche, Irony. These express similarity, difference, wholeness and opposition respectively.

- Affirmation of identity between things and their inner meanings is typical of Metaphor. In this way a relation of meaning between *different* things also becomes possible.
- Denial of this identity, a denial which separates out the things and places them alongside each other without any other connection than that of external causality, characterizes metonymy.
- The submerging of both this identity and this difference into a super-ordinate unity characterizes synecdoche. That is, metaphor and metonymy are integrated at a higher level.
- Denial of both the positive and the negative is the privilege of sceptical irony: there is neither an intrinsic meaning to things nor a purely externalized reality; nor are particularities held in the iron grip of a superordinate system. Instead, they are bathed in a mild but all-embracing light, which in itself is unexplained, but colours all things in

	A	Not A
1.	X	—
2.	—	X
3.	X	X
4.	—	—

Figure 2.10 The fundamental dialectics of thought according to Madhyamika. "X" denotes "Yes" and "—" "No".

the world. In this light, rationality, inner meaning and strong systems all appear as delusions and illusions.

Thus, it becomes clear that the four fundamental categories of dialectics can be conceived as rhetoric's four major ways of expression; or rather, that the four basic categories of dialectics *are* rhetoric's four fundamental ways of expression. Conversely, the four major ways of expression of rhetoric can be conceived as, *or are,* the four fundamental categories of dialectics.

Because of the affinity between rhetoric and the two other main ingredients in our poetics – method and organizational drama – what we have just stated can easily be transferred to the latter.

Murti, like the Madhyamikan dialectics to which he refers, provides rather similar examples from the history of philosophy, even though rhetoric (or more generally poetics) as such is not touched upon in the context.[72] Thus, despite the fact that the two traditions live largely in different worlds there is a convergence at their core.

This theme can be developed through a more concrete example. Madhyamikan dialectics is in fact applied in a number of areas. Of particular interest for our purposes is its analysis of four accounts of causality, listed below with schools of thought in brackets:[73]

- Self-generation, from within the phenomenon itself: *identity* cause-effect, action-result (Samkhya).
- Denial of this, and generation solely from an external source: *difference* cause-effect (Vaibhasika).
- Synthesis of the two above: *unity* between them (Jainism).
- Sceptical denial of all the three above, and thereby of causality itself; events have no rational causes, but just occur, e.g. by chance: *opposite* of the preceding three (Svabhava-vadin).

As we see, the main dialectical categories of causality lie close to the "basic relationships" developed in our discussion of the four methods of poetics in Chapter 1. Thereby, they also provide a good characterization of the types of causality that appear in the four theoretical approaches to organizations we have studied; for the methods of these approaches are variants of those of poetics.

Human Relations (and its later echo in the actors' perspective) saw the source of what happens in organizations in terms of the attribution of meaning by human beings, the inner ground from which actions emanate. By contrast, the causality of the rational classics was external, mechanical; the world consists of discrete, intrinsically meaningless units which affect each other according to deterministic laws. The systems perspective integrated both of these in a (teleological) *functional* causality. Which of the two was applicable depended on which best filled the function of preserving the system, given varying degrees of environmental uncertainty. The cultural perspective takes a sceptical distance from all these types of causality, which explains its irrational tinge.[74],[75]

So, what is the upshot of all this? That a two-thousand-year-old dialectic has been resurrected in modern organizational theory and practice? A new version of the horror movie *The Mummy*? No, but it is scarcely a coincidence that the same four tropological categories which have surfaced in organizational theory and practice have also appeared in nineteenth century historiography, in drama and in modern literature.

This suggests that these categories have a strong hold on our thinking, and that the Buddhist philosophers of old were not simply jumping to conclusions. These men were razor-sharp analysts who devoted centuries of painstaking labour to investigating the mysteries of thought. For them, this offered a key with which to unlock the nature of reality. Madhyamika constitutes the fruits of their efforts.

Nor should it appear as coincidence that the same fundamental categories come up in two quite separate ideational and cultural spheres – in the Western philosophers Aristotle and Vico as rhetoric, in Indian Buddhists such as Nagarjuna in the form of dialectics. This suggests that very basic frames of reference are involved; frames which also shape our modern thinking on organizations.

3 The tragic power machine of the rational classics

In this chapter, we consider the organizational approach represented by the rational classics. We begin by looking at the "concrete organization theories", to use the terminology from Chapter 1, i.e. the main authors within the approach.

First, Taylor and scientific management are discussed. Taylor's passion – or rather obsession – for neatly cutting up and dividing work motions into separate parts marks his style of thought as clearly Metonymic. His drama is that of Tragedy – the movement from an unregulated, crude state of affairs, in this case characterized by the pre-Taylorian regiment of gang bosses, to a well-regulated rule of enlightened groups of educated foremen. Taylor's method, based on measuring motions and establishing scientific laws, is shown to be clearly Scientistic in nature.

Then Fayol and his principles of administration are presented. Fayol's Metonymic style of thought is revealed both in his proceeding from isolated "facts" as the ultimate constituents of reality and in his division of managerial activities, as well as the organizations themselves, into tidily distinguished compartments. Fayol's organizational drama is generalized from his personal experience as a top manager of previously crisis-ridden companies, which are rescued by the application of the principles of administration, thus expressing a Tragic drama with its movement from an unstructured social reality to the discovery and rule of laws. The method of Fayol appears as explicitly Scientist, built on the observation, registering, and classification of facts, in order to establish general rules or principles for administration.

The next section discusses Weber and his theory of bureaucracy and charisma. Weber's style of thought can be characterized as fundamentally Metonymic, proceeding from a fundamental subdivision of reality into separate actions and individuals. His organizational drama is basically Tragic, in that the organizational movement is seen as proceeding from an un-ruled state to a super-efficient, mechanic bureaucracy. This Tragedy, however, has different overtones than in the other rational classics, since Weber regards it with a combination of loathing, or even horror, and fascination. It is, as we shall suggest, enacted in a different genre (or rather, two different genres). Weber's method stands out as more complex than the preceding ones, including traits of both Idiography and Scientism, the former represented by his focus on the qualitative understanding of social action (the typical German *Verstehen* sociology), the second by his suggestion to complement this with a statistical-analysis approach.

A modern classic, Simon, represents the fourth and last name of this group of theorists. Simon's thought style, too, is basically Metonymic, in his case based upon the division of organizational reality into "decision premises" as its ultimate constituent units. His organizational drama is dual. Predominantly it is enacted as a revisionist Tragedy, more sophisticated than in the previous cases, but still Tragic, with the organization regarded as an instrument of power, albeit a subtly hidden power, working through the decision premises. Not without a certain historical irony, Simon criticized the Fayol-inspired theorists for irrationally advocating "rules of thumb" for the governing of organizations. Instead, working from the principles of satisficing and indirectly achieving influence through decision premises, Administrative Man succeeds in making the organization efficient. There is a secondary element of Comedy, though, in Simon's view of the organization as a stakeholder system, balancing various interests against one another. His method, finally, is explicitly Scientist, adopting a logic positivist stance and adhering to operationalism.

After these presentations of the concrete organization theories within the rational classic approach, the continued influence and presence of it is discussed, showing that it still alive and operative in every way (even though we do not subscribe to the claim of some – mostly critical – observers, that the approach is virtually all-powerful).

The chapter concludes with a deepened inquiry, fleshing out the poetics of these organization theories. Here, these are discussed as belonging to the *separative* organizational style. That is, the rational classics constitute a variant of this style, and within this variant, Taylorism, Fayol, Weber, and Simon provide examples of concrete organization theories. Each of these has its special traits, including tensions or mixes within sub-styles (of thought, drama, or method), and often even discernible genres within the dramas. Within the separative style, Metonymy is the ruling trope, or style of thought. It is interesting to note that the issues of power and influence in organizations are crucial to the rational classics – either in open form as in Taylor, Fayol, and Weber, or more indirectly but no less important, as in Simon. This has often led to criticism of élitism against these authors. In fact, according to Vico, the trope of Metonymy is closely associated with just the type of community where there is a sharp division between a ruling élite – an aristocracy – and the broad mass of people:

> This creates a division within socialized humanity both in practice and in consciousness, in that members of the servile class are denied the status of men, are defined as beasts, and are treated as such. . . . For

among the strongest and most powerful and among the weakest and most servile, the social order is sustained by acceptance of the divided social order as being in the nature of things.[1]

There is an affinity between this master trope of Metonymy, the Tragic organizational drama or narrative, and a Scientistic method. Thus, the field is seen to be prefigured by this tropological structure, leaving its imprint on every concrete organization theory developed within this particular style, the first in organization theory and design. This structure is pre-critically, pre-analytically adhered to, i.e. it comes "before" any rational, objective account of "reality". However, displacements and permutations are possible between stylistic elements of the structure, creating interesting and often fruitful imbalances within the poetic field.

3.1 Taylor, the stop watch and the slide rule

We found that this gang were loading on the average about 12 and a half long tons per man per day. We were surprised to find, after studying the matter, that a first-class pig-iron handler ought to handle between 47 and 48 long tons per day, instead of 12 1/2 tons. This task seemed to us so very large that we were obliged to go over our work several times before we were absolutely sure that we were right. Once we were sure, however, that 47 tons was a proper day's work for a first-class pig-iron handler, the task which faced us as managers under the modern scientific plan was clearly before us. It was our duty to see that the 80,000 tons of pig iron was loaded on to the cars at the rate of 47 tons per man per day in place of 12 1/2 tons, at which rate the work was then being done. And it was further our duty to see that this work was done without bringing on a strike among the men, without any quarrel with the men, and to see that the men were happier and better contented when loading at the new rate of 47 tons than they were when loading at the old rate of 12 1/2 tons.

Our first step was the scientific selection of the workman. In dealing with workmen under this type of management, it is an inflexible rule to talk to and deal with only one man at a time, since each workman has his own special abilities and limitations, and since we are not dealing with men in masses, but are trying to develop each individual man to his highest state of efficiency and prosperity. Our first step was to find the proper workman to begin with. We therefore carefully watched and studied these 75 men for three or four days, at the end of which time we had picked out four men who appeared to be physically able to handle pig iron at the rate of 47 tons per day. A careful study was then made of each of these men. We looked up their history as far back as practicable and thorough inquiries were made as to the character, habits, and the ambition of each of them. Finally we selected one from among the four as the most likely man to start with. He was a little Pennsylvania

Dutchman who had been observed to trot back home for a mile or so after his work in the evening, about as fresh as he was when he came trotting down to work in the morning. We found that upon wages of $1.15 a day he had succeeded in buying a small plot of ground, and that he was engaged in putting up the walls of a little house for himself in the morning before starting to work and at night after leaving. He also had the reputation of being exceedingly "close," that is, of placing a very high value on a dollar. As one man whom we talked to about him said, "A penny looks about the size of a cart-wheel to him." This man we will call Schmidt.

The task before us, then, narrowed itself down to getting Schmidt to handle 47 tons of pig iron per day and making him glad to do it. This was done as follows. Schmidt was called out from among the gang of pig-iron handlers and talked to somewhat in this way:

"Schmidt, are you a high-priced man?"

"Vell, I don't know vat you mean."

"Oh yes, you do. What I want to know is whether you are a high-priced man or not."

"Vell, I don't know vat you mean."

"Oh, come now, you answer my questions. What I want to find out is whether you are a high-priced man or one of these cheap fellows here. What I want to find out is whether you want to earn $1.85 a day or whether you are satisfied with $1.15, just the same as all those cheap fellows are getting."

"Did I vant $1.85 a day? Vas dot a high-priced man? Vell, yes, I vas a high-priced man."

"Oh, you're aggravating me. Of course you want $1.85 a day – every one wants it! You know perfectly well that that has very little to do with your being a high-priced man. For goodness' sake answer my questions, and don't waste any more of my time. Now come over here. You see that pile of pig iron?"

"Yes."

"You see that car?"

"Yes."

"Well, if you are a high-priced man, you will load that pig-iron on that car to-morrow for $1.85. Now do wake up and answer my question. Tell me whether you are a high-priced man or not."

"Vell – did I got $1.85 for loading dot pig iron on dot car to-morrow?"

"Yes, of course you do, and you get $1.85 for loading a pile like that every day right through the year. That is what a high-priced man does, and you know it just as well as I do."

"Vell, dot's all right. I could load dot pig iron on the car to-morrow for $1.85, and I get it every day, don't I?"

"Certainly you do – certainly you do."

"Vell, den, I vas a high-priced man."

"Now, hold on, hold on. You know just as well as I do that a high-priced man has to do exactly as he's told from morning till night. You have seen this man here before, haven't you?"

"No, I never saw him."

"Well, if you are a high-priced man, you will do exactly as this man tells you to-morrow, from morning till night. When he tells you to pick up a pig and walk, you pick it up and you walk, and when he tells you to sit down and rest, you sit down. You do that right straight through the day. And what's more, no back talk. Now a high-priced man does just what he's told to do, and no back talk. Do you understand that? When this man tells you to walk, you walk; when he tells you to sit down, you sit down, and you don't talk back at him. Now you come on to work here to-morrow morning and I'll know before night whether you are really a high-priced man or not."

This seems to be rather rough talk. And indeed it would be if applied to an educated mechanic, or even an intelligent laborer. With a man of the mentally sluggish type of Schmidt it is appropriate and not unkind, since it is effective in fixing his attention on the high wages which he wants and away from what, if it were called to his attention, he probably would consider impossibly hard work.

What would Schmidt's answer be if he were talked to in a manner which is usual under the management of "initiative and incentive"? say, as follows:

"Now, Schmidt, you are a first-class pig-iron handler and know your business well. You have been handling at the rate of 12 1/2 tons per day. I have given considerable study to handling pig iron, and feel sure that you could do a much larger day's work than you have been doing. Now don't you think that if you really tried you could handle 47 tons of pig iron per day, instead of 12 1/2 tons?"

What do you think Schmidt's answer would be to this?

Schmidt started to work, and all day long, and at regular intervals, was told by the man who stood over him with a watch, "Now, pick up a pig and walk. Now sit down and rest. Now walk – now rest," etc. He worked when he was told to work, and rested when he was told to rest, and at half-past five in the afternoon had his 47 1/2 tons loaded on the car. And he practically never failed to work at this pace and do the task that was set him during the three years that the writer was at Bethlehem.[2]

This quotation, as long as it is notorious, is taken from a book by the father of the rationalization movement, Frederick W. Taylor, first published in 1911. It shows how the founder of the so-called *scientific management* viewed the "grassroots" of the company, and also which factors within an organization he considered the most important to shape or change. Taylor is also the father of modern organization theory – or rather one of its two fathers; the second is Weber, whom we shall take up later in this chapter.

A closer reading of Taylor makes it apparent that his system has been considerably misunderstood by posterity. This assertion justifies the relatively in-depth study of his work that follows here.

In Taylor's view, Schmidt had two prominent features: greed and stupidity. The first meant that there was a carrot to hold in front of his nose ("A penny looks about the size of a cart-wheel to him"); the second that he could be expected to run after the carrot without reflection. Taylor realizes that this would not have worked with an intelligent person, but with Schmidt, it was possible to "*fix his attention away*" from what he would otherwise have felt was "*impossibly hard work*".

This attitude of Taylor also shines through in his way of talking to Schmidt as to a simpleton: "For goodness' sake answer my questions and don't waste any more of my time." This said in a situation where poor Schmidt could scarcely get a word in edgeways.

In addition, Schmidt possessed great physical strength; he seemed unaffected after a day's work and used to walk the long distance to and from the workplace. Finally, he was so docile that he could be treated like a beast of draught or a robot: The foreman "stood over him with a watch", ordering, "pick up . . . walk . . . sit down . . . rest . . . walk . . . rest," etc. Schmidt did not "talk back", but meekly did what he was told.

The citation does not constitute just a single slip of the pen. Taylor returns to Schmidt time and again in his book *The Principles of Scientific Management*:

> This work is so crude and elementary in its nature that the writer firmly believes that it would be possible to train an intelligent gorilla so as to become a more efficient pig-iron handler than any man can be.[3]
>
> Now one of the very first requirements for a man who is fit to handle pig iron as a regular occupation is that he shall be so stupid and so phlegmatic that he more nearly resembles in his mental make-up the ox than any other type . . . . He is so stupid that the word "percentage" has no meaning to him, and he must consequently be trained by a man more intelligent than himself into the habit of working in accordance with the laws of this science . . . .[4]
>
> . . . a man of the type of the ox . . . so stupid that he was unfitted to do most kinds of laboring work, even.[5]
>
> And besides this, the man suited to handling pig iron is too stupid properly to train himself.[6]

We also know that it was precisely the story of Schmidt that Taylor loved to tell on his lecture tours.[7]

With all desirable clarity, the above shows an élitist feature of Taylor and scientific management. On the one hand, there is the illiterate, beastly stupid labourer; on the other the urbane, intelligent trainer – i.e. Taylor himself, or one of his pupils.[8] Taylor's view of man is a variant of the Tragic, which regards the individual as governed by simple laws.

Thus far scientific management makes an astonishingly simplistic and brutal impression. So Taylor, the father of organization theory and modern corporate management, was a callous misanthropist and capitalist exploiter? Well, even though this has become the received view, the truth is not quite so simple. As we saw in Chapter 2, Hegel said that the true is the whole, and we shall now try to place our account in a wider perspective. It will become apparent that *Taylor's scientific management was something quite different from what would eventually go by that name* and emerge victorious throughout the entire industrialized world. Taylor has also been misunderstood in organization theory. We must go back to the source, and to the historical origins.

A key to what we have said so far lies in Taylor's background.[9] After a childhood when he seems to have been especially interested in – or rather obsessed by – organizing the other children's games through rules, and in inventing various mechanical aids, he embarked upon a career as an engineer. In the USA of that time this primarily meant a practical education, where trainees started on the shop floor and worked themselves up. Taylor obtained apprenticeships first as a pattern maker, then as a machinist at a hydraulics company in central Philadelphia, positions he held for four years. He lived a kind of double life: physical labour during the days; a comfortable upper-class existence in the evenings and at weekends, including playing tennis and cricket in his family's societal circle.

After his trainee period, Taylor took employment at the Midvale Steel Works in Philadelphia, a company which had become successful through the use of product standardization and the application of scientific, in particular metallurgical methods. For a couple of months he worked on the shop floor as a day labourer and then again as a machinist, before obtaining the position of "gang boss" (sub-foreman). In the beginning of this job he had an experience which appears to have been traumatic for him, and which can be regarded as the very genesis of scientific management. It can be placed in the context of a wider movement, called *systematic management*.

As a background, therefore, we start by providing a brief account of this movement, originating in the USA among American mechanical engineers. These technicians especially criticized the relationship between foreman and worker, which they meant had two important shortcomings.

First, the foreman's area of competence was too large; he was in charge of a number of technical functions for which he was not specialized; these were of a "scientific" nature. Second, the foreman's setting of wage rates was often arbitrary, and in relation to this he also lacked in insight as to how much work could be demanded.

As solutions, the proponents of systematic management strived, in the first case, to relieve the foreman of a good deal of his technical tasks; in the second, a number of experiments were made with the sharing of productivity gains, incentive payments and the like.

Taylor's experiences as a freshly appointed gang boss at Midvale can be seen as an example of the conditions which had given rise to the systematic management movement. From his time on the shop floor he was well aware that workers held down their work intensity so as not to put upwards pressure on the piece rate. As gang boss, however, he had the task of getting as much out of the workers as possible. Taylor was a stubborn and systematic person, who did everything he could to break the resistance of the workers by traditional means. Against him stood a united gang of workers, who had long experience of fighting too effective job supervisors.

The result was a struggle which seems to have left deep scars on Taylor's personality; he testifies time and again to the bitterness of this conflict, and how hard it was to be surrounded by enemies throughout the working day. His text, otherwise engineering-like efficient and rational, here begins to pulsate with emotion:

> I want to call your attention, gentlemen, to the bitterness that was stirred up in this fight before the men finally gave in, to the meanness of it, and the comtemptible conditions that exist under the old piecework system . . . . My anger and hard feelings were stirred up against the system; not against the men. . . . I was a young man in years, but I give you my word I was a great deal older than I am now with worry, meanness, and contemptibleness of the whole damn thing. It is a horrid life for any man to live, not to be able to look any workman in the face all day long without seeing hostility there and feeling that every man around is his virtual enemy. . . . This life was a miserable one, and I made up my mind either to get out of the business entirely, and go into some other line of work, or to find some remedy for this unbearable condition.[10]

This conflict lasted for three whole years.

We now leave the biographical background. The conclusions Taylor drew were far-reaching. Such conflicts, such work conditions could not be reasonable. The workplace should function without friction. With his aristocratic background and the intermediate social position he occupied between worker and management, Taylor could not wholeheartedly identify himself with either side. Their conflicts had to be levelled out. A "mental revolution" in favour of more "scientific" management methods was urgently needed.

A recurring refrain in Taylor's writings is the lack of "efficiency". If the workers could do more work, they should also do so. But then they must be paid for it, without having to fear a reduction in the piece rate if they increased their efforts. The increased amount of work must furthermore be based on scientifically accurate studies so that it was optimal, involving neither too little nor too much work. The latter was also important to avoid possible friction; everything should run in a smooth and well-oiled manner; nobody would lose, but everybody would gain from the new system.

The core of all this was time measurement. Taylor started to experiment with time studies in 1882 and therefore also refers the origins of Scientific Management to this time. Of the five figures in his book, one is of a stop watch. Another illustrates a "watch book" with "one, two, or three watches" concealed in the right-hand side of a "frame . . . bound in a leather case resembling a pocket note-book". [11] The watches can be started or stopped by covertly pressing on the outside of the frame. The left-hand side contains the time-study sheets. Using this veritable James Bond contraption makes it possible to time the worker furtively, without his notice. The third illustration is an enlargement of the forms in the note-book. The fourth shows an instruction card for inspection of bicycle balls, with a time specification for each stage of work.

The stop watch, and the slide rule, recur time and again in Taylor's text – instruments for and symbols of the measurement of work motions in time and space. In this way, it would be possible to establish the fastest and most efficient movements – just as with the croquet game that Taylor had studied so diligently as a boy. The trope that imbued Taylor's conception of reality, i.e. his style of thought, was clearly that of Metonymy.

To this was linked a "bonus" remuneration system. If the workers achieved the optimal level, they were rewarded with a bonus payment; if not they were punished, in the short term by a minor reduction in wages, in the long run by job transfer or dismissal.

Further, *functional foremanship* was important. The coarse drill-sergeant types of old had to be replaced by teams of scientifically trained professionals, each of whom fulfilled their own specialist function. [12] Every worker would thus have several foremen to turn to – eight to be more precise, each with his own carefully delimited subfunction. Four of these would constitute a planning department, located in a special planning room; the remaining four would function as representatives of the planning department, supervising current activities on the shop floor.

This meant that the old principle of unity of command was heaved overboard; effective management involved "*abandoning the military type of organization*". [13] The functional foremen were to operate as friendly, tactful trainers and instructors of the worker, and he should be able to consult them with confidence in order to obtain (scientifically grounded) information on various work issues. That Taylor advocated a transition to a more humane form of job supervision did not derive from philanthropy, but from his perception that the system would not function without it. His personal experience had taught him this; he also considered that the motivation of employees was governed by scientific laws as exact as those of engineering, albeit more complex by nature. [14] Conversely, the worker should accept the orders of supervisors without question.

Thus, the main idea of Scientific Management was that of achieving a "mental revolution" in both workers and management. This involved two things:[15]

*   Acceptance of a scientific attitude towards work, which would lead to rising productivity.
*   Acceptance of cooperation instead of conflict, in order to share the increased surplus (profit) thereby obtained.

The latter element is Taylor's solution of the conflict between labour and capital, and should be seen in light of the fact that the growing labour movement, in the USA of that time primarily represented by militant trade unions, regarded conflict between the two sides over the distribution of the surplus as irreconcilable.

These two "absolutely essential elements" found concrete expression in the four famous "principles of scientific management":

> *First.* They [the managers] develop a science for each element of a man's work, which replaces the old rule-of-thumb method.
>
> *Second.* They scientifically select and then train, teach, and develop the workman, whereas in the past he chose his own work and trained himself as best he could.
>
> *Third.* They heartily cooperate with the men so as to insure all of the work being done in accordance with the principles of the science which has been developed.
>
> *Fourth.* There is an almost equal division of the work and the responsibility between the management and the workmen. The management take over all work for which they are better fitted than the workmen, while in the past almost all of the work and the greater part of the responsibility were thrown upon the men.[16]

We note here that Taylor, typically enough of his time, refers to the workers solely as men. However, some of his own experiments also involved female workers (inspectors of bicycle ball bearings).

The argumentation, and thereby the mode of explanation, both here and elsewhere, is strikingly Scientistic in its reference to "science", which for Taylor meant engineering science. In his text, he returns over and over to the "laws", or "rules and laws" that, in accordance with this science, should govern the activities of the organization with exact precision.

> ... management is not yet looked upon as an art, with laws as exact, and as clearly defined, for instance, as the fundamental principles of engineering ... Management is still looked upon as a question of men ....[17]
>
> Under scientific management ... it becomes the duty and also the

pleasure of those who are engaged in the management not only to develop laws to replace rule of thumb, but also to teach impartially all of the workmen who are under them the quickest ways of working. The useful results obtained from these laws are always so great that any company can well afford to pay for the time and the experiments needed to develop them. Thus under scientific management exact scientific knowledge and methods are everywhere, sooner or later, sure to replace rule of thumb, whereas under the old type of management working in accordance with scientific laws is an impossibility.[18]

The fourth principle requires a comment. It implies that the entire responsibility for the planning of work during the day was removed from the workers to the foremen, since this planning had now to be based on the "scientific" time studies. Even if they possessed the ability, the workers did not have time for current planning, but had to devote themselves efficiently to their tasks without scattering their attention and efforts.

The system of scientific management, according to Taylor, had to be introduced cautiously and gradually, so as not to risk setbacks.

> In reaching the final high rate of speed which shall be steadily maintained, the broad fact should be realized that the men must pass through several distinct phases, rising from one plane of efficiency to another until the final level is reached.[19]

Furthermore, it was appropriate to first select a suitable pilot subject ("Schmidt" in the introductory quotation), and then successively extend the circle of those concerned. Moreover, the system had to be seen as an *integrated whole*. Breaking some parts out of it and applying these separately was worse than doing nothing at all, for these methods were so powerful that, applied in isolation, they constituted explosive stuff. Taylor warned specifically against using piece-rate remuneration operated by the old type of foremen, and equipping these with the time measurement system. This would result in – and had been observed by Taylor to result in – increased confrontations, for example in the form of strikes, and ultimately in conditions worse than initially. One had to take

> *the time and the trouble required to train functional foremen, or teachers, who were fitted gradually to lead and educate the workmen.*[20]

And now we come to the point. Through the irony of history it was just the opposite of this which came to be called scientific management, both in theory and practice. Taylor's functional foremanship was almost never applied, since it was considered impractical and contrary to the principle of unity of command. His scientifically based bonus remuneration was also swept under the carpet as providing too little incentive.

Hence, only time measurement remained of the entire system; otherwise, the old foremanship plus piece-rate wages were employed – i.e. *precisely what*

Taylor had warned against! Also in organization theory Taylor's functional foremanship tends to be passed over in silence,[21] or misunderstood [22] and his bonus remuneration is generally not mentioned at all.[23] Yet these were cornerstones of the system, and if they are missing it is not even possible to talk about scientific management in Taylor's sense.

And his attitude towards "Schmidt"? Against the background of Taylor's biography, this might be explained as the result of a combination of an old-fashioned aristocratic patriarchalism derived from his upbringing and the feelings of superiority generated by his scientific training as an engineer rather than as an expression of a capitalistic contempt for the worker. As we have seen, Taylor wanted to take a position between labour and capital.

Without defending Taylor's (indefensible) attitude, there is nothing indicating that he would have been personally hated or even particularly disliked by the workers he was involved with; rather, the opposite seems to have been the case.[24] Once more, it is an irony of fate that precisely Taylor, who wanted to adopt a scientifically harmonizing intermediate position between – or above – company management and worker, has come to symbolize the crass and misanthropic capitalistic exploitation of wage earners.[25] Taylor's scientific management was something quite different from the scientific management which came to be realized historically.

So, after persistent delving into the matter, we can state that the established truth about Taylor and his scientific company management was the very opposite of the historical truth.

Taylor's entire style of thought is permeated by Metonomy in its purest form; the division of reality into discrete units of time, space and motion is the ideal expression of this. The drama enacted is that of Tragedy: human beings and organizations are conceived as being governed by inexorable laws of fate. Dramaturgically, as Frye has noted, Tragedy is the epiphany of law.[26] The law will be revealed through the radical crisis the hero undergoes. And this law is manifested in Taylor's account by the class conflicts which tear companies apart, owing to the latters' lack of rationality.

The conflict has its foundation in the struggle over the distribution of the economic surplus. It is focused personally and palpably in the figure of *the foreman*. Focus on the opposite side is *the trade union*. These both materialize the Tragedy's evil forces, and thus constitute its demons. The lack of rationality – an ill-conceived remuneration system and, above all, unscientific work motions – makes for competition over the economic surplus. Yet this is not necessary. There is a better solution, namely Taylor's. According to this, work motions in time and space are measured with the greatest accuracy, and are subsequently carried out scientifically. A rational wage system is implemented, and a functional foremanship which can operate according to the scientific laws governing both technology and human beings. Only thus can the demons of irrationality be vanquished.

Hence, in Taylor's dramaturgy the company plays the role of the Tragic hero. The hero is marred by a fatal flaw, *hamartia*. His most prominent feature – the dynamics of industrial-technical development – transforms into *hubris*, presumption, which throws him into a decisive life-crisis. A crisis with which Taylor had made personal and very painful acquaintance as gang boss at Midvale. The crisis, however, brings to light the laws of which the hero had been unaware. And these laws are none other than those of scientific management. Here Taylor adopts the role of enlightening chorus. The audience can now, as in every tragedy, learn to act in accordance with these inescapable laws. The fixation with measurements of different kinds obtains its explanation as a Scientistic method for creating the "scientific" laws by which the new principles are justified.[27] Taylor's organizational drama was Tragic, and he himself stood for the disclosure of its laws, in true Scientist spirit. Like the other dramas, Tragedy includes various genres. This is an example of *triumphant Tragedy*, in which the main emphasis is placed on the hero's victory after the overcoming of difficulties.[28] Thus, in the characteristic course of events, the phase that dominates is the one immediately following the crisis that represents the mid-point.

From the perspective of poetics, Schmidt plays a particular role. He has the important function of heightening the Tragedy by creating *pathos*. Typical of the pathetic character is to face threat of exclusion from some social circle, at the same level as the audience/readership is assumed to be found in, and with which it accordingly is able to identify.[29] Schmidt is duly threatened with exclusion from the circle of the "high-priced" and with a continued existence in pre-Taylorian darkness amongst the "cheap fellows" if he does not obey Taylor's instructions. This also explains the striking inarticulateness of Schmidt in the introductory citation. For precisely the speechless, dumb, in a character serves to further heighten the pathos. Helplessness has the same function.[30] Through the contrast between the lumbering, pathetically insentient Schmidt, the equivalent of a Caliban, and the slender rationality of the final state, we are driven to further admire the triumphant resolution of the crisis.

There are interesting parallels between Taylor and Marx.[31] Both pointed to the distribution of the economic surplus as the root of class struggle between labour and capital. Both held that development was governed by inexorable laws, and also that the system did not work in its present state. For Marx the solution lay in a violent revolution followed by a planned economy; for Taylor in the planned rationality of companies. The differences are of course considerable: Marx's socialist society was based on the expropriation of the expropriators, i.e. the obliteration of one pole in the class conflict, while Taylor's scientifically managed companies would preserve and further both poles. Yet the dramaturgical similarities are no less striking for this.

As mentioned, posterity did not employ Taylor's system, but only the part of it concerned with the effectivization of work – something he had explicitly warned against.[32] It is interesting to speculate about how much social conflict might have been avoided in the twentieth century, had Taylor's advice been followed.

That the functional job supervision was impractical seems to have become almost a truism, probably for conservative reasons and since it looks much messier on an organization chart than a simple line organization. But, as Herbert Simon points out, there is actually no empirical evidence that the functional supervision would have been either worse or better than the competitor which emerged victorious from the struggle, namely the principle of unity of command.[33] If anything, Joan Woodward's empirical findings, presented after the appearance of the first edition of Simon's book, rather indicate that it would have been advantageous.[34] (It is tempting to pursue the comparison with the other great Tragedian, Marx, whose analyses, when applied, had to give way precisely to the "obviously practical".) It appears that Taylor's style of thought and method, but not certain parts of his organizational drama were picked up by others.[35] The reason for this is that he had a powerful competitor in these parts in Henri Fayol, who, as we shall see, very strongly advocated unity of command in organizations and objected to Taylor's functional foremanship. With its clear subdivision of responsibilities, and of power at every organizational level, the principle of unity of command is more congenial to the Metonymic style of thought than the idea of a functional foremanship which smacks of teamwork among supervisors, hence has a certain bearing on Synecdoche.

The main criticism that can be directed against Taylor – and which has been aimed at him – is of course that his view of (wo)man builds on an abstraction which is not even approximately realistic: economic man. This one-eyed Metonymic image of the human being as driven solely by economic incentives certainly has much in common with much of modern economics (see, for example, Myrdal's critique).[36] Yet, as with the latter, it makes his conception of organization cover only a restricted part of the reality in question. Within this restricted part, scientific management nevertheless has had lasting importance in at least four ways.[37]

First, time studies have become an established element in corporate activities. The following text gives an inkling of this:

> Of these various systems of "predetermined work time," the most popular is Methods-Time Measurement, put out by the MTM Association for Standards and Research in Ann Arbor, Michigan. This association publishes "Application Data" in booklet form. In this system, the time standard used is the TMU, which is defined as one hundred-thousandth of an hour, equal to six ten-thousandths of a minute or thirty-six thousandths of a second. It offers refinements of the therblig to apply to many conditions. *Reach,* for instance, is tabulated separately for objects in fixed or varying locations, for objects jumbled with others, for very small objects, and so forth, and for distances varying from three-fourths of an inch up to thirty inches. For example, to reach a single object the location of which may vary slightly from cycle to cycle, twenty inches away, consumes according to the MTM chart 18.6 TMU or .6696 second (not, we ask the reader to note, two-

thirds of a second, which would be .6666 second; a difference which, in an operation repeated a thousand times a day, would add up to three seconds).

Move is defined for objects from 2.5 to 47.5 lbs: to either hand or against stop; to approximate or indefinite location; to exact location.

Turn and apply pressure is given for pressures up to 35 lbs., and for vectors of 30 degrees to 180 degrees, in increments of 15 degrees.

Position: loosely, closely, or exactly; for easy-to-handle and difficult-to-handle objects (its opposite, *Disengage,* is also given for the same conditions). *Release* is given not only for normal release (by opening fingers), but for contact release (releasing typewriter key).

Body, leg and foot motions are set forth for the various movements of Bend, Sit, Stop, Walk, etc., for varying distances. And finally, a formula is given for Eye Travel Time:

$$ET = 15.2 \times \frac{T}{D} \, TMU$$

with a maximum of 20 TMU. Eye Focus is defined as occupying 7.3 TMU.[38]

Such measuring of eye movements has been specifically developed for the rationalization of office work, which increasingly has come to supplement the earlier exclusive focus on manufacturing. Further:

More recent research has attempted to overcome the defects inherent in standard data, which, in breaking down motions into elementary components, neglect the factors of velocity and acceleration in human motions – motions which take place as a flow rather than as a series of disjunctive movements. Efforts have been made to find a means of gaining a continuous, uninterrupted view of human motion, and to measure it on that basis. In the course of this research, the use of radar, accelerometers, photoelectric waves, air pressure, magnetic fields, capacitive effects, motion pictures, radioactivity, etc., have been invest-igated, and in the end, sound waves, using the Doppler shift, have been chosen as the most suitable. An inaudible sound source (20,000 cycles per second) given off by a transducer is attached to the body member under consideration. Three microphones, each ten feet from an assumed one cubic yard of work area, are placed in such a way that each represents one of the three spatial dimensions, and they pick up the increased or decreased number of cycles per second as the sound source moves toward or away from each of them. These changes in cycles are converted into changes in voltage, the output of which is therefore proportional to the velocity of motion. The three velocities are recorded on magnetic tape (or plotted on oscillographic paper) and can then be combined into a total velocity by vector summation. Total acceleration and total distance can be derived, and can then be handled mathematically, and by computer, for analysis and prediction. This device goes by the name Universal Operator Performance Analyzer and Recorder (UNOPAR), and is said to be, if nothing else, an excellent timing device accurate to .000066 minutes, though not to be compared in this respect to electronic timing devices, which are accurate to a millionth of a second. (But these last, we are told ruefully, are useful only for experimental purposes, and not in the workplace.)

Physiological models are also used for the measurement of energy expenditure, for which oxygen consumption and heart rate are the most usual indicators; these are charted by means of oxygen-supply measuring devices and electrocardiograms. Forces applied by the body (as well as to it) are measured on a force platform, using piezo-electric crystals in the mountings. In another variant, we read, in an article entitled "The Quantification of Human Effort and Motion for the Upper Limbs," about a framework called "the exoskeletal kinematometer," which is described as "a device which mounts *externally* upon the human subject for the purpose of *measuring* the *kinematic* characteristics of his limbs during the performance of a task." The measurement of eye movements is done through photographic techniques and also by electro-oculography, which uses electrodes placed near the eye.

In this "brave new world" the Metonymic style of thought that Taylor advocated so passionately has come out in full bloom. It is also interesting to note the extremely Scientistic method.[39] As a dramatic theme, *derkou theama,* the torture of observation, is a common element in a certain genre of Tragedy to which we shall return in connection with Weber.[40]

The well-known organization researcher and consultant Peter Drucker summarizes:

> [Underlying] the actual management of worker and work in American industry . . . [is the concept of] . . . Scientific Management. Scientific Management focuses on the work. Its core is the organized study of work, the analysis of work into its simplest elements and the systematic improvement of the worker's performance of each of these elements. Scientific Management has both basic concepts and easily applicable tools and techniques. And it has no difficulty proving the contribution it makes; its results in the form of higher output are visible and readily measurable. Indeed, Scientific Management is all but a systematic philosophy of worker and work. Altogether it may well be the most powerful as well as the most lasting contribution America has made to Western thought since the Federalist Papers.[41]

Second, the various Metonymic rules not related to time studies, which Taylor arrived at as consequences of his system, have become an integral component of working life in general:

... many of Taylor's detailed recommendations have become standard practice, certainly throughout manufacturing industry, and to an increasing extent, in the services sector. It is these practices, such as job descriptions, planned flow of work, systematic stock control, detailed unit cost accounting, etc., which we may describe as the "bedrock" of contemporary management, and to the extent that they are universal features of management they no longer exist as strategic choices ... in decision-making terms.[42]

Or as another writer puts it:

If Taylorism does not exist as a separate school today, that is because, apart from the bad odor of the name, it is no longer the property of a faction, since its fundamental teachings have become the bedrock of all work design. ... In other words, Taylorism is "outmoded" or "superseded" only in the sense that a sect which has become generalized and broadly accepted disappears as a sect.[43)]

Third, in current ideas of *empowerment*, Taylorist ideas of rationalization and control via measurement have entered into a dialectic interaction with ideas of autonomy and corporatism, by, as it were, internalizing rationalization in the workers. While scientific management targeted the non-discursive, physical practices, the focus of empowerment consists in discursive – informational, institutional – practices. Empowerment also presupposes a far more active and flexible role on the part of the employees, and also teamwork as the medium through which to realize this role. In this synthesis, Taylorism constitutes one of the two strands in a kind of managerial double helix. Or, to use the dramaturgical language of the present book: the organizational drama of modern empowerment is played as a Romantic Tragedy. An example is the popular TQM.[44] In fact, if we are to believe Drucker, Taylorism and empowerment may have another feature in common too: the idea that there is one right way of managing; the prevalent conception of this way is at present, according to Drucker, team structure[45] – which is, as we just saw, also crucial to empowerment.

Fourth, the classical, radical, Tragic kind of organization to which Taylor subscribed still survives today – even though it has faced competition from other types. We shall return to this in section 3.5 below.[46]

3.2 Fayol and hydraulics

Taylor interested himself exclusively in shop management, not in top management. The latter was instead the focus of Henri Fayol, whose book *General and Industrial Administration* [Administration industrielle et génerale] came out in 1916.[47),48)] Fayol worked in France and, like Taylor, was an engineer by training (specialized in mining). He advanced to the position as top manager for the concern Commentry-Fourchambault, a post that he handled with outstanding success.[49]

In the following quotation, Fayol refers to three theories which he had been successful in generating; but as the modest – and, presumably, didactic – person he was, the French engineer did not ascribe the merit of this to himself, but to his method:

> I discovered a theory of fires in mines; I discovered a theory of geological formations; I founded the theory of administration, and these works will endure. The wise man, poet, mystic and great teacher Ternier has said, "I do not know which we should admire the more; the discoveries themselves or the methods used to make them." But the theory of fires did not lead me to the theory of geological formations, nor did the problems of administration lead me to investigate the problems of life. Each of these challenges was thrust up by the pressure of the [scientific] method, the unique and universal method, applicable to everything and for everyone.[50]

The method in question is described in greater detail in Fayol's book, in connection with the important task for corporate management that consists in "improvements". Without these, a company is quickly left behind by its competitors. The method through which the improvements were to be implemented is as follows:

> *Method* consists of observing, collecting and filing facts, interpreting them, trying out experiments if need be, and from the study as a whole, deducing rules which, under the management's impetus, may be introduced into business practice. Most developments which have raised business science to its present level emanate from the same method, which in actual fact is none other than the Cartesian one.[51]

The Cartesian approach is certainly also known for its analytical technique. But Descartes was a rationalist, who proceeded from simple to more complex *ideas*, following the method that had proved to be successful in mathematics (geometry and algebra); and then from these more complex ideas to reality.[52] Fayol's method, as described here, is rather the opposite, since he starts from empirical facts and inductively derives rules from them. Although both of these methods are indisputably Scientistic, it should be pointed out that Fayol is not a Cartesian rationalist but an empiricist.[53)]

As was mentioned, in his book Fayol devoted himself more to the overall managerial apparatus than Taylor, who had concentrated on the production system and management at shop-floor level. But in one section of his chapter on "Organizing", he also states his position on scientific management. Fayol warmly advocated Taylor's ideas – with one exception, the "functional foremanship" which conflicted with a principle that was more important to him, namely unity of command. The problems of competence relating to the individual gang boss/foreman, to which Taylor had referred, could, according to Fayol, be solved otherwise. Fayol is the theoretical progenitor of the *line-staff organization*. By combining the path of command down to supervisor level (the line) with advisory staff units it was possible, in Fayol's view, to remedy the problem of the foreman's lack of competence while keeping the principle of unity of command, given that the staff had an exclusively advisory and not a command function.

We remember that Taylor had rejected the military-style unity of command as too unsophisticated for civilian purposes. Fayol, in contrast, held that the military organization had already solved this problem. Here, he referred explicitly to the staff function within "the army". The French had experienced the efficiency of the military staff – a Prussian discovery – during the Franco-Prussian War of 1870–1, and thereafter quickly adopted the idea. Staffs should not only exist at the lowest level in a company; more important for Fayol was that they functioned as auxiliary and supportive organs for the company management. Here too the issue of specialized competence was central.

Thus, Fayol focused on the conditions of administration. "All operations to which enterprises give rise" could in his doctrine "be divided into the following six groups", also identified as "essential functions".[54] These are introduced without further ado or argument direct in the first paragraphs of his book:

1 *Technical* (production, manufacture, transformation).[55]
2 *Commercial* (buying, selling, exchange).
3 *Financial* (search for and management[56] of capital).
4 *Security* (protection of assets and persons).
5 *Accounting* (stocktaking, balance sheets, costs, statistics).
6 *Administrative* (foreseeing,[57] organizing, commanding, coordinating, controlling).

The last-mentioned – administrative – functions were, according to Fayol, more unexplored than the other, more technical ones, which motivated making the former the object of his study. For him, the administrative group of operations, shown in Figure 3.1, *defined* the overall concept of administration. But administration was *not* to be conflated with *management*.[58] Management constituted the integrated handling of all six essential functions. Administration was only one of the six functions, albeit the most important one for higher-level managers. For lower-level staff, the remaining five "professional" functions were more important. Fayol particularly emphasized that his theory was valid for all organizations – big and small, profit and non-profit, private and public, industrial and commercial.

Foresight has innumerable manifestations, the most important of which is the *programme of action* – one of the most essential and most difficult tasks

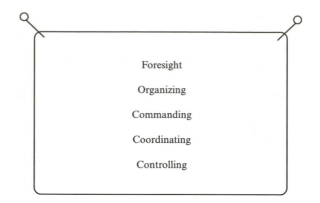

Figure 3.1 The administrative functions.

in any enterprise. The proper programme of action is generally characterized by *"unity, continuity, suppleness, and precision."*[59]

Organizing is to "furnish [the enterprise] with everything that is useful to its functioning: raw materials, tools and machinery, capital, personnel."[60] Fayol primarily discusses formal organizational structures, but also recruitment and training of personnel.[61]

Commanding is identified with "making the personnel function".[62] But in accordance with Fayol's general view of organizations, to which we shall come later, the exercise of command also includes stimulating initiative from subordinates. The commander/manager must also know his personnel; be able to "eliminate the incapable"; serve as a model for others; have a good grasp of all agreements, to avoid "redoubtable conflict"; extensively use organizational diagrams;[63] make intermittent inspections, arrange conferences, and be capable of delegating.[64]

Coordinating the different departments is necessary in order for these to keep in mind the interests of the whole organization, not just their own. This is best achieved through weekly conferences attended by departmental heads.[65]

Controlling, finally, that "everything occurs according to the programme adopted, the orders given, and the principles established" should be separated from company management and the line (and thus be a staff function). Otherwise, a "duality" in managerial relations would arise, conflicting with the unity-of-command principle.[66]

Like Taylor's, Fayol's view of organizations reflects an engineering-science attitude. This comes out clearly in his metaphors, where the organization is compared with mechanical, hierarchical systems of various kinds:

> The social body of enterprises is frequently compared with a *machine*, a *plant*, an *animal*.
>
> The expressions "administrative machine", "cogs and wheels of administration" convey the idea of an organism which obeys the driving

force of its manager and in which all parts are well interrelated, moving together and concurrently towards the same goal. And this is excellent. . . . And the sap carries life to all the branches and the most tender twigs, just as the order from above carries the activity even to the very lowest and most distant extremities of the body social. . . . The nervous system, in particular, shows great analogies to the administrative service. . . . The body social has, like the animal, its reflexive or ganglionic actions, which are effected without immediate intervention of superior authority. Without the nervous or administrative action, the organism would become an inert mass and rapidly deteriorate.[67]

Thus, the organizational drama is Tragic. Fayol regarded the organization principally as a machinery for the transmission of authority. It is especially interesting, and symptomatic, that Fayol uses the very word organism here as equivalent to machinery.[68] However, an element of initiative was needed at lower levels. In the case of physical transmission, power is lost at every stage, Fayol noted, but this must not happen in an organization.[69]

The principles for the transmission of authority are given in Figure 3.2 (Fayol's fourteen famous "general principles of administration").[70]

Comments:

1 By division of work Fayol meant specialization according to function.
2 Authority and responsibility should accompany each other.
3 "Discipline is the principal force of armies," Fayol states with approval.
4 Unity of command has already been commented upon.
5 Unity of direction: "One manager only and one programme only for a set of operations aiming at the same goal."
9 Hierarchy: All communications should follow the same route, "passing through all the degrees of hierarchy", i.e. the whole "series of managers"; those "which start from the top authority as well as those which are addressed by it". Exceptions *may* be allowed – for instance, middle managers can take direct contact with each other without having to go via their superiors; the latter, however, should then always be kept informed (Fayol's "gangplank").
10 Order: "One place for every person and every person in his place." "Cleanliness is a corollary of order. No place is reserved for dirt."
12 "Stability of personnel" refers to the rate of personnel turnover, which must not be too high.
13 Initiative should be encouraged, as it strengthens the manager.
14 The unity of the personnel must not be jeopardized by a policy of "divide and rule"; moreover, it can be damaged by the exaggerated formalism involved in the "abuse of written [in preference to oral] communications", since the former often exacarbates frictions that are easily avoided or smoothed over by face-to-face talk.

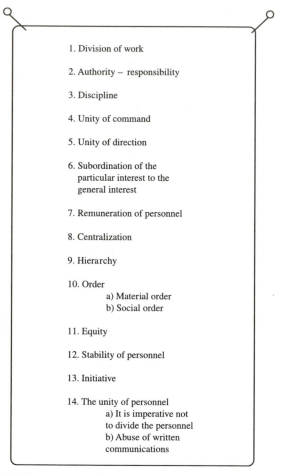

1. Division of work

2. Authority – responsibility

3. Discipline

4. Unity of command

5. Unity of direction

6. Subordination of the
   particular interest to the
   general interest

7. Remuneration of personnel

8. Centralization

9. Hierarchy

10. Order
    a) Material order
    b) Social order

11. Equity

12. Stability of personnel

13. Initiative

14. The unity of personnel
    a) It is imperative not
    to divide the personnel
    b) Abuse of written
    communications

Figure 3.2 The general principles of administration.

The other points are largely self-explanatory.

Fayol's organizational drama was that of Tragedy, i.e. companies are governed by mechanical laws of fate. As with Taylor it can be ascribed to the genre of triumphant Tragedy; Fayol has generalized his experiences of the rescue of crisis-ridden companies. By means of an inductive, Scientistic method, the true laws – the general principles of management – are brought to light by Fayol, and the companies just have to apply them.

It would seem to be no exaggeration to characterize Fayol's style of thought as strongly Metonymic; the organization is divided neatly and tidily into different compartments – or, as one of his mottoes went: "A place for everyone and everyone in his place." Discipline, cleanliness, tidiness, "no appointed place for dirt" are the key words and phrases, typical of the striving of Metonymy for separate units with clear boundaries between them. (I will not here go into psychoanalytical interpretations; a Freudian would certainly have other comments to make.) The strength lay in the relatively simple, almost military tone of the message. The army is undeniably the simplest form of power machine. But in this strength lay also its weakness, which has made Fayol's theses, like Taylor's, a popular target of attacks from later writers.

The principles in question were not subjected to any scientific, empirical testing before the 1950s, when Joan Woodward claimed to have evidence that they did not provide a general explanation for corporate success; different companies required different methods.[71] On a more theoretical level, they have been subjected to sharp criticism by, among others, Herbert Simon, who maintained that they amounted to little more than inconsistent rules of thumb.[72] We do not present a critique of our own here; but we shall return to both these authors.

Although an English translation of Fayol's book had to wait until 1949, he already had very influential followers in the USA in the 1930s, among them the General Motors' managers Mooney and Reiley, and the researchers Gulick and Urwick.[73] Fayol's thinking and the ideas it inspired came to be known as the "administrative management school". Its theses, like those of Taylor, proved to have a very strong impact in practice. It is true that one author has maintained the opposite:

> Serious students are beginning to recognize that Fayol's ideas achieved only a relatively brief flowering in continental Europe during the 1920s and early 1930s, and lost their following after the Second World War. There was a brief interest in England and in North America during the 1950s, stimulated by the publication of . . . [a] translation of Fayol's major work.[74]

Who these serious students are, however, is not revealed. In fact it may well be a matter of the same kind of "death" as in the case of Taylor: Fayol's ideas are so generally applied that their originator is no longer referred to. The theoretical criticism that has been aimed at them should not obscure their widespread practical influence. What strikes a modern reader on first reflection is the ubiquity of the line-staff organization and the controller task.

But there is also broader evidence. In an article, presenting the results of an extensive review of the literature, two authors seek an answer to the question: "Are the classical management functions useful in describing managerial work?"[75] Here, the following interesting findings are reported:

- The Canadian management policy researcher Henry Mintzberg, to whom we shall return in Chapter 5, has strongly criticized Fayol's descriptions of the work of company managers (the administrative functions) and proposed categories of his own.[76)] Yet, Mintzberg's classification has drawn criticism too, *inter alia* for unclear boundaries between categories, and for a superficial observational approach. Empirical studies of its validity have given mixed results. On the other hand, several empirical studies of corporate executives in the USA show that their work – with certain complements – is well described in terms of Fayol's functions. Thus, modern American managers can be said, without any greater exaggeration, to work in accordance with Fayol's principles.

- Empirical studies also show a positive relationship between the success of a company and the degree to which its management devotes itself to Fayol's various classical functions. Thus, modern American companies are successful (among other things) to the extent that they follow Fayol's ideas.
- Two different, statistical surveys show that Fayol's management functions are still the "most favored description" of the work of managers in modern American textbooks. If reference to Mintzberg's categories is made, this generally takes place alongside those of Fayol, without integration of the two. Thus, rather unexpectedly, Fayol's ideas from the beginning of the century still dominated the training of American managers towards the end of it.

A broad survey study,[77] whose results were published after the above article, found that four types of activities constituted the main bulk of managerial work:

- Communication activities (corresponding to Mintzberg's picture) represented nearly a third of managerial time and effort.
- Traditional activities (corresponding to Fayol's administrative operations) represented a third.
- Human Resource Management represented a fifth.
- Networking activities[78] represented approximately a fifth.

Thus, even though it may be undecided whether Fayol's classical administrative operations are wholly dominant in today's managerial world, or rather serve to complement other activities of more or less equal weight, the empirical evidence suggests that they continue to play a very important role.

3.3 Weber's rule machine

If two of the classical organization theorists were engineers, and criticized by detractors for having engineer minds, we meet in the third a genuine German *Gelehrter*, a scholarly giant with an enormous erudition in his academic baggage. He wrote his doctoral thesis in law before becoming a professor of economics. Weber's most important academic achievements, however, were in the field of sociology, especially his major work *Economy and Society*.

The research on Weber is extremely extensive, and ever increasing;[79] his influence on the social sciences in general has been as exceptional, and can only be compared with that of Marx:

> At first sight, there is a look of *embarras de richesse* about the subject, Max Weber and modern social science. Is there any modern social science without Max Weber? He has been called an "authority", a "founder", even a "law-giver". The list of those who see themselves in the succession of Max Weber is long and distinguished, the list of those who acknowledge some debt to the Weber tradition reads like a *Who's Who* of social science.[80]

Economy and Society first appeared posthumously in 1922; it provides both a theoretical summary of Weber's entire output and contains his pioneering work in the field of organization theory. This work has set its stamp on succeeding research to such an extent that it is even claimed that modern organization theory is just a series of footnotes to Weber.[81] A highly influential translation of Part 1 into English by Henderson and Parsons was published in 1947 under the title *The Theory of Social and Economic Organization*, which is also the text generally referred to here.[82]

Fundamental to this reputation of Weber's is his theory of bureaucracy. If Taylor is known for his ideas of rationalization and Fayol for his principles of management, Weber's reputation as an organization theorist rests to a large (though not exclusive) extent on his analysis of the nature of bureaucracy. To understand this we must put it into its larger context.

A cornerstone of Weber's method was his well-known concept of *"ideal type"*. An ideal type for Weber was an abstraction which selected out and exaggerated certain aspects of a real phenomenon. This abstraction could then be used to create a theoretical concept, or a model, with which reality could be compared.

Weber's concept of an ideal type has often been mystified, but it is not so difficult to comprehend. For example, he regarded the laws of economics as ideal typical, since reality only approximately corresponds to them; further factors, not incorporated in the models, always remain. In fact, Weber's ideal types were what in modern scientific-philosophical terminology are usually called *idealizations*.[83] They provide us with knowledge of reality even though this knowledge is not complete; their advantage is that they are compact and easy to handle.

One example, taken from Weber himself, can be mentioned: "a physical reaction which has been calculated on the assumption of an absolute vacuum";[84] another well-known example is the calculation of the falling velocities of bodies on the assumption of the absence of air resistance. In fact, the whole of physics and the natural sciences consists of such simplifying but effective idealizations. Thus, the ideal type is a manifestation of a Scientistic mode of explanation.

Weber derived his ideal types from his own extensive empirical research and literary studies. The types are usually not justified, but simply stated; nor are reasons offered for the transitions between them. This lack of dialectics makes the reader sometimes feel faced with a catalogue of concepts. Yet the concepts generally have something intuitively reasonable and fruitful about them, so that Weber's theory still remains alive and relevant.

Central to Weber's theory is the concept of "*social action*". In *action* "is included all human behaviour when and in so far as the acting individual attaches a subjective meaning to it".[85] This is the very Metaphorical foundation stone of Weber's perspective on society, which in turn paves the way for an Idiographic method. However, even here at the foundation of his theory there is a Metonymic element, in the form of the analytical subdivision of an object of study into its smallest components; the social action was so to say the atom in Weber's conception, that from which everything else is built up.

"Control" of whether the outside researcher has understood the meaning of this action rightly can take place in three ways: through statistical analysis, through comparison, and through intellectual experiment. The first method is to be preferred to the second, and this in turn to the third. Unfortunately, however, statistical analysis is only applicable to a limited extent, which is why, in Weber's view, one frequently has to remain satisfied with comparison or even thought experiment.[86] Or, in our tropological terms: the Scientistic method is desirable as a complement to the Idiographic, but unfortunately not very applicable. As we remember there was also a corresponding duality in style of thought which came to expression in the concept of the ideal type.

On the other hand, Weber's view of the Functional method was more sceptical. He held that it was "convenient for purposes of practical illustration and for provisional orientation"; the Idiographic method, though, was far more advanced:

> Action in the sense of a subjectively understandable orientation of behaviour exists only as the behaviour of one or more *individual* human beings. . . . [F]or the subjective interpretation of action in sociological work these collectivities must be treated as *solely* the resultants and modes of organization of the particular acts of individual persons, since these alone can be treated as agents in a course of subjectively understandable action. . . .
>
> [T]he method of the so-called "organic" school of sociology to attempt to understand social interaction by using as a point of departure the "whole" within which the individual acts. . . . How far in other disciplines this type of functional analysis of the relation of "parts" to a whole can be regarded as definitive, cannot be discussed here; but it is well known that the bio-chemical and bio-physical modes of analysis of the organism are on principle opposed to stopping there.

For purposes of sociological analysis two things can be said. First this functional frame of reference is convenient for purposes of practical illustration and for provisional orientation. In these respects it is not only useful but indispensable. But at the same time if its cognitive value is overestimated and its concepts illegitimately "reified," it can be highly dangerous. Secondly, in certain circumstances this is the only available way of determining just what processes of social action it is important to understand in order to explain a given phenomenon. But this is only the beginning of sociological analysis as here understood. In the case of social collectivities, precisely as distinguished from organisms, we are in a position to go beyond merely demonstrating functional relationships and uniformities. We can accomplish something which is never attainable in the natural sciences, namely the subjective understanding of the action of the component individuals. . . .

We do not "understand" the behaviour of cells, but can only observe the relevant functional relationships and generalize on the basis of these observations. This additional achievement of explanation by interpretive understanding, as distinguished from external observation, is of course attained only at a price – the more hypothetical and fragmentary character of its results. Nevertheless, subjective understanding is the specific characteristic of sociological knowledge.[87]

The Functional method thus could at most serve heuristic ends, but it was in principle defective, since it focused on "collectivities" which strictly speaking did not exist other than as conceptual constructions; the only things that *really* existed were individuals, whose actions should be understood sociologically. Weber rightly designates this latter method, which was his own, as "individualistic".[88]

"Action is social in so far as, by virtue of the subjective meaning attached to it by the acting individual (or individuals), it takes account of the behaviour of others and is thereby oriented in its course."[89] There are four ideal types of social action:

- Goal rational
- Value rational
- Affectual
- Traditional

Goal rational action takes the goals as given and uses the best means to achieve them. Here, the emphasis is consequently on the means.[90] Value rational action focuses on certain goals as having a value in themselves. Here the emphasis lies on the goals. (Thus it is perfectly feasible to combine goal rational and value rational action.) Affectual action is an expression of the actor's emotional state. Traditional action is taken by force of long-accustomed habit.

One might wonder where these types come from, what principle lies behind the typology. Two underlying dimensions can be tracked down: rationality and meaning locus. The first dimension concerns whether the action is rational or non-rational; the second whether the meaning of the action lies in the action itself or outside it. It is no coincidence that just these two dimensions were selected; they were both quite central for Weber. On the basis of these two dimensions the types can be constructed as in Figure 3.3.

The figure is not drawn as a conventional two-by-two matrix, but has continuous scales on each axis, in accordance with Weber's notion of ideal types which correspond to extreme values, but at certain values transform into each other. For this reason the boundaries between the cells are also marked as dotted lines.

The rationality dimension perhaps requires least comment. That goal and value rational action, by contrast with affectual and traditional action, are rational is clear from their names. In value rational action, as in affectual, the meaning lies in the action itself: in the first case as a conscious value, in the second as spontaneous emotion. In goal rational as in traditional action the meaning is located outside the action itself, separated from it: in the first case as a goal-means relation, in the second as a relationship to external tradition.

The transition from single individual actions to more complex phenomena such as power and organizations is effected by the concept of a *social relationship*. This consists in the social action of "a plurality of actors", who mutually orientate themselves to one another. Through this emerges the

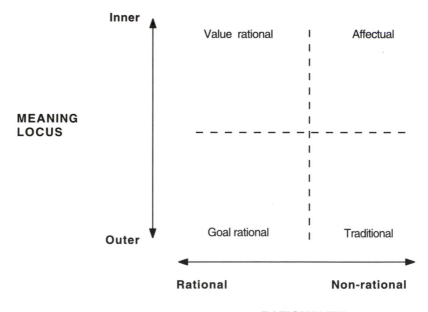

Figure 3.3 Clarification of the four types of action according to Weber.

"probability that there will be, in some meaningfully understandable sense, a course of social action."[91]

A social action or social relationship can be ascribed legitimacy on the basis of its (1) having "been established in a manner which is recognized to be *legal*"; (2) value rationality; (3) affectuality; (4) tradition.

Power [Macht] "is the probability that one actor within a social relationship will be in a position to carry out his own will despite resistance, regardless of the basis on which this probability rests." *Authority* [Herrschaft] "is the probability [*sic*] that a command with a given specific content will be obeyed by a given group of persons."[92]

There are three main types of legitimate authority: (1) legal authority, (2) charismatic authority; and (3) traditional authority.

Legal authority rests on the notion of rationality – either goal rationality or value rationality. This expresses itself in the form of the prescribed order's "formal legality".

Charismatic authority is based on magical conceptions of extraordinary properties that are ascribed to the person furnished with the authority in question.

Traditional authority rests on respect for the person who has gained his position by virtue of the tradition.

Legal authority, by contrast with the others, is "impersonal", tied to and restricted by the formal rules manifested in the different positions of authority (offices); charismatic and traditional authority, on the other hand, are linked to persons, not to formal rules. On the whole, central to legal authority is that it "consists essentially in a consistent system of abstract rules".

From these general characteristics of legal authority follow, according to Weber, certain more concrete properties:

- The duties of office are continuously exerted.
- Delimited spheres of competence.
- Hierarchy.
- "Specialized training" to master the role system.
- Employees not owning the means of production.
- No personal right of possession to offices.
- Written documentation.

The purest type of legal authority is bureaucracy. It is characterized by the following:

1 [Individual officers] are personally free and subject to authority only with respect to their impersonal official obligations.
2 They are organized in a clearly defined hierarchy of offices.
3 Each office has a clearly defined sphere of competence in the legal sense.
4 The office is filled by a free contractual relationship. Thus, in principle, there is free selection.

5 Candidates are selected on the basis of technical qualification. In the most rational case, this is tested by examination or guaranteed by diplomas certifying technical training, or both. They are *appointed*, not elected.

6 They are remunerated by fixed salaries in money, for the most part with a right to pensions. Only under certain circumstances does the employing authority, especially in private organizations, have a right to terminate the appointment, but the official is always free to resign. The salary scale is primarily graded according to rank in the hierarchy: but in addition to this criterion, the responsibility of the position and the requirements of the incumbent's social status may be taken into account.

7 The office is treated as the sole, or at least the primary, occupation of the incumbent.

8 It constitutes a career. There is a system of "promotion" according to seniority or to achievement, or both. Promotion is dependent on the judgement of superiors.

9 The official works entirely separated from ownership of the means of administration and without appropriation of his position.

10 He is subject to strict and systematic discipline and control in the conduct of the office.[93]

Weber considers that bureaucracy in this sense functions equally well in private "capitalistic" companies as in public organizations, in profit as in non-profit associations, and in socialist as in capitalist systems. This is because the organizational form

> is, from a purely technical point of view, capable of attaining the highest degree of efficiency [*zum Höchstmaß der Leistung vervollkommenbare*] . . . It is superior to any other form in precision, in stability, in the stringency of its discipline, and in its reliability [,]

predictability and "in intensive efficiency and in the scope of its operations".[94]

Weber actually means, a point to which he returns several times with prophetic clairvoyance, that a functioning socialism requires a still more developed bureaucracy than capitalism.

Bureaucracy exercises its authority through *knowledge*. This is of two kinds: expert ("technical") knowledge and internal organizational knowledge which officers absorb in the practice of their occupations ("official secrets", commercial secrets, etc.).

The only one superior to the bureaucrat in terms of knowledge is the small private entrepreneur. But the "need for stable, strict, intensive, and calculable" operations is what "gives bureaucracy a crucial role in our society as the central element in any kind of large-scale administration".[95] The only thing, therefore, that would be able to diminish the importance of bureaucracy would be a return to "small-scale" operations in all societal areas.

Weber is particularly emphatic on the machine-like character of bureaucracy:

> The decisive reason for the advance of bureaucratic organization has always been its purely *technical* superiority over any other form of organization. The fully developed bureaucratic apparatus compares with other organizations exactly as does the machine with the non-mechanical modes of production. Precision, speed, unambiguity, knowledge of the files, continuity, discretion, unity, strict subordination, reduction of friction and of material and personal costs – these are raised to the optimum point in the strictly bureaucratic administration. . . .[96]

Weber paints a rather bleak picture of the relentlessness of the bureaucratic machinery, both for employees and clients:

> Where administration has been completely bureaucratized, the resulting system of domination is practically indestructible.
>
> The individual bureaucrat cannot squirm out of the apparatus into which he has been harnessed. . . . [T]he professional bureaucrat is chained to his activity in his entire economic and ideological existence. In the great majority of cases he is only a small cog in a ceaselessly moving mechanism which prescribes to him an essentially fixed route of march. The official is entrusted with specialized tasks, and normally the mechanism cannot be put into motion or arrested by him, but only from the very top. The individual bureaucrat is, above all, forged to the common interest of all the functionaries in the perpetuation of the apparatus and the persistence of its rationally organized domination.
>
> The ruled, for their part, cannot dispense with or replace the bureaucratic apparatus once it exists, for it rests upon expert training, a functional specialization of work, and an attitude set on habitual virtuousity in the mastery of single yet methodically integrated functions. If the apparatus stops working, or if its work is interrupted by force, chaos results, which it is difficult to master by improvised replacements from among the governed. This holds for public administration as well as for private economic management. Increasingly the material fate of the masses depends upon the continuous and correct functioning of the ever more bureaucratic organizations of private capitalism, and the idea of eliminating them becomes more and more utopian.
>
> Increasingly, all order in public and private organization is dependent on the system of files and the discipline of officialdom, that means, its habit of painstaking obedience within its wonted sphere of action. The latter is the more decisive element, however important in practice the files are. The naive idea of Bakunism[97] of destroying the basis of "acquired rights" together with "domination" by destroying the public documents overlooks that the settled orientation of *man* for observing

the accustomed rules and regulations will survive independently of the documents. Every reorganization of defeated or scattered army units, as well as every restoration of an administrative order destroyed by revolts, panics, or other catastrophes, is effected by an appeal to this conditioned orientation, bred both in the officials and in the subjects, of obedient adjustment to such [social and political] orders. If the appeal is successful it brings, as it were, the disturbed mechanism to "snap into gear" again.[98]

There was, however, a deep chasm between Weber's Metaphorical conception of reality and the Tragically threatening shadow of a spiritually evermore dead machine-society, to which his own researches were leading. Testimony to this is the following revolutionary outburst, where he rips the mask off scientific objectivity and denounces the whole modern way of organizing:

> . . . as if we knowingly and willingly *should* become people who need order and nothing but order, who become nervous and cowardly if this order wavers for an instant, and helpless if they are torn away from their unqualified adaptation to this order . . . [the central issue is] what we have to *resist* this machinery so as to keep a remnant of humanity free from this parcelling of the soul, from this exclusive supremacy of bureaucracy's ideals of life.[99]

The rationalization process resulted in a loss of meaning to which Weber gave the apposite name *disenchantment* (*Entzauberung*). The only force capable of offering an alternative to bureaucracy is charisma.[100),101)] However, the latter was, according to Weber, in the short term "unstable", and in the long term exposed to erosion. This is because the charismatic leader always believes that his magical properties are intrinsic, wheras in reality they are conferred on him by his followers. However, the proof of charisma is success. If this fails, sooner or later the followers will desert, and the charisma fade away.

In the long run, the charismatic organization is inexorably hollowed out, particularly by the economic forces which always work in the same direction: towards bureaucracy. Of central importance, thereby, is the need for calculability, and consequently discipline. Weber took most of his illustrations from the white-collar sphere, but there are also comments on the situation on the shop floor. To him, scientific management lay, interestingly enough, at the utmost limit of rationality and discipline, and thus also close to the ideal type. Here the Metonymic style of thought is formulated with unsurpassable acuity:

> . . . [O]rganizational discipline in the factory has a completely rational basis. With the help of suitable methods of measurement, the optimum

profitability of the individual worker is calculated like that of any material means of production. On this basis, the American system of "scientific management" triumphantly proceeds with its rational conditioning and training of work performances, thus drawing the ultimate conclusions from the mechanization and discipline of the plant. The psycho-physical apparatus of man is completely adjusted to the demands of the outer world, the tools, the machines – in short, it is functionalized, and the individual is shorn of his natural rhythm as determined by his organism; in line with the demands of the work procedure, he is attuned to a new rhythm through the functional specialization of muscles and through the creation of an optimal economy of physical effort.[102]

Charisma is alien in principle to economic interests, and generally to any form of structured activity, while the opposite is the case for the efficient and well-ordered bureaucracy. The consequence is that the latter will gain the upper hand in the long run: back to business as usual. This phenomenon Weber gave the well-known designation *routinization of charisma.*

This dialectic between bureaucracy and charisma integrates at a higher level the conceptions of Marx and Nietzsche, the two writers whom Weber himself regarded most highly.[103),104)]

For Marx the loss of meaning in human relations was the result of the economy of commodity production, and in particular the dominance of its capitalistic form. By contrast, Weber maintained that, instead of economy, organizational *power* was central; that this power best expressed itself in a bureaucratic, i.e. meaning-less form; that capitalism had by necessity to take on a bureaucratic shape; but that capitalism was just *one* of bureaucracy's possible manifestations. We even find, interestingly enough, a generalization of Marx's theory of alienation. In the latter, the separation of the direct users of the means of production from the means provides the basis for the entire system. This alienated system is extended in Weber from capitalism alone to a much more encompassing bureaucracy:

> The relative independence of the artisan or cottage outworker, of the landowning peasant, of the holder of a benefice, of the knight and the vassal depended on the fact that he himself owned the tools, supplies, financial means, or weapons with whose help he pursued his economic, military, or political function and from which he lived during his performance. Contrariwise, the hierarchical dependence of the worker, salesman, technician, academic assistant, *and* state official and soldier rests on the fact that those tools, supplies, and financial means which are indispensable for organization and economic existence are concentrated in the hands of either the entrepreneur or the political lord. . . . The "separation" of the worker from the material means to his activity takes many forms; he is separated from the means of production in the

economy, from the means of war in the army, from the material means of administration in public administration, from the means of research in the university institute and laboratory, from the financial means in all of them. It is the decisive foundation common to the capitalist private enterprise and to the cultural, political, and military activities of the modern power state.[105]

Unlike in Marx, human relations could regain their lost meaning not through a violent revolution – this would only lead to either anarchic chaos or a new bureaucracy – but through sporadic eruptions of charisma.[106]

History for Weber, by contrast with Marx, has *no purpose*. Here the influence of Nietzsche's "supra-historical" conception is palpable.[107] According to this, the value of history does not lie in its pre-determined end, but in the gleams of a more sublime consciousness which, in the form of outstanding, creative personalities, illuminates its generally grey, monotonous and mediocre course.[108),109)] The difference as against the aristocratically individualistic Nietzsche was that the social scientist Weber placed these charismatic gleams in an organizational context.[110)]

Thus, Marx's view was unsatisfactory because it confined the critique of modern dehumanization to being valid only for capitalism. On the other hand, Nietzsche's great, freely creative individuals were too isolated from their surrounding society. Weber therefore extended the Marxist theory of alienation from capitalism to bureaucracy, of which capitalism was only one aspect. As a complement, he extended the Nietzschean thesis of pattern-breaking, creative individuals to apply to charismatic personalities in the world of organizations. Weber's dialectic between bureaucracy and charisma therefore constitutes a synthesis at higher level of Marx and Nietzsche.[111),112)] See Figure 3.4, where the shorter arrow symbolizes charismatic revolution of bureaucracy, and the longer routinization of charisma.

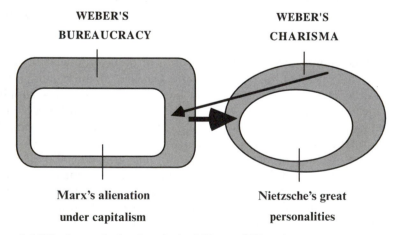

Figure 3.4 Weber's organizational synthesis of Marx and Nietzsche.

The parallel to Taylor's dramaturgy is also striking. In both Taylor and Weber, the well-oiled machinery of rationality succeeds a pre-rational state of arbitrariness and lack of order. For Taylor this takes place through the crisis of foremanship and the resolution by means of scientific management. For Weber, the crisis instead takes the form of the routinization of charisma or tradition. Yet, the Tragic process through which the law of reason reveals itself is common to them both.[113]

The difference is that Taylor perceived the novel state arrived at as the best of all possible worlds. For Weber, rational bureaucracy was certainly the perfect solution to the organizational problem, but at the terrible price of rendering the world empty, sterile, and cold, by depriving it of all inner Metaphorical meaning.[114]

Thus, his organizational drama is enacted in the genre of *fatalistic Tragedy*, where the heroic element is played down and the determinism of the laws of fate becomes the main point of the narrative, instead of the victory over the crisis. As with Taylor and Fayol the emphasis is on the state following the crisis, but we are now more temporally distant from this mid-point of the characteristic course of events. The fatalistic genre tends slightly towards an Ironic conception "by putting the characters in a state of lower freedom than the audience"[115] (this, by the way, may explain the interest of the postmodernists in Weber, to which we alluded in the beginning of the present section). Frye describes this in wordings that might actually have been formulated by Weber himself:

> [T]he central idea that crystallizes . . . is the idea of inscrutable fate or external necessity. The machinery of fate is administered by a set of remote invisible gods, whose freedom and pleasure are ironic because they exclude man . . . . They demand sacrifices, punish presumption, and enforce obedience to natural and moral law as an end in itself. . . . [A] society held together by a kind of molecular tension of egos, a loyalty to the group or the leader which diminishes the individual, or, at best, contrasts his pleasure with his duty or honor.[116]

In lighter moments Weber could take a more optimistic stance, but his main view was that charisma, even though it constituted the only hope of a counter-force to the dehumanizing bureaucracy, would have difficulties to make headway against it.

Taylor – and Marx – belong to the radical, Weber by contrast to the resigned Tragedy authors.[117] For the former the law appears as a divine revelation. For Weber, on the other hand, it takes on other, quite opposite features. In the citations given above, he describes the condition of the bureaucrat in characteristic, pictorial language: "painstaking obedience . . . chained . . . squirm . . . forged . . . cog in a ceaselessly moving mechanism . . . domination . . . parcelling of the soul . . . mechanization and discipline . . . shorn of natural rhythm . . . methodical division of muscular functions."[118]

"Demonic" archetypes with deep roots in both mythology and psychology.[119)]

Much has been written about the machine metaphor in the classics. In Weber, this metaphor has a double function: as an instrument for maximum efficiency, and as a torture mechanism for the individual. Bureaucracy as an instrument of fate for the achievement of maximum efficiency is played out as a fatalistic Tragedy. Yet, in the infernal vision we are given a taste of here, this fades over into another genre, *demonic Tragedy*, with tearing apart [*sparagmos*], torture and mutilation as central themes.[120)] The genre leans towards absurd Tragic Irony. It lies still further than the previous (fatalistic) one from the middle of the characteristic course of events, thereby marking a Tragedy on its way to grotesque dissolution. Weber's organizational drama oscillates between the two genres, fatalistic and demonic Tragedy. Demonic Tragedy is usually too harsh on the audience for it to appear on its own; for the most part it is mixed with other types, as here with the fatalistic genre.[121)]

Against both laws of fate and such diabolical instruments of control as were just touched upon, the irrational forces of charisma fare badly in the long run. But as we recall, there was another alternative to bureaucracy, namely the small businessman. So, might not the entrepreneur act as a counter-force? Weber suggests this in passing, but does not follow up the clue, possibly because he considered it self-evident that large-scale operation and thereby also bureaucracy would inevitably dominate the economy. (At the beginning of the twenty first century, with the very edge of the advanced economies consisting of a dynamic sphere of small, but fast-growing, flourishing knowledge enterprises, targeted on new technology, this is, of course, far from self-evident – one only has to bring to mind terms like Nasdaq and the Internet.) But it is also the case that the entrepreneur does not really fit into Weber's ideal-type schema of tradition, charisma and bureaucracy.

Argumentation is also lacking for Weber's list of the ten characteristics of bureaucracy. These have given rise to a great deal of puzzlement in later research: Why just these and no others? the reader asks. Are they a divine revelation, or where do they come from?

The answer, as far as can be judged, lies in the fact that they are the result of an *analytical comparison with the two other ideal types*. It is a question of properties that the legal type of authority in an organization "should" have owing to its rational orientation, where the most efficient means are used to realize its goals. By contrast, traditional and/or charismatic organizations, either by definition or historically, lack these properties.[122)] Moreover, with one possible exception, the properties are selected so that they apply to the individual occupant of an "office", not to the organization as a whole. This is in accordance with Weber's Metaphorical style of thought, with its focus on individual actors.

Let us elaborate what has just been said by studying the ten characteristics of bureaucracy point by point.

1 *Personal freedom, and subjection to authority only with respect to impersonal obligations.*
   Officials in traditional bureaucracies are usually personally unfree – they were, for example, slaves in the Roman and Ottoman Empires. In charismatic organizations by definition, subordination is linked to a person (the charismatic leader) and is not a question of impersonal duties.
2 *Clearly defined hierarchy of offices* and
3 *Clearly defined spheres of competence.*
   Hierarchies and spheres of competence, i.e. formal structures, are unclear in traditional and charismatic organizations, both historically and for reasons of definition.
4 *Free contractual relationship.*
   Employment contracts do not arise in the case of tradition or charisma, again for both historical and definitional reasons.
5 *Technical qualification (as proven by examination).*
   There are no requirements for examinations in charismatic organizations (although they can be found in traditional organizations, e.g. the Mandarin system in imperial China).
6 *Remuneration by fixed salaries in money.*
   Fixed remuneration is not customary in either traditional or charismatic organizations.
7 *The office as the sole or primary occupation.*
   The office as the sole or primary occupation is no necessity in either charismatic or traditional organizations.
8 *Promotion by seniority or achievement.*
   Promotion according to criteria of seniority or achievement is not the rule in traditional or charismatic organizations.
9 *Separation from ownership of the means of administration and non-appropriation of position.*
   In traditional organizations, the occupant of an office can, for example, own land as the economic basis for the service provided. The office can also be inherited.
10 *Strict and systematic discipline and control.*
   Strict and systematic discipline and control in the conduct of an office is generally conspicuous by its absence in both traditional and charismatic organizations.

It might then be wondered, both whether there are not other characteristics of bureaucracy which do not emerge from such a comparative conceptual analysis, and whether there are not different kinds of bureaucracy which embrace different points on the list. That at least the latter query might be warranted is demonstrated by empirical studies suggesting that actual bureaucracies possess the listed properties to a highly variable extent.[123]

The uncanny machine-like efficiency of bureaucracy by which Weber was both fascinated and repelled was also questioned by the later researchers of the functionalist school after the Second World War, whose interest was directed to the systemic defects of bureaucracy, its so-called "dysfunctions".

One might wonder whether Weber had not unconsciously created a rod for his own back by both proceeding from a largely Metaphorical basic position and devoting so much of his research to one organizational form, bureaucracy, which he had *defined* as impersonally and rationally instrumental – thus as Tragedy. In this way, even from the start, a vast gulf is built into his theory, between view of reality and of organization, between style of thought and dramaturgy.

It is possible to point to psychological background factors as a reason for this.[124] As always in such cases, these in no way render Weber's research findings less valid. They help to explain how the latter were arrived at, not whether they are justified. What remains is that Weber, despite, or rather thanks to, the seminal tensions in his authorship and through his intuitive clear-sightedness, has provided the impulse for so much later research that he more than anyone else can be designated as the "founding father" of organization theory. The organizational research in Weber's footsteps is vast and still swelling; we shall not even attempt an overview here, since this would require several separate volumes of its own. In a more general sense, it has been claimed that Weber even forestalled the postmodern critique of modernism, though of course without indulging in the Ironic quietism besetting so much of deconstructionism;[125] social reality, for him, was to be explained, not merely shrugged away as a trans-textual nonentity.

But, do Weber's analyses have any practical importance for us? Is his description topical? Do Weberian organizations exist today? They surely do, and what first comes to mind are probably bureaucracies within the public sector. However, one easily forgets that there are also modern and very well-known examples from private business. Here is one with which most of us will have made acquaintance at some time:

> Rules and regulations are the gospel at McDonald's. The company's operating bible has 385 pages describing the most minute activities in each outlet. The manual prescribes that certain equipment – cigarette, candy, and pinball machines – is not permitted in the stores. It also prescribes strict standards for personal grooming. Men must keep their hair short and their shoes black and highly polished. Women are expected to wear hair nets and to use only very light makeup. The store manager is even provided with a maintenance reminder for each day of the year, such as "Lubricate and adjust potato-peeler belt."
>
> McDonald's has a passion for standardization of products and work activities. The basic hamburger patty must be a machine-cut, 1.6 ounce chunk of pure beef – no lungs, hearts, cereal, soybean, or other fillers – with no more than 19% fat content. Hamburger buns must have 13.3% sugar in them. French fries are kept under the light for only seven minutes. A flashing light cues the cook to the exact moment to flip the

hamburger patties. Specially designed scoops determine the precise number of fries to fit in each pouch. The standardization of work reduces discretion of employees, but provides uniformity and consistency of products for consumers.

McDonald's uses its well-defined hierarchy. Field service managers visit each store regularly. An inspector will observe each store for three days, timing the counter and drive-through operations, and checking cooking procedures. Grades of A through F are given for cleanliness, quality, and service. If low grades are received, the inspector will come back unannounced and check again. If problems persist, the franchise may be taken away from the owner.[126]

Each store has a refined division of labour and qualified personnel. Assistant managers are assigned to cover each shift, and crew leaders are responsible for specific periods, such as breakfast or lunch. Cooks and waitresses know exactly what to do. Trainers teach new employees the exact procedure for greeting customers and taking orders. Hostesses are assigned the task of helping young children and old people, and they coordinate birthday parties and make sure customers are comfortable.[127]

3.4 Simon and the decision mechanisms: the last of the classics

It is not usual to count Herbert Simon as one of the classical writers.[128] But as indicated by the title above, we shall regard him as the last of the classics. Even if he revises them in important respects, his text expresses the same fundamental style of thought as the great rationalists.

In his book *Administrative Behaviour,* published in 1947,[129] Simon directed sharp criticism at the then hegemonic administrative management school, represented by Fayol and successors:

> It is a fatal defect of the current principles of administration that, like proverbs, they occur in pairs. For almost every principle one can find an equally plausible and acceptable contradictory principle. Although the two principles of the pair will lead to exactly opposite organizational recommendations, there is nothing in the theory to indicate which is the proper one to apply.[130]
>
> [M]uch administrative analysis proceeds by selecting a single criterion, and applying it to an administrative situation to reach a recommendation; while the fact that equally valid, but contradictory, criteria exist which could be applied with equal reason, but with a different result, is conveniently ignored.[131]

In his introduction to the second edition of the book ten years later Simon characterizes the current thinking of administration (that of the administrative management school) as at "best . . . homely proverbs", at "worst . . . pompous inanities".[132]

This is attributable to a focus on rules that might suit individual situations, but not the organization as such. In any study of this, total effectiveness has the central place. Even in the preface, he asserts that "realistically and significantly describing even a simple administrative organization" involves:

> describing it . . . in a way that will provide the basis for scientific analysis of the effectiveness of its structure and operation.[133]

Or, as he expresses it a little later:

> The theory of administration is concerned with how an organization should be constructed and operated in order to accomplish its work efficiently.[134]

Efficiency here denotes the maximization of output in relation to input:

> . . . this maximization is the aim of administrative activity, and . . . administrative theory must disclose under what conditions the maximization takes place.[135]

To anticipate our further discussion in Chapter 7 below, this is the Metonymic style of performance (there are others). The administrative management school had missed this overarching aspect, and treated various principles of management in isolation from one another. Furthermore, like all previous theory in the area (with one exception), it had concentrated solely on formal lines of authority and functional divisions, while bypassing the important way in which efficiency in organizations is carried through in practice, that is through *decisions*.

Simon took the idea of the central importance of decisions from Chester Barnard's influential book *The Functions of the Executive*,[136] and he adhered to this to the extent even of claiming that "decision-making is the heart of administration".[137]

Decision-making, thus, is central to organizational practice. Yet it is, still according to Simon, far too "gross" a basic unit to be manageable for organizational analysis:[138] a decision can be likened to a "great river, drawing from its many tributaries the innumerable component premises of which it is constituted"; it is impossible to say who *really* has made the decision[139] (and, one might add, *when* it was actually made).

Hence a "more appropriate unit of analysis"[140] is required. And Simon finds such a one in *the decision premise*. This corresponds to the tributaries just referred to; the decision premises constitute the myriads of conditions that precede the decision. Such an analytical division of reality into its constituent units is typical of the Metonymic style of thought: Taylor divided into American engineer-style work motions, Fayol into empirical facts and events, and Weber into social actions of German *Verstehen* philosophy.

Thereby, the behaviour of the individual also becomes rational, since it can be regarded as a "process of 'drawing conclusions from premises' ".[141] Behaviour in this way becomes the result of a purely logical calculus (cf. von Wright's rational action theory.)[142] In this context, Simon rejects the sociological role theory of action, developed by Parsons[143] and others, contending that this dramaturgical conception ends up in irrationality, since it presupposes that the individual merely plays a role, without any underlying reason.[144]

Thus, it is an axiomatic truth for Simon that human action is "rational"; a first principle and point of departure which cannot be disputed. This, together with a style that analyzes down to the smallest constituent units, is a clear indicator of a thinking whose basic perspective is coloured by the trope of Metonymy.

Organizational efficiency, therefore, is achieved by *influencing the decision premises of organization members*, and not only through authority and functional division as in the administrative management school. This influence is all the more necessary since individuals always act under *bounded rationality*. Simon rejects the traditional micro-economic picture of "economic man" (*homo economicus*).

This picture has of course been criticized many times before.[145)] What is special about Simon's critique, though, is the famous alternative he presents – the so-called *administrative man*. Because the number of decision premises applying to each individual decision is so great,[146] and given that time and other resources are limited, the decision-maker in the real world has to act with two constraints:[147] (1) restriction of the number of decision premises to a subset of those which actually exist; (2) a minimum rather than a maximum level as regards decision acceptance, i.e. choice of the (first) decision that *satisfices* rather than the one that maximizes.

This, then, is how administrative man operates. Even if such a picture has the merit of taking account of the lack of rationality in the real world, yet by this very token it creates considerable scope for irrationality, which is in clear conflict with Simon's fundamentally Metonymic conception. An organization, for Simon, has the function of exercising "control" over the irrationality of the individual: "administrative theory is concerned with control of the nonrational".[148] The rationality of the individual in decision-making is an island in a sea of irrationality, which means that there is a need for something that can extend the boundaries of human reason, reclaim the sea by building dykes.[149]

That something, which can increase the rationality of individuals, so that their behaviour comes to accord with the organization's overall striving for efficiency, is the various "mechanisms" (a term that recurs time and again) constituting the *raison d'être* of the organization, and the means through which the organization can modify the decision premises of the individual. Among the mechanisms in question can be mentioned the authority and functional division of the administrative management school, but also communication and the development of loyalty (internalization of values, identification). [150]

Through these mechanisms, the organization exerts *influence* on the individual,[151] but in a more indirect and smooth way – via decision premises – than the administrative management school (and the early classical writers in general) had imagined.

Regarding, for example, the development of loyalty – one of the mechanisms referred to – Simon expresses himself as follows:

> The organization trains and indoctrinates its members. This might be called the "internalization" of influence, because it injects into the very nervous systems of the organization members the criteria of decision that the organization wishes to employ.[152]

The power machine still remains, and serves the same purpose (Metonymic efficiency), but now functioning in a more sophisticated and indirect manner (see Figure 3.5).[153] The early classics are represented to the left. Here, there is a direct and simple line of power from the organization to the single individual. In Simon, to the right in the figure, the organization exerts its power on the single individual through his or her decision premises, as illustrated by the black arrows. The shaded arrows represent the result of this, which is similar to that of the early classics. The double arrows (compared to the single arrow depicted in the early classics) represent the higher sophistication and thereby efficiency of Simon's revisionist approach: the organization can influence the individual in more and better ways.

Why then do individuals accept to let themselves be steered? Here we come to a second, but subordinate part of Simon's theory (treated in

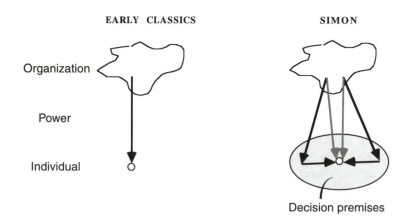

Figure 3.5 The power machine according to the early classics and according to Simon.

Note: The shaded arrows indicate indirect power.

Chapter 7, which he himself characterizes as a "digression" in the introduction to the second edition). As with the decision focus, Simon has drawn the idea here from Barnard.[154] The organization is regarded Synecdochically as a system with input and output flows. Inputs and outputs are considered as *contributions* and *inducements* respectively. Only if contributions and inducements are in equilibrium can the organization keep its members; in particular is mentioned "the employees". The work effort the latter put in should be balanced against, be in equilibrium with, their payment, if they are to stay. This seems reasonable at first sight, even though the position of the equilibrium naturally depends on the supply of and demand for labour.

Simon now maintains that this balancing act is compatible not only with the goal of the organization to survive (which comes in here) but also with its overarching "criterion of efficiency".[155] However, this means, as we remember, the maximization of output in relation to input. But here a fundamental contradiction emerges. *Either* a company aims at maximizing the exchange from work and keeping down wage costs. *Or* it strives to keep them "in equilibrium". It cannot do both at the same time. The alternatives are in fact mutually exclusive: they are based on two quite different, and in this case conflicting, performance goals – on the one hand efficiency and on the other (systemic) effectiveness (cf. Chapter 7 below).

So, at this central point, a fundamental inner contradiction befalls Simon's theory – a symptom of its rhetorical split between Metonymy and Synecdoche. The two parts – the organization as a masked Tragic power mechanism and the organization as the friendly contribution/inducement system of Comedy – simply do not hang together. In line with his basic style of thought, Simon wants to claim one single, overriding Metonymic efficiency, i.e. output/input; at the same time, he is forced to admit that there is also Synecdochic effectiveness, i.e. system survival. He then forcibly subsumes the latter under the former; which cannot be done, for they are in opposition to each other, both theoretically and empirically.

As a result of this striving for a Metonymic regime in style of thought we then obtain two organizational dramas – a sophisticated Tragic main performance and a Comic shadow-play which are acted out partly independently, partly in collision with each other. This involves a clash of styles since "comedy can contain a potential tragedy within itself, [but] . . . to reverse the procedure [is] almost impossible".[156)]

Yet, this striving for a Metonymic regime has also led to further problems in the theory. More specifically, these concern the decisions as the Metonymic heart of the organization; or expressing it differently, as its smallest but one set of rational components. The smallest, as we remember, were the decision premises. Thus, everything in an organization consists of decisions which can be divided up into premises, like molecules which can be divided into atoms. The question arises if this is a reasonable picture of organizational reality. Are there not, in addition to these Metonymic decisions, for example Metaphorical courses of events as well? But there are several other objections that could be directed against the decision approach which has even been characterized as a "paradigm"[157] in organization theory.[158)]

In Simon's conceptual interpretation, decisions appear as something which precedes every human behaviour, of whatever kind, from pure reflex actions to complicated planning activities. It is further stated that decisions are either conscious *or unconscious.* The common meaning of the term is thus extended to cover the mental background to all human behaviour. This background is identified by Simon as the individual's choice of an action from among those that are "physically possible".[159] Thus, choice between actions or behaviours (the words are used in the same sense by Simon) is synonymous with decision.

It seems dubious, however, to maintain that an individual reaches a decision, or makes a choice, when he/she actually does not do this, in the normal sense of the word. By incorporating even unconscious "decisions" or "choices" and reflex actions, Simon has extended the concept so far as to make it virtually meaningless – it encompasses every conceivable situation and therefore designates practically nothing, ending up in triviality: psychological factors lie behind human action. To call all these factors "decisions" or "choices" is really not to add any determination at all to them. What can the psychological background to a reflex action have in common with the background to a complex planning process? Is it reasonable, for example, as Simon does, to maintain that even the contractions of the leg muscles involved in walking have "minute decisions" as their background?[160] Is it reasonable to suppose that one can reach unconscious decisions? If so, what do these have in common with conscious ones? Furthermore, between these two cases – reflex actions and complex planning activities – plus conscious and unconscious backgrounds to action – there is a range of intermediate forms, with major differences between them, for which it is hard to find any underlying unity.

It is difficult to avoid the conclusion that the function of the concept is to tie up all organization theory around decisions; thus the concept is extended to cover everything, and so in reality nothing.

The centring around decisions leads to an excessively rationalistic outlook: the human being is seen as the decision-making animal. While Simon distances himself from a "rationalistic bias", [161] this mainly involves marking the distinction between a "maximizing" decision-making and other types.[162] Later authors have, for example, studied "nondecisions"[163] (note that the terminology is still locked into the decision paradigm), from which it transpires that decisions are not the one and only saving faith. It has been further pointed out that a fixation with decisions leads to an uncalled-for overshadowing of *action.*[164] Also, routinized and anomic organizational types, for example, are left outside the framework. In the former, activities are governed by rules rather than goals; in the latter there are neither rules nor values.[165]

It can further be argued that fundamental aspects of organizational activities, such as problem seeking, problem solving (at least a broad spectrum of problem-solving tasks, where patterns are discovered, but choices between alternatives not made) become neglected when there is a one-sided focus on decisions. Such activities are usually regarded as characteristic of "organic" organizations and "flexible" planning. Even the intuitive and visionary *élan,* which characterizes the charismatic entrepreneur, has little in common with rational decision-making – whether this be maximizing or bounded (i.e. satisficing).

Moreover, a focus on decisions leads to the centring of interest – something which Simon explicitly recommended[166] – on the individual/the decision-maker. At a supra-individual or collective level Simon's decision concept becomes even more unmanageable: then a decision can be conceived of as an action, carried out by a group or a number of individuals ("Now, we come to the decision!"), and, as an action, must according to definition have a further decision as background etc. – thus, one ends up with an infinite regress. Furthermore, it is easy to point to cases where the action takes place, for example, on the basis of a general consensus, entirely without any decision.

In summary: decisions *can,* but *need not* be part of a process within a certain organization (there are decision-less processes). *If* the process involves a decision, it does not go without saying that this stage in the course of events is the central or key occurrence; this depends both on the nature of the course of events and on the basic problem addressed by the investigation.

To the above can be added intuitive actions, changes that are not problem-driven,[167] rationalizations after the event with post- rather than pre-mises,[168] etc.[169)]

The basic Metonymic perspective in his style of thought, together with his criticism of the administrative management school, has driven Simon to a focus on decisions as the last bastion of rationalism. To sustain his thesis on the decision as the organization's molecular unit he is compelled to give a persuasive definition of a decision so that it covers more or less everything that goes on in the administrative part of an organization, whether or not this be a decision in the usual sense of the word. The result is shifts and contradictions between this "usual sense" and "everything".

A further criticism commonly aimed at Simon is that the empirical side of his work is mostly based on public organizations, and that – in consequence – "administrative man" should be confined to these, while "economic man" could maintain his grip on private organizations, in particular privately owned companies. In the light of Chester Barnard's foreword to the book, this criticism is hard to agree with. He stresses that in his experience as a corporate executive – which can scarcely be questioned – Simon's theory is applicable to both the private and the public sector.

A few words on Simon's method. On several occasions he professes himself an adherent of "logical positivism". The administrative management school is criticized for not presenting "operational" concepts, something which Simon himself claims to have done. (This seems mainly to have been a question of good intentions, for it is hard to see any difference in degree of operationalization between the administrative management school and Simon.) Nevertheless, his stance in principle justifies the classification of Simon in terms of method as Scientistic.

In summary, Simon can be described as a Tragic revisionist. He saw clearly the deficiencies in the Metonymic classics. To repair the theory but still retain its Metonymic base he was forced into constructions and assumptions that generated contradictions in the depths of its structure. He criticized the administrative management school for presenting inconsistent rules of thumb, but himself came to recommend the application of other rules of thumb (those of bounded rationality) within the framework of an inconsistent theory. A further criticism against the administrative management school concerned its lack of empirical moorings. Simon's administrative man did not possess any more of this, and was only later on subjected to empirical testing.[170] (It is true that Simon covers himself by claiming that he has only proposed a "vocabulary" for the description of organizations, but he glides the whole time between this more modest linguistic ambition and actual descriptions,[171] even concrete recommendations.[172],[173]

What has lasted over the years are the ideas of satisficing and focus on decisions. In themselves both can be disputed on anti-Metonymic grounds. Decision-making is not always as central as Simon thought. Nor does it always proceed as a logical syllogism, with premises and conclusions standing to attention; often it takes place intuitively, involving rationalizations after the event, etc.

For his work, Herbert Simon was awarded the Nobel prize for Economics in 1978 – so far the only organization theorist to gain this recognition otherwise mostly reserved for economists in the more narrow, disciplinary sense.

Simon revised the rational, Tragic classics in the field of organization theory. Instead of the cold bureaucracy of the naked power machine he posited a more sophisticated and subtle apparatus, which exercised its power by indirect routes. The Metonymic style of thought could thereby be retained as the basis. In Chapter 4 we shall encounter an approach whose own empirical findings gradually drove it to abandon this very Metonymic foundation.

3.5 The classical organization (theory) lives on

The classical, Tragic organization theory still exists in what might be called sublimated form. Even though it has often been something of a punch bag for easy-won polemics, the best expression of its current state at a more sophisticated theoretical level is that it has been *generalized*. That is, later research has shown that the classical organization model is not generally valid, but can be regarded as one design among several possible. Much succeeding research has been concerned precisely with the limits of applicability of the classical organizational model, what these are due to and what lies outside them. As we shall see, there are various perspectives here, and the discussion to a large extent has been about the form into which the classical model should be generalized. That such generalization is needed, most researchers agree upon, on account of empirical findings that have demonstrated other models extant.

Yet, the empirical data also make it apparent that the classical model lives on. Burns and Stalker found it, alongside an alternative model, in their twenty case studies of the management of innovation in British companies in the 1950s.[174] Woodward found the same pattern in her survey study of manufacturing firms in south Essex in the 1950s.[175] Similar results – with varying interpretations and terminology – were presented over the following decades by the Aston school, by Lawrence and Lorsch, and by numerous authors in their wake.[176)]

In later decades, the classical models still hold their ground. Miller and Friesen's taxonomy from the 1980s, based on factor analysis of a selection of 52 corporate reports gives the classical type 12 percent of the sample.[177)] The classical model also appears, with varying names but similar content, in other more modern typologies: Mintzberg's and Lawrence's machine bureaucracy; Pfeffer's bureaucratic decision model; Enderud's bureaucracy; and two of the author's bureaucratic planning cultures, technocracy and routine.[178,179)]

The classical model is also a constant ingredient in *organizational life cycles*, where it appears as a phase or stage. Cameron and Whetten constructed a synthesis of nine empirically based models of organizational life cycles and arrived at four phases or stages as common to them. They then replicated all four phases in a simulation experiment. The third of these phases was the classical organizational model.[180]

The rumour of the imminent demise of bureaucracy[181] is thus much exaggerated. It is quite clear that the classical model is still going strong, both in theory and practice[182)] – even though it now has competitors.

Simon's thinking on decisions has had exceptional influence on both organization theorists and practitioners, especially through the so-called Carnegie Tech school, with Simon himself, March and Cyert as its most prominent representatives. (The name comes from the Carnegie Institute of Technology, now renamed the Carnegie-Mellon University, where Simon and his disciples were active.) Cyert and March's behavioural theory of the firm,[183] and March's and others' well-known Garbage Can Model of decision-making[184] are offshoots of this school. Even a more recent, topical approach such as transaction cost analysis has its roots in the Carnegie Tech school, with which its founding father, Oliver Williamson, was associated.[185)] It would lead too far for us to describe here all the areas where decisionism has found application; as we saw earlier, it has even been regarded as a kind of organizational "paradigm". Provided its totalizing claims to cover everything organizational are peeled away, it still remains applicable and fruitful.[186]

3.6 The poetics of the classical organization

The trope of metaphor is based on *similarity*. Examples: "the moon is a yellow cheese"; "the heart is a lonely hunter". By contrast, the trope of metonymy is based on *contiguity*. Examples: the crozier in hand, which symbolizes the bishop; the mortar board which symbolizes the doctor of philosophy; "a good Burgundy" – the product symbolized by its place of origin. (The bishop, the doctor or the wine certainly do not *resemble* the crozier, the mortar board, or the part of a country; rather, in some sense, these *lie near at hand*).[187] The Metonymic style of thought is fundamentally analytical, separating, divisive: reality consists of discrete, contentless pieces.

The Metonymic style of thought has a natural affinity with a method that seeks to reveal the rational laws of the organization. This is, of course, the *Scientistic* method, mentioned in the Introduction. The type of facts selected are single, individual events, devoid of meaning, which is most clearly illustrated by classical physics, where the objects are determined only by their movement or state of rest in time and space. The intrinsic emptiness of the events makes them easy to measure, which in turn enables the positing of regularities for multitudes of similar events – laws. Causal explanation through law-like regularities is a central element, and means that the events are subsumed under a certain law (with the specification of initial conditions). Thus – to use the categories presented in the Introduction – the interpretive model is causal explanation; the basic relationship is event-law, where a multiplicity of separate, intrinsically meaningless events constitute the object of study and the law is the ground sought for.[188]

This in turn paves the way for a Tragic organizational drama, where the organization is seen as a number of separate parts, governed by iron laws of fate. The human being in the organization thereby becomes a mere "cog in the wheel". The characteristic course of events is that the organization ends up in radical crisis through ignorance of the true nature of the laws. The crisis leads to the epiphany of laws.[189] The course of events is deterministic.[190]

The organizational style which brings together the elements of this triad we denote as *separative*. In its ideal state the rational, classical organization is a variant of the separative organizational style which forms the triad of style of thought, organizational drama and method shown in Figure 3.6.

In the concrete organization theories of Taylor and Fayol, the representatives of engineering science among the classics, reality corresponds well with the ideal. The fundamental Metonymic outlook is proclaimed both in Taylor's manic division of work motions into discrete temporal and spatial units and in Fayol's view of the external world as consisting of individual facts and events. After Scientistic measurement or classification of these analytical units, the laws or principles which control/should control the Tragic organization can be deduced. These laws are revealed through the organization's crisis, which is the *peripeteia* the drama undergoes. The organization is the Tragic hero, and after its purification a new, rational and

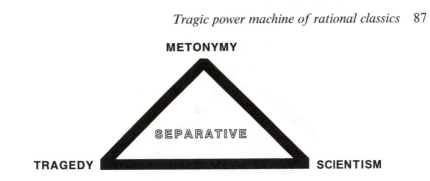

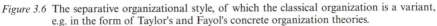

Figure 3.6 The separative organizational style, of which the classical organization is a variant, e.g. in the form of Taylor's and Fayol's concrete organization theories.

better world springs forth on the ruins of the old. The main emphasis is placed on the plan-drawn happiness after the crisis; the drama thus is enacted in the triumphant genre. Taylor and Fayol play both the role of Cassandra and that of the enlightening and commenting chorus. Their Tragic vision is the radical, utopian one. Thereby, their approaches are normative; and it is also in practice rather than in research that their ideas live on.[191]

In the self-divided and brooding Weber the tensions are greater, but so too is the depth. In his style of thought Weber had been influenced by contemporary German, neo-Kantian philosophy, with its Metaphorical, anti-Metonymic orientation. Metaphor is the basic figure of rhetoric (trope). As was mentioned previously, Metaphor is based on *similarity*. It represents something *as* something else.[192] Example: "A is a real gem." This similarity is not just something external and casual, but comes from the nature of the individual items themselves. A *is* a gem, by virtue of her very personality: her essence. All creatures and things in the world have an *inner meaning*.

As a consequence, Weber's method concentrated on understanding, focused on meaning. To that extent the method was Idiographic; the fundamental unit of understanding was the individual human actions. The advocacy of a division into individual actions was combined with explicit polemic against the Functional method, which presupposes a supra-individual unit of analysis. The strong rejection of such supra-individual unities renders the breakdown into individual atomic actions an almost analytical character, giving a certain Scientistic touch to the method. Clearer elements of the Scientistic method, though, are found in the ideal types suggested by Weber, and in his recommendation of supplementary statistical analyses. The strong inner tensions between Idiography and Scientism are, however, kept in rein in Weber's method, contributing to, instead of undermining, its fruitfulness (see Figure 3.7). Henceforth, striped markings on the triangle of our poetic figure will denote conflicts of style. In this case, the striped circle does not break the method corner, but reinforces it.

Weber's organizational drama, finally, was resigned Tragedy. From an original state of unreason (tradition or charisma) and ignorance of the laws, all organizations are led inexorably along the path towards a thoroughly

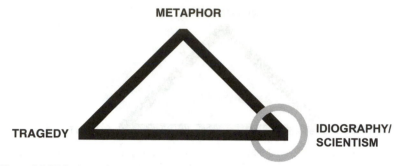

Figure 3.7 Weber's poetics.

regulated, efficient, and mechanically operating bureaucracy, a bureaucracy that can only sporadically be broken by the spontaneous eruptions of a perpetually losing, irrational charisma.[193] The genre is that of *fatalistic Tragedy*. But even more strongly: bureaucracy in Weber's vision took on clearly infernal features, with torture and mutilation as the central figurative elements. The text belongs to a particular dramaturgical genre, the *demonic Tragedy*, whose main theme is *sparagmos*, "the tearing apart of the sacrificial body".[194] Against the infernal reality of the bureaucracy stands the ever dubious, apocalyptic hope of salvation through charisma. Weber oscillates between these two genres, the fatalistic and the demonic Tragedy.

Weber, in contrast to the two other classical writers, was not normative but descriptive; for this reason, his ideas have not had such great influence in practice, but live on – or rather flourish – primarily in the context of research.

Herbert Simon, through his Metonymic analysis, saw clearly the defects in the classics of the administrative management school. To enable his concrete organization theory to repair the damage while still retaining the Metonymic basis, he made the assumption of decision premises, which holders of power could influence more indirectly than by merely giving orders. Thus, his text is a revisionist Tragedy.

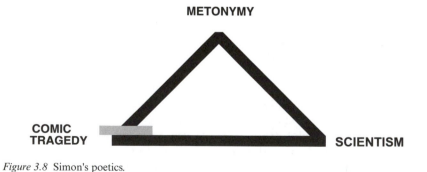

Figure 3.8 Simon's poetics.

The question why members of the organization should accept such indirect control led him, as with the centrality of decisions, to the ideas of Chester Barnard. Here, systems thinking, and more precisely a stakeholder model, provided the solution. But systems thinking basically narrates a Comedy, in which the organization seeks to obtain harmony and balance, in spite of temporary disturbances. In this way, therefore, his – somewhat moderated – Tragic organizational drama obtained an element of Comedy with which it was not fully compatible. A comic tragedy has difficulties in avoiding discontinuities of style, as is illustrated in Figure 3.8 by the shaded marking in the corner for the organizational drama.

Simon's method, finally, is explicitly Scientistic, and more precisely logical empiricist. Shifts between different levels of ambition – terminological development, description, and norm – have helped to keep his ideas alive linguistically, theoretically, and practically.

4   Romance with Human Relations

The Human Relations movement is the second major organizational wave we inquire into. The following account is based on the standard work, Roethlisberger and Dickson's *Management and the Worker* – an enormously rich book, not least because it boldly enough describes the entire research process and not, as is of course most common, only presents the polished final results. Just as with scientific management there are myths to strip away. One of these concerns the famous experiment on illumination which usually occupies the most prominent place in accounts of Human Relations.[1]

In reality the illumination experiment, or rather experiment*s*, as there were three of them, carried out between 1924 and 1927, figured merely as a *prelude* to the real Human Relations study. This took place through cooperation between the Industrial Relations Branch of the company investigated and a research team from Harvard University led by Elton Mayo; it lasted twelve years, 1927–39.

The place was the Hawthorne plants, located in Chicago and the neighbouring town of Cicero in Illinois. Hawthorne was the largest factory of the Western Electric Company, suppliers of telephone equipment to Bell Systems. The size of the company can be illustrated by its labour force, which, when the study started, amounted to about 29,000, with sixty or so different nationalities represented.

In what follows, we first look at the illumination experiment. As was pointed out above, this was carried out in the scientific management spirit, and did not deviate from the poetics of that movement, with its Metonymic thought style, its triumphantly Tragic drama, and its Scientistic method, which we elaborated on in the previous chapter. The aim of the experiments was to measure the effects on workers' performance of varying the illumination.

However, the results of the experiments were inconclusive, puzzling, and paradoxical, and led on to the case study of the "relay assembly test room", which we consider next. In this study, the researchers still followed a Metonymic style of thought. Yet, they had concluded that the investigation of a single variable such as illumination (which might not even be very central) was too narrow a focus. Instead, the new study was to investigate the effects on performance of pauses and shorter working hours. It was deemed advantageous to study a small group of people, in conditions somewhat analogous to laboratory tests, so as to keep potential disturbances under control. The results of this Metonymic study were again intriguing. The researchers discussed several plausible hypotheses to account for them, but, after excluding other possibilities, finally settled for a Metaphoric answer. The findings were related to the change in social relationships, inadvertently introduced when setting up the test room, and more precisely related to the changed conditions of supervision. The experiment became regarded as a "carrier of social value", and the *meaning* ascribed by the workers to events became crucial, not just external happenings.

These new insights led to the Metaphorically-based main phase of the whole study, which we treat in the next section. It is interesting, in this connection, to note that Vico saw the projection of inner fears onto imagined gods as characteristic of the Metaphoric phase: [2]

> As Vico says, they [the men of the Metaphoric period] lived in fear of themselves, that is of these aspects of their own natures which they had projected onto the physical world and conceived as gods. In their consciousnesses, men were nothing, and the gods were all, even though the gods were products only of their own imaginations and nothing but projections of their own animal and human capacities.

The study of irrational fears, or "sentiments", projected onto the organization and its managers, was in fact typical of the Metaphorical phase of the Hawthorne investigation.

The method of this phase was Idiographic, consisting of large amounts of interviews with employees. The quest by individuals for a true inner meaning was central to the Romantic organizational drama; symptomatically, the researchers in this phase were influenced by ideas from psychoanalysis and development psychology. However, during the course of this phase of the study, it eventually became clear that the interpretation of employees' attitudes and behaviours in terms of inner meaning had to be broadened, and the wider social background taken into account.

This was done in the final phase of the study, the "bank wiring observation room", which we treat next. Here, a Functionalist method was used, inspired by social anthropologists of this inclination. In general a Synecdochic thought style, expressing a systems view, prevailed. The function of management Comically was conceived as keeping a *social system* in equilibrium. This phase even brushed upon the Ironic thought style in the shape of a cultural approach.

The penultimate section discusses Human Relations' continued relevance for and influence on organizational theory and practice.

In all phases of the investigation, the preliminary and the three subsequent, one step led naturally to another, following a poetic logic, as is argued in the concluding section of the chapter. Here the threads are also drawn together in an analysis of styles, in which the poetics of the Human Relations movement is seen retrospectively as one of a mix between Metaphor and Synecdoche, with their concomitant organizational dramas and methods, and with the former dominating, the latter as shadow. The genres of the dramas and themes within these genres are also uncovered, thus completing and filling out the picture of the Human Relations poetics.

To elaborate: the Human Relations approach – the second major organizational approach – is mainly prefigured by a Metaphorical style of thought, with its affinites to a Romantic organizational drama or narrative, and an Idiographic method. Together these, with their mutual affinities, form an *expressive* organizational style, and Human Relations basically constitutes a variant of this style. Once adopted, this tropological structure works like a kind of precognitive filter that is inserted between researcher and "reality", establishing the linguistic protocol used to describe an object of study. This dominating style is supplemented by an integrative shadow style, with its particular affinities between its master trope, Synecdoche, and the associated Comic narrative and Functionalist method. The organizational drama of Human Relations, thus, becomes a Comic Romance – i.e. a Romance tinted with Comedy, and aptly described by the researchers' term "the social system". Within this drama, and within the specific "dualistic" genre employed, typical role characters and themes are discerned, such as the churl, the heavy father (*senex iratus*), the tricky slave, the beleagured castle, and the beauty and the beast.

4.1 Prelude: the experiments on illumination

In November 1924 Western Electric, in collaboration with the National Research Council of the National Academy of Sciences, embarked upon its study of "the relation of quality and quantity of illumination to efficiency in industry." The studies were in line with the tradition of Scientific Management; Gilbreth, a follower of Taylor, had taken an interest in the same issues. The experimental period lasted until April 1927. Three series of experiments were conducted over these two and a half years.[3]

In the first experiment, which covered three different departments at the factory, a start was made by measuring the rate of production under conditions of normal illumination. Then the intensity of illumination was increased in intervals, different for each department. However, no relationship between intensity of illumination and production efficiency could be established. In the first department, production went up and down without any relation to the strength of the illumination; in the second, efficiency increased steadily throughout the experiment, though unrelated to the increases in illumination; in the third, production efficiency at the beginning of each interval was higher than normal, and did not always fall even when the intensity of the illumination was reduced.

The second experiment on illumination involved an experimental group for which the intensity of illumination was varied, and a control group for which it was kept constant. It was found that production rose by roughly the same amount in both groups.

The third experiment, as the second, involved an experimental group and a control group. To remove possible influences from daylight, only electric lighting was used. This time, reducing the illumination by fixed intervals was tested. Nonetheless, the production of both groups increased right up to the point when they could no longer see what they were doing.

4.2 Phase 1: the relay assembly test room

From the illumination experiment, the persons in charge drew two conclusions. First, illumination intensity is only a minor factor among all that might influence work performance. Second, it was not possible to measure just one factor, as others were not controlled for; moreover, it was impossible to single out just one of many influences.

For this reason, it was considered to be desirable for the future to isolate a smaller group of employees, who would be studied, so to say, under laboratory conditions. Then it should be possible to avoid uncontrollable external disturbances, thereby at least reducing the number of factors and making it easier to observe their effects. A Metonymic style of thought still lay behind the procedure, with a focus on measurement, passing over the inner meaning of actions.

A group of six female workers was selected. These were placed in a special room. For statistical purposes, among others, the assembly of relays had been deemed as the suitable kind of work. This meant fitting together telephone relays from about thirty-five small components. Assembly took about one minute per relay. A converted printing telegraph, which perforated holes in a moving paper tape, was employed for the measurement of job performance. Each row of holes represented a worker, and each hole a completed relay. Every time one of the participants had a relay ready, she dropped it through a hole in her work bench. On its way down to the chute, the relay passed through a "flapper gate" which, when opened, closed an electric circuit. This transmitted an impulse of current, causing the perforator of the telegraph machine to make a punch in the paper tape and a numerical counter to advance one step.

At this time, fatigue as a consequence of repetitive work was a controversial issue in industrial circles. The test room experiment at Hawthorne was, in line with this, to establish the effects of rest pauses and shorter working hours on production. Here, too, the tradition of Scientific Management and Taylor's pupil, Gilbreth, was followed.[4]

The experiment was divided into three phases, of which the first was introductory. The second and third studied the results of different kinds of rest pauses and shortened working hours. The experiment continued for five whole years, 1927–32, but even by 1929 preliminary results had emerged that fundamentally changed the entire Metonymic orientation of the study.[5]

In the introductory phase, the women, among other things, underwent medical examinations; these were continued at regular intervals during the following phases. The women were also assured that the experiment did not aim at maximizing job performance. If the changed work conditions, such as the rest pauses, made them work better, fine; then both they and the company had gained from the affair. But they were urged not to *exert* themselves to work faster.

In the experiment itself the women were placed together with a "test room observer" who would make notes on events and maintain a "friendly atmosphere" in the room. The observer, furthermore, had the task of sharing job supervision with the ordinary foreman (who was placed outside the room) and of keeping a journal with "a complete account of the daily happenings in the test room",[6] including conversations. Further information was obtained as early as August 1927 by requesting the participants to answer a questionnaire about their private background conditions (family etc.), these being considered as one of the factors that might influence the experiment.

The second and third phases involved experimenting with various kinds of rest pauses and shortened working hours. The group of participants became more and more closely knit and began to arrange parties and other joint activities, such as visits to the theatre and dance halls, in their free time. The test room observer, playing something of a dual role, began to have some difficulties in maintaining discipline. There could, for example, be too much talk. But production did not suffer. The following episode testifies to the free and easy atmosphere and the relationship with the observer/supervisor. It occurred the day after he had warned them for "excessive talking".

The participants asked how long the experiment would last, and emphasized that they wished for it to go on for a long time, since they liked it much better in the test room than out in the main department. The observer replied that conditions in the department were generally the same as those in the test room.

> *Operator 2:* "Yes, but you can't scream and have the good times out there that we do in the test room, and the *fun* in the test room is what makes it worth while."
> *Operator 3:* "Yes, there are too many bosses in the department."
> *Operator 1:* "Yes, [the observer] is the only boss we have."
> *Operator 2:* "Say, he's no boss. We don't have any boss."
> *Observer* (starting to speak) "But you know . . ."
> *Operator 3:* "Shut up."
> *Operator 2:* "Look at that. Look at the way she tells her boss to shut up."[7]

Although the exchange of opinions had a bantering character, and took place during one of the parties arranged immediately after a round of physical examinations (to ameliorate the anxiety with which these were initially associated), it says a good deal about the atmosphere in the test room. Just compare the relationship between Taylor and Schmidt, taking place in the same country and general industrial era!

The outcome of the experiments that were conducted with great care during the second and third phases can be summarized in the following way:

> In many respects these results were puzzling to the investigators, for they were not what they had expected. The general upward trend in output independent of any particular change in rest pauses or shorter working hours was astonishing. The improvement in mental attitude throughout the first two years of the experiment was also perplexing.[8]

Thus, the same phenomenon demonstrated by the experiment on illumination was repeated: production increased continuously, *independent* of test variations in the form of changed job conditions.

Five hypotheses or interpretations were proposed to explain these anomal results:[9]

H1 *Improved occupational environment.* The ventilation in the test room had been improved by installing a fan, in contrast with the department outside. Illumination was more evenly spread. The mechanism for dropping assembled relays into a chute through a hole in the work bench was an improvement on the previous procedure. The test room also had other environmental advantages in comparison with the department.

H2 *Reduction in cumulative fatigue.* If fatigue is cumulative rather than fluctuating, the continually rising rate of production could be explained by a gradual reduction in stored-up tiredness.

H3 *Reduction in job monotony.* Variations in rest pauses and working hours might conceivably have had the effect of reducing monotony at work.

H4 *Increased wage incentive.* The factory operated a group piecework system. In that the group in the test room was so much smaller, increased job performance had a much clearer impact on wages.

H5 *Changes in methods of supervision.* As we have seen, other forms of job supervision had emerged in the test room. Proponents of this line maintained that the test room experiments served in the first instance as "carriers of social value". Improved supervisory conditions also had other advantageous social effects. Thus, according to hypothesis 5, "social factors" provided the explanation.

Hypothesis 1 on the work environment was rejected rather quickly. For example, the fan was only on in the summer. Given the results of the earlier experiment on illumination, the quite marginal improvement in lighting in the test room should have had no significance at all.

The other hypotheses were subjected to in-depth testing. Hypothesis 2 on cumulative fatigue could be falsified after a variety of physiological tests (it was assumed that only somatic, not mental fatigue could be cumulative). Hypothesis 3 on the reduction in monotony could be neither verified nor falsified, and hence was to be investigated in greater detail, in conjunction with a study of the general attitudes of the subjects. To test hypothesis 4 on wage incentives, two control experiments on new groups were carried out. In one, wages were held constant, but all other factors changed as in the test room; in the other, remuneration was changed as in the test room, while all other factors were held constant. Both control experiments showed that the increased productivity in the test room could not be attributed to the changed form of remuneration in isolation; it was inextricably linked with other factors.[10] Thus, hypothesis 4 could be written off, along with the other Metonymic hypotheses (1–3).

Thus, there remained the Metaphorical hypothesis 5 about changed supervisory conditions and the experiments as "carriers of social values". The participants had been removed from their normal environment, brought together in a small group and confronted with a wholly new form of supervision. The social environment had also been changed in other ways:

> There was an intermittent stream of other visitors or consultants: industrialists, industrial relations experts, industrial psychologists, and university professors.[11]

The head of the company's inspection department, who took an intense interest in the experiment, also made frequent visits. Furthermore, during the project, the test room observer had been appointed department head (the test room, hereby, was informally raised to a department in its own right). He still spent a large part of his time in the test room, now assisted by the new test room observer.

The investigators had embarked on the test room study with the Metonymic intention of conducting a scientific laboratory experiment. In their striving to keep all external factors constant and secure the cooperation of the participants, they had introduced so many new factors that they now posed the Metaphorical question whether these factors had not unintentionally become the essential ones. If so, the experiment, through influence of indirect effects, would have been transformed from technocratic into social-psychological.

> With this realization, the inquiry changed its character. . . . [The social] situation included *not only the external events but the meanings which individuals assigned to them* . . . .[12]

Here, the shift in style of thought from Metonymy to Metaphor is expressed with unsurpassed clarity. As we recall from Chapter 3, Metonymy – the trope of prose – builds on contiguity, and Metaphor – the trope of poetry – builds on similarity. While the former stands for an external relation in time and space, in the latter, the focus is switched to some inner, essential, and meaningful relation between two items. Metaphor sees something *as* something (meaningful) else. In other words, rather than looking at external, Metonymic causes and effects, Metaphor looks at the meanings of entities:

> ... the effects of the experimentally introduced changes in working conditions ... had proved to be *carriers of social meaning rather than mere changes in physical circumstances.*[13]

On the basis of the experimental results, company management took two sets of measures. First, they introduced rest pauses for the workers to an ever increasing extent. Even though it had not been demonstrated that these as such brought increased efficiency, they were, to judge from the reactions of the test room personnel, much appreciated, and could therefore lead to improved relations between management and employees without any negative effects. Second, management gave the green light for a further, more extensive, stage of the investigation which would map the attitudes of employees, as a further follow-up of the Metaphorical hypothesis 5.

In the secondary literature, this hypothesis has often gone under the name "the Hawthorne effect"; it has both been linked to the so-called "illumination experiment" and acquired the meaning that productivity increases, if workers only receive more "attention". That this is a gross misinterpretation should be evident after the account presented here. Moreover, empirical data do not indicate that attention as such would increase productivity.[14]

4.3 Phase 2: the interview programme

At about the same time as these new interpretations of the test room experiment began to gain the upper hand, the company held a training course for supervisory staff in the form of a conference. The subject was work morale, which company management thought had been given too little attention. Many opinions of the course participants were ventilated, and they often proved quite contrary to one another. To resolve these differences in views, there was obviously a need for a wider and more systematized factual base. When this was discussed within the company one of the test room observers hit upon the idea of interviewing employees, asking them about their attitudes for and against various aspects of their work environment.

The idea fell on fertile ground and a decision was made to start with the 1,600 employees in the Inspection Branch. At a second phase, the programme was extended to the Operating Branch, and at a third to all employees of the

Hawthorne plant. The activities became very extensive. In total, over 21,000 interviews were conducted in the course of the programme, which reached its peak in 1930.[15] The programme was discontinued in 1931, both as a result of the depression which now was hitting Western Electrics with major force, and because the prevailing Metaphorical research orientation had begun to be called in question, in favour of a new line.

In the first phase, the interviews were structured under six headings: job conditions, supervision and work; for and against. The questions corresponded to these headings. Each interview took about half an hour and, when written down, covered about 2 1/2 typed pages, single-spaced.

This way of proceeding proved impractical, however. First, the interviewers were continually forced to specify and concretize, since these questions were too general. Second, the interviewees tended to start talking about things they themselves thought were important, rather than answering the questions. And it was here that the really interesting information often emerged. As a result, the orientation was changed from the previous "direct" method of interviewing to an "indirect" one. The latter meant that the respondents themselves could choose the subject, and were not interrupted when they spoke of things which interested them. Expressed in modern terms, there was a transition from semi-structured to unstructured interviews. Each interview now took about 1 1/2 hours, and covered about ten typed pages.

The massive interview programme had several advantages. Recurring complaints could be used to adjust unsatisfactory conditions. Supervisors obtained a broad information on attitudes among the personnel. The interviewees were offered an opportunity, for once to ventilate their own problems; the interviewers gave eloquent accounts of how positively this was perceived – the programme even came to function as a real "lift" for the whole personnel. Finally, the researchers obtained an invaluable database at their disposal.

The question now was how this huge database should be interpreted. At first, the analytical team set up simply tried to group positive and negative judgements according to various factual areas. This, however, soon proved to constitute too simplistic a classification. In many cases, for example, it was difficult to verify the objective ground for a complaint; or there was no such "objective referent" at all.

In the latter case, the complaint had a "subjective" or inner referent – that is, it was the manifest expression of latent attitudes in the interviewees. These were also termed "sentiments".[16] As an example can be mentioned the respondent who kept complaining of bad air, even though measurements showed that there was nothing wrong with the air. On investigating the personal background of the person concerned, it emerged that his brother, a man in his prime, had recently died from pneumonia. Another example is the worker overreacting to an event which otherwise would have passed by as a minor irritant; a quarrel with his wife over breakfast earlier in the morning forms the background.

It thus became important to place the interview responses in a larger context of meaning, a social background. The leaders of the study also laid down that such a conceptual framework should be utilized even by the interviewers. To begin with, this context was conceived, as in the examples above, as the interviewee's *personal* background. (As we remember, there was a precursor to this interest in the test room experiment, which had also included a survey of the personal background of participants.) Thereby, the Metaphorical stage of the investigation with its concomitant Idiographic mode of explanation had reached its peak. In this style of thought, the investigators were influenced by psychoanalysis (Janet, Jung) and development psychology (Piaget).

However, it seemed more and more plausible that the personal backgrounds of the interviewees only constituted a partial explanation for their complaints. Thus, for example, it became increasingly clear that the monotony of repetitive tasks prepared the ground for brooding and compulsive thinking, which might find any outlet whatsoever. A lack of supportive job supervisors and co-workers gave free rein to these tendencies.

In a later stage of the interview programme, the background was therefore extended to include also the social context *at the workplace*. This marked a sliding towards a more Synecdochic style of thought, with a Functional mode of explanation. In this respect, the inspiration came from a systems approach, with sources in functionalist sociology (Durkheim) and social anthropology (Malinowski, Radcliffe-Brown). An economist, Pareto, "contributed probably most to the *systematic understanding of a social system*".[17]

Here, then, we have it in black and white that the Human Relations movement did in fact anticipate the systems approach, something which is not usually apparent in the secondary literature, where at the most its interest in the emergence of informal groups is touched upon. The conventional picture of the development of organization theory is that systems theory started in the 1950s, while Human Relations, as its name implies, was concerned with interpersonal relations, at the very most within small groups.[18] Yet, an important difference in comparison with later systems theory is that people were still not regarded merely as system components, but as meaning-creating individuals.

> We are intentionally referring to the social organization as a social equilibrium in order to emphasize what we conceive the chief character of a social organization to be: an interaction of sentiments and interests in a relation of mutual dependence, resulting in a state of equilibrium such that if that state is altered, forces tending to re-establish it come into play.[19]

The third and final stage of Human Relations, thus, in our tropological terms, can be described as a Synecdochic style of thought on Metaphorical ground; the organizational drama was enacted as a Comic Romance; and the method, as it came to expression in the final phase of the investigation, was Functional-Idiographic.

4.4 The bank wiring observation room

The deepening depression made it difficult to sustain the massive interview programme. The new focus on the social context of the workplace at the same time made it more attractive to study small groups. The investigators, therefore, began interviewing whole work teams. Hereby they stumbled on a number of new phenomena which had previously eluded them, the most important of which was the *restriction of production which seemed to be imposed by informal groups.*[20]

The researchers, however, felt it as a shortcoming, not being able to observe the course of events, but having to rely on the interviewees' statements about this. A more complete study thus would include both interviews and "direct observation",[21] to comprise both words and actions of the actors.

This also became the way of proceeding in the study of the bank wiring observation room.[22] It lasted from November 1931 to May 1932. The aim of the study was to acquire knowledge of informal group formation within the company.

The research leaders would have preferred to study an entire shop department *in natura,* to prevent the kinds of changes in social situation that had occurred in the test room for relay assembly. Unfortunately, this was infeasible because of the size and complexity of the workshops. The investigation instead had to be concentrated on a smaller group which was placed in a special room.

For this reason, a series of measures were taken to avoid social side effects. For example, the observer was given no supervisory responsibilities and besides had strict orders to keep a low profile. The work results were recorded in the workers' absence. One indicator that these measures succeeded is that the group's production did not change appreciably during the investigation.

The observer recorded data according to the following criteria:

- Deviations from formal organizational plan.
- Evidence of informal organization in the form of recurring interaction or signs of group solidarity.
- Functions fulfilled by this informal organization, if it was observed.

The observer kept a diary of his observations. Ultimately this came to cover over 300 typed pages, single-spaced.

Data was collected in the following categories:

- Production quantity
- Production quality
- Observations
- Interviews
- Physical examinations
- Tests of intelligence and skills

On the basis of various criteria, the department for the assembly of office telephone exchanges was arrived at as the most suitable for the study, and within this the operation of bank wiring. The banks were mounted on fixtures placed on the workbenches, and had terminals (100 or 200) for the attachment of the wires. The banks were assembled into what were called *equipments*, ten to eleven banks wide and two to three banks high. The wire was attached to a whole such equipment according to a wiring diagram. There were two types of equipments, *connectors* and *selectors*, which differed in that a connector was eleven banks long and a selector nine.

Three types of workers (called *operators*) were required: wiremen, solder-men, and inspectors. The wiremen attached the wires to the terminals, the soldermen soldered them tight, and the inspectors checked that the connections functioned. Three wiremen were allocated to one solderman. (In addition, there was a trucker, who loaded the completed equipment onto trucks and transported them away.)

The workers' earnings consisted of two parts.[23] A group piece-rate was given for main tasks, such as wiring and soldering. Individual *day work credits* was the form of payment for subsidiary tasks, such as cleaning away particles of solder from the work bench, but was also given for time wasted through disruptions to the supply of materials and other halts to production arising though no fault of the worker. Group piecework payments were distributed to individual workers in accordance with utilized piece-rate time (and estimated individual skill). This meant that if the time for day work credits increased, the time for group piece-rate payments would diminish, and thereby also the overall piecework payment to an equivalent extent. The *bogey* was a kind of maximal production norm, a target which the workers were expected to aim at; thus, it was only designed to function as a benchmark for them.

In the observation room was placed a group of nine wiremen, three soldermen and two inspectors, together with the observer. The immediate supervisor, the *group chief*, spent about half his time in the room and half outside it, since he had also to supervise personnel in the workshop outside the room.

Both interviews and observation soon demonstrated the existence of a limit to production. This was based on an unofficial norm. Two equipments were regarded as "a day's work". The operators simply stopped working when they had completed two equipments during the day. How just this norm had emerged is uncertain. It was justified by the argument that if there was too much deviation from it – especially through increased pace of work – "something might happen".[24] This "something" ranged from raising the bogey to raising or lowering of the piece-rate, lay-offs, and pressure being placed on slow workers by the foreman.

A further discovery was the existence of two sub-groups or cliques, A and B. The cliques in question each comprised three wiremen and one solderman; in addition, the first group also included an inspector. This pattern of sub-groups found expression in many ways, which the investigators represented in the form of sociograms: participation in gambling activities, in controversies over whether the window should be kept open or closed, in job exchange, in mutual assistance, in relations of friendship, in antagonisms.

The question now arose of how to account for these cliques. At first sight two factors seemed reasonable.

Spatial relations constituted the first. The cliques coincided to a great extent with the men's position in the observation room. By the participants themselves, they were also called the "group in front" and the "group in back".[25] However, there were exceptions to this rule, which made it insufficient as an explanation. For example, in the middle of the "group in front" was stationed a wireman, who had been excluded from this clique.

A second explanatory factor lay in job tasks. Connector wiring had a higher status than selector wiring. The wiremen in the former category belonged to Group A, and those in the latter to Group B. This, however, does not explain why an inspector was included in Group A but not in Group B; nor why soldermen had been included. Inspectors were ascribed a higher status than wiremen, and the soldermen a lower. On the other hand, the trucker, who had the lowest status, did not belong to either group. So, neither is this factor sufficient for an explanation.

A third factor had to do with job performance. Members of Group A proved to have considerably higher productivity than Group B. This difference could not be related to intelligence, manual skill, or physical ability, all of which were measured or controlled for in tests or other investigations.

Some workers had been excluded from the groups because they either deviated too much from the group's internal production norms or did not follow certain other informal social rules. These rules can be reduced to the following four:

1 You should not turn out too much work. If you do, you are a "rate-buster".
2 You should not turn out too little work. If you do, you are a "chiseler".
3 You should not tell a supervisor anything that will react to the detriment of an associate. If you do, you are a "squealer".
4 You should not attempt to maintain social distance or act officious. If you are an inspector, for example, you should not act like one.[26]

Group A observed all these rules. Group B observed all but (2). The reason for this was that B used this rule precisely in order to define itself, while at the same time establishing a distance from Group A. This was a means through which B subordinated itself to A. Excluded individuals either produced too much, acted in a superior or officious manner, or squealed to the job supervisor. Thus, group membership was an instrument of social control. (There were also other instruments, such as sarcasm, ridicule and "binging", the latter meaning that the norm-breaker was corrected by a more or less friendly blow on the upper arm.)

Thus far about the internal functions of the clique formation. But it also had an external function. The group members' level of production was in fact remarkably constant whether, as in A's case, it was near the informal norm or, as in B's, below it.

The group members regulated their output so that it would remain constant by demanding more or fewer daywork credits. The supervisors were helpless in the face of this. As we remember, such credits could be demanded for irregular work or for time lost through disturbances to production. The workers could always demand daywork credits and refer to production disturbances. If, on investigation, the supervisor did not accept the particular disturbance referred to, they could always point to some other disturbance, and, when this was investigated, yet a third, etc. The supervisors simply did not have time to check all the claims.

This meant that the workers did not function as "*homo economicus*". If so, they would have tried to increase their wages under all circumstances, driven by economic incentives. But the daywork credits were lower than the piecework payment. Even though they worried that the piece-rate would be increased if they produced too much,[27] they would at least have produced according to their *own* norm, had they been primarily motivated by financial interest. But, as we remember, Group B went slow in accordance with their self-appointed role as the "bad boys", and came considerably under this norm.

The conclusion was instead that both cliques, and thereby the whole informal group formation in the bank wiring observation room, aimed at *resistance to change*. Above, the four informal, internal rules were listed. As to external relations, one single informal main rule governed the behaviour of the workers. It can be expressed as follows: "Let us behave in such a way that we give management the least possible opportunity to interfere with us."[28]

This the workers in the observation room achieved by keeping production constant, so that external forces would have neither reason nor excuse to intervene. The *level* at which this constant production was maintained was determined in part by the group's norm for a single day's work, in part by the game played between the two groups; this involved A keeping their production close to the norm, and B below it.

Interventions might come from the two external parties with whom the workers had direct contact: technicians and supervisors. From the technicians, new time measurements were feared, and perhaps a changed remuneration system. The supervisors had the task of maintaining discipline through rules the workers perceived as arbitrary and meaningless. For example, they were forbidden to help each other at work, since this was considered to lead to a decrease in efficiency. The workers thought the opposite, and besides mutual aid was an expression of social relations.

The conclusion the authors drew from both the study in the observation room and the preceding investigations was that a company functions as a social system. We have earlier seen that the experiment with the test room for relay assembly led to a transition from a Metonymic to a Metaphorical style of thought. The research findings from the interview programme led to the latter beginning to be supplemented by Synecdoche: a development that became even more palpable during the study of the bank wiring observation room. This is expressed very clearly in the following quotation:

> ... the function of management [is] that of maintaining the social system of the industrial plant in a state of equilibrium such that both the external and internal purpose of the enterprise are realized.[29]

The function of management thus is to keep the system in equilibrium. There are two sides to this. External equilibrium keeps the company in financial balance by ensuring profitability. Internal equilibrium maintains the social organization through which the workers can satisfy their personal needs and desires. These two equilibrium goals are related to each other. If the personal needs of individuals are not fulfilled, the company's financial targets cannot be met – as evidenced by the bank wiring observation room. And the other way round: if the company's financial targets are not secured, security for individuals cannot be guaranteed.

In the observation room, these two goals conflicted. In the test room for relay assembly, by contrast, they were in harmony, for the investigators had unintentionally made the group function as an amplifier for the goals of the company. In the test room, it became apparent that no changes can be introduced in isolation without them having effects on the system as a whole.

And the authors even went one step further, hinting at a cultural perspective:

> According to this point of view, every social act in adulthood is an integrated response to both inner and outer stimuli. To each new concrete situation the adult brings his past "social conditioning." To the extent that this past social conditioning has prepared him to assimilate the new experience in the culturally accepted manner, he is said to be "adjusted." To the extent that his private or personal view of the situation is at variance with the cultural situation, the person is called "maladjusted."[30]

This, however, remained just a hint. Even so, it sufficed to underline the Ironic touch in the endeavours of the company management to increase production and the workers' efforts not to bust the piece-rate. The former resulted, as we have seen, in a remuneration system that led to restriction of production. The latter were meaningless, seen from a rational perspective.

The principal criticism which can be directed at the study is that it fails to take sufficiently into account historically inherited subcultures, as, for example, those of the working class. Resistance to "rate busters" in capitalistic countries and "Stachanovites", i.e. model workers, in the East is a historical-cultural phenomenon, building on experiences and not confined to one company.

The systems perspective possessed considerably more flesh on its bones. Yet it was not applied to the full. Even though the work group in the observation room was mapped in detail, its external relations were presented more sketchily. Here, the authors also end up in a tautological explanation:

> The chief function of the informal group in the Bank Wiring Observation Room was to resist changes in [the members'] established routines of work or personal interrelations.[31]

But, to an essential degree, these personal interrelations consisted precisely of informal group formation. Obviously one is going round in circles if this group formation is explained Functionally by asserting that it exists in order to maintain itself.

The focusing on small groups also implies that the systems perspective still does not function as a means of conceiving *the organization as a whole*. This is in fact related to the previous point. If the system is the organization as a whole, then every part of it – according to functionalism, the systems school to which the authors mainly adhere – has as its purpose to maintain the whole in one way or the other. But the authors have in fact only closely investigated one part of the organization as a system, namely the small group in the bank wiring observation room, and so they can only speak of the latter.

According to the systems perspective and functionalism, every system aims at maintaining itself. Therefore, the authors end up in the tautology alluded to, or spurious explanation, when they simultaneously treat the small group as a part (with external function) and as a whole (a system with the goal of surviving). The *relevant system* has not been specified, to use later systems jargon.[32] The basis of Synecdoche, the part–whole relationship, is, in other words, undeveloped.

A third criticism is that the assumed "equilibrium" or "balance", a fundamental aspect of Comedy's organizational drama, seems loosely pasted on. It is never really explained in detail.[33])

Nonetheless, we can establish that Human Relations points forwards, towards the systems as well as the cultural perspectives.

4.5 Lasting significance

Despite its defects, Roethlisberger and Dickson's *Management and the Worker* still today appears as an astonishingly rich book, from which to scoop ideas and empirical material. It has also proved extraordinarily far-sighted in anticipating the systems approach to organizations and even touching upon the cultural perspective.

The book was no isolated swallow. Among other works within the same orientation can be mentioned T. North Whitehead's *The Industrial Worker*, 1938; Roethlisberger's *Management and Morale,* 1941; Elton Mayo's *The Social Problems of an Industrial Civilization*, 1945. After the war, a host of books were published, and the activity still continues. Human Relations came in fact to have a major and lasting posterior influence on the organizational world:

> The Hawthorne trunk has given rise to numerous research and reform offshoots, each of which has produced many individual branches. The major research issues pursued include studies of the work groups in the organizational environment, leadership behavior, and the impact of worker background and personal attributes on organizational behavior. Reform attempts include the use of personnel counselors, leadership training, job redefinition, and participation in decision making. . . . [A]ll of them are still flourishing.[34]

In the field of organizational science/analysis, there is a subdivision between *organization theory* and *organization(al) behaviour.* The former focuses on the organization as a whole, the latter (OB) on groups and individuals within the organization. Practically everything within the subject area of organizational behaviour ultimately stems from Human Relations, which is thus the origin of the field's division.[35)]

The following is a sample of areas occupying a central position within Organizational Behaviour, as this is taught to prospective managers in English-speaking countries today, and which all go back to Human Relations:

- Foundation of individual behavior (includes values, attitudes, perception, and learning)
- Personality and emotions
- Basic motivation concepts
- Individual decision making
- Foundations of group behaviour
- Understanding work teams
- Communication
- Leadership and creating trust
- Power and politics
- Conflict and negotiation

All these are chapter headings in a modern textbook on Organizational Behaviour.[36] And this is how two of the three main *parts* of another are described.[37]

- Individual Processes and Behaviour. (Includes the chapters: Personality, Perception and Attribution. Attitudes, Values, and Ethics. Motivation at Work. Learning and Performance Management. Stress and Well-Being at Work.)
- Interpersonal Processes and Behaviour. (Includes the chapters: Communication. Work Teams and Groups. Decision Making by Individuals and Groups. Power and Political Behaviour. Leadership and Followership. Conflict at Work.)

The remaining main part contains chapter headings such as: Jobs and the design of work, Career management, and Managing change, but also Organizational design and structure and Organizational culture. These chapters are written from the point of view of how organizational macro variables affect individual behavior and group dynamics in organizations.[38]

As well as in organizational behaviour, Human Relations has demonstrated its development potential in three other, partially overlapping, directions. One of these is *Organizational Development* (OD), which has been popular for almost half a century as a means for planned intervention to change organizations. In OD, the influence of Human Relations is combined with Kurt Lewin's Gestalt psychological field theory from the 1940s, and with elements from systems theory. A processual and group-dynamic orientation is favoured, as is the idea of "change agents", individual catalysts for change who are often, but not always, consultants. OD discourse is coloured, to some extent, by a medical perspective; in particular the metaphor of "diagnosis" is frequently used. A set of change technologies has been elaborated, of which the classical one is T-group training, but there are many others: currently used tools include survey feedback, organizational mirroring, intergroup confrontation, role negotiation, process consultation, team building, and life and career planning.[39]

The *sociotechnical school* represents a second important current. It is rooted in Human Relations' interest in the relationship between the technical and the social system in processes of change. This was studied at the famous Tavistock Institute in England, whose full but less known name was the Tavistock Institute of Human Relations. One of the more influential outcomes of this research was the ideas about autonomous work groups. These have had, and still have, a strong influence in organizational change throughout both Europe and the Unites States.[40]

Human Resource Management (HRM) is the third line of development, whose aim is to promote the growth of the abilities of personnel, thereby increasing their creativity and productivity. (The techniques for organizational development referred to above are sometimes included in HRM.) In the 1980s Harvard Business School introduced HRM as a compulsory course – the first in twenty years. This could be taken as a sign, one among many, that the interest was more than just a passing fad.[41] The movement is now very strong and established, not least in the USA, where it has an organization of its own, the Society for Human Resource Management (SHRM) and a magazine, *HR Magazine*. SHRM was initiated in 1948 under the name of the American Society for Personnel Administration (ASPA). From a modest start with twenty-eight individuals operating on a voluntary basis, the organization has swelled to over 120 000 members in 1999 and a permanent staff of 175 persons. SHRM acquired its current name in 1989.[42] Human Resource Management has succeeded in taking over a number of the roles that were previously played by Organizational Development, and has more or less absorbed traditional personnel administration. One reason for the great and increasing impact of HRM in theory and practice may be that, at least since the end of the 1980s, it has been linked to innovation in firms.[43] Another, related reason may be the interest in the linkage to performance, which has been referred to as the currently hottest area for HRM.[44]

Empirical findings also show that Human Relations' Metaphorical, humane organization model lives on. In their twenty case studies of British innovative companies in the 1950s, Burns and Stalker found it coexisting alongside the classical model we discussed in the previous chapter.[45] It comprised two-thirds of the cases in Woodward's whole population study of manufacturing companies in South Essex in the 1950s.[46] Similar results – with varying interpretations and terminology – were presented over the following decades by the Aston school, researchers such as Lawrence and Lorsch, and a host of other authors in their wake, which would require a separate volume just to report on.[47]

If we move on to the 1980s we find that the human model still maintains its position. Miller and Friesen's taxonomy, based on Q-factor analysis of reports from a sample of fifty-two companies, gives the humane type a share of 12 per cent, thus approximately the same as that of the classical model.[48] (Jointly therefore the rational classics and Human Relations comprise a quarter of the cases in Miller and Friesen). The humane model also appears, with varying names but similar content, in other newer typologies: Mintzberg's adhocracy, Sköldberg's collegial planning culture, and in Bordt's "collective" type (comprising 27 per cent of the 113 women's non-profit organizations she studied).[49]

The humane model has also been a common ingredient in *organizational life cycles*, where it appears as a phase or stage. Cameron and Whetten constructed a synthesis of nine models of organizational life cycles and arrived at four phases or stages which they had in common. They then replicated the same four phases in a simulation experiment. The second of these phases was the humane organization model.[50]

Thus, it is quite clear that the humane model is still going strong, both in theory and practice; even though there are alternatives.

4.6 The poetics of human relations

The Hawthorne studies involved a journey through all four tropes, which can be summarized and elucidated in Figure 4.1.

Metaphor is in capitals, since it is here that the main emphasis of the investigation lay. Irony is in smaller type, since the investigation only touched upon the cultural approach.

The preliminary study – the experiment on illumination – was carried out in the best scientific management tradition, almost in the spirit of Taylor's pupil, Gilbreth. The same applied to the design of the first study – that of the test room for relay assembly. Thus, they were clearly stamped by the basic Metonymic conception of this tradition: the world consists of separate parts. The method was Scientistic; measurement and separation of the variables was of the essence. The view of the relationship between man and organization was scientific management's Tragic picture of the mechanically functioning economic man.

The results of the research, however, suggested that this very basic picture was wrong. The investigators, therefore, shifted their fundamental style of thought, and turned to the trope of Metaphor with inner meaning as the centre. Human beings were no longer described as economic automatons, governed by Tragic laws, but as individuals, Romantically involved in a quest for meaning.

As compared to the beginning of the investigation, interest had thereby been displaced from event-data to people. A psychological angle of approach, with ideas from psychoanalysis and development psychology, now placed the

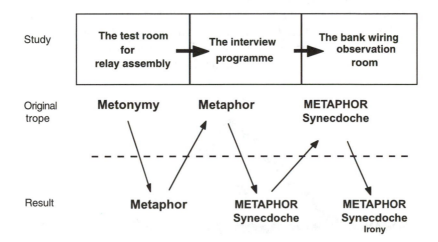

Figure 4.1 Human Relations' journey through the tropes.

individual and his/her development at the centre. For the purpose of studying the individuals, the massive *interview programme* was launched – based on an Idiographic technique, which was designed to capture the meanings involved. The style of thought was (still) Metaphorical.

The Metaphorical style of thought is based on inner meaning. The method corresponding to this style of thought is the Idiographic, which picks out as facts singular individuals/episodes within organizations, each imbued with a meaning of its own. The model of interpretation is understanding and the basic relationship is expression-meaning, where the expression is the immediate object of study and the meaning is the ground sought after.[51)]

Yet the founders of the Human Relations School assigned an even greater importance to the interview programme. Influenced by psychology, Elton Mayo strongly recommended using clinical interviews, not only as a research method but also as the panacea against irrational ideas among the workers – ideas which would otherwise lead to conflicts, thus undermining industrial effectiveness. In other words, the disturbances of the industrial society ultimately had its roots deep in the disturbed psyche of the individual worker. Once the unconscious disorientations of the worker vanished, the harmonic communications between individuals would be (re)established, and thus also undisturbed industrial effectiveness.[52] Corresponding to this is a Romantic organizational drama through which separate individuals, after an original period of estrangement, rediscover their inner meanings, and thus their own true self. Only in this way can they regain understanding, even between one another.

The organizational style for this triad is the *expressive*[53] (Figure 4.2). This is the chief organizational style of Human Relations.

The interview programme, however, demonstrated the existence of informal small groups and restrictions on production. Since such groups are obviously wholes formed by parts, the Synecdochic style of thought became relevant. A Functionally planned study was started, with the purpose of investigating informal group formation: the study in *the bank wiring observation room*. An Idiographic orientation still remained, manifested among other things by the

Figure 4.2 The chief organizational style of Human Relations.

design of the study, whose aim was to reveal both individual meanings and functions at the system level.

In fact, the system was thought to consist of individual meanings, which stand in a relationship of equilibrium or balance with one another. Thus, the organizational drama enacted is a combination of Comedy and Romance with the latter as fundament: a Comic Romance.[54] The underlying style of thought is Synecdoche on Metaphorical ground. Yes, even a cultural perspective was touched upon, which we shall analyze in Chapter 6 on the basis of the trope of Irony.

To summarize: in the concrete organization theory which became the final result, Human Relations combined two variants of the expressive and integrative organizational styles, with the former predominant (see Figure 4.3).

Thus far the development of the investigation over time. We now take leave of this, and look a little more closely at the organizational drama that the Hawthorne researchers finally reached, the Comic Romance. Retrospectively, this also came to imbue their view of earlier phases in the investigation, for instance the test room experiment. Its essence is captured by the key concept "the social system", by which, to reiterate a previously quoted passage, was meant:

> an interaction of sentiments and interests in a relation of mutual dependence, resulting in a state of equilibrium such that if that state is altered, forces tending to re-establish it come into play.

The state of equilibrium, which is restored by various forces if it is disturbed, forms the Comic component of the drama; "sentiments and interests" its Romantic component. This Comic Romance is enacted in a *dualistic* genre. The dualism applies to both components, the Comic and the Romantic. In the case of the Comedy, this means that both the deficient and the desired states, between which the drama moves, are clearly presented – i.e. the disturbed and the restored state of equilibrium. For the Romance, the dualism means consolidating achieved self-realization, as against external pressure.[55]

Figure 4.3 The poetics of Human Relations.

The portrayal of the observation room corresponds to one pole in this dualism – the deficient state and lack of self-realization. The other pole – the desirable state and self-realization – is represented by the story of the test room.

The presentation of the observation room as an originally deficient state, which should be replaced by a better one, comes close to the nature of classic Comedy. One of the most prominent features of this type of drama is the so-called "blocking characters" (see Chapter 5), who have the function of obstructing the drama's happy ending – the transition from the deficient to the desirable state. A blocking character

> is usually someone with a good deal of social prestige and power, who is able to force much of the play's society into line with his obsession.[56]

In the observation room, the central blocking character is company management with its meaningless and deleterious rules. Company management corresponds to that most favourite of blocking characters, the typical *senex iratus* – the heavy father who does everything to prevent a happy ending, in the form of bringing together the young couple, here represented by groups A and B.[57]

But even these have their (unwritten) rules, which express a lack of Romantic, individual self-realization; enchantment in a non-human form of behaviour. This defect has strongly Comic overtones through the ritual compulsiveness with which the informal groups follow their unwritten laws. Their almost farcically mechanical way of acting, which typically enough aims at resisting change, is just a reflection of company management's own ritual behaviour – the way in which a *senex iratus* succeeds in obstructing development by forcing an entire society into his obsession. In Comedy, the blocking characters, through their stereotypical compulsiveness, provide much of the comic element; and this is also the case with the bizarre rules, of both management and the informal groups, which are described in the observation room.

Another comic figure is the *churl*, a "miserly, snobbish or priggish" type, who does not understand jokes, opposes the light-hearted atmosphere of the Comedy, and thus by his very nature creates a striking contrast to the fundamentally merry tone of the drama.[58] All these regrettable properties seem to adhere to the poor inspector who had been excluded from Group B; he could in fact have been directly modelled on Malvolio, the killjoy in Shakespeare's *Twelfth Night*. Among the informal groups, there is also a cheery element of games and play, mutual help, joking and other social activities which point away from the defective towards the desirable state.

The nature of this desirable state emerges from the portrayal of the test room. Roethlisberger and Dickson's retrospective story of events in the test room is radically dissimilar to the Taylorian design and carrying through of the experiment. It has elements of Comedy from the final phase of the whole investigation, but is dominated by Romance. The light-hearted tone is characteristic of the first-mentioned dramatic form.

Especially typical of Comedy are the incessant *festivities* occurring.[59] (Their counterparts in the observation room are the recurring games around which much of its social activities revolved.) In the test room drama, there also appear *assisting characters* whose task in Comedy is to bring the drama to a happy ending (see Chapter 5) and who thereby constitute the counter-pole to the blocking characters. These roles, more specifically, are occupied by the Hawthorne researchers themselves, whose influence ensured that the drama reached a happy conclusion. One of the most common types of assisting characters is the *tricky slave* or *scheming valet* [dolosus servus]. A better characterization of the research team hired would be hard to find. The most common means through which the tricky slave manages to turn the drama around are *complicated manipulations* and the *revelations of weighty secrets*.[60] In the former we recognize the complicated change in supervisory conditions; in the latter the researchers' findings which were expected to lead to better conditions at Hawthorne (and in other organizations as well).

The main theme, however, is that of Romantic *consolidating*: the self-realized hero's defence of his inner integrity against external attack. There is a predeliction for this to be symbolized by two images. The first concerns the group, the second the individual.[61] Both refer to the defence of the purity of the heart against external threat, of ideal against reality.

1 *The beleaguered castle*.[62] A Romantic court which defends itself from the attack of an external enemy. This image characterizes the test room, where the workers "perplexing improvement in mental attitude", i.e. their self-realization, is the central theme, and is only matched by an equally strong resistance to the dissolution of the group and the termination of the experiment.
2 *The beauty and the beast*.[63] The virgin who tames a monster (lion, satyr, rhinoceros etc.). The Gorgon's head on Pallas Athene's shield crystallizes this archetype.[64] The duel between the female workers and the male observer – symbol of the boss/beast – illustrates this other favourite image of the genre. Typical is the jestingly disrespectful treatment of the monster in question, after certain initial fears.[65]

Some of the most important *dramatis personae*:

Company management	Tyrannical father-ruler
Groups A and B	The young couple
The Hawthorne researchers	The tricky slave
The test room	The enchanted castle
Operator	Virgin
Observer	Monster, which is tamed

We can now provide a summary reconstruction of the Narrative of the social system.

RESUMÉ:
This Comic Romance starts with a tyrannical father-ruler attempting to prevent the young couple from being united by having them bewitched into automatons. Owing to the manipulations and revelations of a tricky slave, there is a happy turn to the drama. After their liberation, the main characters are placed in an enchanted castle which is besieged by miscellaneous evil forces. The decisive effort in the defence of the castle is made by a maiden who tames a monster. The drama concludes with festivities and scenes of rejoicing lasting for seven days.

This is, then, how the drama of the social system looks. Amazing? Not if we remember what was said in Chapter 2: everyone who wants to *narrate* something about something must ultimately always go back to the forms of narrative that already exist, and have been crystallized since the dawn of time as the most effective ones. We continuously assimilate these archetypical forms, right from childhood, in speech and writing. Consciously or unconsciously, we then fall back on them when we ourselves are to produce our narrations. They comprise the repertoire from which all narrations have to start – thus even narrations about organizations, in this case the social system at Hawthorne.

The systems approach in Roethlisberger and Dickson, however, appears undeveloped and partly confused. It is not clear what is part and what is whole. The whole sometimes seems to be the entire Hawthorne factory, sometimes a small group studied within it. As a result of this undigested Synecdoche the investigators end up in circular explanations. Furthermore, it is unclear what is really meant by the harmonic balance/equilibrium to which the Comedy leads. The emphasis, therefore, does not lie on the system but still on the meaningful human relations. This is why we have characterized the organizational drama as a Comic Romance.[66]

As we have seen, Comedy shows how a whole acts to regain its basic equilibrium despite disturbances; Romance, on the other hand, focuses on the single individual's combating of perils, in order ultimately to find inner meaning and thereby also remove the conflicts with his social sphere. A Comic Romance as an organizational drama thus plays out a *double* harmony, both on the level of the whole and on that of the individual, which, moreover, mutually reinforce each other. This can be compared with fictional literature; the most typical form of this drama here expresses, for corresponding reasons, nostalgia for the dreamlike innocent world, in which every conflict is resolved and everything breathes peace, joy, and tranquility.[67] This most typical form, which also characterizes the drama of Human Relations, involves precisely the dualistic genres of Comedy and Romance, which here fade into each other. The action in this Comic genre is presented on two social planes, of which one is preferred and consequently in some measure idealized. . . . This dream world collides with the stumbling and blinded follies of the world of experience . . . , and yet proves strong enough to impose the form of desire on it . . . not as an escape from "reality," but as the genuine form of the world that human life tries to imitate.[68]

And Romance? Well, as we have seen

the central theme of this [genre] is that of the maintaining of the integrity of the innocent world against the assault of experience.[69]

In terms of the course of events typical of Comedy, this genre represents a point just beyond the middle of the story, where the desired state starts to predominate over the deficient. In a similar way the corresponding Romantic genre represents the situation of consolidating, just after self-realization.

The *real* world in Human Relations' dualistic organizational drama is an idealized world of a community of interests, harmony, and happiness. This is illustrated by the predominantly Romantic test room. The *unreal* world is the one in which unnecessary conflicts, misunderstandings, and disharmonies occur. This is illustrated by the predominantly Comic observation room.

Therefore it is no coincidence that Human Relations has been strongly criticized for exaggerating freedom from conflict as an organizational ideal, fostering an idyllic representation of existence.[70] This especially applies to the project leader's (Elton Mayo) influential interpretation of the Hawthorne findings, which takes harmonization still further, so that it assumes sheer pastoral features,[71] and we find ourselves in "the green world"; an important theme for precisely the dualistic genres of Comedy and Romance.[72] However, there is nothing new under the sun – the same critique for being pastoral has long since been directed at the comic romance in fictional literatre.

Mayo's book is a popularly written, in part social-philosophical, and not very voluminous collection of essays. Roethlisberger and Dickson's book is a thick and fact-laden account of a major research project. Elton Mayo's easy-to-read representation strains the Hawthorne findings in a strongly harmonic direction. Unfortunately, it has tended too much to block the view of Roethlisberger and Dickson's work – heavier to be sure, but richer in nuances and points.

5   The Comedy of the self-regulating system

This chapter first traces the roots and development of the systems approach and then elucidates the general notion of a system. Basically, it is contended, the poetics of the systems approach expresses the regime of Synecdoche – the third master trope and style of thought, relating part to whole. Periods when this trope is ruling are, according to Vico, exempt from any pre-conceived, necessary or self-legitimizing hierarchy; rather, Synecdochic societies can be characterized as "commonwealths", functioning for the good of each and all, i.e. the whole community.[1] The dramaturgy of systems thinking in general is viewed as Comic – the system trying to maintain a happy, harmonic equilibrium despite external disturbances. The method is Functionalist, relating the parts of the system as structures to the over-arching function of the system, especially survival and growth.

The next section provides an outline of functionalism. Parson's function-alism (especially that of his later years) provides a good representative of the poetics of the systems approach, as delineated above, with a Synecdochic style of thought, a Functional method, and a Comic organizational drama, aiming at friendly balance and harmony. Merton's and his followers' (dys)functionalism, on the other hand, essentially employed a Functionalist method to study Tragic organizational dramas.

Then follows a presentation of the breakthrough in the late 1950s and early 1960s of systems theories as applied to organizations – the third major organizational approach. Mechanistic and organic management systems, and, in connection with this, contingency theory, are first discussed. The poetics of Burns and Stalker's pathbreaking analysis is outlined, with a special emphasis on its Comic dramaturgy, including the specific genre in which the drama is enacted – dualistic Comedy, with thematics from the "green world" of that genre, and typical role characters that either block or contribute to the drama's happy solution.

Thereafter, we turn to the issue of the technological imperative – the impact of technology on the organization. Woodward's investigation is discussed, and its poetics outlined. The organizational drama is played out in the same (dualistic) genre of Comedy as was Burns and Stalker's. However, the role characters are different, and the contributing characters take most of the limelight.

Next, some critical and reformist views are taken up: strategic choice, the actor's frame of reference, loosely coupled systems, and garbage can. All these stand out as Romantic rebellions or oppositions of various kinds within the general poetics of the system approach.

The penultimate section treats organizational "configurations" and meta-morphoses between these (Mintzberg and Miller). The configurational school adheres closely to the poetics of the systems approach. What marks their style out as specific, however, is their genre of Comedy – that of *picaresque*, in which the hero-picaro-manager is seen as continually jumping from one of the system's several states to another.

Finally, the poetics of the systems approach to organizations is discussed. In general, it follows the poetics of the systems view as such, outlined above: there is a basic affinity in this approach between a Synecdochic style of thought, a Functionalist method, and a Comic organizational drama. This provides the general linguistic protocol that prefigures any concrete organization theory within the approach with a certain style. Thus, even before more rational analyses are undertaken, a certain view of organizational reality is already pre-critically adopted. The organizational style is thus the *integrative* one, linking in a precognitive, tropologic structure its particular style of thought, method, and drama, as described above. Within the concrete organization theories, however, there are interesting tensions of style. In particular, Burns and Stalker's method was Contextual, and made use of a cultural analysis well ahead of its time, at least as organization theory goes. This created a discrepancy *vis-à-vis* their Comic dramaturgy. Moreover, the Contextuality of their method tended to feed back on their basic style of thought, which thus came to assume the character of Irony rather than that of Synecdoche.

Even stronger were the tensions between Woodward's method and her dramaturgy. As we saw earlier, Woodward's organizational drama, like that of Burns and Stalker, was enacted as Comedy. Her method, though, bore the imprint of Scientism. In Woodward's poetics, there was an even stronger tension between organizational drama and method than in Burns and Stalker. Here, though, the clash of styles is taken to so far as to stop being productive; instead, it has detrimental effects for the substance of the analysis. Interestingly, this does not seem to have caused the theory of the technological imperative to lose any of its rhetorical force.

5.1 Background

The roots of the systems perspective reach far back in time.[2] A short history of the development of the general systems idea is necessary here too, as background to its application to organizations. The first great proponent was Aristotle, who directed his attention to all the branches of knowledge at the time, but especially interested himself in biology, which also came to colour his perspective on the whole; he had a Synecdochic tendency to treat all objects of investigation as organisms or analogous to organisms, and therefore governed by purposes, i.e. teleologically. As we recall, Synecdoche is one of the four master tropes, or styles of thought; in particular it is the *holistic* rhetorical figure, relating part to whole. The Synecdochic way of thinking focuses on wholes; to use a popular expression, it is "holistic". It is well illustrated by Doctor Pangloss, for whom we live in the best of all possible worlds – provided that the whole is kept in sight.

Aristotle's writings disappeared from Europe in conjunction with the fall of the Roman Empire and were only rediscovered in the beginning of the High Middle Ages (the twelfth century) through translations from the Arabic. His thoughts, which had been originally greeted as a breath of fresh air in the hitherto anti-scientific, theological darkness, rapidly became predominating and were transformed into dogma in the form of the so-called Scholasticism.

The end of the Middle Ages, and the Renaissance heralding the New Era, marked a break with Aristotelianism and its Synecdochic idea of teleological causes, as well as with the conception of the entire universe as a large organism, harbouring various suborganisms. The so-called Copernican revolution, with Copernicus, Galileo, and Kepler as foremost advocates, later synthesized and developed by Newton, meant the transition to a completely different, Metonymic world-view with interest tied to parts instead of wholes and to mechanical causality instead of teleology: modern natural science became the pattern for knowledge at large.[3]

The Synecdochic view of reality did not really recover until the nineteenth century,[4] in the beginning of which Hegel emerged as the paramount philosopher and theorist of science. "The true is the whole" was a sentence that Hegel coined, and it says perhaps most of what needs to be said about his predilection for a Synecdochic style of thought. Hegel's philosophy is an endeavour to synthesize earlier philosophical approaches. Among those who occupy the highest rank in his system is Aristotle. Goal-governed activity is, according to Hegel, something that takes place at a higher, more important level than ordinary causality. Hegel had a great influence on philosophy and the theory of science in Germany during the first half of the nineteenth century.

But even after Hegelianism as a school had fallen apart into various fighting factions and finally vanished entirely from the scene, major parts of its intellectual heritage were preserved within Marxism. In fact Marx started his career as a (radical-liberal) left Hegelian, and Hegelian thinking came, even after his radicalization and conversion to socialism, to impregnate his entire perspective.[5] Marx's main work, *Das Kapital*, is predominantly marked by a Synecdochic, if not to say a systems perspective. (There are exceptions, e.g. the section on the fetishism of commodities in the first volume.)

The idea that societies can be compared with organisms was put forth during the second half of the nineteenth century by the influential social philosopher Herbert Spencer. At about the same time, various "vitalist" approaches began to flourish within the biological sciences. Vitalism (Reinke, Driesch, Ostwald, related theories put forward by the better-known French philosopher Henri Bergson with his "*élan vital*") maintained that organisms could not be reduced to physical/chemical processes, but that there was some kind of governing "life force" within them. Generally speaking, vitalism came out as the loser of the paradigmatic struggle in biology of the nineteenth and twenteeth centuries, largely because the "life force" was conceived as some kind of metaphysical element, believed to exist within the organisms. The Synecdochic perspective, however, was important for the vitalists, by contrast with their Metonymic opponents.

Spencer associated social function with structure.[6] Later in the nineteenth century, the French sociologist Émile Durkheim – called the "father of sociology" – promoted the idea that the division of labour in society could be related to its integrating *function* there. Two well-known social anthropologists from the beginning of the twentieth century, Malinowski and Radcliffe-Brown, are usually regarded as founders of functionalism.

In the 1920s, Köhler founded the so-called "Gestalt theory" school, with a decided Synecdochic orientation: the whole, the "Gestalt", is prior to the part, a mode of thinking which found application within such diverse disciplines as physics, biology, and psychology.

During the same decade Whitehead presented his philosophy of "organic mechanism", Cannon launched the concept of "homeostasis" (self-regulation or dynamic equilibrium), and Bertalanffy began to outline how biologists could study organisms as wholes, as systems. Thus, a resurgence for the Synecdochic style of thought seemed to be in the making.

However, fascism and war intervened; and it was not until after the Second World War that a number of currents with Synecdoche as common denominator really came to break through, right from the beginning in clear opposition to the dominating Metonymic positivism of the first post-war years.

During the war the interest of the military had already been directed to the precursors of today's computers and to self-regulating machines, especially anti-aircraft guns. The idea of servo-mechanisms had an ancestry as far back as the eighteenth century and the centrifugal regulator in Watt's steam engine. Norbert Wiener's epoch-making *Cybernetics* established at a stroke a wholly new science with that same name.[7] It described self-regulating machines in terms of input and output, plus a control system governing via feedback.

How was this governing exercised? The answer lay close at hand: through *information*. The concept of information was also investigated by Wiener, and especially by Shannon, likewise at the end of the 1940s.[8] The concept became even more attractive when a striking similarity was discovered between the mathematical formula for information and that of entropy, the latter of which (roughly speaking) measures the (lack of) order in systems. All the Synecdochic relations between parts of the whole, components of the system – control, communication, feedback, hierarchy (i.e. order) – could in fact be interpreted as the transmission of information.[9]

By the end of the 1940s functionalism had also seriously established itself in American social science, with Talcott Parsons as its most prominent figure.[10]

In 1954 the Society for General System Theory was founded, with the biologist Ludwig von Bertalanffy, the economist Kenneth Boulding, the physiologist Ralph Gerard, and the bio-mathematician Anatol Rapoport as its foremost names. The purpose of the society, as indicated by its name, was to create a general theory of systems, both organic and inorganic. The year 1956 saw Ashby's influential book on systems theory, *Design for a Brain,* based on a cybernetic perspective.[11]

Post-1950s developments in the systems approach (some of which may overlap) include Prigogine's theory of dissipative structures,[12] Pribram's holographic paradigm,[13] ideas of a second order cybernetics (integrating the observer),[14] self-organizing systems[15] and autopoiesis[16] – all highly interesting,[17] if perhaps a bit far-flung sometimes. Having emerged mostly at a time when Synecdoche no longer is the ruling trope, these have certainly inspired some seminal writings in organizational theory,[18] but have not (yet) had an impact on the field comparable to that of earlier systems thinking. On the other hand, these orientations have been able to incorporate aspects of other styles of thought. Thus, for instance, Metaphor has been included, in the form of a subjective, "Radical Constructivist" view of knowledge.[19] Even more importantly, Irony has been placed on the agenda, in the form of the acceptance of paradoxes, contradictions, and even downright post-modernism, within self-organizing systems.[20] This assimilation of extra-Synecdochic tropes should contribute to making their reception by organization theorists a more promising affair.

5.1.1 Systems

As has already emerged, the systems approach draws from two separate main sources: the biological concept of an organism and the theory of servo-mechanisms.[21], [22] Therefore, it cannot be explained by a single "root metaphor". Moreover, both general systems theory and cybernetics are substantially empty, content-free.[23] That is, the physical analogies – organisms and servo-mechanisms – are used as crutches, to throw away as the theory is generalized.[24] That it would still be marked by the crutches remains to be proved.

In Hegel's terminology,[25] the theory has rather risen from a "sensuous" to a "conceptual" level of consciousness; and the latter cannot be reduced to the former. (This is for instance clearly seen in Bertalanffy's development from a systems-oriented biologist to a general systems theorist.)[26] Instead, the systems approach is an expression of an underlying style of thought – the Synecdochic – and the analogies, as already stated, are merely preliminary aids in the beginning, the role of which should not be exaggerated. This also applies to the application of the systems approach to organizations.

There may be reason to pause here and take up the question of definition. What *is* a system? Following Bunge we shall define a system as a number of components which have an environment and interact with each other.[27] Interaction between components constitutes the difference between system and *aggregate*; if the components do not interact, they do not form a system but an aggregate. Further, a system may or may not interact with its environment; in the former case it is denoted as *open*, in the latter as *closed*.[28]

On the other hand, the cybernetic model of systems as input-output mechanisms is too narrow as a definition. It treats systems as black boxes, which automatically excludes studies of their inner differentiation.[29] In addition, the system becomes purely reactive and cannot be changed through signals from the inside, only through input from the environment (Figure 5.1).[30]

However, we cannot follow Bunge when he claims that a system does not necessarily have a goal. Bunge's concept of goal, which includes freedom of choice and learning,[31] becomes too narrow at the more restricted end, and excludes by definition target-seeking missiles, for example. The interaction within the system and, where this applies, between the system and its environment, must drive it in some direction. The state towards which the system is driven by virtue of its internal and external relations is its goal.[32]

Survival/maintenance and growth/expansion are typically mentioned as systemic goals. In relation to this, we may also distinguish between internal and external system goals. Internal goals concern the system as such; external goals will also affect the environment. Survival is, then, an internal system goal. In particular, the system should maintain its balance, so that it can survive despite external disturbances. This can also be expressed by saying that it is in dynamic *equilibrium* (homeostasis). Here we see a re-action on

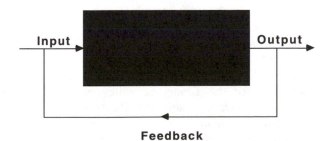

Feedback

Figure 5.1 The cybernetic model.

the Synecdochic style of thought of its organizational drama, Comedy. The principle of the latter is to unravel into harmony and general reconciliation despite temporary complications. Growth is an external system goal. In fact it is the principal means through which change is usually expressed in the system approach. Control over the environment can be an internal or an external system goal, depending on whether the environment in question is conceived as inner or outer.[33] We return to these system goals in connection with our discussion of organizational effectiveness in Chapter 7.

5.1.2 Functionalism

Functionalism conceives the dynamic equilibrium as maintained by the parts of the system, its *structures*, having advantageous *functions* for the whole (the system). It goes without saying that the method is Functional. Parsons, probably Functionalism's weightiest author, also refers explicitly to Cannon's biological concepts of organism and function.[34] Interestingly enough, in his early works Parsons had presented a Metaphorical theory, focusing on the meaning-orientation behind action. By contrast, his later works were characterized by a Synecdochic systems approach, where people have disappeared and been replaced by actors, who are mere structural elements in roles entirely determined by external expectations.[35] There is a striking analogy with organisms, containing different organs, which in turn consist of cells. The element of Comedy is a main thread in Parsons' systems theory, with its recurring theme of equilibrium.

Robert Merton, a pupil of Parsons, was another of the great functionalists in the 1940s and 1950s. Merton applied functionalism to various societal phenomena, which had previously been investigated from other aspects. In particular, he discussed so-called *dysfunctions*, that is, the negative effects for the whole of certain structures – "social diseases", to follow up the analogy to organisms. Deviant behaviour was such a phenomenon. In 1947 the first English translation of Weber's magnum opus *Wirtschaft und Gesellschaft* had appeared, which would prove seminal. Merton now launched a second research programme: the application of functionalism to the *phenomenon of bureaucracy*. Among other things, he put forth the famous thesis of *goal displacement*, according to which one dysfunction consists in the transformation of the means in a bureaucracy into ends in themselves.[36]

Merton's research programme generated a host of star researchers, all of whom conducted case studies to investigate the dysfunctions of bureaucracy. In particular should be mentioned Selznick's study of a public development company for the Tennessee Valley; Gouldner's study of a plaster factory near the Great Lakes; and Blau's book about structural change in two government bureaucracies.[37] All these are inspiring variations on the theme of bureaucratic dysfunctions and goal displacements. Later, the Frenchman Michel Crozier made a synthesis of this research, also based on personal empirical research (two major case studies of public organizations: the French state tobacco monopoly and the Parisian head office of a public utilities agency). The result was a theory of "the vicious circle of bureaucracy" where external disturbances drive the bureaucracy into creating internal rules, whose outward effects reinforce the external disturbances, which in their turn generate new rules . . . and thus the circle is in full swing.[38]

What these researchers did, following in Merton's footsteps, was to employ a Functional method to study a Tragic organizational drama. Thus the interest in even radical crises and "breaks" in development, which otherwise are rather alien to systems thinking.[39] Significantly, Merton also compares this Tragically influenced systems thinking with Marxism.[40] True enough, the same combination of – or tension between – a Functional analysis and a Tragic dramaturgy can be found in Marx.

5.2 The great synthesis: Burns and Stalker

The most significant new approach to organization theory which emerged in the 1950s in the wake of the systems wave was, however, *contingency theory*.[41] It is particularly associated with the studies of Burns and Stalker, and Woodward. We begin with the former and treat Woodward in the next section. Neither of these uses the systems view in detail, but it finds expression in overall features of the works. Nor do they adopt any particular part of systems theory, such as cybernetics, general systems theory, or functionalism; their assimilation of it is more universal in character.[42]

Burns and Stalker studied management systems in twenty British companies, of which fifteen were in the electronics industry and four had a major focus on R&D.[43] The investigation took place in three phases. Burns began with two pilot studies, then, in cooperation with Stalker, investigated eight Scottish companies, and finally conducted a study of ten English companies. Regretfully, we cannot go in greater detail into this stimulating and well-written book, which in the secondary literature has too often been reduced to a dry formula, summarizing the authors' main thesis.

The main thesis in question was as follows. The authors found that the companies' management systems clustered around two opposite poles. One pole can best be described by words such as bureaucratic, hierarchichal, specialized, and formalistic. They termed this type of system *mechanistic*. The second pole consisted of a more flexible, loose, and unspecialized type of system which the authors termed *organic*.

More specifically the two types were characterized by the following:[44]

Mechanistic system

(a) the specialized differentiation of functional tasks into which the problems and tasks facing the concern as a whole are broken down;

(b) the abstract nature of each individual task, which is pursued with techniques and purposes more or less distinct from those of the concern as a whole; i.e. the functionaries tend to pursue the technical improvement of means, rather than the accomplishment of the ends of the concern;

(c) the reconciliation, for each level in the hierarchy, of these distinct performances by the immediate superiors, who are also, in turn, responsible for seeing that each is relevant in his own special part of the main task;

(d) the precise definition of rights and obligations and technical methods attached to each functional role;

(e) the translation of rights and obligations and methods into the responsibilities of a functional position;

(f) hierarchic structure of control, authority and communication;

(g) a reinforcement of the hierarchic structure by the location of knowledge of actualities exclusively at the top of the hierarchy, where the final reconciliation of distinct tasks and assessment of relevance is made;

(h) a tendency for interaction between members of the concern to be vertical, i.e. between superior and subordinate;

(i) a tendency for operations and working behaviour to be governed by the instructions and decisions issued by superiors;

(j) insistence on loyalty to the concern and obedience to superiors as a condition of membership;

(k) a greater importance and prestige attaching to internal (local) than to general (cosmopolitan) knowledge, experience, and skill.

Organic system

(a) the contributive nature of special knowledge and experience to the common task of the concern;

(b) the "realistic" nature of the individual task, which is seen as set by the total situation of the concern;

(c) the adjustment and continual re-definition of individual tasks through interaction with others;

(d) the shedding of "responsibility" as a limited field of rights, obligations and methods (problems may not be posted upwards, downwards or sideways as being someone's else's);

(e) the spread of commitment to the concern beyond any technical definition;

(f) a network structure of control, authority, and communication. The sanctions which apply to the individual's conduct in his working role derive more from presumed community of interest with the rest of the working organization in the survival and growth of the firm, and less from a contractual relationship between himself and a non-personal corporation, represented for him by an immediate superior;

(g) omniscience no longer imputed to the head of the concern; knowledge about the technical or commercial nature of the here and now task may be located anywhere in the network; this location becoming the *ad hoc* centre of control, authority and communication;

(h) a lateral rather than a vertical direction of communication through the organization, communication between people of different rank, also, resembling consultation rather than command;

(i) a content of communication which consists of information and advice rather than instructions and decisions;

(j) commitment to the concern's tasks and to the "technological ethos" of material progress and expansion is more highly valued than loyalty and obedience;

(k) importance and prestige attach to affiliations and expertise valid in the industrial and technical and commercial milieux external to the firm.

The mechanistic system was, according to Burns and Stalker, most suitable in stable environments, and the organic in rapidly changing environments.[45] Between these poles were transitional types.

Environment in this study referred to technology and/or market. Since most of the companies studied were exposed to rapid changes in technology and markets, it became pertinent to try to discover why these did not all pass from a mechanistic management system to an organic. The transitional types just mentioned were in fact systems that had not been wholly transformed into organic ones, and in which their mechanistic properties played the role of "dysfunctions". The authors found the answer in the existence of two further internal systems within the organizations besides the management system – those of power and status, which stood in the way of a successful adaptation to the environment.

A systems view permeates the investigation. The management system constitutes a structure whose function it is to preserve the achievement of the goals – identified as "survival" and "expansion" – of the company/the whole/the system, this in the face of disturbances from the external world. If no such palpable disturbances arise, that is, the environment is relatively stable, a mechanistic system is appropriate; if there are major disturbances, that is, the environment is relatively dynamic, an organic system is preferable. Later authors have labelled these environmental properties "*uncertainty*",[46] a central term in every description of the contingency theories.

The organizational drama thus enacted is the Comedy of the systems approach. Especially typical is the distinction between two organizational states, where the original is deficient and the final integrates the particularities into an overall whole. The balance between these two, the fact that they are both equally clearly represented, characterizes the *dualistic Comedy* genre, by contrast with the other genres of this drama, where either the deficient or the desirable state dominates (to a varying extent).[47] Otherwise expressed, the emphasis lies near the middle of the typical course of events: at the beginning of the story the deficient state predominates; at its end, the desirable. The interest of Burns and Stalker focuses in particular on the transition from the mechanistic type, characterized by strict and formal regulation (i.e. laws), to the gentle and friendly organic type. As we saw in the Introduction, the general theme of Comedy is one of transition from law to community.

The metaphors Burns and Stalker use for their organizational states provide further dramaturgical material. In fact, the *mechanistic* is what is Comic in this drama – the machine-like repetitiveness characterizing the humorous actions in it. (A striking illustration is provided by slapstick movies – Chaplin, Buster Keaton, etc. – where this has been taken to an extreme.) The *organic* metaphor points to the relevant genre of Comedy as the *dualistic*, since a very typical theme of this genre is *the green world*, the "organic", integrated, whole, summer-like world, as distinguished from the rigid, quasi-rational, law-abiding world which isolates people from each other in a cold and wintry domain.

Further, the Comic course of events differs from the Tragic in not being deterministic; the transition can fail, and what the result will be depends on the characters acting for and against a happy ending.

In Burns and Stalker's theory, the character who assists the happy ending of the drama is uncertainty. It is interesting to study its place in the drama a little more closely. Uncertainty (1) is something non-corporeal,[48] (2) comes from outside, (3) creates unease, but still (4) does good, in the sense of promoting a happy (i.e. successful) ending. In Comic imaginative literature, a common type of corresponding figure is the *spirit of Comedy* or *benevolent vice*: an ethereal being, which "enters invisibly" from the outside and, as unpredictable as it is mischievous, still leads the action towards a happy ending (e.g. Puck, Ariel).[49] In fact, it is hard to find any better character-ization of uncertainty in Burns and Stalker than this prankish sprite – the mischievous yet basically benevolent "vice".

In portraying the transition, great attention is also paid to another thematic feature – "blocking characters". These are identified as the power and the status systems. The most common blocking character in Comic literary drama is the irate old man, or *heavy father* [*senex iratus*], who through his irrational, rigid authority puts spokes in the wheels of the drama's happy resolution.[50] In the previous chapter, we have seen how company management played a similar role at the Hawthorne factory. In Burns and Stalker, the power and status systems have the same function. Just the company management at Hawthorne they – through the properties just mentioned – account for a large part of the comedy in the drama, being unwittingly funny. In other words, the blocking characters are also the main *humorous* characters.[51]

We now turn to the method, which makes a surprisingly modern, Contextualist impression:

> The methods of study we have followed are those common to what is called field sociology and to social anthropology. These are simply directed towards gaining acquaintance, through conversation and obser-

vation, with the routines of behaviour current in the particular social
system being studied, and trying thereafter to reach an appreciation of the
codes of conduct which are supposed by the members of the system to
underlie behaviour. All this is very far removed from any method of
investigation which could possibly be called scientific.[52]

By "scientific" here is meant the Scientistic method. The reason why the
authors use a Contextual method is that behind the two opposed systems of
management – the mechanistic and the organic – they find two separate
cultures:

> The differences between the two kinds of management system seemed to
> resolve themselves into differences in the kind of relationships which
> prevail between members of the organization, whether of the same or of
> different rank, and thus into the kinds of behaviour which members of
> an organization treat as appropriate in their dealings with each other. It
> was possible to distinguish various modes of behaviour used by
> individuals according to a single dimension of conduct: the bounds set
> to what – in the way either of requests, instructions, or of considerations
> and information – the individual would regard as feasible, acceptable,
> worth taking into account, and so forth. The observable way in which
> people in a concern dealt with each other – the code of conduct – could
> therefore be regarded as the most important element in a concern's
> organization, given the structure of the management hierarchy and the
> skills and other resources at its disposal. It expresses the *framework of
> beliefs* [my italics] which decision-making invokes. In a realistic,
> operational sense, it *is* the organization.[53]
>
> Every firm is a community, with its own particular flavour, its own
> social structure, its own style of conduct. Newcomers are very conscious
> of this quality of uniqueness. Indeed, they have to be, since they have to
> learn the *culture*, and until they do, until it is other places which begin to
> have a disconcertingly unfamiliar smell, they have neither been accepted
> not accepted their position.[54]

Thus, the management systems are both cultures. The difference is that the
organic management system, by contrast with the mechanistic, is a "shared
culture":

> In exploiting human resources in this new direction, such concerns have
> to rely on the development of a "*common culture*", of a dependably
> constant system of *shared beliefs* about the common interests of the
> working community and about the standards and criteria used in it to
> judge achievement, individual contributions, expertise, and other
> matters by which a person or a combination of people are evaluated. A
> system of shared beliefs of this kind is expressed and visible in a code of

conduct, a way of dealing with other people. This code of conduct is, in fact, the first sign to the outsider of the presence of a management system appropriate to changing conditions.[55]

How familiar this sounds for a contemporary organization theorist, having experienced the wave of symbolism and cultural studies from the beginning of the 1980s! Yet it was written more than twenty years earlier, at the very inception of contingency theory and when the systems perspective on organizations was just beginning to take off. The style of thought which imbues the whole book is in fact that of Irony – the true reality is not the immediately given, for behind this hides *another*, secret world of meanings and significances, expressed in the code of conduct. Also, various subcultures and relationships – especially oppositions – between these are investigated, such as those between R&D personnel and others. Yes, the authors even go so far as to describe the production process as an "interpretive system".

Moreover, the theory of the two management systems integrated classical organization theory and the Human Relations school. Burns and Stalker criticized the former for its one-sided interest in the mechanistic system. Human Relations, again, had according to the authors first taken a "Manichean" stance by introducing a distinction between the formal (i.e. mechanistic) organization which represented the evil in our existence, and the informal organization which accounted for the good. In later years, however, Human Relations had adopted a diluted "Freudian" position, with the mechanistic organization as the rigid super ego, against which the repressed informal organization is up to a lot of mischief.[56] Human Relations' informal organization corresponds, as the reader will have guessed at this stage, to Burns and Stalker's organic management system.

As we have seen, the authors contended instead, as their main thesis, that neither one system nor the other could be generally recommended, but that which one was appropriate depended on the situation – a sceptical or relativistic slant, also typical of Irony.

Thus, Burns and Stalker integrate the classical and the Human Relations schools under Comedy's overarching systems perspective, but with an Ironic style of thought as base. In Human Relations the systems view had stopped at an attempt, and the cultural perspective at a hint. Not until Burns and Stalker's study were both developed to the full. But their immediate successors solely retained the systems perspective. The cultural perspective was rediscovered in the 1980s by a new generation, in reaction to a then dominating systems approach.

The criticism that can be aimed at the book is that its main thesis is weakly substantiated as to the claim that the more successful companies, those better adjusted to the environment, etc., should have a certain – in the authors' study primarily an organic – management structure. The authors Darwinistically interpret adjustment to the environment as resulting in "fitness for survival". Here, they in fact end up in a circle, just like Roethlisberger and Dickson. The criticism against evolutionary biology's concept of "survival of the fittest" for tautology is well known: The fittest survive because they are fittest. For what? Well, for survival. (As we remember, Burns and Stalker themselves stated survival as a goal.)

An independent criterion is therefore required. Darwinians themselves usually eschew the accusation of tautology by translating "the fittest" into "those who have the greatest reproductive capacity".[57] This escape route – which moreover has been called into question with reference to bacterial capacity in the area – is not open to organization theorists, for natural reasons. In passing, it can be mentioned that this is also a weakness in the foundation of the modern theoretical approach usually denoted as population ecology, which is based on the analogy to Darwinian development biology.[58]

Besides, all the companies investigated by the authors were still alive. But perhaps the goal of growth, which Burns and Stalker also specify, may be a criterion for successful adaptation? In biology, from where the analogy is taken, this is not the case – we need only refer to the dinosaurs. Nor is it so in the world of companies, where too strong expansion is well known to bring calamity.

Burns and Stalker finally state that other companies' judgements have been one of the criteria of a company's success. Yet in such judgements, psychological factors play so great a role that the former cannot be taken very seriously.

The book, then, lacks a more comprehensive or systematic exposition of the degree of success and adaptation of the companies, and of how these relate to type of management system. But this is hard to achieve with the method selected. The systems view and Burns and Stalker's, in Geertz's words, "thick description" of culture[59] are not quite compatible. In other words, there are splits in the seams between the authors' Contextual method and their Comic organizational drama.

Burns and Stalker's work was epoch-making. It was followed by a flood of contingency research, which largely confirmed the authors' thesis, but which we shall not even attempt to survey.[60] We shall, however, briefly touch upon two of the more important works. In their *Organization and Environment* Lawrence and Lorsch codified the terminology, which has been in use since then: *uncertainty* from the environment and *contingency* became henceforward the standard conceptual terms. The authors measured uncertainty and the internal structural properties of differentiation and integration in ten companies in the plastics, food, and container industries. Differentiation referred to differences between subunits within the companies, and integration to cooperation between these same subunits.

The results of the investigation agreed very well with those of Burns and Stalker. Successful companies in a swiftly fluctuating, thus uncertain environment such as the plastics industry proved to have a high degree of differentiation between subunits, and therefore also to require more flexible, sophisticated forms of integration. On the other hand, successful companies in the stable, more secure industry were less differentiated and could therefore manage with simpler forms of integration, such as the traditional command hierarchy. We recognize here Burns and Stalker's organic and mechanistic types. Lawrence and Lorsch showed that the difference between organic and mechanistic, depending on environmental uncertainty, also held for subunits within companies: for example, research and development departments were more organic than manufacturing departments.

The latter point is related to what J. D. Thompson, on a purely theoretical basis, maintained in his influential book *Organizations in Action*: uncertainty was the main thread in all organization theory. Organizations had a technological core which, provided that it was protected from the uncertainty of the environment, could function mechanically. The protection consisted of special *buffer units*, which *absorbed* the uncertainty.

What, then, is meant by uncertainty? There may be reason here to briefly account for the development of the concept within the systems approach to organizations,[61] and to conclude this with some critical reflections, leading to a tropological diagnosis.

In a first phase – to which Burns and Stalker belonged – authors were mainly interested in objective, uncertainty-generating properties of the external environment. In a second phase, this *objective uncertainty* was complemented by the so-called *perceived uncertainty* of the organization's actors. This phase, which had a transitional character, can be exemplified by Thompson. In a third phase, during which Lawrence and Lorsch were pioneers, interest was displaced more and more towards the latter type, perceived uncertainty. Efforts to find statistical relationships between objective and perceived uncertainty have provided conflicting results. The debate between "objectivists" and "perceptionists" continues. Uncertainty about the concept of uncertainty therefore increased, with the result that – although still central – from the 1980s it has not been quite as much in vogue as in the previous decades.[62]

However, it would seem that the polarization between objective and perceived uncertainty rests on a misunderstanding of a semantic and meta-scientific nature. It is necessary to distinguish between the *definition* of a concept and its *operationalization*. The former refers to the meaning-content of the concept;[63] the latter provides the concept with indicators (measures or qualitative criteria). The concept of "operational definition" has caused a lot of mischief, as it erroneously identifies definition with operationalization, meaning-content with indicator. Yet that these are entirely different phenomena, modern, post-positivist philosophy of science generally agrees upon, despite differences on other issues.[64]

Organizations are symbol-processing devices.[65] Uncertainty can be defined as the degree of difficulty for the organization in rendering an unequivocal interpretation of the received symbols. The same definition is given by

March and Olsen and also in "fuzzy set theory", which has provided several precise, quantitative measures of it.[66]

We note first that this definition applies to the whole organization. The experiences of individual actors are at this stage irrelevant. Second, it concerns a *relation between* organization and environment. The controversy between objectivists and perceptionists stems from the fallacious assumption that uncertainty is a *property* of *either* the environment *or* individual actors within the organization. This is a category error,[67] similar to asking whether a marriage is an attribute of the husband or something perceived by the wife. It is neither, but a relation between the two. And this is the case with organizational uncertainty, also. Statements that environmental properties or single individuals' experiences have value as indicators of the concept are – just as statements on the mutual relations between the two – *empirical hypotheses*, not definitions.

Otherwise expressed, a Scientistic method here clashes with a Comic organizational drama. The thesis concerning operational definitions, like the thesis that everything can be reduced to measurements at the individual level, belongs to a logical-empirical tradition which tallies badly with the systems perspective (besides, as we have just seen, being superseded in the scientific-philosophical domain).

5.3 The technological imperative: Woodward

A more extensive empirical material than Burns and Stalker's is found in Joan Woodward, the second major British contingency theorist of the 1950s. From 1953 to 1958 Woodward led a research project at the newly established Human Relation Research Unit in South Essex College of Technology. A hundred companies in south Essex were made the object of a survey study. Covering 91 per cent of all the manufacturing companies in the region with 100 or more employees, it can in practice be classified as a whole population study. The results of the survey were supplemented by case studies. The findings of the project were then followed up by further studies between 1958 and 1963. Thus, Woodward's investigation extended in total over nearly ten years, 1953–63.

The project had a dual aim. On the one hand, there was a general explorative intention: to examine "how the firms studied were organized and operated". Then, there was a more specific purpose, to establish

> whether any particular form of organization was associated with management efficiency and commercial success.[68]

In the survey the research workers concentrated on formal organizational aspects, leaving the informal side to the case studies. Data were collected under four headings:

1   History, background, and objectives.
2   Description of the manufacturing processes and methods.
3   Forms and routines through which the firm was organized and operated.
4   Facts and figures that could be used to make an assessment of the firm's commercial success.[69]

Under (2), a large quantity of data was gathered on the firms' technologies, something which would prove to be important. As to (4), Woodward pointed out in particular the risk of ending up in "the circular argument that an arrangement works because it exists".[70] Data under (4) therefore included "any available information having a direct or indirect bearing on [the firm's] achievements". The data, however, were considered as sufficient only for a crude classification in low, medium and high success. In the construction of measures for these three classes, the various success variables were weighted.[71]

Woodward found a wide variation between different organizational principles. For example line, line-staff, divisionalized, and functional organizations à la Taylor (numbering two) were all represented.[72]

Burns had released a research report on the difference between mechanistic and organic organizations. In Woodward's material, these types accounted for around a third and two-thirds respectively, a distribution which probably depended on industry in south Essex, being new and still developing, favouring the organic type.[73]

The number of hierarchic levels and the span of control (the number of workers under a first-line supervisor) also varied strongly.[74]

The question now arose as to the reason for this. Woodward tried several explanations, but, as she says:

> Although the analysis of the information had shown that firms differed considerably in the way they were organized and operated, it was not easy to find the common threads underlying these differences.[75]

The differences were, for instance, unrelated to type of industry or company size.[76] Nor did the researchers consider that the personality of managers or the historical background and tradition of the companies had had any effect.[77]

Moreover, with respect to the success variable the classical perspective had little explanatory value.[78]

Woodward therefore turned to *technology*, the remaining category for which data had already been collected, under (2), Description of the manufacturing processes and methods. Here, the companies were originally divided into nine classes according to the nature of their production, but for practical application, these were re-grouped into three: unit and small batch, large batch and mass, and process.[79] In what follows, we shall, for the sake of convenience, simply write "unit" instead of "unit and small batch", and "mass" instead of "large batch and mass". Unit production manufactures non-standardized goods on customers' demand (such as individually tailored suits or prototypes of electronic equipment). Mass production, for instance that of the assembly line, manufactures standardized, discrete products (such as aspirin tablets or machine parts). Process production is concerned with standardized, continuous flow products (such as acetylsalicylic acid, or more generally "liquids, gases and crystalline substances").[80]

These three production technologies when compared were, according to Woodward, chacterized by increasing complexity. Mass production is newer and more complex than unit production; in turn, process production is newer and more complex than mass production.[81]

A linear relationship emerged between, on the one hand, technological complexity and, on the other, the degree of administration (according to various indicators).[82] This result appears intuitively reasonable, since a more complex technology demands more planning.

Curvilinear relationships, on the other hand, emerged between technological complexity and organizational structure (see Figure 5.2).

The span of control (number of workers controlled by a first-line supervisor) tended to be highest in mass production, lower in unit and process production. Correspondingly, mechanistic organizational structures tended to appear in mass production and organic in unit and process production.

The picture was reinforced when the success variable was controlled for. It emerged that the companies successful within the different technological categories tended to cluster around median values with respect to span of control. The opposite was the case for less successful companies. The same applied to organizational structure (mechanistic or organic): successful companies were likely to be found in organic, mechanistic or organic structures depending on whether they worked with unit, mass or process production.

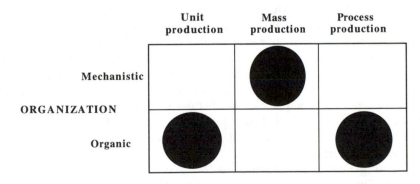

Figure 5.2 Technical complexity and organizational structure (mechanistic, organic), according to Woodward.

Thus far the conclusions of the study and the conventional picture painted by posterity. If we now scrutinize a little more closely the statistics which underlie the conclusions, we find the following:

Success. Even if a number of different variables are mentioned, there is no systematic account of them, their quantitative indicators, or how they were weighted.

Organizational structure. The presentation is based on bar charts without stated frequency values.

Type of industry and size vs. organizational structure. Here a multivariate analysis is required, instead of the descriptive bar charts (with frequencies omitted), in order to weigh the influences of the different factors against each another. Size should have been measured by more than one indicator (number of employees). A glance at Woodward's bar chart for the relationship between size and span of control of first-line supervisors, however, reveals a marked difference between companies with 100–250 employees and those with a greater number: the frequency of less span of control is higher in the former.[83)] Woodward, however, found no relationships.

Mechanistic and organic organizations. There is no mention as to which indicators have been used to distinguish between these.

The relationship between tradition and organizational structure. No arguments are provided that such a relationship does not exist; this is presented more as an article of faith:

> The research workers felt, however, that while it was obviously true that such factors [historical background and tradition] were variables in the situation and influenced it, they did not adequately explain it; the observed differences between firms either in organizational patterns or in the quality of human relations could not in all cases be related to personality or tradition.[84]

The relationship between the success variable and classical approach. Two pieces of evidence are offered for the absence of such relationships:[85]

First, according to a principle of management, presented by a follower of Fayol, the span of control at the *highest* level may not exceed six. By contrast, Woodward found that in "five successful firms the chief executive controlled more than twelve immediate subordinates".[86] However, this tells us nothing, considering that the number of successful companies was twenty in total,[87] and that nothing is revealed about the spans of control in the fifteen remaining successful companies. Nor are the spans of control of the successful companies compared with those of the non-successful. Both would have been a necessary requirement for discussing the validity of the principle of management referred to.

The non-successful companies (below average) are said to have "wide variations in the size of the span of control" – variations which are not specified more precisely.

Of the other principles of management, *none* was examined for its possible relationship with business success. According to the received view, Woodward falsified the classical principles of management empirically, showing that they did not lead to success for the company. This conventional wisdom is thus inaccurate.

Second, "Advanced production control techniques were not in operation in all successful firms".[88] How many is not specified; nor what is meant by "advanced". Thus, Taylor's principles were not refuted either.

Linear relationship organization-technology. On the other hand, the linear relationships Woodward found between organization and technology seem to be substantiated, as far as can be gathered from the bar charts. Furthermore, here several indicators are used for the same organizational variable – degree of administration. Moreover, a table with exact data is presented – one of two tables with such content occurring in the book.

Curvilinear relationship organization-technology. The case is more doubtful with the curvilinear relationships, which have come down as the received view of Woodward's own contribution to organization science. What is corroborated is that span of control is wider in mass production (median value 49) than in the relatively similar unit production (23) and process production (13).[89] As to a more general curvilinear relationship between mechanistic/organic organization and production technology, however, this is not confirmed at all.

Relationship between production technology, organizational structure (span of control) and business success. For the relationship between these variables, reference is frequently made to the book's second and final table with exact numbers.[90] It is intended to show that successful companies in each technological category cluster around the median value of span of control for that category, while on the other hand non-successful companies are found around the extreme values. But the number of cases (individuals controlled) in the cells is far too small,[91] and the boundaries between categories too uncertain, to make any definite, statistical conclusion.[92] Minor measurement errors or adjustments in the boundaries between categories can turn the pattern upside down. Given the problematic nature of success measures, and also the complicated procedure with weighting of various indicators, which Woodward hints at but does not account for, the results become even more problematic. In summary, it can be said that this table – one of the two with exact values in the book – provides too fragile a basis for the conclusions drawn.

Yet these are, as we shall now see, the only data presented for the thesis concerning the relationship between production technology, organizational structure, and success.

Relationship between production technology, organizational structure, (general) and success. Here no data are offered, but Woodward simply asserts:

The figures relating to the span of control of the chief executive, the number of levels in the line of command, labour costs, and the various labour ratios showed a similar trend [as in the table above].[93]

Relationship between production technology, mechanistic/organic organizational structure, and success.

It was also interesting to find that, in terms of Burns's analysis, successful firms inside the large batch production range tended to have mechanistic management systems. On the other hand, successful firms outside this range tended to have organic systems.[94]

When it comes to quantitative or other evidence for this, the reader is left in the dark, however.

In other words, the defects in the Scientistic investigation are striking; such a statistical description would have difficulties in being accepted at the basic level of academic training in most social sciences. This criticism is not anachronistic, since the statistical science was well developed at the time. Is it not astonishing, then, that a researcher of Woodward's calibre could have made such misses? Maybe so, but only if we disregard the underlying dialectical poetics.

For the defects can be explained, not by personal properties, but by virtue of Woodward having already prefigured her investigation in a Synecdochic style of thought.[95] Consider the four groups of variables for which data were collected (see the beginning of this section). Success (4) clearly constituted the system goal. Organizational design (3) provided the structure which Comically had the function of sustaining this system goal against environmental influences. Now, there were, to judge from the data, *different* types of structures. This must – in line with the systems approach to which Woodward adheres[96] – be explained by the influence of the environment.

Two variables then remain, tradition and technology. Tradition (1) is not an environmental factor and rather tends towards a Metaphorical perspective with Idiographic explanations of particular cases. This also explains why it is rejected so summarily. Consequently, the only group of variables in the investigation that, within the framework of a systems approach, could be linked to degree of success and organizational structure was *technology* (2). Moreover, Burns, with whose work, as we have seen, Woodward was familiar, had already used this as an environmental variable.

Thus, the investigation was already pre-analytically – tropologically – destined to find a relationship between technology and organizational structure with respect to business success. Hence, the Metonymic theories of the classics had to be rejected in favour of Synecdochic conclusions, and hence a statistical treatment which even Woodward herself admits was "too crudely expressed for general acceptance".[97] Also contributing is that the Synecdochic style of thought clearly clashes with the Scientistic method of investigation.

More justice is done to Woodward's talent in the Functional case studies, which she conducted to follow up the survey. They aimed at comparing the three technological groups (unit, mass, and process production) with respect to line-staff organization, relations between the main functions of R&D, manufacturing and marketing, and also production organization.

Dramaturgically, the organizational drama, just as with Burns and Stalker, falls within the genre of *dualistic Comedy*. Some Comic genres focus on the deficient, over-regulated state, leaving the integrated, desirable state rather vague in contours; others concentrate on the final, happy state and give a rather shadowy picture of the rigorous, law-abiding state. Dualistic Comedy provides a clear display of both the states between which the action moves – the originally deficient and the final, desirable. The mechanistic state of affairs in mass production appears as a de-humanized community, which has neither the organic charm of the old or individualistic ways in unit production, nor the equally organic benefits of a modern process industry, emancipating the workers to autonomous thinking, co-determination, and responsibility.

The transition between the deficient and the desirable state does not take place deterministically, also in similarity with Burns and Stalker. However, by contrast with these authors, the blocking characters do not occupy a prominent place in the drama. Instead, decisive weight is placed on an assisting character, one which releases the change between the states. In Woodward this role is played by technology. Technology is, of course, the servant of humankind, but also a disquietingly "clever" and independent one. In literary Comedy, alongside the benevolent, spiritual "vice" the *eiron* role is played most commonly by the *scheming valet/tricky slave* (*dolosus servus*) who – equipped with intelligence as much as independence – turns the action towards its happy ending.[98]

We have already seen, in the Comic Romance of Human Relations, the figure in question appears under different guise. There, however, the means through which this character acted were clear: manipulations and the revelation of secrets. Here, by contrast, it remains unclear just *how* technology might bring about the structural transition between the states. This is a dramaturgical weakness (*deus ex machina*), which also signals a weakness in Woodward's theory.

We shall not go any further into the case studies, since the survey was the pathbreaking work, which has remained a subject of interest and discussion. It stimulated a veritable deluge of research, especially of a Scientistic nature, about the impact of technology on structure, something which came to be called the "technological imperative". In sum, it can be said that while later research generally confirmed the results of the other contingency theory classic, Burns and Stalker, it tended on the whole to either strongly modify or run counter to those of Woodward.[99]

The Aston school – named after the University of Aston in Birmingham, England – is the primary exponent so far of such research. In the 1960s it conducted a more full-fledged Scientistic study, with a thoroughly Metonymic style of thought, of the relation between (among other things) technology and structure.[100] The research team conducted a multivariate statistical analysis of a random sample of forty-six organizations in the Birmingham area. The thesis of the technological imperative could only be confirmed to a highly modified extent.

The analysis of the Aston research team indicated instead that *size* played a far more decisive role in structural design. (By contrast, as we remember, Woodward had not found any relationship between size and structure.) For this group, size was the main assisting character, typical of Comedy, for effecting change from one (structural) state to another.[101] Technology only influenced structure secondarily and in smaller companies. The latter was because more employees in such companies come into immediate contact with technology/the shop floor. In larger companies such influence was limited mainly to those structural aspects which were in direct contact with the technology in question. Even though the statistical analyses of the Aston school can be disputed at certain points,[102] their results have been corroborated by later Scientistic research in the field.[103]

5.4 Critics and reformists

At the beginning of the 1970s, a researcher from the "third generation" of the Aston school directed a fundamental critique against the principles of contingency theory. In a very influential article in the journal *Sociology*, John Child claimed that the theories grossly over-estimated the importance of the system's environment at the expense of the opportunities for "strategic choice" which decision-makers in organizations possess.[104]

The contingency theorists had, according to Child, represented change in organizations as an automatic reflex to changed environmental conditions. As against such determinism, he instead put his finger on the necessary inter-mediate processes – the judgements of the actors in the organization through whom the change must be realized. A main objection was that statistical investigations in the Aston school style neglected the *understanding* of events.

The article is highly compressed and very rich in ideas. Strategic choice functions as something of an umbrella concept for many organizational phenomena. Its chief components can be summarized as follows:

- Impulses from the environment – e.g. uncertainty – are not transmitted mechanically, but via the interpretations of decision-makers, who constitute a "dominant coalition", that is the organization's group in power.[105] Thus, for example, perceived uncertainty is important, not just objective uncertainty. But decision-makers can also, in a wider sense, mentally create their own environment.[106]
- To this subjective medium through which the impulses of the environment must be refracted, and which counteracts them, should be

added a number of different objective conditions within the organization. Among these can be mentioned the so-called "organizational slack" – buffers in the form of surplus resources which dampen the impacts of the environment, preventing them from having having an immediate effect.[107]

- This means that decision-makers have considerable degrees of freedom as to designing organizational structures in accordance with their own wishes.
- Decision-makers can also choose to influence the environment, for example by manipulating its uncertainty. Here, the direction of causality is reversed; instead of the environment affecting the organization, the organization, via its decision-makers, affects the environment.
- They can also decide to choose a suitable environment, for instance with a degree of uncertainty which suits the organizational set-up.

Child was influenced by David Silverman's book, published in 1970, which criticized organization theory from an "actor's frame of reference". Silverman wrote on a more fundamental level, that of the style of thought, and had in turn been inspired by phenomenological philosophy, where the experiences of the individual are central. He can be characterized as a Metaphoric rebel against the Synecdochic systems approach. Child's text is more concretely oriented to organizations. With his emphasis on the individuals' ability to express themselves through meaningful interpretations and free action, it constituted a Romantic revolt against the prevailing dominance of the organizational Comedy. In line with this, Child recommended the Idiographic method as against the Aston school's Scientism.

Thus, instead of environmental properties, the consciousness of decision-makers becomes the factor which ultimately explains everything, but itself is unexplained. Against Child one might object that the conception of such an uninfluenced consciousness of decision-makers is a hypothesis which remains to be proven – just like the hypothesis of the unaffected environment. Might not the case be, for example, that the environment affects organizations *through* influencing the actors' interpretations?[108] Dialectical ideas of interaction between organization and environment have also been presented, under criticism of both contingency theories and strategic choice on the grounds for one-sidedness.[109] A further angle is represented by resource dependence theories, where the organization is seen as dependent on, and therefore striving (through strategic choice) to control scarce resources.[110] Here the resources of the environment constrain the strategic choice.

Both the dialecticians and the resource dependence theorists sought, each in their own way, to *combine* the systems approach and Child's revolutionary Romance into a hybrid – a Romantic Comedy.

Child pursued a Romantic rebellion against the systems approach. A Romantic striving for reform *within the framework of Comedy* is represented, on the other hand, by Weick. The main point was a transition of genres from the normal dualistic genre of the systems perspective, to another Comic genre. Weick's "loosely coupled systems" are characterized by weakened goal orientation and control. Through "enactment of the environment", the organizational members individually endow the environment with meaning.[111]

> The crucial links in a loosely coupled system occur among small groups of people, including dyads, triads and small groups[112]

In Weick, the drama's choice of words, its metaphors, are those of Comedy; its content that of Romance. The genre corresponds to the collapsing phase of Frye's Comedy, which faces onto Romance.[113] This *disintegrating* Comedy, corresponding to the end of this drama's characteristic course of events, is marked by

> the collapse and disintegration of the comic society [. . .] In this phase the social units of comedy become small and esoteric, or even confined to a single individual.[114]

We note here how well this matches Weick's loosely coupled systems; and also that the Comic society's disintegration in favour of the esoteric – "the sense of individual detachment from routine existence"[115] – points towards Romance.

In the same genre runs Cyert and March's behavioural theory of firms as "coalitions", in which many separate interests can be represented and goals are fragmented.[116]

To the same genre also belongs the so-called "garbage can" model of decision-making, in which streams of problems, solutions, participants, and choice opportunities are mixed together; as too does the corresponding organizational model of "organized anarchy", characterized by problematic goals, unclear technologies, and fluid participation.[117)] Weick identifies organized anarchy as a loosely coupled system.[118]

Weick's loosely coupled systems, Cyert and March's coalitions, March *et al.*'s garbage can model, and organized anarchies – all these forms which resemble and more or less flow into each other – are variants of one and the same genre: the disintegrating Comedy, where the transition to Romance lies close at hand.

Even Scott's well-known classification of organizations can be interpreted in the light of the above. He starts with a categorization into "rational, natural and open systems".[119)] Later, he constructs a "slightly more complex" typology by inter-relating the two dimensions rational/natural and closed/open systems. In this way a two-by-two matrix with four types is obtained. Type I, closed rational systems, enacts the Tragic organizational drama; type II, closed natural systems, the Comic Romance; and type III, open rational systems, the normal, dualistic Comedy. Thus they correspond to the dramas of our first three dominant organizational approaches, and also the division of the traditional textbook version.[120]

It then becomes interesting to see what Scott's type IV corresponds to. In this section we have discussed a number of Romantic critics and reformists of the "normal" Comedy genre. *Scott's fourth type refers precisely to Romantic reformists of the normal, dualistic Comic genre.* These alternative organizational dramas belong primarily to the disintegrating genre of Comedy which we just touched upon: Weick's loosely-coupled systems,[121] Cyert and March's coalitions, March and Olsen's organized anarchies; further dramas in the same genre are Hickson's "strategic contingency" (subgroups with varying degrees of environmental unsecurity and therefore power) and Meyer and Rowan's "decoupling" between subsystems.[122),123)]

5.5 Configurations and metamorphoses: Mintzberg and Miller

The classical organizational school regarded the rational type of organization as universally valid. By contrast, Human Relations advocated a more social organization. In contingency theory (Burns and Stalker, Woodward, Lawrence and Lorsch) the possible states of the organization/the system were conceived as two: the mechanistic and the organic. These two correspond to the organizational types favoured by the classics and Human Relations, which contingency theory now showed to have validity under different environmental conditions. Thus, contingency theory represented a higher-level synthesis of the two earlier main branches in organizational research. But might there not be more organizational types/system states than just two?

From the 1980s onwards, researchers linked to McGill University in Montreal, Canada, have extended the sphere of possible system states. Their studies also hark back to some previously constructed organizational typologies.[124] By contrast with the latter, however, the types are no longer conceived as static *taxa* in the Plato-Linnéan tradition, that is as mundane representations of an unchanging world of ideas, but as coherent clusters of properties in dynamic systems. By virtue of this, it also becomes interesting to study the transitions – the metamorphoses – between the various states, or organizational types.

5.5.1 *Mintzberg*

The Canadian management policy researcher Henry Mintzberg set out by discerning three "modi" of business behaviour. Two of these correspond to the mechanistic and organic types. But to these Mintzberg added a third, an *entrepreneurial* type. Here, the organization is flexible, as in the organic type, but leadership is strong, as in the mechanistic. Yet it is no simple combination of the other two, from which the entrepreneurial type differs by virtue of properties like intuition, vision, and charisma.[125]

Mintzberg later developed these three types into his famous five.[126] These include:

• The machine bureaucracy
• The adhocracy

- The simple structure
- The divisionalized form
- The professional bureaucracy

The machine bureaucracy is the mechanistic organization. The adhocracy is the organic. The simple structure corresponds to the entrepreneurial type just described.

The divisionalized form is, as its name indicates, simply a divisional organization, with (more or less) independent divisions. Other authors have discussed – and propagated – it as the "M form" of organizations (M for "multidivisional").[127]

In earlier research, the professional bureaucracy has been found mainly in public higher education organizations (universities), but also hospitals and the like. It has been labelled with well-known, graphic designations, such as organized anarchy and the "garbage can" model for decision-making (see section 5.4 above).[128] Unclear goals, uncertain means, and fluid participation are characteristic. Leadership is weak and the organization decentralized.

The types have been derived inductively from a broad study of literature on organization and management. However, it proves also possible to link them to the different main components of an organization between which Mintzberg distinguishes. These are five, too:

- Technostructure (the "analysts", responsible for planning, scheduling, work studies, etc.)
- Support staff (e.g. R&D, legal resources, payroll department, PR, post room)
- Strategic apex (top management)
- Middle line (line managers at intermediate level, not including "middle management" in the technostructure or among support staff)
- Operating core (the shop floor, but also salespersons and purchasing agents)

Now, a strong technostructure carries with it, according to Mintzberg, a tendency to machine bureaucracy, since the work of analysts (staff) is to plan and standardize operations for the organization. In the same way, if the support staff has a strong capacity to pull the organization in its direction, an adhocratic structure emerges; we can, for example, think of R&D departments which traditionally are built this way. A strong force of attraction from the strategic top prepares the ground for a simple structure with powerful management. If the middle line dominates, divisionalization can easily emerge from the tug-of-war between the different line managers. Strength in the operating core – as for instance represented by non-administrative hospital personnel, or university teachers/researchers – brings about a professional bureaucracy.

In his book about power, Mintzberg has further developed his typology, this time to seven types.[129] He has divided machine bureaucracy into two: Machine bureaucracy as instrument and Machine bureaucracy as closed system. The former primarily refers to goal-governed, rationally planned bureaucracy in the private sector as a tool for the owners. The latter mainly refers to the Weberian, rule-governed bureaucracy within the public sector. The divisionalized form is subsumed under Machine bureaucracy (in particular as closed system).[130]

Also, an additional type appears, the Missionary: an ideologically governed organization with a rather loose structure.

Mintzberg has also, especially in his book on power, discussed transitions, or to use Starbuck's term metamorphoses,[131] between the different types.[132)]

Like his pupil Miller, Mintzberg has a pronounced systems perspective. Mintzberg emphasizes that contingency theory is inadequate, since it often just states how particular traits of the environment are reflected in particular traits of the organization:

> And so recent management theory has moved away from the "one best way" approach, toward an "it all depends" approach, formally known as "contingency theory." . . . [The] "it all depends" approach does not go far enough, . . . structures are rightfully designed on the basis of a third approach, which might be called the "getting it all together" or . . . the "configuration" approach. Spans of control, types of formalization and decentralization, planning systems, and matrix structures should not be picked and chosen independently, the way a shopper picks vegetables at the market or a diner a meal at a buffet table. Rather, these and other parameters of organizational design should logically configure into internally consistent groupings. Like most phenomena – atoms, ants, and stars – characteristics of organizations appear to fall into natural clusters, or configurations.[133]

This is the very foundation of Mintzberg's and Miller's typologies. The organizational drama is still Comic, but the genre has changed into *picaresque* – a never-ending journey between different states, with Ironic–Satirical overtones, since one state is as good as the other, and complications in one state eventually will lead to a flight to another. The company manager is the hero, in the role of *picaro*, the smart and charming but rather unprincipled adventurer-rogue who, with feline agility, leaps between the various tin roofs on his journey before they get uncomfortably hot.[134]

Organizations act according to Comedy's rules for maintaining their "packages" of basic properties, and thereby harmony and stability. It is precisely these packages which constitute the different types. For this reason, organizations can only be transformed in "quanta", that is, in leaps between the various types. Gradual changes of one property at a time lead to imbalance and therefore do not work, or as Mintzberg says:

It is presumably its search for harmony in structure and situation that causes an organization to favor one of the pure types.[135]

Thus, the method is Functional.

5.5.2 *Miller*

In Danny Miller we encounter a fruitful stylistic tension between the Comic organizational drama and a Scientistic method.[136] Miller and his colleague Friesen applied so-called Q factor analysis[137)] to a selection of case histories of fifty-two firms. Miller's taxonomy was created on the basis of this analysis. ("Taxonomy" by contrast with "typology" is used here to denote that the types have been sorted out inductively from a data material, with the use of statistical machinery.)

Their taxonomy included the following archetypes:

* "Entrepreneurial", whose properties are indicated by its name (7.5 per cent of the sample)
* "Adaptive, S_1B", an organic type (12 per cent)
* "Adaptive, S_1A", a mechanistic type (13 per cent)
* "Stagnant", i.e. dysfunctional bureaucracy (12 per cent)
* "Headless", an organized anarchy with emphasis on anarchy (8 per cent).

From the factor analysis four further archetypes also emerged. The percentage for Entrepreneurial seems unexpectedly low. But there is an additional "Impulsive" archetype (13 per cent) which appears to be Entrepreneurial at

MINTZBERG'S CONFIGURATIONS	MILLER'S ARCHETYPES
Simple structure; Missionary	Entrepreneurial; Impulsive
Adhocracy	Adaptive S_1B
Machine bureaucracy (Instrument)	Adaptive S_1A
Machine bureaucracy (Closed system)	
	Stagnant
Professional bureaucracy	Headless

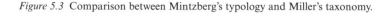

Figure 5.3 Comparison between Mintzberg's typology and Miller's taxonomy.

the beginning of transition to other types. If we count it in, the types referred to account for two-thirds of Miller's total sample. His remaining four types, which we shall not go into any further, covered in all 22.5 per cent of the sample. In a replication of this study, using fifty-two other companies as data sources, Kets de Vries and Miller found that 80 per cent of the companies could be classified as belonging to the already established taxonomy.

The similarity to Mintzberg's typology is striking (see Figure 5.3 for a comparison).

The critical views that can be directed at Mintzberg and Miller are the following. Mintzberg has worked inductively on the basis of reviews of the literature. There are no arguments in his book for why just the typology presented has emerged from the studies of the literature, rather than any other. It stands out as something of an impressionistic work of art, immediately attractive to the eye but perhaps not so seriously grounded, and therefore less convincing in the long run.

Miller, on the other hand, impresses with dazzling mathematical-technical virtuosity. But the virtuosity obscures the fragile ground on which the analysis rests. The empirical data have not been selected at random, since the cases were sifted out so as to fit in with the variables upon which the researchers (Miller and Friesen) had already decided in advance (on the basis of the literature). The cases were taken from *Fortune*, the Harvard Case Clearing House series, plus a number of "textbooks". It is, however, crucial to use a random sample as the basis for the construction of taxonomies.[138] To this can be added that factor analysis is known to be dirigible more or less to where the researcher wishes. Still, there is something intuitively plausible about both Mintzberg's and Miller's findings.

An integration of these and other prominent typologies with theories of organizational transitions and culture is provided by the author in the theory of "planning cultures".[139] Within the compass of the present style analysis, its organizational drama could be best described as a Satirical Comedy, uniting a systems and a culture perspective from a relativist stance.

5.6 The poetics of the system

The Synecdochic style of thought relates the part to the whole. This finds expression in a method which investigates organizations by placing separate parts of these in a functional relation to the whole. We call this method the *Functional*.[140)] The selected facts are neither meaningful nor meaningless singular entities as in the two preceding cases, but wholes consisting of parts. As we have seen, the model of interpretation employed in the Idiographic method focused on understanding, and in the Scientist on causal explanations. By contrast, the Functional method's model of interpretation is the one usually called "finalistic": it focuses on means-end, which is here the basic relationship, as the purpose of the part is to serve the whole. The means, i.e. the part, is the immediate object of study, and the end, i.e. the function in relation to the whole, is the ground one seeks.[141]

The corresponding organizational drama is Comedy, which evens out all disturbances and conflicts in particular parts, in favour of an overall harmony of a whole. Thus, the development points towards neither the self-realization of the individual nor the impersonal rule of the law, but towards a balancing, a reconciliation of the social forces in the embrace of the benevolent whole. The organization/the whole moves between two states – one original and deficient, the other final and desirable. The end state means the natural integration of the participants, despite opposing, resisting forces. The course of events is, in contrast to that of Tragedy, not deterministic. The organizational style of this triad is what we have termed the *integrative*.[142]

The systems approach constitutes a variant of the integrative organizational style, which in its ideal state forms the triad of style of thought, organizational drama and method shown in Figure 5.4.

The systems approach is based on a Synecdochic style of thought. The relationship between part and whole becomes the essential. The part is seen in terms of its relation to the whole, not conversely. For the Functional method the parts in the system have no other function than to serve the system's whole, enabling it to survive. The corresponding organizational drama is that of Comedy: the play through which the organization's fundamental harmony and stability is maintained despite temporary disturbances.

There are two basic systems orientations. First, the cybernetic model launched by Norbert Wiener, in which the system is conceived as a servo-mechanism, receiving inputs and transforming these into outputs; the stability is achieved through (negative) feedback. Second, the open system, in which the system is regarded as an organism, maintaining through metabolic processes its internal balance, despite variations in the environment.[143] Given that these *two* models are joined in the systems perspective, it is clear that one cannot speak of a single "system metaphor".

Parsons, the pioneer of the systems view of organizations,[144] had been influenced by general systems theory. He represented a functionalist

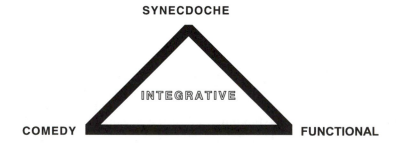

Figure 5.4 The integrative organizational style, of which the systems approach is a variant.

perspective, where the parts were structures having the task – function – of guaranteeing the right to existence of the whole. The harmony perspective was prominent here. His disciple, Merton, focused the attention on dysfunctions of the structures. Merton's pupils Gouldner, Selznick, and Blau, conducted empirical investigations based on their teacher's methodology. With his theory of the vicious circle of bureaucracy, the Frenchman Michel Crozier presented a synthesis of the "dysfunctionalists" ideas.

Yet, the epoch-making system current in the organizational field was contingency theory. It integrated the two contending schools – the Rational Classics and Human Relations – under one hat. Both had been right *and* wrong. It depended on the *environment* which organizational type was most appropriate, the "mechanistic" of the classics, as it now came to be called, or the "organic" of Human Relations.

"Contingencies" in the environment manipulate the drama towards a happy, that is, organic ending. The contingencies (uncertainty and technology) have four main features. All these properties also characterize the *assisting characters* in literary comedy (spiritual "vices" and tricky slaves):

- They are *uncontrollable*.
- They are *boundary-transcending*, coming "from outside" the system, or the world enacted on the scene.[145)]
- They appear as *disruptive elements*.
- They function as *catalysts* for the happy ending.

We draw the conclusion that in the dramatic narrative of contingency theory, *contingency serves as the assisting character*.

Burns and Stalker's concrete organization theory was based on the systems approach. Their organizational drama was that of the dualistic Comedy with its two states clearly represented, one original, defective; the other, final, desirable and harmonic. In this organizational Comedy the power and status systems emerge as the primary blocking characters, corresponding to the Comic *senex iratus*, the heavy father of imaginative

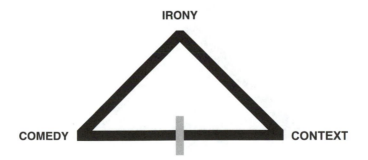

Figure 5.5 Burns and Stalker's poetics.

literature. As contingency, alias the *eiron* figure that promotes the happy ending, uncertainty performs, homologous to the benevolent "vice" of imaginative literature. The degree of uncertainty in the environment determined which of the two types – the mechanistic or the organic – was most advantageous. Or in other words, the power of the benevolent vice was decisive as to whether the drama was to end in the "green world" or remain in the realm of rules and laws.

Burns and Stalker, however, used a Contextual method involving cultural analysis. This also marked their overall style of thought, which can be denoted as Ironic in that it focused on interpretative patterns lying behind the system – the meaning-content behind observable behaviours. A discrepancy came to prevail between the authors' Comic organizational drama and their Contextual method (see Figure 5.5).

As to the mechanism which would guarantee the restoration of stability and harmony, they in fact subscribed to a Darwinian perspective based on the natural selection of the "fittest". However, the Contextual method in conjunction with cultural analysis obstructed the production of an independent criterion of fitness, or success.

Woodward's concrete organization theory also integrated the Rational Classics with Human Relations under the dualistic organizational drama of Comedy. She had been inspired by Burns and Stalker's distinction between mechanistic and organic organizations. In her investigation of industrial firms in south Essex, however, technology instead of uncertainty was the external, determining factor – the contingency. Woodward found that in companies with mass production, the mechanistic organization was dominant, while in companies with unit and process production, the organic organizational form prevailed. In Woodward's organizational Comedy, technology appears in the subsidiary role, the homologue to the "tricky slave" of imaginative literature. This character is generally sympathetic and helpful to the happy conclusion of the drama, yet at the same time unpredictable, both because it comes from an external sphere and because it wants to regain its freedom.

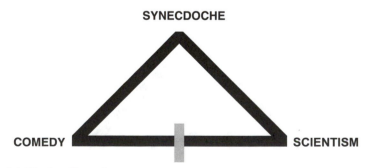

Figure 5.6 Woodward's poetics.

Woodward proceeded from an overall systems approach. This also coloured her style of thought, which was explicitly Synecdochic. In a consequent discourse, the method would have been Functional. As a result, however, of the original study design it was Scientistic: the law of the technological imperative would essentially emerge from statistical data analysis (even though the statistics in three particular areas were followed up by Functional case studies). The organizational drama, supported by the style of thought, therefore comes to dominate, at the expense of the deviating method. An even stronger discrepancy obtains between organizational drama and method than in Burns and Stalker; the tension becomes too great, so that the analysis is weakened (see Figure 5.6).

Later contingency research, especially the Aston school and its successors, has both employed and reinforced Scientism as a working method, with repercussions for the Synecdochic style of thought, which is undermined in favour of Metonymy. As contingency, alias assisting character, size most often appears; but other occupants of this role are also found. The Scientistic corner of the triangle has been stabilized, and ever more refined statistical techniques are in the foreground, but the influence exerted by the method, both directly and via the style of thought, has weakened the Comedy.

On the other hand, Child's critique of contingency theory, based on the idea of strategic choice, involved a Romantic revolt against Comedy and the advocacy of an Idiographic method.

For their part, Weick's loosely coupled systems, Cyert and March's coalitions and March *et al.*'s garbage can model and organized anarchies constitute closely related Romantic strivings for reform within the framework of the systems perspective. Their genre is that of disintegrating Comedy, where the transition to Romance lies close at hand.

The metamorphosis researchers, Mintzberg and his pupil Miller at McGill University, introduced further system states than the two thus far, the mechanistic and the organic. Both adhered explicitly to a Synecdochic systems perspective, which was well matched to a Comic organization drama. The genre is picaresque with the characteristic course of events consisting of an incessant journey between different states, occasioned by the complications arising within these. A certain lack of principle is an element of the genre, since the states are regarded relativistically as equivalent. Thus, it verges in certain respects towards Irony and Satire. Mintzberg has employed case and literature studies with a Functional orientation. Thereby, from among the concrete organization theories we have discussed here, his is the one that best matches the ideal poetic logic of the systems variant. Miller has succeeded in a fruitful way in utilizing the tension between a Comic organizational drama and a Scientific method involving statistical data analysis. If there is an Achilles' heel in both these McGill researchers, this is to be found in their data material, the empirical ground of their works.

As Burns and Stalker had already realized, we can interpret mechanistic and organic system states as cultures.[146] In other words, the boundary between the systems and cultural perspectives is not absolute, but dialectical, shifting. We now turn to a discussion of the latter perspective.

6 Satire

The contrary culture

The mode of presentation in this chapter is thematic rather than linked to specific authors. The background to this is the very multitude of influential texts in this the fourth and last major approach to be studied here, in contrast to the few highly regarded and much-quoted classics in Chapters 3–5. In other words, there are no really heavy "classics" in the cultural approach, but a veritable host of important books and articles. One may speculate about the reason for this. One possible explanation might be that this is the latest approach, and it has not yet begun to be superseded by another. As Hegel said, the owls of Minerva only begin to fly at twilight, meaning that the historical structure of a period can only be ascertained when it is coming to an end. We are still very much in the midst of the cultural approach, so it is possible that the "big names" have not yet crystallized. Another explanation seems perhaps more plausible, or at least complementary: the general Ironic and Satirical aspect of the approach tends to counteract the rise of "big names", favouring instead a fragmentation of the textual field. Be that as it may, the absence of really heavy classics is reflected in the more thematic disposition of the present chapter, as compared to the previous ones. Another way of saying this is that the present chapter does not distinguish "concrete organization theories" within the cultural approach. Also, the critique, laying bare tensions and inconsistencies within the approach, is tied here to themes rather than particular authors.

The chapter begins with a historical background of the organizational culture approach, and the time-line is also drawn to the present, showing that the approach is still very vital. Next, the method used in this approach is considered – the Contextual method which provides understanding of a social phenomenon – a community – in terms of a general spirit or atmosphere, surrounding as well as permeating it.

The following section provides a conceptual discussion of the culture concept. Cultures are seen as basically symbolic contexts. Since there are in principle an unlimited number of such contexts, depending on the infinite possibilities of variation of symbols, the culture approach has an inbuilt tendency to relativism, hence scepticism and an Ironic style of thought. Such a relativism is of course the very opposite of the one-solution character of the rational classics. But it became increasingly noticeable in the systems approach, mostly so in the writings of the McGill school (Mintzberg and Miller). Yet, in these texts, the number of possible organization types was limited to a handful, whereas in the cultural approach it has no upper limit, since every culture is its own unique symbolic context. It is interesting to note, in this context, that scepticism was central to Vico's conception of the Ironic master trope.[1] Irony is fundamentally sceptical and undermining towards all other tropes. Yet at a certain point this will turn inwards and undermine any effort to maintain a stable or at least enduring community – even a sceptical one. As one of the possible antidotes to the dissolving force of scepticism, Vico pointed to strong leaders; and, of course, strong, charismatic leaders have often been associated with strong organizational cultures. Attention is also drawn, in this section, to the Satirical drama of the cultural approach. The symbolic context it elicits tends to be polemically counterposed to the world of ordinary or superficial common-sense observations, attitudes, or expectations, which are often ridiculed. The section ends with an elucidation of the nature of the symbolism in this symbolic context.

After this, the notion of subcultures is looked at, and it is observed in this connection that harmonic, consensuous subcultures are generally favoured by adherents of the culture approach, in contrast to disharmonic, dissensuous ones. And this favouring has its roots in the organizational drama and method, which both presuppose a minimal unity – of the play and the symbolic context, respectively. The harmonic cultures are often regarded as "strong", the disharmonic cultures implicitly as "weak"; and linked to ideas of cultural engineering with concomitant conceptions of "quick fixes", a further association to good performance (high profits) for the former and bad performance (low profits) for the latter is then close at hand. Yet the favouring by both the organizational drama and method in this approach of harmonic cultures and subcultures is basically counter to the whole thrust of the Ironic style of thought, thus creating a tension within the culture approach. It is argued that dialectical and more truly Ironical "rainbow cultures", involving a mix between harmony and difference, may be an underestimated alternative to the harmonic/disharmonic cultures which mainly figure in the literature.

A typology of symbols is then suggested, based on cognitive, emotional, and pragmatic aspects. In the mediation of symbols, interesting imbalances, tensions, and contradictions between these aspects appear and are possible to study, once we move beyond the general presupposition of harmony in the cultural approach and realize its Ironic potential.

The following sections continue to deal with issues of organizational symbolism: different meanings, different meaning loadings, change in meanings, conflicting symbols, and symbols and power. The main thread that runs through all these themes is that more Ironic, dialectic thinking in studies of organizational symbolism and culture, true to the thought style of the approach, would open up many more seminal ways of research and praxis within this major approach.

Thereafter, some points for further research are taken up, also linking to the need for more Irony and dialectics: the psychopathology of organizations, disturbances of the symbol-processing capacity of organizations, collapses of meaning, fusion and fission of symbols, and meanings in quest for their symbols.

The chapter concludes with a discussion of the poetics of the organizational culture approach, with especial focus on its inbuilt tensions, and how to resolve this in terms of more emphasis on a more heterogeneous and paralogic organizational symbolism. It is contended that the culture approach is precognitively, tropologically structured by the master trope of Irony, and its affinities to a Satirical drama and Contextual method. Together this prefigures the approach in the *permeative* organizational style, shaping the study of organizational "reality" by establishing a particular linguistic protocol to follow, even before the study begins. The inbuilt tensions alluded to occur between on the one hand the Ironic master trope of the style and on the other its Satirical drama and Contextual method. While the former leans towards contradictions, collisions of meanings and heterogeneity, the latter share a greater benevolence towards harmony and homogeneity, which runs counter to the overarching thought style of the approach. The tendency towards immobility in traditional culture studies is another dimension of this, and in this sense, an opening up of the concept towards more collisions and tensions between symbols would also facilitate more mobility and transformation in organizational cultures. Finally the genres of the organizational culture drama are considered, one tending towards renewal and innovation, and the other towards fossilized tradition and stagnation, reflecting the general tension between thought style and method/drama within this approach.

6.1 Introduction

The cultural perspective is the latest organizational approach of the four studied here.[2] It first really took off during the 1980s. But its roots lie considerably further back in time. In Chapter 4, we saw that Human Relations already touched upon the cultural approach. As its pioneer, Elliott Jaques can be considered; his *The Changing Culture of a Factory* came in 1951, and was probably the first book in the field with a purely cultural orientation. Burns and Stalker (see Chapter 5) combined the systems and cultural approaches in their book, which appeared in 1961. Turner in 1971 used a clearly cultural perspective in *Exploring the Industrial Subculture*. Meyer and Rowan's article from 1977 on institutional myths underlined the importance of "ritual conformity", and was thereby close to a cultural conception, even though the word itself was missing.[3] Handy's book

Understanding Organizations, 1976, with four cultural types named after Greek gods, was also influential.

The development accelerated at the beginning of the 1980s, to virtually explode around 1982.[4] Andrew Pettigrew's influential article, 1979, "On Studying Organizational Cultures", is often referred to as the starting shot. Three books, all written in a more or less consultant-oriented spirit, and published in the USA in 1981–2, added further coal to the fire: Ouchi's *Theory Z,* Peters and Waterman's *In Search of Excellence* and Deal and Kennedy's *Corporate Cultures.* The growth curve has striking similarities to the rapid increase in so-called "exponential growth".[5] The interest has continued well into the late 90s, showing no signs of abating.[6] Both academics and practitioners are involved[7] – a criterion of a dominating organizational approach.

Although the approach has thus been and still is very popular, it is not on this account unproblematic. Studying the literature can bring about a certain feeling of frustration: what is treated is mostly not what seems central to investigate about organizational cultures and symbols. All too often, cultures and symbols are conceived as something static, homogeneous, harmonious and interaction-free. In other words, a main thread in what is lacking appears to be the *dialectical perspective.* This is the literature's general *centre of gravity*, even though there are exceptions. These occur, however, only as relatively insignificant elements in writings on the subject; moreover, they are spread out over different authors, so that no overall picture emerges. In a dialectical perspective, on the contrary, such items as change (even in the case of radical transformations), heterogeneity, contradictions, opposition, and interaction would constitute the central object of study.[8]

A conception supporting this angle of approach has been put forward by J. Lotman in his semiotic dialectics, a good account of which is available in Shukman.[9] The following text harmonizes well with the ideas on which this chapter is grounded:

> Human culture, argues Lotman, is different from other supra-individual unities such as the anthill in that each individual, being part of the whole, does not lose its own integrality. The relationship between the parts is thus not axiomatic but presupposes semiotic tensions and collisions, sometimes of a dramatic character. The structure-formation principle works in two directions: within the individual consciousness, as it develops, psychological "personalities" arise; while at the same time the separate individuals are grouped into semiotic units. "It is the richness of the internal conflicts", concludes Lotman, "which ensures that culture, as the collective intelligence, will have exceptional flexibility and dynamism".

Contrariety, and thereby Irony as the preferred dialectical style of thought, thus is, or should be, central to the cultural perspective. It appears mysterious that in practice such has not been the case to any greater extent; on the contrary, this style of thought has been largely swept under the carpet in practical applications. We shall attempt to explain this. The present chapter aims at laying the provisional ground for a unified dialectical framework of concepts for the study of organizational symbols and cultures. Empirical applications are taken both from the literature on the subject and from my own field studies of the institutional organization of higher education in Sweden after the reform implemented in 1977.

6.2 The method

The method of the culture approach is Contextualist, posing the question of which atmosphere of meaning permeates the organization.[10] This appears most typically in Geertz's very influential "thick description" of culture, which we shall use as an illustration:

> ... a semiotic concept of culture is peculiarly well adapted. As interworked systems of construable signs (what, ignoring provincial usages, I would call symbols), culture is not a power, something to which social events, behaviours, institutions, or processes can be causally attributed; it is a *context*, something within which they can be intelligibly – that is, thickly – described.[11]

In a single, central sentence Geertz distances this, his Contextualist method, from all others:

> If ... we take, say, a Beethoven quartet as an, admittedly rather special but, for these purposes, nicely illustrative, sample of culture, no one would, I think, identify it with its score, with the skills and knowledge needed to play it, with the understanding of it possessed by its performers or auditors, nor, to take care, *en passant,* of the reductionists and reifiers, with a particular performance of it or with some mysterious entity transcending material existence.[12]

1. *Understanding possessed by performers or auditors.* This refers clearly to Idiography. Of those he criticizes, Geertz is most positive towards this approach, on the grounds of its interpretive outlook.[13] His main objection is that it is confined to the psyche of individuals. Against this, Geertz, with the support of Ironic philosophy (the later Wittgenstein), maintains that private meaning is impossible, and "that culture consists of socially established structures of meaning in terms of which people do ... things". "Culture is public because meaning is".[14]

   One might perhaps add that private and public uniform meaning need not necessarily be mutually exhaustive alternatives. Fragmented, temporary, patchy, colliding, contradictory, etc., meanings fall outside Geertz's dichotomy.

2. *A particular performance.* This is explained more extensively on the same page:

> "that [culture] consists in the brute pattern of behavioral events we observe in fact to occur in some identifiable community or other; that is, to reduce it".

Here Scientism is criticized because the dimension of meaning disappears and only external behaviour is counted.

3. *Some mysterious entity transcending human existence.* This is also explained in the same place:

> "there are a number of ways to obscure [the truth]. One is to imagine that culture is a self-contained 'super-organic' reality with forces and purposes of its own; that is, to reify it".

This criticizes the Functional method. (The influence of Weber is palpable here.)

   What, then, is the correct interpretation, according to Geertz? Well, a Beethoven quartet is

4. "[A] coherent sequence of modeled sound".[15]

What does this coherence mean, transferred to culture?

> *"we begin with our own interpretations of what our informants are up to, or think they are up to, and then systematize those"*.[16]

> "Cultural systems must have a minimal degree of coherence . . . ; and, by observation, they normally have a great deal more".[17]

Thereby, the contraries, the dialectics, have also correspondingly been ruled out, already methodologically. The method consists in first gathering the symbols from the single individuals, and then *systematizing* them, so that they attain at least a "minimal degree of coherence", and in normal cases "a great deal more". There is no better way of expressing that the cultural method is a Contextualist one, aiming at provisional integration, under a permeating "spirit". This Contextualist method also influences the definition of the concept of culture, to which we now turn.

6.3 The concept of organizational culture

What *is* an organizational culture? Even though a strict definition in positivist style should not be demanded of a concept which provides the grounds for what has been called a new "paradigm" in organizational research,[18] since too strict demands should not be imposed on new concepts,[19] the progressive elucidation of central concepts is a key element in all research. Conceptual ambiguities and contradictions that are initially fruitful can in time be transformed into obstacles.

Deal and Kennedy refer to *Webster's New Collegiate Dictionary*, where culture is defined as:

> the integrated pattern of human behavior that includes thought, speech action, and artifacts and depends on man's capacity for learning and transmitting knowledge to succeeding generations.[20]

For corporate cultures in particular they refer to Marvin Bower, the former managing director of McKinsey and Company: "the way we do things around here."[21] From this we are perhaps not much the wiser. Similar, rather vacuous conceptualizations are common in the literature; moreover, almost every author offers their own interpretation. The question then becomes whether there is any common denominator to the concept of corporate culture, or if it bears the character of a "family concept".[22]

In order to track down such a common denominator it may be rewarding to go back to the historical development of organization theory, to two of the three previously dominant organizational approaches – the rational classics and the systems perspective. Despite major dissimilarities these share certain common features; in fact, the systems perspective might be considered as merely a more sophisticated form of the classical – organizations being regarded no longer as *mechanical* machines, but as *self-regulating, goal-driven* machines (either cybernetic[23] or open, metabolic[24]).

Since organizations can be regarded as condensations[25] of human relations, it is clear that these perspectives are both characterized by the particular *absence* of something; more precisely the absence of the specifically human, the "*spiritual*" (in a non-religious sense) or *symbol-creating* aspect.[26)] Insufficient weight therefore has been placed on the meanings and significances with which members of organizations imbue their behaviour. Both the machine and systems perspectives might hence with a polemical term be designated as *robot perspectives*.

The robot perspective thus appears one-sided and reductionist – the organization as a whole is not investigated, only certain external aspects; the interest in structure and technology, for example, is striking. The alternative was Human Relations, and Organizational Behaviour in its wake. But these focused on the individual and group level, and were thus incapable of combining interest in meanings and significances with a holistic conception.[27)] The latter, however, is likely to be a precondition for studying *organizations*.[28]

There was a social anthropological tradition to tap from, which met these requirements. Authors like Geertz and Lévi-Strauss have served as sources of inspiration.[29] A consistent theme is that culture is conceived Ironically as the direct converse to the naive conclusions of observation. In addition, the full consequences could be drawn from a train of thought which had already been embarked upon by the systems thinkers, more specifically the contingency theorists, and even more so the metamorphosis researchers of the

McGill school: there are *different* organizational forms and none of them is absolutely better than any other. This line of thinking is, as we pointed out in Chapter 5, relativistic and sceptical, hence Ironic.[30] In the systems thinkers, the number of these forms is still restricted to a mere few – two for the contingency theorists, around half a dozen for the metamorphosis researchers. For the cultural perspective, on the other hand, the number of equivalent forms is in principle unlimited: there are as many organizational cultures as organizations. In this way, relativistic Irony is driven all the way, as an overarching style of thought.

It is against this backdrop that the "explosive"[31] development of the cultural perspective during the early 1980s should be seen: it filled a gap in previous machine and systems ways of thinking; while at the same time approaching the study of meanings and significances from a holistic perspective – that of culture, not from an individual perspective as with Human Relations or the "actor" school.[32] Moreover, the ground had already been prepared, by the latter's, so to say, subversive operations against the dominant modes of thought of the 1970s.

Thus, explicitly or implicitly, the common denominator in the cultural approach to organizations lies in the focus on *symbolic context*.[33] The organizational drama becomes Satirical – the true, symbolic reality behind the appearance is quite a different one than for the uninitiated. Three examples from several presented in a book on culture in organizations[34] illustrate this Satirical vein:

- A girl scouts' camp displayed a strongly obscene culture;[35)] the energetic guides' nightly excursions to the neighbouring town even culminated in intervention from the local police for disturbing public order.[36)]
- An organization of Mormon missionaries, in the eyes of the outsider such grave, suit-clad men, showed a culture strongly characterized by practical jokes and other forms of antics.[37]
- The management of a large health care organization propagated with genuine pathos lofty ideals for their activities; the members' culture ridiculed these, among other things by the epithet "walnut heaven" – an allusion to the central administration's luxurious furnishing.[38]

Similar examples can be supplied *en masse*. Thus, the culture indicates a hidden and different context behind the superficial and apparent. At this point, however, the conceptions of the various authors already start to diverge. What does the "symbolic context" in question look like? Smircich, for example, in a now classic article, refers to "five different programs of research that flow out of linking the terms culture and organization." The first two are coloured by functionalism and structural functionalism, respectively,[39)] and therefore presuppose a harmonic perspective. Of the others, two presuppose "shared cognitions" or "shared symbols" (also "shared meanings"). The fifth is structuralist, and therefore assumes a uniform deep structure underlying the manifest culture.[40]

Thus it can be established that *all* the orientations in the study of organizational cultures, analysed by Smircich, share a common basic view of the cultures in question as a kind of homogeneous, invisible "jelly", in which the organizations are encapsulated, and which keeps them together. We will term these "harmony cultures". By these approaches, hence, non-uniform cultures are already discarded by definition – they simply do not not count as organizational cultures.

Against this, Gregory and Riley, for example, have offered a more heterogeneous conception of organizational cultures, in which these appear as "mosaics" of subcultures.[41] As Gregory points out, consultant-oriented authors, such as Deal and Kennedy or Peters and Waterman, have conceived harmonic cultures as strong and successful, mosaic cultures on the other hand as weak and pre-destined for failure.[42]

However, if, as I shall do, one conceives *organizational culture* as *the sum of the symbols in an organization*, such a conceptual interpretation contains both the uniform and the mosaic types; but beyond this also other possibilities – what we shall term "rainbow cultures". Nor is it certain that a homogeneous culture is more guaranteed of success than a heterogeneous one. (I shall return later to a discussion of the concept of "symbol". Here it suffices to say that in what follows a symbol refers to the unity of meaning and behaviour.) On this interpretation, the symbol is therefore "the atom" of the organization('s culture). The mediation of meaning via symbols is the organization's fundamental transmission process.

A short comment on point of view: we hereby agree with the notion that culture is something that an organization "*is*", as opposed to something that it "*has*" (in addition to many other components/aspects)[43] – a culture being comparable to a Wittgensteinian "life form".

Other authors have distinguished between symbolic and what they call "substantial" action in organizations.[44] Symbolic action, e.g. symbol management, would then refer to myths, rituals, ceremonies and the like; substantial action, by contrast, to cash flow, production control and other more tangible processes.

The problem is merely that *all* actions, of whatever kind, are interpreted symbolically by both the actor and others, since they must always be inserted in some mental frame of reference to be understood.[45] Money and products, to pursue the examples above, are only meaningful concepts in the first place for someone with experience of a market economy; how they are further regarded and treated is of course also a result of the entire culture into which the person has been socialized, including the education he or she has received, whether that consists of compulsory schooling or training in economics at some university.

This, of course, does not gainsay the fact that physical things always lie at the bottom of the activities; but the nature of, in this case, money or products is wholly determined by the symbolic social network within which they are enclosed. Without interpretation, money is at best mere slips of paper, or in the cash-less society, a little flicker on a computer screen.

Is there then no difference between more or less symbolic activities in an organization? Yes, there is such a difference, but it is dialectical, not mechanical: certain symbolic activities, e.g. myths, rites, and ceremonies as above, *refer to other symbolic activities* – e.g. cash flow and production. It follows that they operate at a level one step higher than the latter and might therefore, strictly speaking, be termed "*meta*-symbolic".

Thus, we draw the conclusion that all organizational activities are symbolic. Naturally this does not turn (organizational) reality into a purely "subjective construction" which we can modify freely at will, if we just can overcome our own false consciousness and alienation before it.[46] Once symbolic contexts have arisen they are just as "objective" and real as anything else; they follow their own laws, which every attempt to change must heed, if it is not to run aground on utopian underwater reefs.

6.4 On subcultures: harmony, mosaic, or rainbow?

For the sake of convenience, we shall hitch the discourse on subcultures to set-theoretical concepts. If a culture consists of symbols, then the symbols can, in consequence of what has just been said, be conceived as *elements*, and the culture in which they are included as a *set*. Subcultures in an organization can then be regarded as *subsets* of symbols.

The more the subsets – the subcultures – overlap, the greater the homogeneity in the organization's culture as a whole. On the other hand, the more they are disjoint, the greater the heterogeneity of the whole organizational culture.

The organizational culture as a whole is thus regarded as a set of subcultures. The sum of all distances – non-overlapping symbols – between subcultures then becomes a measure of the heterogeneity in the organizational culture. The more the symbol sets of the subcultures are disjoint, the greater the heterogeneity in the organizational culture. The reasoning is illustrated in Figures 6.1 and 6.2.

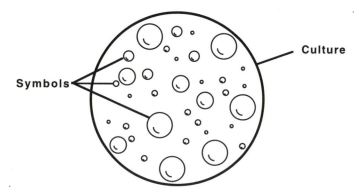

Figure 6.1 Homogeneous organizational cultures (harmonic cultures).

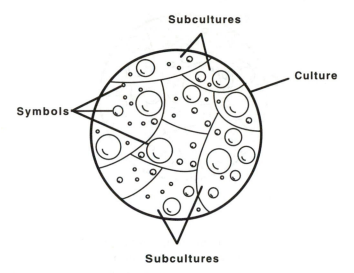

Figure 6.2 Heterogeneous organizational cultures (mosaic cultures).

Both unity cultures and mosaic cultures express a Contextualist mode of explanation. For unity cultures this is obvious, since organizational phenomena are explained against the backdrop of the all-pervasive invisible culture. But a mosaic culture is simply a sum of a number of unity (sub-)cultures, and thereby consists of several subcultures, each of which requires a Contextualist mode of interpretation.[47)]

As pointed out earlier, in the literature on cultural management, a number of authors have propagated the advantages of harmonic cultures. However, it is also possible to claim that a mosaic culture can be beneficial, in particular for innovative thinking and development. Such a view has been linked to the recommendation of "networks" between different subcultures.[48] The point of such networks should be that they can lead to fruitful "over-lappings" (i.e. intersecting subsets). Thus, networks are just a special case of factors that can promote overlapping subcultures. In such cases, however, we use the denotation "rainbow cultures" (see Figure 6.3). We reserve the term "mosaic culture" for the situation where there are subcultures, yet no overlappings, but watertight bulkheads between them.

A reasonable hypothesis seems to be that an entirely heterogeneous, mosaic culture is not advantageous for the organization as a whole, but that neither need an entirely homogeneous, unity culture lead to success; in the latter case, this naturally depends on the nature of the culture. By contrast, rainbow cultures appear in themselves fruitful for development and new ideas.

Two case studies conducted within the framework of a programme following up the reform of Swedish higher education in 1977 provided support for this thesis.[49] On *the university board in B-city* ("case B"), from the outset major conflicts prevailed between the various categories of

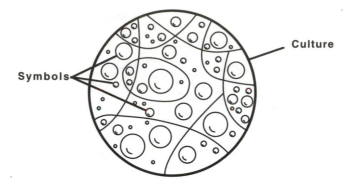

Figure 6.3 Partially overlapping subcultures (rainbow cultures).

representatives, resulting from their backgrounds in different organizational cultures. These were especially intense between the categories representing the "public interest" (trade unionists and political appointees) on the one hand, and staff representatives on the other. The conflicts were so virulent that they blocked opportunities for bringing about any development of the way the university operated.

In course of time, however, the "old" ways of thinking, manifested in the staff representatives, came to predominate; the representatives of the "public interest", who had initially presented all but revolutionary demands for transforming activities, rather soon became quite socialized into the academic culture. Since this had a "conserving" character, initatives to change the organization in a positive direction were absent in this new situation as well. Thus, we have a transition from a mosaic culture to a harmonic culture with stagnation as a result.

The opposite picture was presented by *the university board in C-city* ("case C"). Even if certain groupings were formed, especially some of a political nature and others concerning the student representatives, there were no definitive lines of demarcation similar to those in case B. The situation can therefore be described as an organizational culture with partially overlapping subcultures. The fruitful interaction between different organizational cultures had the consequence, among others, that policy issues together with educational and research matters dominated the board's activities, by contrast with case B, where routine matters accounted for the bulk of activities. (This, according to both agenda statistics and board members' subjective perceptions, as presented in interviews.) In addition, the board had arranged specific Policy Days, and was in the process of working out a policy document. The rainbow culture thus proved favourable to constructive developments.

The dominant orientation in research on organizational cultures regards these as entirely homogeneous harmonic cultures – which is presented as an advantage – while certain oppositional authors instead advocate subcultures and heterogeneity. These would at first sight appear to be mutually exclusive alternatives, but as we have just seen, there is also room for a third view: intermediate forms – rainbow cultures – exist, with partial inner overlappings, and the case can be made that these are beneficial for the vitality of the organization.

The cultural approach appears on the whole to have been afflicted with an inner conflict between its style of thought and its method. The style of thought is Ironic, i.e. contrariety is central, since human culture, unlike anthills, "presupposes semiotic tensions and collisions, sometimes of a dramatic character", as we saw in the introductory quotation from Lotman. On the other hand, the method is Contextualist, which requires a fairly unitary context. To this it should be added that even though Satire as such is especially prone to clashes of style and fragmentation, as an *organizational drama* it also has a striving for coherence, for unity of plot. The result is that the cultural approach is incapable of developing all potentialities inherent in a more symbolic conception.

Another critical point that can be made against the discussion of organizational subcultures in the literature is that these are usually seen as concentrated around various *actors* – individuals, subunits,[50] while sub-cultures hitched to distinct *forms of activities* are correspondingly margin-alized. Naturally, the latter should also be investigated, and they do not necessarily coincide with the former.[51] A further interesting task in this context is to study *the relation between* actor cultures and activities cultures.

6.5 Symbols: a typology

We have previously said that cultures can be conceived as sets of symbols. Symbols in their turn can be interpreted as meaning-laden behaviours. The meaning put into the symbol can be cognitive, emotional and/or pragmatic. On the other hand, the symbol can be either an expression of or a trigger of meaning. Thus, we obtain the typology schematically presented in Figure 6.4.

Of course, these are idealized pure types, and in reality every symbolic meaning will have elements of cognition, emotion, and action-orientation.[52]

		Cognition	Emotion	Action
	Expression of	I	II	III
Symbol as				
	Trigger of	IV	V	VI

Figure 6.4 A typology of symbols.

Thus, the types can more properly be conceived as expressions of the *dominance* of one of these aspects, where the others enter as subordinated elements.[53)] In the literature, some particular aspect of these is often isolated in the discussion of symbols/cultures. Thus, for example, Deal and Kennedy maintain:

> Values are the bedrock of any corporate culture. As the essence of a company's philosophy for achieving success, values provide a sense of common direction for all employees and guidelines for their day-to-day behavior.[54]

This corresponds to our pragmatic aspect, more precisely type VI.

By contrast, Eoyang treats symbols as something purely cognitive (types I and IV):

> I propose that the process of understanding is fundamentally similar to symbolization. Specifically, just as cognitions are associated into a symbol by some functional relations, so symbols themselves are incorporated into our cognitive structure . . . Thus, the meaning of a sign is generated when the sign is translated into the existing framework of previously retained knowledge and experience.[55]

The third aspect, the emotional (types II and V), is not as prominent in the literature, but elements of it still appear. Dandridge, for example, states:

> There are three ways in which symbols can function to control energy of organization members or of outsiders. First, they can be used to inspire members, to attract new recruits, or to repel undesired outsiders. . . . In each of these cases a symbol has functioned as it influenced people's feeling about the organization, changing their level of energy . . . Second, symbols facilitate re-experiencing of a feeling by the user alone. Third, symbols serve the function of controlling energy as they provide acceptable venting of feelings for organization members.[56]

This corresponds to our type V.

As has been already mentioned, in general all three aspects – the cognitive, the emotional, and the pragmatic – are likely to be integrated into the particular symbols, and thereby into the organizational culture, even though one of the aspects will normally prove dominant.

"Expression of" or "trigger of" can be interpreted in terms of sender or receiver of the symbolic message, as illustrated in Figure 6.5. At the sender, a meaning is expressed; at the receiver, a meaning is triggered.[57)] Here, certain possibilities occur for conflicts between sender and receiver of the symbolic message, namely when the types have *different aspects*. To take an example: In the study already referred to, of higher education in Sweden, "planning"

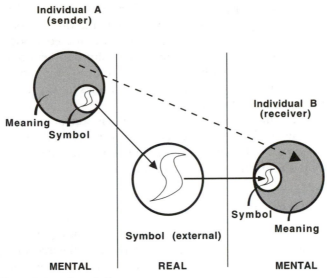

Individual A
(sender)

Individual B
(receiver)

Meaning
Symbol

Symbol

Symbol (external)

Meaning

MENTAL   REAL   MENTAL

Figure 6.5 Transmission of symbolic messages.

was assumed by the higher authorities to be an action-oriented concept (type III) for the various newly set-up units. For the regional boards studied the concept operated instead as a "trigger of cognition" (type IV), whereby knowledge appeared in the form of pronouncements on the financial requirements of the higher education institutions (universities and colleges).[58]

Other examples of "aspect disparity" emerged in the interview situations. For us, an "interview" was something which mainly had to do with the acquisition of knowledge (type IV). However, in a number of interviews, the respondent reacted according to type V – perceptions of threat, feelings of revenge, discontentment and joy were examples of such pervasive emotional colours.[59]

The process of the mediation of meaning – the organization's fundamental transmission process – is therefore only in *balance* under the necessary condition of aspect compatibility (see Figure 6.6 – S_m and R_m refer to sender and receiver of meaning respectively).[60]

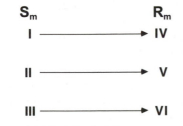

Figure 6.6 Mediation in balance.

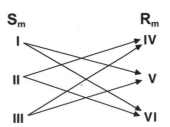

Figure 6.7 Mediation in imbalance.

In the case of aspect disparity, on the other hand, imbalance and conflicts arise; the arrows in Figure 6.7 below demonstrate the various combinations.

The traditional, Contextualist, method of cultural theory does not allow for such possibilities, since it presupposes the culture to be a homogeneous and transparent medium without inner differences or oppositions. This constrains the Ironic style of thought's opportunities for expression. A more symbolic conception avoids these limitations.

To a great extent lacking in the literature is, further, a discussion of contradictions in symbols.[61] These can be of various types, and we discuss them in sections 6.6–6.11 below. At the same time, we take the opportunity to exemplify the Satirical vein of organizational cultures.

6.6 Different meanings

A symbol can have two or several different meanings ("polysemy"). The concept of polysemy has been the object of intricate theoretical discussions. Without going further into these,[62] we raise an empirical example of such semantic equivocity that came up in our investigation of the Swedish higher education reform, namely "bureaucracy". Criticism that the administration of higher education is bureaucratic is widespread (as it has always been); anyone working in the Swedish organization will hear acrid comments on the subject virtually every day. A general and intuitively plausible supposition is therefore that members at the operative level – the level of departments – have a strongly negative attitude towards the flora of new organs which have flourished in and around universities and colleges over the past decades.

Yet, an attitudinal survey conducted at the departmental level showed, surprisingly enough, that such was not the case.[63] When analyzed by both administrative region and educational sector, the consistently held view was that the number of superordinate organs was of a reasonable size (the only exception being the strongly critical culture and information sector – the place of deportation for the classical education and the humanities in the new and over-centralized study programme system). On the other hand, extensive criticism was voiced concerning the increased administrative burden, and certain superior organs' *way of functioning.*

Criticism of bureaucracy thus proved to have two distinct senses – a stereotyped image of the ways in which members think and a real such image, depending on various interpretive possibilities.

The different senses may be overt or covert. One example of this is the participation in courses and conferences of different kinds, which only seemed to be increasing. The overt meaning of this phenomenon lies, of course, in the acquisition of knowledge. At the same time, growth would probably not have been so rapid, were it not for other, covert meaning-contents in course participation. To all appearances, courses and conferences also met a need for social contact, something which was frequently admitted in private conversations. A study of course and conference participation as a social phenomenon would therefore be of great interest.

Other examples are the *hidden power games* behind different, apparently innocent and "neutral" aspects of organizations. The following examples of the language of power give food for thought: [64]

- Why is an inaccurate net income forecast called "exceeding the budget"?
- When I purchase something I am called a "buyer". When I purchase labour I am called an "employer". Why *employer* and not *labour buyer*? Why *employee* and not *labour seller*? After all, this takes place in a business world where everything else is a matter of buying and selling.
- Why is the construction of data called "data-gathering"?
- Why is a human being referred to as a "component" in systems language?
- Why is the one-dimensionalization of information called "decentralization"?
- Why are systems for the handling of uncertainty described as "security systems"?
- Why is "waging war" now "struggling for peace"?
- Why is it called "housing benefit" and not "housing subsidy" for the rental market?

From the angle of the organizational drama the Satirical nature of these double meanings is, of course, obvious. Such Satirical style provides a complement to the often too uncritical presentations in the organizational culture literature in question (an illustrative case is Evered who investigates language usage in the American Navy, without at all penetrating underlying power functions).[65]

6.7 Varying strength of meaning-content

A symbol can be laden with meaning of varying strength or weakness, and this can differ between actors/groups of actors. (If this is something which permeates the entire organization, then the issue of strong/weak cultures comes in here, not under the the perspective of subcultures.) This aspect has unfortunately been marginalized in studies of organizational symbolism.[66] Yet, it must be of fundamental importance *how strongly* we perceive as true, feel, or are prepared to act with respect to a particular symbol (of cognitive, emotional, or pragmatic meaning-content, respectively).

A good example of a symbol with a varying strength of perceived meaning-content is provided by Smircich.[67] In the Insurance Company, a major conflict had previously prevailed between two groupings, one of which had formed around the company's executive vice-president, and like him was recruited from an outside corporation. When the vice-president died after a period of illness the president of the company decided not to replace him and to go in for a policy emphasizing intra-company unity and harmony, so as to finally smooth over the old and festering conflict between the company's "insiders" and "outsiders".

One element in this policy was to create a visual symbol for the company.

It took the form of a slogan "Wheeling together" and was represented by an actual wagon wheel mounted on a flat base. The various spokes on the wheel represented the different parts of the Insurance Company; at the center was the customer. The wheel, about 4 feet high, was kept at the top of a file cabinet and was moved around from department to department. Lucite paper weights were produced embedded with the wheel image. There were even "Wheeling together" rubber stamps for use on outgoing mail.

. . . The symbol of the wheel and the slogan "Wheeling Together" were intended to communicate a spirit of interdependence and teamwork. But at the time of the study the symbol and its accompanying slogan were clearly not alive as a positive image for the staff. In fact, the symbol became a shared image but in a negative way; it gave the staff members a common way to understand and talk about how poorly they worked together. "Wheeling Together" was the counterpoint or antithesis of their experience and they used it derisively to mock and ridicule their own behavior. One staff member talking about a series of incidents which demonstrated the hostile behavior between two departments summed up with a sarcastic "now that's wheeling together." For the most part the executives were sympathetic to the ideal the symbol represented but questioned its applicability to their group. "The philosophy was that each of the departments was a spoke of this wheel and if all the spokes were there and functioning you had a smooth-riding trip. But some of the departments are a little splintered and as a result the thing isn't really working together." Another staff member joked "Actually we've got four wheel drive, but every wheel is going in its own direction."

The wheel symbol in the Insurance Company thus was laden with a meaning which radically differed in strength for the president as compared to other members of management: strong for the former, but very weak for the latter. We also note the strongly Satirical element in the company's real culture, pregnantly formulated in the image of a vehicle whose four wheels go in separate directions.

Deal and Kennedy provide another good example. This refers to the company Procter and Gamble in its initial phase.

From the earliest days of P&G, its founding fathers always had an eye clearly fixed on what might be important to customers. One morning in 1851, William Proctor noticed that a wharfhand was painting black crosses on P&G's candle boxes. Asking why this was done, Proctor learned that the crosses allowed illiterate wharfhands to distinguish the candle boxes from the soap boxes. Another artistic wharfhand soon changed the black cross to a circled star. Another replaced the single star with a cluster of stars. And then a quarter moon was added with a human profile. Finally, P&G painted the moon and stars emblem on all boxes of their candles.

At some later date, P&G decided that the "man in the moon" was unnecessary so they dropped it from their boxes. Immediately P&G received a message from New Orleans that a jobber had refused delivery of an entire shipment of P&G candles. Since these boxes lacked the full "moon and stars" design, the jobber thought they were imitations. P&G quickly recognized the value of the "moon and stars" emblem and brought it back into use by registering it as a trademark. It was the beginning of brand name identification for P&G and the first of many times that P&G listened to its customers.[68]

Here, it was company management which perceived the symbol's meaning as very weak. For the company's customers, however, it was so strongly laden with meaning that an attempt to dispense with it led to a refusal to accept deliveries! Here too, the Satirical element is striking, since a mark on the cardboard boxes, which had originally come about by chance, eventually became more important than their physical contents.

If, finally, we view the strength of symbols as a continuous scale, two extreme cases can be envisaged. At one end, the symbol loses its meaning altogether. It then ceases to be a symbol. At the other, the symbol obtains maximum strength, becoming the object of almost magical awe and veneration by crystallizing in itself all the positive values of the organizational culture. It has then been transformed into an *emblem*.[69] In both cases, we are faced with the limits of Satire, since the symbol either evaporates, or congeals and in itself encloses the entire organization.

It should be a research endeavour of central importance to investigate *what it is that makes* organizational symbols laden with meaning of varying strength. If we localize these factors, we might well be able to put our finger on, and tap, the most fundamental hidden energy potentials of organizations.

6.8 Change in meaning

A symbol's meaning can also change over time (thus, contradiction over time[70]). Nor are studies of change in this area common within the "culture literature", where symbols are far too often regarded as something static. An account worth considering, however, is provided by Smith and Simmonds – a narration of how a charismatic leader-hero, virtually inevitably, is transformed into the organization's principal scapegoat.[71] *Dethroning* is a Satirical theme with ancient roots in the carnival tradition and the saturnalities of antiquity; in imaginative literature, for example, it has a prominent place in the grotesque Renaissance masterpiece by Rabelais.[72]

This theme is also interesting in that it points to the further possibility of *inverting* a symbol's meaning: a hero is assuredly a symbol of success, and a scapegoat can therefore, as a symbol of defeat, be regarded as the inverted value of a hero.

Such transformations, therefore, should be fruitful to study more generally. In, for example, the author's study of the administration of dental training in B-city, it thus became apparent that the budget had undergone this kind of radical transformation. Here, it was a question of inversion from a symbol of *compulsion* ("everything is handled by the central planning unit here at the Institute, we [the dentists' programme committee] have no say in budgetary matters") to a symbol of *freedom*. This occurred when the committee went into open conflict with the planning unit, and set to work at changing the budget process via programme budgeting into an instrument for realizing its own goals. The Satirical ridiculing of the planning unit was, incidentally, a striking feature in the process.

6.9 Conflicting symbols: myths as solutions and the organization's "dreams"

Further, we have the phenomenon of conflicting symbols in a culture. Although this problematic has been treated extensively in structuralist anthropology,[73] this orientation has not had any major impact on research in the field of organizational symbolism.[74] A consistent theme in Lévi-Strauss is that *myths* in organizations have the double function of both solving and presenting problems, whereby "problem" here can be conceived as tantamount to symbols in conflict. Even though a more "harmonizing" perspective prevails in the literature on organizational cultures, there are some exceptions. One of these is Abravanel's treatment of "mediatory myths".[75]

The concept of "myth" has been endowed with various meanings by different authors. (In Jönsson and Lundin, for instance, it corresponds most closely to our type VI above – a complex of symbols that mobilizes to action.[76]) Different interpretations are thus possible. Here we use Abravanel's definition:

> The word myth designates a story about past, present or future events. The truth of these events is asserted as dogma or taken for granted.[77]

Abravanel now links the function of myth to a distinction between "fundamental" and "operative" ideology, i.e. vision and reality, the myth functioning as a bridge-builder between the two. This constraint does not seem wholly warranted. Instead, a reasonable working hypothesis, in line with the role of myth in structuralist anthropology, would seem to be: the rational, analytical, and logical thinking, according to which "both A and non-A" constitutes an impermissible contradiction, is inadequate for handling the contradictory symbols which emerge within a culture. The function of myth is to integrate the two poles into an intuitively apprehensible whole, governed by dialectical logic,[78] where A can be both A and non-A.[79]

One example of such a myth emerged in the author's case study of the university board in B-city.[80] The board had received instructions from super-ordinate authorities to ensure that, in accordance with the Higher Education Ordinance, the economic planning should function at the university; clearly, this also concerned the operative units – the departments. At the same time, the board was characterized by a very traditional academic mode of thinking, which among other things meant maximum freedom to both the university as a whole and the separate departments within it. It is also clear that effective financial planning would involve increased opportunities for control, of both the entire university and individual departments. Classical official loyalty thus stood in radical opposition to academic freedom, with respect to financial planning.

The solution to this dilemma, as well as the form in which it externally manifested itself, was found in a story, narrated, in various versions, by the interviewees. In short, it consisted in the departments *not wanting to have* a realistic budget process, in contrast to the prevailing, fictive system (based on standard assessments). This story, however, was not empirically founded, since no systematic inquiries on the subject had been made at the depart-ments; furthermore, it emerged that two of these had started to operate on their own precisely such a new economic system as was wanted by the higher authorities, and that this proved to function quite excellently.

Thus, the story was a myth, which dialectically solved the contradiction between "A" (official loyalty) and "not-A" (academic freedom). At the same time, this contradiction was reflected in the myth as in a focal point. Such tales from within an organization can consequently function as possible clues to hidden contradictions and conflicts within its symbolic context – the culture. In this way, an otherwise seemingly harmonious and unbroken cultural façade may prove to have almost invisible cracks, which in the course of time frequently turn out to be deep-going and fundamental. Thus, the study of myths can also serve as a *methodological* angle in the investigation of organizational cultures. With a comparison drawn from psychoanalysis we might therefore say that myths are the organization's "dreams".[81]

6.10 Rites as complementary symbols; the organization's Yin and Yang

Rites too can be interpreted from a dialectical perspective. Rites can in fact be conceived as complexes of symbolic actions, repeated in structurally identical forms at regular intervals.[82] The aim is to periodically confirm certain symbolic values that are not elicited during intervening periods. Thus, the values of the rite serve the purpose of *complementing the intervening periods' non-ritualized values,*[83] which means that both sets of values within the organization are interrelated in a dialectic dance of unity and contradiction.[84)] Rites and other more ordinary activities thus presuppose and contradict each other like the Yin and Yang symbols of Taoism.

Religious rites also provide good examples of this, complementing the more prosaic values practised by members in their everyday life. If the contrast becomes too strong, what is usually called double morality emerges, with a Satirical effect.

Parties constitute other good examples Here, the organization's members are given the opportunity, in a well-structured form, "to do everything which they are not usually allowed to do" – the phenomenon of *"inversion"*. Through these symbolic actions, the participants actually complement and reinforce the everyday values, paradoxically by virtue of signalling their very opposite. Such rites naturally often serve as safety valves, when the pressure for organizational adaptation in one direction has become too strong. The Satire against everyday existence, in the shape of these inverted party behaviours, has ancient roots in carnivals and other popular festive traditions.[85]

A third example of the rite's dialectical, complementary function occurred in the planning system of the university board in B-city. Here, the budget process functioned as a rite, which by its "quasi-planning" nature served to complement other activities that lacked even the *semblance* of planning.[86]

6.11 Symbols and power

Which actors/groups of actors account for the changing or conserving of symbols? This can be directly linked to the issue of *power* in organizations.[87] The combination of power and symbols occurs relatively sparsely in the literature; to the extent that it is made, symbolic power is often conceived as an ideological superstructure on, or as a derivative from, power over *resources*.[88] The influence from a Marxist conception ("economic base – ideological superstructure") is palpable here, as too from exchange theories.

If, however, we see the exchange of *symbols* as the fundamental process in organizations, then it is here that we should seek the source of power, rather than conceiving it as a derivative of resources. Pfeffer, for instance, holds that such a view stems from a confusion between the *base* of power (resting on the resources) and its *exercise* in the form of symbol creation.[89] But if we proceed from the conception of culture (the set of symbols in circulation) as something an organization *is*, rather than something it *has*, then the criticism instead affects the resource perspective: Power over resources becomes something derived from the more fundamental power over culture (symbols).

This was very noticeable in our study of the reformed higher education system in Sweden. In accordance with the institutional frameworks of the Higher Education Ordinance, the "tangible" power resources were identical within all three groups investigated – regional boards, university/college boards, and programme committees. Yet it turned out that more symbolic aspects of power, and by that token the entire character of the investigated units, greatly diverged. Individual actors or groups of actors within these units on several occasions managed to hold the balance, tipping the scales of the boards or committees in favour of new activity patterns; or they prevented such transitions by functioning as shock absorbers. This was especially the case with the new external representatives (the "working life" and "public interest" categories) who first became members of these units as a result of the reform.

This confirms the trends in modern organization theory, in which the behaviour of organizations is not just seen as a reflex reaction to external environmental conditions in accordance with the stimulus-response model, but as emanating from quasi-"subjects", changeable on the basis of inner impulses. Our results suggest that staff composition within an organization could be one of the most important factors behind its way of functioning as a whole.[90] Even though the weight of intra-organization relations and the nature of internal activities already was part of our theoretical presuppositions, it was still quite surprising to note the extent of their importance for the overall functioning of the cases investigated.[91]

In this context, studies of what we may call *"non-culture"* also seem worthwhile to conduct: which actors or groups of actors have the power to prevent certain symbols even from surfacing in an organization? Smircich provides the following illustrative example of – in this case – conflicts as non-culture:

> The dominant interpretation that the executive staff used to account for their way of life was the belief that, in their group, differences or problems which may be difficult or painful to handle were submerged. There was widespread agreement that "if you've got anything that is controversial, you just don't bring it up."
>
> They saw their mode of behaviour as a direct result of the style and preferences of the company president. The staff claimed that the president "likes to keep it cool," "doesn't like to see any friction or animosity" and "doesn't like to hear if things are bad." Consequently, there was a belief that in the company "people say what they know everyone else wants to hear." Problems get "buried" instead of dealt with directly because "it's easier to handle that way." Staff members perceived the president as having the philosophy that "you shouldn't air problems or disagreements." They feared that if they were to surface a disagreement they would be labelled a "troublemaker" or accused of "pointing a finger." The atmosphere in the organization was described as "a fiction, not reality."[92]

Here too, Satire is prominent as the organizational drama.

6.12 Future research

Further aspects of the dialectical perspective on organizational symbols are:

- *Organizational neuroses.* If neurosis in an individual is the inadequate transference of symbolic reaction from one situation to another, there is much to support the view that this applies to entire organizations as well. A good example is the successor crisis at the transition from Henry to Edsel Ford, which came close to destroying the whole corporation, since certain symbolic patterns were almost impossible to break, despite changed environmental conditions.[93] It would be interesting to study such "irrational" reactions from the perspective of the *psychopathology of organizations.*[94] By which methods are such organizational neuroses *cured?* Creativity training – "redemption courses" – psycho-technologies? This should be evaluated empirically.
- Various forms of *disturbances to the symbol-processing capacity of organizations,* cognitively, emotionally, pragmatically. In other words, difficulties in forming the knowledge necessary and in obtaining functioning emotional relations, and paralysis of action.
- *Meaning collapses.* What does it signify for meaning to disappear from a symbol/symbol system? Through which processes does this phenomenon arise? – This is, among other things, the problem of alienation/anomie.[95]
- *Fusion/fission of symbols' meaning-content.* Through which processes can the meaning-content of several symbols be merged, and what does this imply for the strength with which they are laden with such new content? Analagously for the division of meaning into several symbols.
- *Meanings in quest for their symbol* ("unsigned meanings"). Certain cognitions, emotions, and dispositions to act float around in the organization without yet having found the sign which forms them into symbols. Leadership as the capacity to create such symbols (= leadership as "signature").

6.13 The poetics of culture

The Ironic style of thought is based on opposite meaning and is at one and the same time both penetrating and permeating. (There is a built-in relation of opposition between these two properties, as will be shown later in this chapter. Since Irony, above all others, is the dialectical trope, this relation is no coincidence.)

Thus, the method is Contextual, and strives to reveal the spirit which permeates the organization. The events taking place within the organization are rendered meaningful from an overall, "spiritual" perspective, not through an understanding of its individuals/episodes as with the Idiographic method. The facts selected are events within some kind of *epoch.* The model of interpretation for the Contextual method involves neither understanding, causal explanation, nor finalism;[96] rather, it is what we might call *pneumatic:* it attempts as meticulously as possible to reveal the invisible threads which link the events under study to the spirit which envelops and permeates them.

The basic relationship is events–spirit, where the events are the immediate object of study and the spirit the ground one seeks.[97]

The Contextual method thereby becomes "provisionally integrating".[98] In this respect, it differs from and assumes a kind of intermediary position between, on the one hand, the Idiographic and the Scientistic methods (both of which are *dis*integrating in their own way) and, on the other, the Functional method (which is definitely integrating). The Contextual method is critical both of the putative rational ways of proceeding of the Scientistic and Functional methods, and of the way in which the Idiographic method gorges on richly coloured details and their contents, each considered in isolation. The Contextual method views apparently fragmentary events against an overall background which makes them meaningful, but at the same time meaningless, as the background itself is not rational.[99]

The corresponding organizational drama, Satire, critically sees through earlier ideas and praxis, but at the same time constructs its own counter-image which penetrates the organization.[100] Satire has an irrational feature, in that it turns against both the law- or rule-bound rationality of Tragedy and the brighter, harmonic faith in reason of Comedy. It focuses on the organizational level, and is thereby also sceptical of the limitation of Romance to individual opportunities for expression and self-realization. Satire takes a delight in describing the specific type of global irrationality which, like a kind of hallucinogenic gas, colours every form of action in the organization. No development really takes place, it is just illusory; except in the sense that one "gas" can be exchanged for another, one absurdity replaced by another. In such a case, even the exchange occurs wholly at random, irrationally, out of the blue, a new medium inexplicably emerging in the place of the old. Thus, satire is a kind of "anti-narrative" where nothing really happens, despite the fact that it *appears* to do so. Every change turns out to be an illusion.[101] This finds its particular expression in that the Satirical drama *lacks a conclusion* in any real sense. Romance culminates in the triumph of the hero, Tragedy in the revelation of the natural law, and Comedy in a "happy end"; Satire ends up with nothing and is therefore a counter-image to them all.[102]

We give the name *permeative* to this organizational style (see Figure 6.8). It can also be characterized as negative, i.e. contradictory or conflicting.

In this chapter, I have argued that the dialectics of symbols should be given a more central position in organizational studies. Fragments from a variety of authors have been elicited, and I have presented some developments of my own, with the aim of providing a starting point for a relatively coherent dialectical frame of reference.

An organizational culture was defined as the set of symbols in an organization. The symbols are, as it were, the "atoms of the organization". Starting from this simple first conceptual determination it becomes possible to account for both homogeneous "harmonious cultures" (the focus of interest for the predominant schools in the field) and heterogeneous "mosaic

Figure 6.8 The permeative organizational style, of which the cultural perspective is a variant.

cultures" (which incorporate separate subcultures). I have also argued for the importance of studying "rainbow cultures", since these, with their partially overlapping subcultures, seem to be favourable for the renewal and development of their organizations.

Three aspects – the cognitive, the emotional, and the pragmatic – were said to be included in an organizational symbol, and one of these three will generally come to dominate. Balance in the organization's constant mediation of meaning – its fundamental transmission process – presupposes "aspect similarity", i.e. that sender and receiver place the *same aspect* on the symbolic message. By contrast, aspect disparity gives rise to tensions and imbalance.

Polysemic symbols (with two or more different meaning-contents) in organizations were also studied – for instance, standard vs. real images, overt vs. covert contents, including hidden power games. Further, the importance was emphasized of studying (the varying) *strength* with which the symbols are laden with (cognitive, emotional, pragmatic) meaning: the organization's most fundamental energy potential.

The meaning-content of symbols can also be transformed *over time* to its opposite – "*inversion*": the process through which an individual is converted from hero to scapegoat, or one and the same activity from a symbol of compulsion to a symbol of freedom. The mechanisms behind such inversion processes should be investigated more closely.

Myths were interpreted as both presentations and solutions of contradictory symbols within a culture. They thereby function as the organization's "dreams".

Rites are conceived as complexes of symbols which *complement* more mundane values by constituting their polar opposites. They presuppose and oppose one another simultaneously, in accordance with the Yin/Yang model.

Symbols and power: here it was maintained, under criticism of ideas inspired by exchange theory, that power over symbols is the fundamental issue, not power over resources. This also applies to "non-culture" – that is, the power to prevent certain symbols/symbol systems from even surfacing.

Finally, certain guidelines were indicated for future research:

- Studies of "irrational behaviour" in organizations, i.e. organizational neuroses, as the inadequate transference of symbols to new situations. From a wider perspective, the psychopathology of organizations.
- Meaning collapse of symbols/symbol systems (e.g. anomie, alienation).
- Fusion/fission of symbols' meaning-content, including consequences for the strength with which they are laden with this content.
- "Unsigned meanings" – meanings in quest of their symbol. Leadership as "signature".

Three things lastly emerge from the above. Cultures should be studied from their "atomic" aspects – the symbols. These should be investigated as they actually are, with their tensions, transformations, collisions, splits, fusions, etc., rather than from a purely static perspective with accompanying predestined harmony. Myths and rites can also be analyzed from a dialectical perspective; but the study of organizations as cultures cannot be confined to myths and rites: the dialectics of the symbols cannot be locked into certain fixed patterns, but must be investigated on their own, unrestricted terms.

Yet, in the literature about organizational cultures and symbols, the dialectical perspective has occupied a modest place, appearing only in fragmentary form in the works of a number of different authors. This is because the cultural approach proceeds from a Contextualist mode of interpretation, based on a transparent and internally non-contradictory medium which invisibly permeates the organizations. In this way, the expressive potentialities of the Ironic style of thought are constrained by its method. As White has pointed out, Irony is the dialectical trope *par préférence*, being based on contrariety.[103] The Ironic way of thinking lies in ambiguity, the paradoxical, mockery. It is represented, for example, by Colombo, the sharp-witted detective inspector in the TV series of the same name, who (in a Socratic way) loves to present himself as less knowing than he actually is; or, in quite a different way, by the principal character in John Fowles' novel *The Magus,* for whom reality is dissolved in a game of masks behind masks, behind which there seems to be no truth at all.

The Ironic style of thought is based on reverse meaning and – seeing through them all with a jaded glance – turns against both Metonymy's dessicated formalism and Metaphor's impressionistic single meanings, as it does against the Synecdochic whole's patriarchal custodianship over its component parts. The cultural perspective is based on Irony and rejects all other organizational styles of thought as illusions, erecting an irrational, yet at the same time total counter-image. The same style of thought also finds expression in an orientation that is at ground relativistic and sceptical, and therefore Ironic: different organizational cultures, of which there are in principle an unlimited number, are regarded as being of equal value; no one of them has absolute privilege over any other. Thereby we have come as far as it is possible from the classical idea of the single-best organization.

The method is Contextual and poses the question which meaningful atmosphere permeates the organization. It turns against (a) an Idiographic way of proceeding, since meaning is not private; (b) a Scientistic, since meaning cannot be erased from action; and (c) a Functionalistic, since culture is not a hypostasized, "super-organic" system. Instead, it is perceived explicitly as a "context", which is assumed to have "a minimal degree of coherence . . . and . . . normally . . . a great deal more".[104] The task of the investigator is to systematize the particular observations so that they acquire this coherence.

The organizational drama of the cultural perspective is the anti-intellectual or *quixotic*[105] *Satire*, exhibiting the futility of all rational endeavours; beyond their illusions, they are still mere tiltings at windmills. This genre, therefore, finds a special target in theory, systems, philosophy and the like, for placing a strait-jacket on reality and excluding everything that does not fit into the picture. Against rules, the quixotic Satire sets practice; against dogmas, experience, and common sense; against norms and ideals, life.[106] [107] The Satire of the cultural approach wages a two-front war: on the one hand, against the classical and the systems orientations' rationality, radical and evolutionary respectively; on the other, against the Romantically idealized conceptions of individual or group emancipation in the Human Relations tradition.[108]

The cultural perspective would thus represent a variant of the permeative organizational style, in which Irony, Context, and Satire form the three corners. See Figure 6.8 above.

Yet, here is a dialectical tension already built into the poetics of culture and setting its mark on the concrete organizational theories discussed in this chapter. The Contextualist method presupposes in fact a *fundamental unity*. Courses of events are studied against a backdrop of uniform meaning, i.e. an underlying spirit. And this meaning, this spirit is the culture. "Culture is public", as we heard Geertz say, "because meaning is". By "systematizing" the separate meanings and thereby giving them (at least) "a minimal degree of coherence", we gain the unity and wholeness that was already counted on by definition. Geertz' example of the Beethoven string quartet is an excellent illustration of this Contextualist science.

In this chapter I have point by point demonstrated this uniformity, or lack of dialectics, which means that whole chunks of quite decisive importance in the symbolic world of organizations, central themata in their dramas and for understanding them, are swept under the carpet. To recapitulate:

- Differences and imbalances between different types of meaning transmission (cognitive, emotional and pragmatic).
- Different meanings (polysemy) in the symbolism.
- Different strengths in the meaning with which the symbols are laden
- Change in meaning.
- Conflicting symbols.

- Myths as problem solving.
- Rites as complementary symbols, the organization's Yin and Yang.
- Symbols and power.
- Disturbances to symbol-processing capacity.
- Meaning collapses.
- Fusion/fission of symbols' meaning-content.
- Meanings in quest for their symbol.

The list could be made even longer, but we stop here. The Contextualist method that the cultural approach employs has a common denominator in the shared meanings under study, which – be they homogeneous harmonic cultures or heterogeneous mosaic cultures – permeate the whole. In the case of harmonious cultures, the whole is the entire organization, and in the case of the mosaic cultures, some part of it.

Thus, the cultural approach suffers from a lack of dialectics in its method. In conflict with this stands, after all, its underlying style of thought, that of Irony, since it is the trope of dialectics and contradiction *par excellence*. Irony in the cultural approach is limited to two things. First, the organization's covert meaning-content as opposed to its visible "surface". But both meaning-content and surface are *each in itself* envisaged as homogeneous; the former by definition (of the concept of culture), the latter as an (inverted) reflection of the uniform meaning-content. Second, there is Irony in the form of (relativistically conceived) differences *between* organizational cultures: in principle, an unlimited number of cultures exist, and one is as good as the other.

Within the organizational culture there is, however, scant Ironic dialectics; here, uniformity is fundamental. For lack of contradictions the culture hence becomes stifling and immobile in the long run – the more it changes, the more it remains the same. This is of course also basic to the Satirical drama as such, for which every change is only apparent, not real. Thus Satire fundamentally depicts an immobile community. When first established, it is often ahead of its time; eventually the surrounding world catches up; and in the end it is left astern. Just for a fleeting moment, between the avant and derrière garde, is it in pace with its environment. The cultural approach therefore has a built-in risk of slipping backwards, from the *quixotic* to the *conventional Satire*: the genre which from a conventional perspective directs its criticism at the new, the odd, the unconventional.[109] This by contrast with the quixotic, which from an unconventional perspective criticizes conventional dogmas.

These two Satirical genres, representing renewal and stagnation, also reflect the tug-of-war between style of thought and method. While the quixotic genre still contains new ideas and paradoxes despite the impact of the method, not much is left of the Ironic love of contradiction in the conventional genre. It has been reduced to a tired grimace at the modernities of its time. Thus, the style of thought tends to be dominated by its own

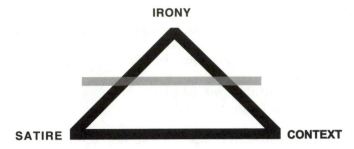

Figure 6.9 The poetics of culture.

method, even to the verge of repression. The arteries that prevent rigidifi-cation by conveying the vital, dialectical force of Irony to the organizational drama are thereby at risk of being cut off. Another circumstance amplifies this risk: even though Satire is uniquely prone to clash of style, fragmen-tation,[110] it is split between this and its striving (as an organizational drama) for at least a minimum degree of coherence in the plot (see Figure 6.9).

It is possibly no coincidence that a perspective characterized by the contradictory trope of Irony ends up in conflict with itself. I have maintained, in all events, that the consequences of its Ironic style of thought should be drawn to the full. But this presupposes in turn that the reverse operation is undertaken – that of cutting loose the moorings to the Contextualist method with its attached unitary definitions, thereby dissolving the entire variant. The cultural perspective might then, rather than being locked as now in an unwarranted unity of meanings, sail on across the dissimilarities, collisions and tensions of real symbols.

7 Da capo
Organizational performance

There is an objection against the cultural approach to organizations which runs roughly like this: Yes, that is all good and well, but surely you must understand that what these companies are *really* after is only to improve their performance (efficiency, effectiveness) by other means? At first sight, this objection seems as cynically clear-sighted as plausible. Of course companies aim to earn as much money as possible and therefore to be as high-performing as possible. When harder methods don't work, gentler ones will be used. But this is just smoke and mirrors; ultimately the goal is the same. Why else all the talk about "excellence"? And must there not be some truth in what economists keep telling us about profit maximizing as *the* goal of the firm?

If this were right, then the differences between the various ways in which organizations function, which we have studied in this book, would be merely chimerical. And the poetics of organizing would be at most an epiphenomenon to the "real", hard-nosed world of performance measures and profitability. However, in this chapter I shall attempt to demonstrate that this is not the case by examining the concept of organizational performance. This will lead up to a "poetic" interpretation of performance itself, demonstrating that not only is performance as a lodestar fully compatible with the poetics of organizing: it even shares the very same poetics.

Performance, like power, is an intricate concept. And, just as with power, this has led a number of prominent researchers to raise doubts about its scientific usefulness.[1] To a not insignificant extent, as with the theory of power, this is due to widespread confusion between the measure and the measured, between quantitative indicators and conceptual content (even, for example, in the otherwise rather perspicacious Bluedorn).[2]

But we will distinguish between semantics and measuring techniques. In what follows we first (7.1) go into the semantic content of the concept, and especially into the associated, or subordinated, concepts of "efficiency" and "effectiveness". Because of semantic confusions pertaining to these two, a preliminary distinction is done instead between the two main aspects of performance which we shall call "input performance" and "output performance". The common ground for both of these is argued to be *degree of goal achievement*, which accordingly is also proposed as a definition of performance.

Section 7.2 takes a closer look at one of performance's ingredients – the goals of organizations. The existence of various kinds or groups of such goals is pointed out, such as profitability and cost-efficiency, personnel-oriented goals, control and survival, and mission. A poetics of performance is discerned in this, enacting organizational goals as Tragic, Romantic, Comic, and Satirical, respectively.

In the literature, there is both qualitative and quantitative evidence for the existence of different goals, associated with different styles of performance. The quantitative evidence in question is based on measures of performance, and these are treated in the more technical section 7.3.

Finally, in 7.4, the various threads of the chapter are tied together around our four tropes, Metonymy, Metaphor, Synecdoche, and Irony. It is argued that organizational performance, just as organizational approaches, is prefigured by these four master tropes, or thought styles. The same holds – with minor differences – for the dramaturgy, which here takes the form of "mode of presentation". The deviation is in the method, which is globally Scientistic, because of the dominance of input performance. Thus, rather than making irrelevant the poetics of organizational approaches, organizational performance has a poetics of its own, supplementing the former.

7.1 Efficiency and effectiveness

> Some leading scholars have expressed impatience with the very concept of "organizational effectiveness", urging researchers to turn their attention to more fruitful fields.
>
> (Kanter and Brinkerhoff 1981)

In popular presentations, the term performance is most often used in the vague, general sense of "doing something (better)". In the fields of business administration and organization theory, performance is a more exact, but also more ramified concept. The concept is usually split into two main compartments – *efficiency* and *effectiveness*.[3] This is usually expressed in the following two manners:

- Efficiency is doing things the right way. Effectiveness is doing the right things.[4]
- Efficiency is the ratio between input and output, in some sense.[5] Effectiveness is goal achievement.[6]

The two definitions/conceptual distinctions hang together, in that maximizing the output-input ratio means that processes are carried out in the right way; on the other hand, goal achievement means that the right things are done. In the former, the most favourable means are employed to achieve a certain specific goal; in the latter, the focus is on a certain goal, regardless of the means. (This distinction, like so many in the social sciences, ultimately harks back to Weber – in this case, his distinction between goal rationality and value rationality, see Chapter 3 above.)

This is the traditional picture. Without delving deeply into the subject, we may note that it is in need of certain (dialectical) refinement. For the confusion is great. We can compare this with Mintzberg's chapter heading "Efficiency as a Systems Goal", for example.[7] Here, efficiency is defined as a systems goal although the classical distinction between efficiency and effectiveness rests on the latter (not the former) being defined in terms of goal achievement. And undoubtedly, the maximization of the output-input relationship is *also* to be regarded as a (particular kind of) goal.

"Doing the right things", correspondingly, ought to be a task for the person who intends to optimize the output-input relationship; while those who focus the activity of the firm on a certain goal, for instance growth, must act "in the right way", that is, in accordance with the goal at hand.

For the sake of clarity, it would certainly be better if this traditional distinction were displaced by, for instance, the terms "input performance" and "outlook performance" (where "outlook" refers to goals with a usually more extensive scope in time and space than in the case of the more short-sighted output-input maximizing). The overarching definition for these two types – and hence for performance – can then be stated as *degree of goal achievement*.

However, we do not rest content with such a dichotomy, for as we shall see, there are several different types of outlook performance (or "effectiveness").

7.2 Different types of goals

In the case of input performance ("efficiency"), profitability is clearly the goal referred to. Yet, what "other goals" could then be involved, in the case of outlook performance ("effectiveness")? Is not the criterion of profitability the "real" criterion of organizational performance? Not necessarily. For instance, it is well known that Japanese companies, by contrast with their American counterparts, do not give the highest priority to profit criteria; rather, they focus on increasing market shares, a strategy that time and time again has forced its American competitors to give way, e.g. in domestic electronics and the automobile industry. (The current economic difficulties of the Japanese economy are the result of structural rigidities and over-regulation, unrelated to these strategies.) This is how the problem can look from the American horizon:

> As president I couldn't afford to waste energy on petty disputes. I had to think of the big picture. Where was the company going to be five years from now? What were the major trends we had to pay attention to?

After the Arab-Israeli war of 1973 and the subsequent oil crisis, the answers to those questions became very clear. The world had turned upside down, and we had to respond immediately. Small, fuel-efficient, front-wheel-drive cars were the wave of the future.

You didn't have to be a genius to figure this out. All you had to do was read the sales figures for 1974, a terrible year for Detroit. Sales at GM dropped by a million and a half vehicles. Sales at Ford were off by half a million. The Japanese had most of the small cars and they were selling like crazy.

Gearing up to produce small cars in the United States was a very expensive proposition. But there are times when you have no choice but to make a big investment. General Motors was spending billions of dollars to "downsize" the entire company. Even Chrysler was investing a small fortune in fuel-efficient models.

But for Henry, small cars were a dead end. His favorite expression was "minicars, miniprofits".

Now, it's true that you can't make money on small cars – at least not in this country. And it's becoming more true every day. The margins on small cars just aren't high enough.

But that didn't mean we shouldn't be building them. Even without the prospect of a second oil shortage, we had to keep our dealers happy. If we didn't provide them with the small cars people wanted, those dealers would drop us and sign up with Honda and Toyota, where the action was.

It's a simple fact of life that you've got to take care of the low end of the market. And if there's an energy crisis to boot, that clinches the argument. For us not to be offering small, fuel-efficient cars was like owning a shoe store where you tell the customer: "Sorry, we only handle size nine and up."

Small cars became the bone in Henry's throat. But I insisted that we had to do a small, front-wheel-drive car – at least in Europe. There, gas prices were much higher and the roads were narrower. Even Henry could tell that a small car in Europe made good sense.

I sent Hal Sperlich, our top product planner, across the Atlantic. In only a thousand days, Hal and I put together a brand-new car. The Fiesta was very small, with front-wheel drive and a transverse engine. And it was fabulous. I knew we had a winner.

For twenty years, the bean counters at Ford had given us reasons why we should never build this car. Now even the top people in our European division opposed the Fiesta. My vice-president of international operations told me that Phil Caldwell, then President of Ford of Europe, was violently against it, saying that I must be smoking pot, because the Fiesta would never sell, and even if it did, it would never make a dime.

But I knew we had to go for it. I went to Henry's office and confronted him. "Look," I told him, "our guys in Europe don't want to do this car. So you've got to back me up. I don't want any second-guessing like you did on the Edsel. If you're not with me heart and soul, let's just forget it."

Henry saw the light. He finally agreed to spend $1 billion to do the Fiesta. And it's a good thing he did. The Fiesta was a tremendous hit. Whether Henry knew it or not, it saved him in Europe and was as important to our turn-around there as the Mustang had been to the Ford Division in the 1960s.[8]

Thus far Iacocca, to whom we shall return later for excellent illustrations to different performance styles.

Thus, to focus one-sidedly on input performance at the expense of outlook performance can not only lead astray in theory, but also bring disastrous consequences in practice.

Such a one-sided focus has had strong backing from classical micro-economic theory, with its conceptions of "Economic Man"; let us, for example, quote no less than Milton Friedman:

> . . . unless the behavior of businessmen in some way or other approximated behavior consistent with the maximization of returns, it seems unlikely that they would remain in business for long. Let the apparent immediate determinant of business behavior be anything at all . . . . Whenever this determinant happens to lead to behavior consistent with rational and informed maximization of returns, the business will prosper and acquire resources with which to expand; whenever it does not, the business will tend to lose resources and can be kept in existence only by the addition of resources from outside. . . . given natural selection, acceptance of the hypothesis [of maximization of returns] can be based largely on the judgement that it summarizes appropriately the conditions for survival.[9]

This position, presented by one of the most prominent extollers of modern capitalism, is also shared by Karl Marx on the extreme opposite wing of the political spectrum; his *Das Kapital* presents profit maximization as the real engine of capitalism.[10]

But reality, as we have seen, is more complicated. This simplified micro-economic image lives its own life, despite severe criticism. As Cyert and March point out, with the support of a multitude of references to the literature, the idea of profit maximization can be impugned in two ways. First, there are other goals than profit. Second, it is not certain that profit is maximized, even when it is the goal.[11]

Which, then, are these "other goals", that may occur under outlook per-formance? Mintzberg mentions the following: survival, growth, control and mission.[12] Survival concerns the very long-term existence of the organization, and should not be jeopardized by the achievement of other goals,

such as growth (or more or less short-sighted profitability). Indicators that
the goal of survival is being satisfied are, for example, solvency and liquidity
ratios. Back to Iacocca. Now it is crisis time at Chrysler, for which Iacocca
became president after his time at Ford.

> But saving money wasn't enough. We also had to raise a bundle of cash
> just to pay our bills. At one point we were losing money so badly that we
> sold all the dealership real estate we owned to a Kansas company called
> ABKO. Included were a couple of hundred downtown properties that
> ensured we'd have Chrysler dealers in strategic locations around the
> country. But we were scrambling for cash and we needed the money,
> which came to $90 million. Later, to keep our dealers where we needed
> them, we had to buy back about half of those properties – for twice the
> price.
>   In retrospect, selling the real estate looks like an enormous mistake.
> On the other hand, we needed the cash. At the time, that $90 looked like
> a billion to me![13]

As to growth, the advantages of focusing on this instead of profitability have
already been alluded to.[14)] We mentioned Japanese companies, but there are
also American examples. Such a strategy appears to be one of the main
factors behind IBM's long hegemony on the computer market: instead of
increasing profits, the corporation consistently sought increasing market
shares as a means of dominating the market.[15] (Later failures of IBM in this
respect were due to its persistent, anachronistic efforts to dominate the wrong
market – the shrinking mainframe market instead of the rapidly expanding
PC market. On the latter, its policy of outsourcing key elements such as
processors and operating system to external companies – Intel and Microsoft
– enabled the clone-makers to out-compete its own products with inex-
pensive copies.) Another example is, of course, the market strategy of
Microsoft itself. In his ruling in the recent case against the software giant,

> U.S. District Court Judge Thomas Penfield Jackson . . . noted that
> Microsoft's own studies confirmed that Microsoft could have charged
> only $49 per Windows upgrade and still remained profitable, but that it
> had enough power within the market to charge $89. In addition, Jackson
> said that the company took that additional profit and invested it not in
> its own products but in efforts to keep other companies out of various
> software markets through high "barriers to entry" – in other words, by
> making it more costly to create competing software.[16]

Whether, to the detriment of customers, Microsoft did actually pursue
unfair, monopolistic practices, or – as the company spokesmen maintain –
merely played the role of a vigorous but basically fair competitor, will surely
continue to be debated for a long time to come. Yet, what concerns us in the

present context is that there seems to be little doubt that market dominance was a prime target of the company, at the expense, among other things, of investing its profits in new products, either to make bigger short-term profits, or to go for missionary, entrepreneurial goals. It can of course be argued that, even if it adamantly denies it, the firm had targeted market dominance as a means to reap (or keep) maximum monopolistic profits. But it remains to be proven that this would have been more profitable than reaping the gains from developing new products on a more competitive market, particularly when the certainty of intervention from the juridical-political sphere against blatantly monopolistic practices is added to the picture.

An aggressive growth strategy – albeit not one leading to market dominance – has also been followed by PepsiCo. John Sculley, former president of PepsiCola, the main division of the concern, tells the following story:

> Every two months the marketing gurus of Pepsi – the company's heart and soul – would gather here, on 4/3, the executive floor of PepsiCo's corporate headquarters in the New York City suburb of Purchase, for a private ritual in the public war of the colas between Pepsi and Coke. A.C. Nielsen Co., the country's most prestigious market-research firm, would formally present what became popularly known as the Nielsens – closely guarded market-share figures that showed how we were faring in our competitive battle with Coca-Cola Co. The Nielsens defined the ground rules of competition for everyone at Pepsi. They were at the epicentre of all we did. They were the non-public body counts of the Cola Wars . . .
>
> Every two months, we would meet in the same elegant boardroom with Kendall and Pearson [the chairman of the board of directors/group president respectively] to chart our progress. The meetings served as a constant reminder that Pepsi wasn't the typical, faceless corporation. Rather, there were two demanding taskmasters at the top in Kendall and Pearson, the latter once singled out as one of the toughest bosses in America by *Fortune* magazine. They held our soles to a fast-burning flame called competition.
>
> These sessions weren't always euphoric. Often, the tension in the room was suffocating. Eyes would fix on Kendall to capture his response at every gain or drop in every tenth of a market share. . . . No silent gesture or comment went unnoticed. Kendall and Pearson, always seated at the front of the table, occasionally exchanged whispered remarks about the numbers that everyone strained to hear.
>
> If we had a bad Nielsen period, there would be no backslapping, no cigars. Kendall's steely blue eyes would pierce through the executive whose Nielsens were lagging. You could count on Kendall to be direct and bold.
>
> At Pepsi-Cola, this was our day of reckoning, our day of accountability. The results of every decision made in the field or at corporate

headquarters could be measured here in the fine print of the Nielsens. When you performed, you were rewarded by the approval of your peers, increased responsibility, significant raises, and future promotions. When you didn't, the pressure became intense. We knew our careers rode on swings of a fraction in share point.

An executive whose share was down had to stand and explain – fully – what he was going to do to fix it fast. Clearly in the dock, he knew that the next time he returned to that room, it had better be fixed. It was the kind of experience you wouldn't want to go through very often. Indeed, you couldn't. Those who had trouble quickly repairing the damage didn't get a chance to explain a third time. Either your numbers went up and continued to grow, or you began to comb the classifieds for a job elsewhere. Always, there was another executive in the room, ready to take your place. . . .

We often knew the likely mood of these meetings three weeks in advance. That's when we would get our first glimpse at the numbers in the form of an early Nielsen flash. . . . We knew then whether the next three weeks were going to be horrible or wonderful, whether you would face a reprimand or approval from Kendall.

A week after the flash, the Nielsen decks, 3-inch-thick computer printouts, would arrive. They provided a wealth of detail, a nationwide sampling of how Pepsi was faring in nearly 2,200 supermarkets in 68 areas by brand, product, and package size. The data not only compared performance to other competing soft drinks but to snack foods and detergents, too, so we could account for any marketplace anomalies from strikes to price wars.

Winning, to me, was an obsession. I was driven not only by the competition but by the force of powerful ideas. I demanded the best of myself. If I walked away from an assignment not totally consumed or absorbed to near exhaustion, I felt guilty about it. Dozens had failed at this regimen; but to me, Pepsi was a comfortable home. . . .

Pepsi's top managers, however, would carry in their wallets little charts with the latest key Nielsen figures. They became such an important part of my life that I could quote them on any product in any market. We would pore over the data, using them to search for Coke's vulnerable points where an assault could successfully be launched, or to explore why Pepsi slipped a fraction of a percentage point in the game. [17]

Which is the greatest moment of triumph for such a company, obsessed by the struggle for market shares? The occasion when record annual profits are reported? No; as might be supposed, the sweetness of victory is sipped from quite a different cup:

The moment I entered the boardroom, I knew the meeting would be momentous. For years, these executive sessions had followed a carefully orchestrated ritual. Today, there was a subtle, though telling, difference. Ordinarily, the conference table's 21-foot-long surface, polished to look more like glass than the rare burl of Carpathian elm, would be touched only by PepsiCo board members, and then no more than twelve times a year. Today, the fitted leather covering that hid the gleaming top was removed.

I had been in this room at least a hundred times. I had sat worried at this table and I had nearly soared at it. I had witnessed tense colleagues – friends – being publicly hung for questions of performance, and I had seen them applauded, just as I had been here, for marketing ideas and strategies.

But this meeting was different. The table's exposed top said so. It made the spacious, windowless room all the more imposing. Like nearly everything else at PepsiCo, Inc., the room's stately power and elegance made you stand a little straighter. A large abstract painting by Jackson Pollock's widow, Lee Krasner, dominated the far wall. Custom-designed carpeting in earth-tone colours cushioned the floor. The bronze-plated ceiling, perhaps more appropriate for a church, reflected burnished mahogany-panelled walls. High-backed beige leather chairs, so imposing they could have carried corporate titles of their own, surrounded the boardroom table. . . .

The meeting began precisely after Kendall took his seat and a black butler in a white jacket arrived with his drink on a silver tray: a Pepsi in a Tiffany tumbler set on a napkin in front of him. The recessed lights dimmed as the electric doors on one wall pulled away to reveal a projection screen. A Nielsen official began flashing the latest figures on the screen under Kendall's watchful eyes, explaining the minutiae of data that the company was spending nearly $10 million annually to collect.

Today, there would be no stern warnings, no sharp commands, no snapped orders to the platoon of executives around the table. Kendall's unabashed ebullience proved infectious. He broke out a box of his favourite Cuban cigars early and passed them around the table. Clouds of smoke, even laughter, engulfed the room as the figures revealed an achievement it had taken nearly a decade to create: Pepsi had surpassed Coke in sales as the leading soft drink sold in the nation's supermarkets.

"This is what I've longed for during my entire career," Kendall exulted, "to beat Coke fair and square."[18]

But when this goal is achieved – is it not then time to think of input performance, profit maximizing? Let us listen to Sculley again.

Our celebratory meeting around the yacht-sized conference table acknowledged a milestone, not a goal, in our battle with Coke. Pearson maintained that our victory over Coke wasn't enough. It proved that Pepsi had become a "fine corporation", but we still strived to emerge a "great corporation" in the tradition of a much-admired IBM or Procter and Gamble.

"We can't rest on our laurels," I agreed. "We've got to use this not as a victory but as a strategic building block."

We discussed how to exploit our victory in the supermarkets as a major attack against Coke in international markets, in vending machines, and in fountain sales, all areas in which we still trailed our nemesis. We had to persuade others that consumers preferred Pepsi when they were given a choice.

Now, however, everyone could taste blood.

"We can never relax," warned Kendall. "We have to have it all. We have to have it all. We have to beat Coke in every market. This just proves we can do it."[19]

In a major global study, the international management and consultant firm AT Kearney looked at the development of share prices for more than 1100 companies in twenty-four business areas and thirty-four countries during the period 1987–98. Deep interviews with more than fifty managers were also included in the investigation. The study showed that a prioritization of growth as a goal increased share values with an average of 26 per cent a year, compared to 16 percent for those firms that prioritized profitability. There is consequently a strong relationship between growth and shareholder value. This pattern was valid for all business areas, not only IT and related, but also mature branches. Internal growth factors emerged as equally important as external ones (fusion and acquisition). The investigators concluded, among other things, that it is important to accept temporary losses in profitability over some periods, in order to keep up the growth. As eminent examples of successful growth strategies, Microsoft and Home Depot (the home improvement retailer) were mentioned.[20]

Thus far on growth as a goal. Control over the environment is an important strategy for handling demands and uncertainty from the outside world.[21)] Vertical and horizontal integration, and diversification, are some of the means for gaining control, but there are plenty of others.[22] This goal can be regarded as a means for survival[23] (see the discussion on the resource acquisition approach to performance at the end of section 7.3 below).

Mission constitutes an ideological or ethical goal for the organization. The Salvation Army or AA may be the type of organizations that first come to mind, but the missionary goal is not at all uncommon in profit-driven companies. As Selznick already pointed out:

Efficiency as an operating ideal presumes that goals are settled and that the main resources and methods for achieving them are available. The problem is then one of joining available means to known ends. . . . Leadership goes beyond efficiency (1) when it sets the basic mission of the organization and (2) when it creates a social organism capable of fulfilling that mission.[24]

In the numerous biographies of entrepreneurs that have been written, it is striking what a marginal role goals such as profit, control, survival, or growth have played. Instead, the person in question has believed in and carried through an idea, often over a long period of extreme uncertainty about the company's survival, severe external resistance, bad finances, and real hardships. Let us listen to John Sculley, now recruited by the leading USA headhunter to become president of Apple, the second-largest personal-computer company in size next to "Big Blue", the gigantic IBM, regarded as unbeatable. The latter had established an iron grip on the market with its operating system, the so-called MS DOS, which, by selling licences to prospective producers in the early 1980s, it had managed to establish as the industry standard. It became an axiom that every personal computer with a chance of success had to build on MS DOS, thus in reality be an IBM clone. "IBM compatibility" was the message drummed in by the advertisers.

In 1984 Apple launched the Macintosh, a revolutionary new machine with its own operating system, which ran directly counter to and was a truly Ironic entrepreneurial gesture against the IBM-dominated establishment of the industry. The point of the system, the so-called Mac OS, was ease in use, as opposed to the cumbersome MS DOS, as well as a superior graphics capacity for business charts, visual models, and other presentation material. The Mac was greeted – characteristically enough for major innovations – alternately by derisive laughter, lack of understanding, and wild enthusiasm. Sales went excellently at first. However, by as early as 1985 the corporation was in deep crisis, triggered by a general slump in the industry and worsened by a number of factors: internal conflicts in the organization, too high costs (especially for warehousing), misguided marketing, and too small a memory capacity in the first version of the new computer. What to do?

> Turning the company around wasn't the difficult part. Cutting expenses isn't much of a mystery. Closing down an unprofitable plant or operation, while one of the toughest decisions a manager might make, isn't all that difficult, either. The hard part is knowing what to turn the company into . . . A tremendous amount of advice poured in from all quarters during the crisis. Most of it, in hindsight, was poor advice. We would have destroyed the company if we had followed most of it. *Instead, we held close to our dream and vision* [my italics].
>
> Even in the darkest moments of our crisis, we refused to abandon the things we cared about – our proprietary technology, our alternative to "the standard", our focus on the individual and the future of the personal computer. We resisted entreaties to become just another maker of IBM clones or to license our technology to others in a last-ditch

effort for short-term success. It's important in a crisis not to become consumed with expense cutting, but to set aside enough time to work on the company's values, vision, identity, and directional goals. This is the company's future.[25]

This adherence to the mission became crucial to the corporation's recovery and exceptional successes during 1987, a year when most personal computer companies that had joined the MS DOS standard (including IBM itself) ended up in crisis. For this standard now reflected an ageing product in the downward phase of its life cycle. Mac OS, by contrast, was a young product on its way up. The end of the story – at least for the time being – was IBM's realization towards the end of 1987 that the Macintosh's user-friendly interface and graphic capacity was the melody of the future. "Big Blue" therefore abandoned the standard which it had proclaimed as the only true gospel in 1985, going over to a new operating system (the so-called OS/2), similar to the Macintosh system. The entire market picture was thereby transformed, which is typical of the revolutionary force of Irony. (Eventually, not OS/2 but Microsoft Windows proved a more successful replication of the Mac concept on the PC side; Windows operates as a "front" for DOS, hiding its cumbersome structure from the user.)

Illustrative also is the founder of Apple, the man behind the Macintosh and one of the most renowned entrepreneurs of our time, Steve Jobs. He embodies the modern American dream of the Silicon Valley entrepreneur as the architect of his own electronic fortune. In the 1970s, together with another student dropout, his namesake Steve Wozniak, Jobs started his future multi-billion dollar company, and thereby the entire personal computer industry, in his parents' garage. Typical of Jobs' personality is his conduct on a business trip to the Soviet Union during the Brezhnev period. At a meeting with Soviet dignitaries he held up no less than Leon Trotsky as a model – roughly equivalent to promulgating the merits of Beelzebub in the Vatican. Naturally, this was done quite intentionally. It is hard to think of a more lunatic behaviour if the goal was to conclude a business deal in the Soviet Union. But Jobs just could not control his Ironic, permanently oppositional, and paradoxical personality in such situations, something which ultimately resulted in his exclusion from the company he himself had founded

Jobs has frequently been judged as enigmatic or incomprehensible, as a consequence of his antagonistic, bizarre, and arrogant behaviour, coupled with a charisma and innovative brilliance that bewitched even a superstar of the American business establishment such as Sculley, a man 20 years his senior.[26] Employing our poetic logic, his style of thought is easier to interpret; he appears as the very incarnation of the Ironic entrepreneur. Or as Sculley says:

Steve Jobs had a great ability to shift points of view constantly, to compare, contrast. . . . Steve could see the potential for high technology in a "low-tech" Cuisinart, and prophecy for the computer industry in a Bob Dylan lyric about war. His ability to draw rich contrasts helped make him a genius.[27]

Sculley was eventually demoted, and the company for a while tottered at the brink of disaster – another tale in the continuing Apple saga. After Jobs' unexpected, triumphant return as (interim) manager of Apple, and after the launching of the revolutionary iMac computer had proved a sucess, he was asked about the phase after the "come-back story" for the company: What would the demands for sustained growth, rather than just the turnaround of the company, mean for its stock value? Jobs reply was characteristic: "We are focusing on producing the best computers in the world, and if we do that, the rest will take care of itself." This captures both his own philosophy and the style of mission effectiveness in a nutshell.[28]

The mission, however, does not need to be positive or progressive; it can also achieve the character of a brake on new ideas. Back to another world – that of Iacocca and the Ford Fiesta:

> Right away, Sperlich and I started talking about bringing the Fiesta over to America for the 1979 model year. We saw the Japanese imports on the rise. We knew GM front-wheel-drive X-cars were well on the way. Chrysler was coming out with its Omni and Horizon, and Ford had nothing to offer.
>
> As it stood, the Fiesta was a little too small for the American market. So Hal and I decided to modify it by expanding the sides a little to add more room in the interior. We called our car the "blown Fiesta." Its code name was the Wolf.
>
> By this time, however, a combination of Japanese trade advantages and impossibly high labor rates had made it almost impossible for an American company to build small cars on a competitive basis. It would have cost us $500 million just to build new plants for the four-cylinder engines and transmissions. And Henry wasn't willing to take the gamble.
>
> But Sperlich and I were too hot on this project to give it up without a fight. There just had to be some way to build the Wolf and still make a profit.
>
> On my next trip to Japan, I set up a meeting with the top management of Honda. Back then, Honda didn't really want to make cars. They preferred to stay with motorcycles. But they were already equipped to make small engines and they were eager to do business with us.
>
> I got along wonderfully with Mr. Honda. He invited me to his house and he threw a great party, with a massive display of fireworks. Before I left Tokyo, we had worked out a deal. Honda would supply us with three hundred thousand power trains a year at a price of $711 each. It was a fantastic opportunity – $711 for a transmission and engine in a box, ready to drop into any car we wanted to make.

I was on fire when I came back from Japan. The Wolf just couldn't miss. This was going to be the next Mustang! Hal and I put together a black-and-yellow prototype that was a smash. This car would have knocked the country on its ear.

But when I told Henry about the deal with Honda, he promptly vetoed it. "No car with my name on the hood is going to have a Jap engine inside!" he said. And that was the end of a great opportunity.[29]

To summarize: there are different styles of performance. First, a Tragically law-governed input performance (efficiency), which has as its goal the maximizing of the output-input ratio – preferably through minimizing the amount of input per unit of output. Beside this, outlook performance incorporates various goals. Survival and growth are the classical system goals. They reflect the Comic style of performance. Control, a means for survival, is a (secondary) system goal. In addition, there is mission performance, which stands out as somewhat odd, since it is either ahead of or behind its time; it thus acquires Satirical features.[30]

The fourth, Romantic style also appears and is no less important. In Human Relations-oriented measurement of performance, focusing on "Human Resource Development", we encounter, among others, the following typical personality goals:[31]

1 Strong corporate culture and positive work climate.
2 Team spirit, group loyalty and teamwork.
3 Confidence, trust, and communication between workers and management.
4 Decision making near sources of information, regardless of where these sources are on the organizational chart.
5 Undistorted communication horizontally and vertically; sharing of relevant facts and feelings.
6 Rewards to managers for performance, growth, and development of subordinates, and for creating an effective working group.
8 Interaction between the organization and its parts, with conflict that occurs over projects resolved in the interest of the organization.

A synthesis of different types of performance has been advocated within the "Competing Values Approach", constructed on the basis of the evaluations of panels of experts.[32] The authors arrive at four main types:

• *Rational goals*. Ends: productivity, efficiency. Means: planning, goal setting.
• *Human Relations goals*. Ends: human resource development. Means: cohesion, morale.
• *Open systems goals*. Ends: growth, resource acquisition. Means: flexibility, readiness.

- *Internal systems goals.* Ends: stability, control. Means: information management and communication.

As the term "Competing Values Approach" indicates, these types, according to the authors, compete with one another; thus, the individual company has to make priorities in order to decide where to put the emphasis.

A survey of the goals adopted by American corporations produced the following list:

Reported goals of US Corporations[33]

Goal	% Corporations
Profitability	89
Growth	82
Market share	66
Social responsibility	65
Employee welfare	62
Product quality and service	60
Research and development	54
Diversification	51
Efficiency	50
Financial stability	49
Resource conservation	39
Management development	35

Here are all the kinds of goals that may appear in the organization's four tropes. Profitability and efficiency belong to the Tragic style of performance; management development and employee welfare to the Romantic; growth, market share, diversification, financial stability, and resource conservation to the Comic, harmonic style; while social responsibility, along with product quality and service, function as the environmentally-friendly, Satirical counter-image to the goals of profitability, management development, and growth.

We shall return to the tropes of performance in section 7.4. First, however, a somewhat more technical section, on the problems raised by multiple goals and the measuring of performance.

7.3 Measures of performance

Organizational performance has been interpreted as degree of goal achievement.[34] We now turn to *measures* of this. In the case of input performance,[35] this concerns measures of *profitability*.[36] Measures of this kind have been extensively constructed and discussed in the literature, and we cannot go into them in detail here.[37] Nevertheless, a couple of points can be made.

First, the problems of validity are considerable, which makes it prudent for investigators to employ several, complementary, measures.

Second, we must decide whether it is a question of (a) short-term or long-term profitability, (b) profit maximizing or profit satisficing. Then, under (a) must be elucidated what is meant by "long" and "short" term; a reminder in this context is that what is long-term for, say, an advertising agency or a computer firm may be short-term for a steel mill, for example; the time perspective varies both between industrial sectors and individual companies. Under (b) it is necessary to clarify whether the company is to be regarded as a classical profit maximizer in the tradition of economics, always striving for the greatest possible gain, or if it merely aims at achieving a satisfactory level.

These considerations, moreover, also apply to the other goals which are included in the second component of performance – outlook performance.

There are a number of measures of outlook performance. One possibility is to follow Hall and distinguish between *subjective* and *objective* measures.[38] Subjective, or, as we might also call them, reputational measures, are generated by questionnaires to the members of organizations, in which they are asked to what extent they themselves consider that the goals of the organizations are achieved by its activities. The objective measures assess – through the highly outwards-oriented character of the goals of outlook performance – how these have been realized in the relationships with the environment.

From a source-critical perspective, however, it seems dubious to rely solely, as in the subjective, reputational method, on the organization's own members. The risk for bias from tendentious statements is too great. Probably this is also why Hall has detected a discrepancy between subjective and objective measures. If, for the sake of mutual complementarity and increased validity, both should be employed together, a more reasonable way of proceeding would be to add outsiders to the group of respondents.

Another possible way of proceeding is to be found in Mahoney and Weitzel. The authors acknowledge at the outset the usual definition of outlook performance, "the achievement of a final goal"; this is the "ultimate criterion". Their view, however, is that it can be useful in practice to employ so-called "midrange criteria".[39] For this purpose, one of the authors (Mahoney) has first panned out 114 common indicators of effectiveness, and then by factor analysis reduced these to twenty-four dimensions. At a further stage, the two authors then conducted a multiple stepwise regression analysis of the twenty-four dimensions, from which the four having the greatest explanatory value were sifted out.

These four accounted for 58 per cent of the variance in the ultimate goal, which means that about one-third of the variation in the dependent variable was explained. One of the four dimensions accounted for just about as much of the variance in the ultimate goal as the three others taken together. And here we encounter an old acquaintance. This dimension can in fact be identified as ... input performance. The authors also describe it as "productivity-support-utilization".

The three other dimensions, in order of explanatory value, are: planning, reliability, and initiative. Planning is necessary for focusing on the goal; reliability is necessary for goals to be achieved without constant supervision and control; initiating of new ideas and new ways of acting, finally, is necessary for the fund of variation, without which no goal can be attained in a changeable environment.[40]

These results applied to "general business". In a control study of corporate R&D departments, the authors arrived, at the final stage, at a partially different set of dimensions, something which they reasonably enough referred to the specialized goals of such departments in comparison with general business. There were now three dimensions: reliability, cooperation, and development. They believe, however, that the twenty-four fundamental dimensions remain a good basis for any concrete investigation.[41]

The two measuring methods – according to ultimate goals and midrange criteria – which we have taken up here can be employed as alternatives; if one wishes to strengthen validity, they can also be used as complements. The latter way of proceeding is suggested by the hors d'œuvre offered by Steers. In a survey of seventeen effectiveness studies he found that the following fourteen evaluation criteria had been employed.

Frequencies of evaluation criteria in studies of organizational effectiveness[42]

Adaptability-flexibility	10
Productivity	6
Satisfaction	5
Profitability	3
Resource acquisition	3
Absence of strain	2
Control over environment	2
Development	2
Efficiency	2
Employee retention	2
Growth	2
Integration	2
Open communications	2
Survival	2
All other criteria	2

We note that the variables comprise a mixture of (a) "ultimate" goals, whose degree of achievement can be assessed employing the first, more theoretically-oriented method and (b) "midrange criteria" for which measurement is of the second, more empirical kind.[43)]

We note further that the variables largely fall under three of our master tropes. Productivity, profitability and efficiency is the Tragic style of organizational performance; satisfaction, absence of strain, employee retention and open communications the Romantic, person-oriented;[44] adaptability-flexibility, resource acquisition, control over environment, growth, integration and survival are Comedy's harmonic developmental goals.

7.4 The poetics of performance

To summarize: we can state that performance is a concept with many ramifications; but it can be utilized, provided one is sure which of its branches to sit on – and then not allow these to be sawn off. This can easily happen if theoretical definition is confused with methods of measurement, something which has led to major conceptual confusion in the area,[45] just as in the case of organizational uncertainty, for instance.[46]

To a great extent this can be blamed on lingering "operationalist" aberrations. Operationalism was the 1920s philosophical tradition that identified definition with measuring procedures (thus reducing meaning to technicalities). To paraphrase Keynes: Practical men, who believe themselves to be quite exempt from any intellectual influences, are usually the slaves of some defunct philosopher.

Performance in general can be defined as degree of goal achievement.[47] Traditionally, one particular component of it has been isolated, which we have here termed input performance (efficiency). In the corporate case it can be gauged by profitability measures, but the problems of interpretation that these involve should be constantly borne in mind.

It is, however, of the utmost importance to remember that profitability is not the sole, and often not even the most important criterion of performance, or success. The additional goals of outlook performance must also be taken into consideration; otherwise, there is a risk of ending up as badly off as the American automobile industry did, fixated with short-term cost efficiency. Economic Man does not always succeed well in practice. System goals, such as survival and growth, but also possible ideological/ethical goals, i.e. the company's "mission", must be weighed in with profitability. To these should also be added human resource goals, for instance those which Steers referred to in the final list of the preceding section: job satisfaction, absence of strain, development, employee retention and open communications.

There are two basic forms of performance: input performance and outlook performance. The accounts-governed input performance, pursued by those referred to disparagingly by Iacocca as the "bean counters", reflects the Metonymic style of thought, with its preference for partitioning reality into tightly sealed compartments. But beyond this, there is also (outlook) performance according to personal, system, and missionary goals. These correspond to the other master tropes: Metaphor, Synecdoche, and Irony (see sect. 7.2 above). Consequently, we now have *four* basic types of performance (no longer two) which, just as was the case with organizations, correspond to the fundamental tropological categories. In the research findings presented above, output-input and system goals are a constant feature. Missionary and personal goals are missing on occasions, and some of the variables referred to may be difficult to place tropologically. Yet, the overall picture is clear: different styles of performance fall into place within the four tropes. [48)]

In the analysis of the main organizational approaches, the concepts of style of thought, organizational drama and method were used. These categories must be adjusted somewhat for use in the context of performance. Both the first and the last (style of thought and method) can be applied in the case of performance, too. The second (organizational drama) is not possible to employ, since performance only concerns *one* aspect of the organization, its degree of goal achievement. Here, the corresponding concept will be designated as "mode of presentation". Thus, the categories we employ in our account of the poetics of organizational performance are style of thought, mode of presentation, and method.

For once, we start with method. Organizational performance can, as we have seen, in contrast to organizations themselves, be generally defined in quantitative terms and also be measured, even though the measurement is encumbered with varying degrees of difficulty. Investigations of organizational performance are therefore by sheer definition more or less quantitative in character: more in the case of input performance, less in the case of outlook performance. Thus, the methods of all types are permeated by Scientism. This Scientistic preponderance helps to explain the dominance of input performance, since this type is the easiest and least controversial to measure.

Input performance (efficiency) is basically cost performance.[49)] Its style of thought is Metonymic in its analytical accounting attitude towards reality. Its method is the most Scientistic of all in its reduction of everything to exactly measurable quantifiable units and criteria of profitability. Its mode of presentation is Tragic, and can be illustrated especially clearly by *rationalization,* which leads the organization, following a crisis of performance resulting from unreason, to the promised land of the law of profitability. The genre can be best classified as triumphant with elements of fatalistic. The former emphasizes the successful overcoming of the state of crisis; the latter, the well-oiled impersonal everyday functioning of the apparatus (see Chapter 3). The emphasis can be placed on one or the other genre, according to need and circumstance.

Personal performance argues that the individuals and their perception of meaningful work are the central aspect of the organization. The basic image is of the individual human being who – via Human Resource Management and similar techniques – will be Romantically brought to rediscover his or her mythically lost but true self. The plot focuses on this quest itself, rather than preparations for it or its consolidation; something which marks the *normal Romance* unlike other Romantic genres.[50] The overall style of thought is dominated by inner meaning, thus Metaphorical. Yet, there is an ongoing Tragic and Metonymic invasion of this territory. "Performance Management", a more or less Tayloristic philosophy and set of techniques, and the latest trend in performance appraisal, has during the 1990s become part of Human Resource Management in both private and public organizations.[51] As against this development, it is always possible to argue for a more genuinely Romantic Human Resource Management, for example as a "family friendly" philosophy and practice.[52]

System performance places the part Synecdochically in relation to the whole. The mode of presentation is that of Comedy. Dysfunctions must be eliminated and eufunctions promoted for the lasting benefit of the system – a general harmony and reconciliation, which finds its expression in the system's survival and/or growth. These two types of functions correspond to blocking and assisting characters, respectively. The former, here the dysfunctions, account, as always, for much of the Comics of the play. The genre is *arcadian Comedy*, in which the emphasis is not so much on the difference between two states, one original, deficient and one desirable, as on the harmonious continuance or the expansion of an already established, desirable state.[53] In the story of PepsiCo, we saw how the growth target can be raised to an all-pervasive obsession. This also applies to other goals, especially the one to which we shall now turn.

Missionary performance constitutes an Ironic contrast to the other performance styles. Chief exponent of the missionary style is the entrepreneur (or intrapreneur). Inwardly, his/her vision permeates the organization as an irrational medium. Outwardly, the entrepreneur consistently attracts the ridicule of the environment, as the odd-man-out, or deviant. Such cranky ideas, above all such *novel* ideas, are after all just a laughing-stock. Thus the missionary performer holds up a Satirical funny mirror to conventional wisdom and sententiousness; the genre, consequently, is quixotic. See the story of the Apple Macintosh above.

But what if the entrepreneur is rewarded with success? Whether that happens or not, the saga of the entrepreneur is as brief and shimmering as that of the butterfly. Success is the exception – and then the situation is unstable, as each expanding entrepreneurship is transformed sooner or later into a bureaucracy, if it is not to fall apart under its own weight.[54)]

Those who try to stick to their mission despite environmental change easily end up in the same situation as Henry Ford I, for whom all car colours were fine, as long as they were black – while at the same time, General Motors were fervidly engaged in painting their cars in all the colours of the spectrum, and getting sales accordingly.[55)] The story of Henry Ford II and Doctor Honda further confirms that the mission can also be reactionary. Even then it obtains a Satirical tinge, by being sufficiently out-moded. A mission is not of its time; then it would not be needed. Here, the same transition occurs from quixotic to conventional Satire that we saw in Chapter 6.

In this mode of presentation the organization is thus enchanted by an overall vision – a soap-bubble within which everything happens . . . and at the same time nothing, since the vision does not change. The vision emerges and breaks through suddenly and irrationally; as suddenly and irrationally, it can disappear and be replaced by a new one.[56]

But, the sceptic may ask, how then can the expectant missionaries defend themselves from the attacks of the natives – e.g. in the shape of criticism from the less-than-visionary "bean counters"? As an axiomatically correct argument in all matters concerning missionary performance, the idea of *corporate identity* is presented. The latter has a value in itself, which cannot be rationally disputed, and which for the organization takes precedence over any other consideration – profitability, job satisfaction, or functionality. Compare Henry Ford II above, for whom it was more important to shoulder the white man's burden than to buy the cheap Japanese engines that promised commercial success: "No car with *my name on the hood* is going to have a Jap engine inside!" [my italics]. It is scarcely possible to express the corporate identity argument any more clearly.

In Sweden in 1988 the same opposition between two types of organizational performance was reflected in a conflict between, on the one hand, Jan Wallander and Clas Reutersköld (board chairman and chief executive, respectively) in one of Scandinavia's largest media/publishing companies and, on the other, Albert Bonnier, dominant owner. Despite his excellent record in terms of profitability, Wallander was publicly criticized by Bonnier for failing to safeguard the special character of the company's business, i.e. its publishing operations. After this declaration of no confidence, Wallander resigned in protest and Reutersköld in sympathy with him. This conflict, unique in Swedish business life, concentrates three aspects of performance in a single tale: (1) the existence of different styles of performance; (2) the difference between input performance and missionary performance; (3) that the former will not always emerge victorious over the latter.

In organizational performance we find the same fundamental poetics as in the organizational approaches (see Figure 7.1).

There are deviations. The primary difference concerns method. Each type of performance is permeated by Scientism, but in the organizational approaches, all four methods appear. This can be explained by reference to the basically quantitative nature of performance as a concept, making a measurement-orientation the natural method.

The dramaturgy – here in the form of "mode of presentation", as we recall – is, with minor exceptions, the same for performance as for organizational approaches. The exceptions concern the Romantic and Comic genres, which we have described above in the present chapter. In the first case, there is a difference between dualistic and normal Romance. This simply means that the original Human Relations' more contemplative, descriptive style has given way in its successors to a more action-oriented one. In the second case, it is a matter of a difference between dualistic and

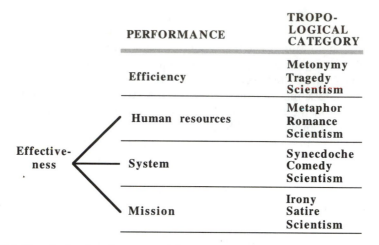

Figure 7.1 Organizational performance and the tropes.

arcadian Comedy. Here, interest – in terms of performance – has focused around the preservation and extension of a certain system state rather than around choice between system states (mechanistic or organic). This too is easy to explain. A change of system state is a major upheaval which occurs relatively seldom in organizations; performance, by contrast, must be looked after continuously (see, for example, the tale of PepsiCo).

A fascinating autobiographical portrayal of how a balance between these goal types can be obtained in reality is provided by Iacocca (quoted above). He had come up the hard way at Ford's, finally reaching the top as an enormously successful president of the corporation. As such, he grew too strong for the owner, and after a period of harassment was summarily sacked. Rather than retiring from business life and cultivating his garden roses he accepted the post of president of Chrysler, a company then on the verge of bankruptcy. He succeeded in turning the trend, and was hailed as a national hero of business life.

In his book Iacocca directs some heavy flak at Ford's "bean counters", fixated on narrow cost accounting at the expense of system goals such as marketing. But he also criticizes Henry Ford's neglect of personnel skills development and the lack of human resource goals.

During his time at Chrysler he was at first borne by missionary goals, seemingly against all reason, such as the K-car and the mini-van. The development work on these proceeded, while the company was judged by all outside observers to be on its way into the grave. It was a matter of just keeping afloat from day to day. But Iaccoca believed in his ideas and persisted with the development work.

During his early days at Chrysler cost performance was the central concern, however, since this was the weak spot. During the worst of the crisis, as has emerged above, cost performance had to be let go, because running payments had to be made – it was a question of survival at any price.

The situation makes ever shifting demands on where to place the centre of gravity among the four styles of performance. In his autobiography Iacocca appears as something of a virtuoso in playing all four.[57] The emphasis here is on "appears": this is no naive value judgment about "what really happened", based on a single and possibly biased source, but a characterization of what picture of himself Iacocca wants to communicate. Whether this picture came through in reality, or is more of an ideal espoused in his book, is an interesting question, though one which – for reasons of bias – cannot be answered merely by studying his autobiography; it would amount to a separate research project, involving interviews with many other people, studying documents, etc. The concern here is with the image of a successful top manager as presented in a book by a highly influential corporate executive, not with the correspondence between textual image and reality.[58] And this image is one of a well-integrated "multiple personality" leader, playing in harmony over the four styles of performance, which are all described as necessary at one time or other, at the changing scene of management.

Sculley is the second major American corporate figure we have cited as an example. He had not only, like Iacocca, changed company but also industry – from PepsiCo and soft drinks to Apple and computers. Even though brutal cost-efficient purges could be made, as a kind of fire-fighting when need arose for such drastic measures, at PepsiCo, growth, a system goal, was the law and the prophets. Woe betide the executives who lost a fraction of a percentage point in market share. Those who won the corresponding amount could, on the other hand, look forward to a time in the sun – that is, until the presentation of the sales reports for the next period. Sculley was self-critical of his lack of consideration for personal performance aspects during his time at Pepsi. His efforts at Apple were characterized to a far greater extent by a desire to stimulate the creativity of individuals. The missionary goal for the new Macintosh computer was, however, prioritized even higher. (This, incidentally, found striking expression in the designation given to the field workers who were to spread the glad tidings: *evangelists*.) The emphasis placed on this goal was so great that the vision was not renounced even when the corporation seemed to be on the verge of collapse, but it succeeded, for the time being.[59] Later, as is well known, the Apple saga continued in a kind of roller-coaster style, with extreme ups and downs, primarily because of strategic failures and successes (we have previously referred to one of the latter, and latest – the triumphant return of Steve Jobs and the launching of the iMac).

Now to a third, concluding example, and a "Mac" of quite different kind – the hamburger chain McDonald's. With his fiery spirit, the corporation's founder Ray Kroc pursued right from the start a line that radically differed from that of other franchisers in the fast food industry. The customary procedure was to make quick money from the granting of licences, and then show little interest either in the franchisees – except for their licence fees, or in the restaurants' customers – except for the payments they made over the counter. Kroc held the view that a franchiser could certainly rake in large profits in that way. Yet, the franchising corporation would not be stable in the long run – survival would be threatened by the lack of solidarity between franchiser, franchisee, and customers.[60]

Nor, as a former salesman, was he interested in profit maximizing. Kroc's goals were quite different – he wanted to build an empire. McDonald's was to become the dominant company in the industry. To achieve this, it was necessary to completely invert the methods of other companies in the sector. Product quality and paying the greatest possible attention to the franchisees became the lodestars. Other franchisers, who initially had better prospects but had exclusively oriented themselves towards input performance, saw their companies bud, flourish, and die. McDonald's continued to expand year after year with clockwork regularity, until it reached its current position, widely surpassing even the dreams of the volcanic Ray Kroc.[61]

Thus, from the very start, Kroc had opted for growth, a system goal, in the sharpest possible contrast to the input performance prevailing in his surroundings. As a secondary goal, to realize this wholly dominant overall purpose, he had used two other performance styles. Missionary performance was best expressed in the ubiquitous, almost manically inculcated slogan of QSC (Quality, Service, Cleanliness).[62] A personal performance style was also adopted, which for Kroc meant standing up for franchisees/restaurant owners in all situations and stimulating their entrepreneurial spirit instead of earning a maximum amount of money from them.[63]

At the outset of his career, Kroc had broken away from the general pattern of efficiency in McDonald's external environment, in favour of a sharply profiled systems approach to performance. At the height of his career he was to see this being undermined by advocates of input performance within his own organization. Harry Sonneborn, financial executive and finally president of the corporation, was more interested in the lucrative real-estate activity and cost-cuttings than in hamburgers, and wished at any price to halt the expansion of McDonald's, which he regarded as hazardous. This all led to a prolonged crisis and ultimately to an acute conflict between Sonneborn and Kroc, chairman of the board and dominant owner. Sonneborn resigned and a more growth-oriented president was appointed. After the battle, Kroc commented on events in illuminating fashion:

> I didn't give a damn about money . . . . All I wanted was to make McDonald's a winner in the hamburger business. That was the thing I romanced. But Harry was strictly a financial man. He didn't know a damned thing about hamburgers. I couldn't talk to him because he

couldn't talk operations. That's what made us drift apart. I was afraid Harry was turning McDonald's into a cold, calculating business.[64]

The conflict between McDonald's president and the chairman of its board incarnates – an expression uncommonly well suited to this context – the opposition between two of the four types of organizational performance: input performance and system performance (survival/growth). It is the former which is forced to yield.

Thus, linking back to the introduction to this chapter, it becomes clear that the claim that there is no "real" difference between organizational approaches (since all are fundamentally designed to promote performance) may refer to any one of the three following things. (Often, there are shifts between the three interpretations below, so that if one is refuted, one of the others is presented, etc.)

First, the meaning can be that a company's way of operating is designed to make it "function better" in the widest possible sense. Then we are into the trivial sense of performance, which was touched upon initially. On account of its utter vagueness, it is difficult to discuss, and strictly (albeit somewhat drastically) speaking, it simply amounts to the assertion that companies (in general) are not led by masochists: who would not want their organization to function better?

Second, the meaning can be that organizational forms and procedures are "really" designed to maximize input performance, efficiency. Then the statement is empirically false, since not all ways of organizing, as we have been seen, aim at input performance (not even indirectly). It is an empirical fact that many companies (especially those under managerial as opposed to owners' control) do *not* aim at profit maximizing, either in the short or long term; instead, profitability plays the role of a constraint which, when satisfied, leaves room for other goals such as security, control and growth. Also, there are a large number of companies (particularly small and medium-sized) which have either their mission (the entrepreneurial type) or stability as the primary goal, and are not at all intent on increasing profit at any price, above a certain acceptable minimum level.[65]

The third interpretation is that the non-Metonymic ways of functioning in question are "really" out to achieve goals within *outlook performance*. This cannot be disputed. But then, as we have seen, we are only saying that these ways of functioning aim at achieving their *own* goals, survival, growth, etc. – which no one could reasonably disagree with. The proposition is in fact tautologic.[66]

Thus, our conclusion is that the claim that all organizations are "really" only out to improve performance, depending on interpretation, proves to be either trivial, empirically incorrect, or tautologic. Like organizations themselves, their conceptions of performance are prefigured by the four master tropes (see Figure 7.2) and cannot be reduced to any single one of these.

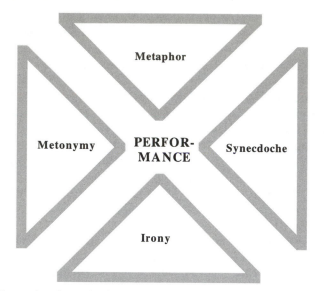

Figure 7.2 The poetics of organizational performance.

In fact, a sound performance policy would appear to resemble the one espoused by Iacocca – playing over all the four styles, making one of them predominate at a time, although not to the exclusion of the others. This is actually what the four-leaved clover in Figure 7.3 suggests. There is always a risk of a particular performance style going too far in its own direction, if only for the reason that "what has worked before must also work in the future".[67] For example, (cost-)efficiency can end up in myopic "bean-counting"; overly personnel-oriented policies can transform companies into staff-driven isolates; strategies of growth and market dominance can develop into monopolistic malpractices, making interventions of the political sphere inevitable; and exaggerated missionary zeal can make the company forgetful about such mundane principles as profitability, relations to the personnel, solvency, liquidity, and market shares. Before one mode of presentation is developed into an extreme (a sure sign of this is that effective blinkers are set up against other modes), and its key players begin to suffer from a danger-ous hubris, it is wise policy to begin toning down this particular style. Tracing back towards the centre of the "clover", the organization can then prepare the transition from there to the next mode of presentation that will be predominating – which one, only circumstances and managerial *phronesis*, the Aristotelian term for practical wisdom, can tell. In this way, the mode of performance will come to resemble a revolving stage, where one main scene at a time is turned towards the audience.

This policy differs from what is implied by the above-mentioned "competing values approach" – to stick to one particular type (or types) of performance, and only to change this in connection with "major reconfigurations" of the organization.[68] What is advocated here is rather a more flexible, sequential principle of "complementary performance styles", alternating between these even between periods of radical transformations, according to the plight of the organization. However, there might be a medium way between these two policies: keeping in general to a dominating, prioritized performance style (or styles), but allowing secondary types to come in when especially called for. Thus, for example, a generally favoured Metaphoric performance style, focusing on human resources, may be temporarily displaced by a Metonymic style when a cost crisis becomes acute, by a Synecdochic style when growth is all-important, and by an Ironic style when mission is first on the agenda. What performance style is prioritized depends, of course, on the strategy chosen by the organization, and more precisely the type of goal, if any, that is placed in the forefront. (This may sound like a tautology, but it is not, since establishing a certain policy is one thing and putting a certain performance style to practical work is another; in particular, the first does not automatically lead to the second, so that they may very well conflict with each other.)

But, to reiterate, some kind of sequential operating over the field of different performance styles is recommended from a tropological point of view. Organizations should also not generally put all their eggs in the same basket, but should remember to keep an eye at any given time on non-prioritized performance styles as well. Of course, in the rare cases when the situation is really desperate it is tempting to let go of the latter altogether; but as we have seen in this chapter, successful managers endeavour to keep their poetic freedom even in very dire straits.

Figure 7.3 The four main styles of performance.

Notes*

*The locations of the original note references are given as part of the running head.

Preface

1 For the dialectics between these aspects, see Ricoeur, 1984a, b.
2 As I shall argue in Chapter 2, the fashion metaphor should be employed with a certain caution in this context, since it presupposes that fashions appear irrationally and inexplicably, and also tends to suggest that they replace each other, so that the old fashions would disappear at the emergence of the new ones. But neither of these features suits the organizational approaches. Here, we use the fashion metaphor provisionally, and with the reservations just given.
3 Vico, 1963/1744.
4 White, 1985a.
5 Frye, 1973.
6 However, the use of poetic logic in organizational studies is of course not restricted to the analysis of styles: see Sköldberg, 1994, for an application to empirical material – eight case studies of organizational change.

1 Introduction

1 Adapted from White, 1985a, b, who used it to study nineteenth century historiography. White's principal theoretical sources of inspiration were Vico 1963/1744, Frye, 1973, and Pepper, 1966.
2 Alvesson and Sköldberg, 2000; Brown, 1977; Bruner, 1986; Czarniawska, 1999; Fisher, 1987; MacIntyre, 1990/1981; McCloskey, 1990; Ricoeur, 1984a, b, 1985, 1988.
3 Lyotard, 1986.
4 For a critique, see Alvesson and Sköldberg, 2000.
5 Alvesson and Sköldberg, 2000.
6 Akin and Palmer, 2000; Boyce, 1996; Gabriel, 2000; Pondy, 1983.
7 E.g. Czarniawska, 1997; Jeffcut, 1993; Sköldberg, 1994.
8 Gagliardi, 1996; Guillén, 1997; Ramirez, 1988; Strati, 1999.
9 Vico, 1963/1744; White, 1985a, b. Indian dialectical thinking had long previously suggested a basically similar cyclical model as a general principle for the development of thought (see section 2.12 for details).
10 For the latter – organizational dramas in practice, see Sköldberg, 1994.
11 From White, 1985, and Frye, 1973 (on whom White builds).
12 The dramaturgic genres are adapted from Frye, 1973.
13 This argument is freely inspired by Hegel's dialectical logic (Hegel, 1967/1812: 2).
14 Adapted from White, 1985a, who builds on Pepper, 1966. Besides (in our terms) style of thought, drama, and method, White also has a fourth category, ideology,

which appeared less applicable in the present context; also, the relationships of the ideologies to the tropes did not seem wholly convincing.

15 Usually, a distinction is made only between "idiographic" and "nomothetic" methods, the latter corresponding to what is here called a "Scientistic" method. This dichotomy is often taken to be exclusive. The terms are taken from German neo-idealist philosophy from the beginning of the twentieth century (Windelband), and the dichotomy reflects this philosophy's fundamental problematic of understanding vs explanation, humanities vs. natural science. Fruitful as this dichotomy has been, if regarded as exclusive it has the disadvantage of leaving more holistic methods out of the picture. These, on the other hand, are incorporated in the present typology, in the shape of the Functionalist and Contextualist styles, which transcend the understanding/-explanation distinction. All four, moreover, can be used – and have been used – in social science.

16 For a discussion of the difference, and relationship, between story (or narrative) and explanatory model, see also Ricoeur, 1984b.

17 The last-mentioned taken in the sense that the organization "has" a culture, rather than "is" a culture; this is the interpretation which is generally to be found in the literature on empirical organizational cultures (although I have proposed the latter, wider interpretation). Culture in the former sense, where thus it is just one side of the organization, corresponds to what I, in the discussion of the concept of culture in Chapter 6 below, call "metasymbolism", i.e. symbols that treat symbols.

18 An interesting further confirmation of Simon's Metonymic world-view is his concept of performance, which corresponds precisely to Metonymic efficiency: *"The criterion of efficiency dictates that choice of alternatives which produces the largest result for the given application of resources."* (Simon, 1957a: 179. Author's italics.)

19 A more recent current, the "actor's frame of reference" of the 1970s (Silverman, 1970), was also thoroughly Romantic, Idiographic and Metaphorical. It constituted, however, something of an underground movement, which is why we have not taken it up in any greater detail in our presentation (which is concerned only with dominant approaches). We touch upon it in relation to the discussion of Child's critique of contingency theory and his concept of strategic choice, which was influenced by Silverman. In the 1990s, something of a similar role was played by Lincoln and Guba, 1985, with their explicitly "idiographic" approach; there is also a Functional element to their perspective.

20 Such a development had moreover already been initiated by the Aston school in its typology comprising four organizational structures (Pugh and Hickson, 1979).

2 Poetics: styles of organizing

1 See, for instance, Astley and van de Ven, 1983; Burrell and Morgan, 1979.

2 See, e.g., Dessler, 1986; Hunsaker and Cook, 1986. Cf. also, Lupton, 1971. (On the other hand, several orientations discussed by the authors in note 1 above are not mentioned in the textbooks.)

3 Scott, 1987: 97 ff. develops his original typology (rational, natural and open systems) into one that is "slightly more complex" – ending up with four types: I. closed rational systems (i.e. the Classical theories); II. closed natural systems (Human Relations); III. open rational systems (the systems perspective); IV. open natural systems. Of these, the first three are identical to those recognized in the textbooks as major themes in organization theory. The final (fourth) type covers *pseudo-systems* – characterized by the attenuation or dissolution of goals,

and thus located on the margin of the systems perspective. (For closer analysis in terms of the "poetic logic", see section 5.4 below.)

The weakness of this account is that everything is pushed by force into a systems suit, which tends to come apart at the seams. For example, organizational culture as a "control system" (pp. 291 f.); or Silverman's focus on actors as a natural open system (p. 106), when this focus is just one polemic against the systems perspective. There is a world also outside the systems.

4 Smircich, 1983a. For a broad review of organization theory from a metaphorical perspective, see Morgan, 1986.

5 For the importance of the cultural perspective, also compare Alvesson, 1993; Alvesson and Berg, 1992. For Human Relations, e.g. Perrow (1986: 114), who even claims that: "the Human Relations school . . . has flourished and *dominates organization theory*" (author's italics) Human Relations certainly emerges as *one* major theme; however, to refer to it as reigning supreme, or even chief among the approaches, would be to go way too far.

6 Hannan and Freeman, 1977b; Williamson, 1975, 1985.

7 Postmodern organization *theory* should be distinguished from postmodern *organizations* (Clegg, 1990). The interaction between these two is much less prominent than in the dominating approaches investigated in this book, which is another reason for not including postmodernism among them. That is, if we agree that there are such entities as postmodern organizations. This, however, is not an uncontroversial issue. In fact, serious doubts have been raised as to the very existence of such a phenomenon in its own right, rather than as another example of relabelling prior knowledge. Thus, Eccles, 1992, views the postmodern (poststructuralist, post-Fordist, post-Taylorist, etc.) organization as merely another name for the time-honoured organic organization. Generated by the rhetorical need for apparent, rather than real, novelty in managerial discourse, such new names crop up now and again; the (counter-bureaucratic) content of their messages remains identical or almost so. (For a similar view, cf. Alvesson and Deetz, 1996.) As to postmodern *theory*, there is a growing suspicion that it may be self-defeating, since its Ironic standard critique against all non-postmodernist orientations for being "grand narratives" seems to provide a perhaps even more adequate description of itself (on this, see, for instance, Alvesson and Sköldberg, 2000). A certain lack of self-Irony in this respect makes the poetics of postmodernism less effective than it might otherwise have been.

8 E.g. Daft, 1998; Mintzberg, 1983b; Scott, 1987.

9 The systems approach is not infrequently regarded as the dominant paradigm in organization research (see, for instance, Hassard, 1993/1990). In their book *Osynligt ockuperad [Invisibly Occupied]*, 1980, Arbnor, Borglund and Liljedahl attack the entire modern approach to business studies as being bewitched by systems thinking. The impact of this perspective has been so strong that, paradoxically enough, the path towards the development of more formal and detailed applications of systems theory has itself been blocked (Ashmos and Huber, 1987).

10 Cf. Stupak, 1998. See also Hofstede, 1986.

11 As verified by any search on the Internet, where sites with this content abound.

12 The natural sciences did not have such a strong impact on nineteenth century historiography, with its long tradition of independence and its humanistic roots. Nevertheless, in 19th century historiography there was a strong positivistic undercurrent, represented most prominently by H. T. Buckle, which White does not take up, and which testifies to the influence of the natural sciences:

"General Introduction to the *History of Civilization in England*. Chapter 1. *Statement of the resources for investigating history, and proofs of the regularity of*

human actions. These actions are governed by mental and physical laws: therefore both sets of laws must be studied, and there can be no history without the natural sciences."
(Henry Thomas Buckle, *History of Civilization in England*. Quoted in Stern (ed.), 1970: 121 f.)

13 Ouchi, 1981. Cf. Alvesson and Berg, 1992.

14 Silverman, 1970.

15 Cf. organizational changes as fashion (e.g. March, 1981).

16 There is evidence, however, that less encompassing managerial fashions than the major organizational approaches studied in the present book do replace one another (Kieser, 1997).

17 Kuhn, 1970.

18 In the debate about "paradigmatic closure" between organizational perspectives (see, for instance, Hassard and Pym, 1993/1990), "paradigm" is something of a misnomer (at least in Kuhnian terms), if it is used to refer to several competing schools of thought, none of which is dominant. This is precisely the kind of context that Kuhn, 1970, labelled "pre-paradigmatic", i.e. not (yet) "paradigmatic". As to "closure", or "radical incommensurability", this appears to over-dramatize the difficulties of communication that always exist, to a greater or lesser degree, between various schools of thought. (For a discussion of how to communicate between perspectives, despite the difficulties, see Alvesson and Sköldberg, 2000.)

19 Newton's paradigm always had two, undefeated competitors: thermodynamics and electrodynamics (Feyerabend, 1985; Prigogine and Stengers, 1984). Furthermore, a corresponding form of pluralism has set its stamp on twentieth century physics, with its fundamental schism into two mutually incompatible schools of thought – relativity theory and quantum mechanics (e.g. Davies and Brown, 1988, eds). Moreover, these persist side by side – when they do not stimulate speculative (and exciting) attempts at synthesis (e.g. in the form of the topical string theory, ibid.). It would be hard to maintain that either the theory of relativity or quantum mechanics is pre-scientific.

20 This also appears to be the view of Pfeffer, 1993, as applied to organization theory. For critiques of Pfeffer on this point, see Cannella and Paetzold, 1994; Perrow, 1994.

21 Feyerabend, 1985: 137, n. 18. Cf. also 18 above.

22 Masterman, 1972. To be fair, it should be said that the difficulty for Kuhn in defending himself against this type of criticism has tropological grounds. Contexts – in which the paradigms belong – are by their nature so holistic and, at the same time, so vague that they are not *capable* of being strictly defined according to Scientistic requirements (cf. Feyerabend, 1985: 24 f.). Kuhn has made the mistake of conducting his defence on the Scientistic terms of his critics, rather than on his own Contextualist grounds; as a result, he has been forced continually to shift his position.

23 Toulmin, 1977: As Toulmin points out, this process has had a direct equivalent in another subject area: geology in the twentieth century, and the dramatic thesis concerning geological revolutions put forward by the "Catastrophic" school, which under pressure from counter-examples was watered down bit by bit, ultimately only to apply to common forms of change. Neither the concept of paradigm nor the theory that the development of normal science is marked by successive, recurring scientific revolutions was new. The former stems from Georg Christoph Lichtenberg, Professor of Natural Philosophy at Göttingen in the middle of the eighteenth century, who introduced it in the sense of overall patterns of thought; in modern times, it has been employed by Wittgenstein. The

latter, the theory of scientific revolutions, had already been presented by the British philosopher Collingwood in the 1940s. (Ibid.) What Kuhn, 1970, did was to combine the word paradigm with the theory of scientific revolutions and cast this mixture in a popular, cogent and suggestive mould. The success of his book was due to the unparalleled consistency and sureness of style rather than its content, of its Satirical drama; something which Hanson and Toulmin lacked, and which Feyerabend drove to absurdity.

24 Toulmin, 1977.
25 Smircich, 1983a; Morgan, 1986.
26 Taylor, 1947b, passim (scientific management not "mechanism"); Fayol, 1916/17: 84. As early as 1950, Worthy coined the phrase "machine theory" for the organizational design of the classical writers.
27 See under section 2.2 above.
28 Alvesson, 1993.
29 Cf. Lakoff and Johnson, 1980.
30 Brown, 1977: 78.
31 Honour and Fleming, 1991: 191.
32 Op. cit.: 171.
33 White, 1985a: 426 ff.
34 Op. cit.: 30 f.
35 White 1985b: 106. Footnote and italics omitted.
36 Cf. section 2.9 below.
37 White, 1985b: 209.
38 White, 1985a. Cf. also a dialectical judgement such as Hegel's (1971/1840: 416): "The Irony knows its mastership over [all determinations]; it takes nothing seriously, it carries on its play with all forms" (my translation).
39 Cf. Ricoeur's, 1988, criticism of White, on p. 154 f.
40 Wittgenstein, 1953; Hanson, 1958; Kuhn, 1970.
41 For a critique of relativism in the context of the philosophy of science, see Siegel, 1987. For a defence, see Feyerabend, 1988.
42 For a similar conclusion, see Morgan, 1986: 340–3. Morgan's argument, however, is conducted on the basis of a discussion of different organizational metaphors. It is maintained in this book that this is far too restrictive; a tropological analysis is more suited to the problematic.
43 Cf. Siegel, 1987.
44 The last-mentioned taken in the sense that the organization "has" a culture, rather than "is" a culture; this is the interpretation which is generally to be found in the literature on empirical organizational cultures (although I have proposed the latter, wider interpretation). Culture in the former sense, where thus it is just one side of the organization, corresponds to what I, in the discussion of the concept of culture in Chapter 6 below, have called "metasymbolism", i.e. symbols that treat symbols.
45 Alvesson and Sköldberg, 2000.
46 Bourdieu and Wacquant, 1992.
47 Derrida, 1973/1967: 84 f., n. 9.
48 Brumbaugh, 1984.
49 The clock metaphor expresses, and has expressed historically, a view on societal phenomena which is rationalistic, deterministic, regulated and rule-governed (Mayr, 1982). – Cf. Heidegger's, 1962/1927, Chapter 6, rejection of this Metonymic and, according to him, "vulgar conception of time" in favour of one which is more Metaphorical, "original". Heidegger considers that the operationalization of the concept of time in the form of clock times leads to an instrumental and relational conception of time, linked to the limited life span of the

individual, emptied of its meaning, and "levelled" simply to a mechanical, endless sequence of individual "nows".

50 A good illustration is the conception of time of a Metaphorical thinker such as Nietzsche, 1969, characterized by the thesis of the "eternal recurrence of the same" course of events. (See, especially, the interpretations in Kaufman, 1974; Deleuze, 1986; Heidegger, 1986.) Wood, 1988, points to (1) the relationship between the trope of Metaphor and Nietzsche's cyclical conception of time; (2) his opposition to a linear and evolutionary conception of time.

51 Roethlisberger and Dickson, 1943: 414. Italics added.

52 Cf. Eliade's, 1974a, thesis concerning modern man's Synecdochic, linear conception of history as against archaic man's Metaphorical cosmos, cyclically recurring in archetypical gestures and events, derived from a mythical Golden Age.

53 The disguised yet at the same time dreamlike unchangeability in this Ironic time, where everything happens, but at the same time *nothing,* is nowhere described better than in novels such as Melville's *Moby Dick* and Kafka's *The Castle* (cf. Brumbaugh, 1984).

54 Cf. Sculley's, 1987, criticism of the cultural perspective on the grounds of its conservatism.

55 Dialectics as a method in organization theory has been employed by Benson, 1977, in particular, and also by Zeitz, 1980. In Berger and Luckman, 1966, it is one element within a more general methodological framework.

56 Taylor's rightly celebrated biography (Taylor, 1986) contributed to increase the interest in Hegel. In my case, the inspiration has a longer history, emanating primarily from Hegel's major work *Wissenschaft der Logik* but also from *Phenomenologie des Geistes,* the first parts of which might have spared later philosophers the burden of a great deal of thought – if they had taken the trouble of immersing themselves in them. Taylor's work fulfils an important function as a counterweight to the inaccurate and hostile treatment Hegel's work has received, for example in Bertrand Russell's history of philosophy (Russell, 1975). Interestingly enough, there is a direct parallel in research on Nietzsche, in Kaufmann's, 1974, biography and Russell's even stranger presentation in the same history of philosophy. Russell's, and more generally the logical empiricists', attitude towards Hegel and Nietzsche appears, from the perspective of poetics, as an example of Metonymic narrow-mindedness in relation to Synecdoche and Metaphor.

57 The most prominent representatives of dialectics in Indian philosophy are Shankara and the Vedanta school within the Hinduist tradition, and Nagarjuna and the Madhyamika school within the Buddhist (Murti, 1980). In China Laotse and Taoism have played a major role in dialectical thought (ibid.). Of the Greek philosophers, well versed in dialectics, Heracleitus was the earliest, and it is in his works that a dialectical theme is most pronounced.

58 Here is a direct parallel with the concept of *maya* in Indian Vedanta philosophy. For Shankara, the founder of this philosophy, maya was the net of illusions, and thereby paradoxical ignorance (*avidya*), which the categories of thought lay between us and true reality (Eliade, 1982).

59 Murti, 1980: 49. Hegel himself expresses the same idea in his typically more abstruse language: "the identity between identity and non-identity" (Hegel, 1952/1807).

60 Alvesson and Sköldberg, 2000.

61 Ricoeur, 1988: 206.

62 For Marxist organization theory, see Benson, 1977 (ed.); Clegg and Dunkerley, 1980.

63 The history of dialectics has sometimes been merged with currents such as hermeneutics and phenomenology (Berger and Luckmann, 1966; Silverman, 1970;

Radnitzky, 1968). These threads go back to the continental European philosophy of the 1930s and have remained intact since then (French phenomenology and existentialism, the German Frankfurt School). It is easy to draw the conclusion that dialectics is one aspect of these currents of thought. But such is not the case. Dialectics has a tradition of its own, with an essentially different problematic and a much older history than either hermeneutics or phenomenology.

64 White, 1985a: 428.

65 See Ricoeur, 1984b.

66 *"Sharpest criticism.* – One criticizes a person, a book most sharply when one pictures their ideal." (Nietzsche, 1969/1887: 176.)

67 See, for instance, Eco, 1985.

68 White, 1985a, b.

69 Murti, 1980.

70 For traditional formal logic of a logical-empirical nature such statements have been an abomination, as within this logic anything may be proved to follow from a contradiction. This is also the reason why its adherents have dismissed dialectics as an irrational delusion, while dialecticians for their part have regarded formal logicians as narrow-minded formalists. Nowadays there is, however, also non-standard logic, which may help to dissolve this polarization. Thus, in modern "fuzzy set" theory multi-value systems of logic have been constructed which can encompass contradictions without any fundamental irrationalism as a consequence (Kandel, 1986).

71 And the Madhyamika school itself? It tried to reach beyond the four categories by a radical, critical-dialectical rejection of them all and by exploding from within all the schools founded on them, laying bare the contradictions to which their own logic had driven them. This may seem destructive; however, according to Madhyamika, truth was not to be reached by thinking but only through *intuition* of the true, i.e. the absolute reality beyond the aberrations of thought (Murti, 1980). Dialectical criticism was no goal in itself, but the only means to sweep away these illusory frames of reference as clouds before the wind, so as to obtain real clarity. (Cf. also the "koans" of the considerably younger Zen Buddhism – insoluble riddles which have the function of radically breaking down our conventional thinking in favour of an insight beyond the categories.) Here, however, we have left the domains of discursive knowledge.

72 Thus, Murti, 1980: 130, places Vedanta philosophy, with its radical focus on the individual's attainment of inner meaning, i.e. the rediscovery of the Self (Samadhi), in Category 1 (corresponding to poetics' Metaphor); Hume, the prophet of British empiricism in Category 2 (corresponding to Metonymy); Hegel's systems thinking in Category 3 (corresponding to Synecdoche); and sceptical philosophy in Category 4 (corresponding to Irony).

73 Op. cit.: 132 ff., 166–78. – "Causality" is considered here in a wide sense; from a narrower perspective, application of the concept is often restricted to what is here called external causality.

74 As those of its relatives – theories of strong organizations (Starbuck, 1983; Brunsson, 1985), myths and wishful thinking (Jönsson and Lundin, 1977).

75 White, 1985a, places Contextuality in relation to functional causality. But the latter is teleological by nature; i.e. characterized by goals; according to the same author, Contextuality rejects teleology in principle, as belonging to a Synecdochic style of thought. To the extent that such elements occur in the Contextualist method – e.g. among the social anthropological classics and in Parsons – they therefore constitute mixed or transitional forms with regard to a Functional method.

3 Tragic power machine of rational classics

1 White, 1985 b: 211.
2 Taylor, 1947b: 42–7.
3 Op. cit.: 40.
4 Op. cit.: p. 59.
5 Op. cit.: 62.
6 Op. cit.: 63.
7 Nelson, 1980.
8 There is neither direct nor indirect evidence for Nelson's palliative judgement (op. cit.: 98, 172) that "Taylor admired [Schmidt] for his self-discipline" and "remembered [him] affectionately as a determined and independent individual, perhaps as a working class version of Frederick W. Taylor."
9 The following is based on the factual presentation in Nelson's, 1980, biography and Taylor's, 1947, own accounts.
10 Taylor, 1947c: 83 ff.
11 Taylor, 1947a: 152 ff.
12 It should be noted that such a team would not constitute any "staff", but is a line unit, which *replaces* the line foreman.
13 Op. cit.: 98, my italics.
14 Taylor, 1947b, c.
15 Taylor, 1947c.
16 Taylor, 1947b: 36 f.
17 Taylor, 1947a: 18.
18 Taylor, 1947b: 104.
19 Taylor, 1947a: 133.
20 Taylor, 1947b: 134, my italics.
21 Scott, 1987; Perrow, 1986.
22 E.g. Abrahamsson, 1986, who writes that functional foremanship is a "hierarchical solution", when in fact it is precisely the opposite. Or Hunsaker and Cook, 1986: 19, who speak of "a line foreman with the help of a planning department", which transforms Taylor's functional foremanship into a line-staff organizational set-up – yet again the direct opposite of Taylor's own system.
23 In the Epilogue to his biography of Taylor, Nelson, 1980: 198–204, in the same way marginalizes both functional foremanship and bonus remuneration. In his case study *Taylorism at Watertown Arsenal,* 1960, p. 29, Aitken disposes of functional foremanship in six lines of his 36–page first chapter on "The Taylor System".
24 Nelson, 1980. This despite bitter conflicts over factual issues, e.g. those with the shop workers at Midvale at the beginning of his career. Instead, he seems, not without justification, to have been treated with a certain amused indulgence as a slightly cranky person with a number of bees in his bonnet.
25 As, for example, in Braverman, 1974.
26 Frye, 1973: 208.
27 For an extensive discussion on Taylor's Scientism, see also Young, 1990.
28 Op. cit.: 221.
29 Frye, 1973.
30 Ibid.
31 Cf. White, 1985a, who places Marx in the Tragic category of historiographer. There are two subspecies of Tragedies; the radical and the resigned. Both Marx and Taylor write in the radical mode, which points the way to a brighter future after disruptive crisis and catharsis.
32 An important link in this chain of development was Taylor's pupil Frank Gilbreth, who broke with Taylor over this very issue. Gilbreth developed time

and motion studies, aided, among other things, by film cameras rather than stop watches, but at the expense of the other parts of Scientific Management (Haber, 1973).

33 Simon, 1957a.

34 Woodward, 1965.

35 I am grateful to Martha Feldman for this comment.

36 Myrdal, 1990.

37 If Taylor was the prophet of scientific management there soon emerged a host of apostles, who as usual worked both with and against their master. In particular the Gilbreths and Henry Gantt can be mentioned. (See e.g. Haber, 1973.) We shall not go into these in detail as the major components of the teaching were laid down by Taylor; his successors could develop or dismantle these, but did not add any new major components.

38 Braverman, 1974: 175 f.

39 MTM is not the only one of its kind; there is an enormous flora of different time study methods – CWD, DWF, RWF, MSD, MCD, MMD, MODAPTS, SPMTS, etc. See, for example, Grant 1983. MTM itself has been developed into MTM-2, MTM-3 . . . etc. (Berggren and Kjellström, 1981; *Introduction to Work Study,* 1978). A somewhat later variant is MTM-X, a faster and more user-friendly system for non-experts (Davies, 1984).

40 Frye, 1973.

41 Drucker, "The Practice of Management", quoted in Braverman, 1974: 88.

42 Kelly, 1982: 25.

43 Braverman, 1974: 87f. For an empirical example of Taylorism in company practice of today, see Jones, 2000.

44 Agre, 1995.

45 Drucker, 1999.

46 Young, 1990.

47 The first English translation of Fayol's book was published in 1929, and printed in merely "a few hundred copies" by the International Management Institute at Geneva, which were all distributed in the UK, not in the USA (Urwick, Foreword to Fayol, 1949). The next translation (by Constantine Storrs) had to wait until 1949. In 1984, Irwing Gray's revised edition was published. Of the available versions, Storr's translation can be characterized as free, and Gray's revision makes it even freer, both deviating rather heavily from Fayol's own text. In the citations that follow, I have translated from the French original.

48 In his Foreword to the 1949 version, L. Urwick regrets that the French term "administration" has been translated as "management", and points out that in the first 1929 translation, "administration" was used as the English term, too. Without going into Urwick's lengthy discussion about the pros and cons of the two alternatives, I tend to concur with his general opinion on this point. Hence, "administration", not "management", will be used in the citations that follow.

49 Urwick, Foreword to Fayol (1949: vi f.).

50 R. Samuel-Lajeunesse (1948) *Grand mineurs français,* p. 195. Paris: Dunod. Cited in Breeze, 1985.

51 Fayol, 1949: 64.

52 Descartes, 1986/1637.

53 This is also evident in his critical attitude towards the use of advanced mathematics in the training of both managers and technicians (Brodie, 1967). By contrast, for Descartes, 1986, mathematics was the queen of the sciences and was the Method with a capital M.

54 Fayol, 1917/1916: 7 f. The use of the word "function" here should not be confused with either 1. Taylor's functional foremanship, to which Fayol was

opposed, or 2. the term's meaning in systems-oriented functionalism, which by contrast with that of Fayol involves the creation of balancing forces *vis-à-vis* the organizational whole (see Chapter 4 below).

55 Gray has added "engineering" at the beginning of the list. Both Storrs and Gray have "adaptation" for the French "transformation".

56 Storrs and Gray have "optimum use" for "gérance" here. But "gérance" simply means "management".

57 Storrs and Gray translate "prévoyance" [foresight] as "planning".

58 Here, Fayol has "gouvernement", which literally means government – or even steering ("gouvernail" = a rudder). In the present context, though, "management" appears more congenial to the French text.

59 Fayol, 1917/1916: 57 ff.

60 Op. cit. 76.

61 Op. cit. 76 ff.

62 Op. cit. 11.

63 "Synoptical tables" showing the authority hierarchy.

64 Op. cit. 138 ff.

65 Op. cit. 147 ff.

66 Op. cit. 153 ff.

67 Op. cit. 81 ff.

68 A whole dominated by one element or level is a feature of a Metonymic style of thought; by contrast, Synecdoche is expressed by a whole with mutually interacting parts (White, 1985a: 36). In another comparison Fayol, 1917/1916: 59, draws a parallel between the company and the nervous system, where the brain is the organ of "direction".

69 Op. cit. 84.

70 Op. cit. second Part, Chapter 1.

71 Woodward, 1965.

72 Simon, 1957a: 20, 36; and see below on Simon.

73 Mooney and Reiley, 1939; Gulick and Urwick, 1972.

74 Breeze, 1985.

75 Carroll and Gillen, 1987.

76 There are ten of these (Mintzberg, 1980): three interpersonal roles (figurehead, leader and liaison); three informational roles (monitor, disseminator and spokesman); and four decisional roles (entrepreneur, disturbance handler, resource allocator and negotiator). One influence on Mintzberg's analysis was Sune Carlson's pioneering Swedish study of the work of executive managers in the early 1950s (Carlson, 1951).

77 Luthans, 1988.

78 The aspect of managerial work focused by Kotter, 1982.

79 Mommsen, 1987.

80 Dahrendorf, 1987.

81 Even postmodern writers claim that the world of organizations never has really managed to extricate itself from the grip of bureaucracy, and that organization theory is fundamentally just about bureaucracy and formal organization – just as Weber would have it. (Cooper, 1993/1990; Kallinikos, 1996; cf. Gergen, 1999.)

82 Weber, 1947. A complete translation of the whole work into English had to wait until 1968 (Weber, 1968).

83 See, for example, Nagel, 1961: 129–45; Suppe., ed.: 1977, passim.

84 Weber, 1947: 110.

85 Op. cit.: 88.

86 Op. cit.

87 Op. cit.: 101 ff.
88 Op. cit.: 107. Schluchter's, 1981, functionalistic reinterpretation of Weber, in the tracks of Parsons and Habermas, is a deliberate, Synecdochic switch of style. As such it is not without interest. But it goes further than, as Schluchter claims, only reformulating the answers to Weber's questions. Any transformation in style of thought also reformulates the problems, not just the solutions.
89 Weber, 1947: 88.
90 A more modern term would therefore be "instrumental action" (Mommsen, 1974).
91 Weber, 1947: 118.
92 Op. cit.: 152. In a footnote (ibid.) Parsons discusses the relative merits of translating *Herrschaft* as "authority" or "imperative control". Roth and Wittich (Weber, 1968) use both "authority" and "domination". In a footnote, Mommsen (1974, p. 72) states that the term is "almost impossible to translate", but prefers "domination". Thus, he consistently refers to Weber's "types of legitimate domination". "Masterdom" would perhaps be the closest translation.
93 Weber, 1947: 333.
94 Op. cit.: 337. Weiss, 1983, maintains that Weber's purpose was to study "domination rather than efficient coordination". This, however, is a constructed opposition, since, for Weber, efficient coordination in bureaucracy was precisely the rational-legal type of domination in its purest form. On the other hand, it is easy to concur with Weiss's claims that Weber, by contrast with certain modern American interpreters, was not prescriptive in his analyses, and that Parson's translation of *Wirtschaft* und *Gesellschaft* has a dubious functionalist bias. But Weber naturally could, and also did, investigate efficient coordination without being either prescriptive or functionalist.
95 Weber, 1947: 338.
96 Weber, 1968: 973.
97 Mikhail Bakunin (1814–76). Revolutionary from Russia and one of the main founders of modern anarchism. A contemporary of Karl Marx; his chief opponent in the First International.
98 Op. cit.: 987 f.
99 Weber, 1951/1922: 414.
100 Weber's account of charismatic leadership and its counterposition to a levelling bureaucracy is influenced by Friedrich Nietzsche's aristocratic individualism – "cultural people" [*Kulturmenschen*] as opposed to "order people" [*Ordnungsmenschen*] (Mommsen, 1974: 112). This distinction still echoes in research about the difference between "transformative" and "transactional" leaders, i.e. radical reformers vs. conservers (Burns, 1978). The former are best described in terms of charisma (Bass, 1985; Kuhnert and Lewis, 1987); the latter in terms of the status quo (Conger and Kanungo, 1987).
101 For a discussion of charismatic leadership in organizations, see Conger and Kanungo, 1987.
102 Weber, 1968: 1156.
103 "One can measure the honesty of a contemporary scholar, and above all, of a contemporary philosophy, in his posture toward Nietzsche and Marx. Whoever does not admit that he could not perform the most important parts of his own work without the work that those two have done swindles himself and others. Our intellectual world has to a great extent been shaped by Marx and Nietzsche." (Eduard Baumgarten, *Max Weber: Werk und Person,* Tübingen, 1964, cited in Mitzman, 1985: 182.)
104 There are also clear parallels with Wilfred Pareto's cyclical élite theory, where calculating, cunning élites ("foxes") are replaced through revolution by élites of

brute strength ("lions"), which in turn are slowly eroded through the infiltration of the cleverly calculating fox élite (Pareto, 1963). However, no direct influence can be shown (Beetham, 1987).

105 Max Weber, *Gesammelte Politische Schriften,* 1958, quoted in Mitzman, 1985: 184.

106 Mitzman, 1985.

107 Ibid.

108 For the similarity between Nietzche's great personalities and Weber's charismatic, see Mommsen, 1974.

109 Kaufmann, 1974. Personalities to which Nietzsche gave the frequently misunderstood name "superman". It is difficult even to mention Nietzsche and especially the concept of superman without triggering off conditioned reflexes, emanating from the totally unrestrained falsifications of the Nazis which have inflamed the subject. Many still believe that Nietzsche's superman was a bellowing, boot-clad German petty bourgeois. It is hard to conceive of anything more in conflict with the truth. The following should be pointed out (ibid.) so that the nature of Nietzsche's influence on Weber should not be misunderstood: 1. Nietzsche detested anti-semitism and German chauvinism above all else – to the extent that he even called his sister an "anti-semitic goose" and proposed that "it might be useful and fair to expell the anti-semitic screamers from the country" (Nietzsche, 1966/1886: 188). Instead, his models were French culture and cosmopolitanism. 2. Nietzsche's superman was a person – often exemplified by Goethe – who had sublimated [*über*winden] his experiences (including negative ones) into elevated creativity of an artistic or philosophical kind. For German beer-drinking chauvinists, in or out of uniform, he reserved his strongest condemnations, in both words and actions. See, for example, his characterization of the three worst misfortunes that had afflicted Europe – Christianity, Germans and syphilis (Nietzsche, 1969/1886: 143); and his break with his previously worshipped friend, Wagner, precisely on the grounds of the latter's propagation of German mastery (op. cit. passim, esp. pp. 247 ff., 317–25). 3. Nietzsche was wont to express himself extremely provocatively and metaphorically, and so also with the term "superman", which makes it easy – consciously or unconsciously – to misunderstand. Thus, even during his lifetime, biological, even racist interpretations of his work had already emerged, interpretations which he rejected with the greatest contempt (Kaufmann, 1974).

This does not of course mean that we should abstain from criticizing Nietzsche, just that we should consider his ideas on their own terms, not on the basis of later misinterpretations or downright falsifications. Only in this way do they become *discussable.* (For modern interpretations of Nietzsche based on the writer himself, see, besides Kaufmann, Deleuze, 1986; Lingis, 1986.)

110 In this he seems to have been influenced by the German circle around Stefan George and its interpretation of Nietzsche, stressing, among other things, the desirability of forming a permanent group around the charismatic personality (Mitzman, 1985).

111 This thesis of Weber's synthesis of Marx and Nietzsche in the organizational area is my own. Weber also integrated these two with respect to their conceptions of history – Marx's materialism and Nietzsche's voluntarist idealism – by maintaining that both material circumstances and individuals could play a decisive role (Mommsen, 1974).

112 Weber's relationship to Marx is well known, but that to Nietzsche is mostly known among specialists. Here Mommsen (ibid.) has yet again been the pioneer; for references to later research on Weber-Nietzsche, see Eden, 1987. But not even the specialists have always given sufficient weight to Nietzsche's influence; thus,

for example, Käsler, 1988, who in his biography of Weber only mentions Nietzsche once, *en passant*.

113 Several writers of this epoch described the same Tragedy: Marx (1967; Marx and Engels, 1968) from personal relations to alienation; Tönnies (Toennies, 1957) from *Gemeinschaft* to *Gesellschaft*; Durkheim (1949/1893) from mechanical to organic solidarity. (It might be imagined that the terms should be reversed in the last case, but this was in fact the way Durkheim expressed the transformation from natural to calculating relationships. The reason was that organic solidarity, by contrast with mechanical, expressed division of labour, just as in biological organisms.) Cf. also n. 45, chapt. 5.

114 Cf. Marx in *The Communist Manifesto*, 2000/1848, on the bourgeois revolution of human relations: "It has pitilessly torn asunder the motley feudal ties that bound man to his 'natural superiors', and has left remaining no other nexus between man and man than naked self-interest, than the callous 'cash payment'. It has drowned the most heavenly ecstasies of religious fervour, of chivalrous enthusiasm, of philistine sentimentalism, in the icy water of egotistical calculation. It has resolved personal worth into exchange value. . . ."

115 Frye, 1973: 221.

116 Op. cit.: 147.

117 For this distinction, see 31 above.

118 The final quotation is a more literal translation than the "functional specialization of muscles" given above.

119 Eliade, 1974b; and the more controversial Grof, 1985.

120 Frye, 1973. E.g. Shakespeare's *Titus Andronicus*; Pasolini's *Salò*. Another ingredient in the same type of tragedy, of which we earlier saw examples in scientific management, is *derkou theama,* the torture of observation. – To my knowledge, Michel Foucault has not discussed the classics of organization theory in his writings. However, the similarity between these classics and his descriptions of the growth of ever more detailed mechanisms of institutional control over the individual is so striking that they ought to be made the subject of a special study. Foucault's (1973, 1979) portrayals of the development of the prison system and the history of madness are demonic tragedies, permeated by *derkou theama* and *sparagmos,* with the shock effect on the reader, typical of the genre (Frye, 1973).

121 Ibid. Cf. Parsons' distinction between authority *via* technical competence and *via* position, often referred to as a criticism of Weber, who supposedly had conflated the two. Gouldner, 1954, sharpened Parsons' distinction into one between "representative" and "punishment-centered" Weberian bureaucracies, which rests on the means through which rule-following is achieved – voluntary consent or obedience by (threat of) punishment. In the first case, an order is obeyed because it is perceived as reasonable, as leading to "some goal"; in the other, because the issuer of the order occupies a certain position (Gouldner, 1954: 22 f).

Yet, in Weber's bureaucracy, knowledge and control do not stand in opposition to each other, but are both outflows from rational legality via "sphere[s] of competence" (pp. 330 f.), and mutually interact. Or, expressing it in terms of our poetic logic: the organizational drama combines the fatalistic and demonic genres of the law-governed Tragedy. Weber's great dilemma was precisely this: that the impersonally effective knowledge led to and presupposed control over individuals. And now we come to the poetical point. Parsons and Gouldner write in a quite different organizational drama, that of Comedy. They therefore interpret Weber in terms of this drama's basic distinction between a deficient and a desirable state, mutually incompatible (see Chapter 4); not in terms of a general conformity to law as in Tragedy and as in Weber – "a belief in the 'legality' of patterns of normative rules" (p. 328), through which the genres can be combined.

122 For traditional organizations as opposed to bureaucracies, cf. Scott, 1987: 41 f.

123 Hall, 1963, 1968; Pugh and Hickson, 1979: 61; Udy, 1959.

124 According to unanimous testimony, Weber was endowed with a "volcanic" temperament, equally matched by strength of will and talent. Even to the point when he suffered a severe mental breakdown, he managed, with rationalist will-power, to suppress his emotions through work-addiction. But this Lutheran asceticism was unable in the long run to curb the chained demon of passions. After his breakdown he gave freer rein to his emotional life. His interest in the rationalization of modern society, and the dialectic between this and an irrational charisma which time after time breaks the iron hold of reason, thus reflects his own psychological disposition. See Mitzman, 1985, who unfortunately deals with this only peripherally, and instead places greater weight on a schematic Oedipal interpretation; his speculations on Weber's supposed sexual problems fail, however, on source-critical grounds (a single, unconfirmed secondary source).

125 Turner, 1992.

126 McDonald's procedures may vary over different countries.

127 Daft, 1986: 178.

128 One exception to the rule, however, is Scott, 1987. Cf. also Perrow, 1986.

129 A preliminary edition appeared in 1945, the first in 1947, and the second (with an extensive new introduction) in 1957. All page references are to the second edition.

130 Simon, 1957a: 20.

131 Op. cit.: 36.

132 Op. cit.: xiv.

133 Op. cit.: xlv.

134 Op. cit.: 38.

135 Op. cit.: 39.

136 Barnard, 1938.

137 Simon, 1957a: xlvi.

138 Op. cit.: xxxii.

139 Op. cit.: xii.

140 Op. cit.: xxxii.

141 Op. cit.: p. xii.

142 von Wright, 1971.

143 Parsons, 1951.

144 Simon, 1957a: xxxi ff.

145 Thus, for example, by Marx, 1961/1867; see also Myrdal's, 1990, classic rebuttal. The Human Relations school, which we discuss in the following chapter, found empirical counter-evidence against the economic man as wage earner (Roethlisberger and Dickson, 1943: 532 ff., 576 f. Interestingly enough, pp. 576 f also provide an explicit critique of "economic man" as an alibi for the Taylorian effectivization of work.)

146 Simon, 1957a: 79 ff.

147 Op. cit.: xxv.

148 Op. cit.: 244.

149 Op. cit.: 102.

150 Op. cit.: Chapter V.

151 Op. cit.: 102 f.

152 Ibid.

153 C.f. also Sugarman, 1999, on these "unobtrusive processes of control".

154 Barnard, 1938; cf. Simon, 1957a: 111, n. 1.

155 Simon, 1957a: 122, 172 ff.
156 Frye 1973: 215. On account of its (dual) character of Comic Tragedy, the organizational drama also eludes any conclusive genre determination.
157 Enderud, 1977: 90, n. 3.
158 The following builds on Månsson and Sköldberg, 1983.
159 Simon, 1957 a: 1 ff.
160 Op. cit.: 4.
161 Op. cit.: 61.
162 Op. cit., pp. xxiv ff., 38 ff., Chapters 4–5, especially pp. 80 f., 240 ff.
163 Bachrach and Baratz, 1963, 1970.
164 Brunsson and Jönsson, 1979: 12.
165 See Sköldberg, 2001.
166 Simon, 1957a: 3, 39 ff.
167 Sköldberg, 1986.
168 Cf. Weick, 1979.
169 It should be added that Simon took an interest in such aspects in his later research (Simon, 1988).
170 The empirical findings provide some but only partial support for "Administrative Man". See, for example, Clarkson's, 1963, study of decisions concerning portfolio investments; Soelberg's, 1966, and Glueck's, 1974, studies of career decisions. – Simon's own optimistic view in the introduction to the second edition of *Administrative Behaviour* (1957a: xxvii), that the thesis of "Administrative Man" had now been "verified in its main features" through simulations "with the aid of an ordinary electronic computer" can be regarded as a reflection of early over-confidence in the decisionist programme.
171 An example taken at random (op. cit.: 218): "Through identification, organized society imposes upon the individual the scheme of social values in place of his personal motives." This is not a statement about language but one about the actual nature of organizations. Similar examples can easily be added.
172 E.g. op. cit.: 108: "No step in the administrative process is more generally ignored, or more poorly performed, than the task of communicating decisions. All too often, plans are "ordered" into effect without any consideration of the manner in which they can be brought to influence the behavior of the individual members of the group. . . . Failures in communication result whenever it is forgotten that the behavior of individuals is the tool with which organization achieves its purposes. The question to be asked of any administrative process is: How does it influence the decisions of these individuals?"
173 For sharp criticism of Simon, see especially Storing, 1962. Cf. Krupp, 1961.
174 Burns and Stalker, 1961.
175 Woodward, 1965.
176 Lawrence and Lorsch, 1967; Pugh and Hickson, 1979; see also Chapter 5 of the present book. An account, from a leftist perspective, of the development of "bureaucratic control" in the workplace during the twentieth century is provided by Edwards, 1979. According to the well-known "threat-rigidity thesis" (Staw *et al.*, 1981), organizations under threat tend to change into the "mechanistic" model described by Burns and Stalker. For an empirical evaluation of this Tragic scenario, see Barker and Mone, 1998.
177 Miller and Friesen, 1984. The designation is "adaptive S_1A". In a replication of this study, Kets de Vries and Miller found, 1985, largely the same pattern in a sample of fifty-two other companies. (Ibid.)
178 Mintzberg, 1983a, b; Pfeffer, 1981; Enderud, 1977; Sköldberg, 2001.
179 Lawrence, 1981, by synthesizing his earlier research with his own and others' later findings, has extended his original typology to embrace more than two

types. However, the classical organization (following Mintzberg, now renamed machine bureaucracy) remains one of the types.

180 Cameron and Whetten, 1981.

181 Bennis, 1971.

182 Quite a few researchers believe that it is not only strong, but totally dominant. For example, Sugarman, 1999, writes: "The old paradigm of management and organization" – subsequently identified as the bureaucratic paradigm – "has been found seriously deficient and a new paradigm is desperately needed." Obviously, this implies that the bureaucracy paradigm still reigns supreme (otherwise we wouldn't be in "desperate" straits). Similarly, Kallinikos, 1996. In the same vein, Allcorn (1997) maintains that we are still "stuck inside of the bureaucratic-hierarchical organizational paradigm or model", which he hypothesizes to explain the apparent lack of development of management thought" during the twentieth century. (It is symptomatic that Bennis, 1974, already revised his earlier prophecy, see previous note, that the death of bureaucracy was at hand.)

183 Cyert and March, 1963.

184 Cohen, March and Olsen, 1972.

185 For a critical discussion of the decision-making approach within transaction cost analysis, see the population ecologists, Bidwell and Kasarda, 1985.

186 See, for instance, Hickson *et al.*, 1986.

187 Naturally, a certain symbol may involve more than one trope. For instance, as we have just seen, from the point of view of its contiguity with the bishop's hand, the crozier is an example of metonymy; on the other hand, from the point of view of its similarity with the shepherd's crook, the crozier is of course also an example of metaphor. Again, the shepherd's crook, if taken to symbolize the shepherd, constitutes an example of metonymy.

188 Examples of the Scientistic method: positivism of various kinds (logical empiricism, Popperianism); Cartesianism.

189 Cf. Frye, 1973: 208: "Whether the context is Greek, Christian or undefined, tragedy seems to lead up to an epiphany of law, of that which is and must be. It can hardly be an accident that the two great developments of tragic drama, in fifth-century Athens and in seventeenth-century Europe, were contemporary with the rise of Ionian and of Renaissance science. In such a world-view nature is seen as an impersonal process which human law imitates as best it can, and this direct relation of man and natural law is in the foreground."

190 Frye, 1973.

191 Guillén, 1997, argues that the "machine aesthetics" of Scientific Management strongly influenced European modernist architecture. In fact, the Metonymic thought style of this architecture, its Scientistic method, and its radically utopian, or triumphantly Tragic, dramaturgy bears a close resemblance to the stylistic design of Scientific Management.

192 Burke, 1969.

193 Thus, the charismatic leader, in his meaningless revolt against a meaningless system, does not play the role of Romantic hero, but is instead reminiscent of Albert Camus' absurd hero in *The Myth of Sisyphus*. The absurd and irrational, but still paradoxically meaningful, and likewise the all-pervading character of charisma, points towards a Satirical organizational drama (more particularly in the *anti-intellectual, quixotic* genre; for this see Chapter 5 below, and Frye, 1973.) Since Weber does not discuss the nature of the modern charismatic organization in detail, but concentrates on older forms, we shall not delve more deeply into this issue; in any case, it belongs more to a book on The Poetic Logic of Power and Leadership. Here it shall be merely pointed out that Weber in his more

pessimistic moments considered the general process of rationalization to be so strong that it reduced all inner meaning to a Romance for particular individuals, thereby repressing the more overarching, revolutionary Satire of charisma:

"The fate of our times is characterized by rationalization and intellectualization and, above all, by the 'disenchantment of the world.' Precisely the ultimate and most sublime values have retreated from public life either into the transcendental realm of mystic life or into the brotherliness of direct and personal human relations. It is not accidental that our greatest art is intimate and not monumental, nor is it accidental that today only within the smallest and intimate circles, in personal human situations, in *pianissimo,* that something is pulsating that corresponds to the prophetic *pneuma,* which in former times swept through the great communities like a firebrand, welding them together." (Weber, 1948: 155.)

194 Frye, 1973: 148.

4 Romance with Human Relations

1 See e.g. Buchanan and Huczynski, 1985; Scott, 1987.
2 White, 1985b: 210.
3 Roethlisberger and Dickson, 1943: 14 ff.
4 Gilbreth and Gilbreth, 1916.
5 Roethlisberger and Dickson, 1943: 29, n. 1. The change was to a Metaphorical approach (p. 183 f.).
6 Op. cit.: 27.
7 Op. cit.: 71 f.
8 Op. cit.: 86.
9 Op. cit.: 87 ff.
10 Op. cit.: 160.
11 Op. cit.: 180.
12 Op. cit.: 183. Italics K. S.
13 Op. cit.: 184. Italics K. S.
14 Op. cit.: 325 n.
15 Op. cit.: 204.
16 Op. cit.: 252.
17 Op. cit.: 272 n. 1. Italics K. S.
18 One exception is Scott, 1987, who, however, strives as one-sidedly in the opposite direction – to incorporate Human Relations, like all other organizational approaches, into his systems-oriented analytical framework
19 Roethlisberger and Dickson, 1943: 365, n. 1.
20 Op. cit.: 379–84.
21 Op cit.: 385
22 Op. cit.: 384 f.
23 What follows is a simplification to the essential features of the rather intricate "wage incentive system" (op. cit.: 409–12) for the bank wiring personnel.
24 Op. cit.: 417, 423.
25 Op. cit.: 508.
26 Op. cit.: 522.
27 A worry which, besides, according to the researchers, was unfounded, since the piece-rate at Hawthorne was not set on the basis of increased or decreased production, but was only changed at the introduction of new production technology.
28 Op. cit.: 525.
29 Op. cit.: 590.
30 Op. cit.: 558.

31 Op. cit.: 561.

32 Checkland, 1981.

33 Even at an early stage, ideologically coloured criticism from the left was directed against Human Relations for manipulating the workers, hiding its true purposes. (The approach was given the derogatory name "cow sociology", since its aim was seen as that of transforming employees into contented milch cows.) See Braverman, 1974, for this type of critique. Cf. Bramel and Friend, 1981. According to O'Connor, 1999, " . . . managerial control . . . was made kinder and gentler by Mayo and the HRS [Human Relations School]."

The thesis of the significance of job satisfaction for productivity has, on the other hand, failed to gain support from later empirical, Scientist research: see, for instance, Organ, 1977; Porter and Lawler, 1968. Sharply critical viewpoints on the Hawthorne studies from a Scientist perspective are provided by Carey, 1967, who maintains that they are "worthless scientifically". Again, Shepard, 1971, holds that Carey is wide off the mark. The field of research was still highly topical well into the 1980s, when the debate on Hawthorne showed no sign at all of abating, rather it was intensifying (Perrow, 1986). If the interest in the Hawthorne studies *per se* has decreased somewhat in recent years, the larger issue of the job satisfaction–performance relationship remains very much in the focus. One recent example among many: in an ongoing research project, linked to Sheffield University and London School of Economics, the researchers "try to find out why relations between job satisfaction and performance are generally only small to moderate," analyzing "data from a two-wave longitudinal study, applying a new statistical approach based on structural equation models" (Dormann and Zapf, 1999).

For the extensive criticism directed at the Hawthorne approach over the first decades of its existence, see Landsberger, 1958. A critical review of the entire Human Relations perspective, including its modern successors, is provided by Perrow, 1986: Chapter 3.

34 Scott, 1987: 58. For an extensive, critical presentation, above all of leadership theory in the wake of Human Relations, see Perrow, 1986: Chapter 3.

35 Cf. Woodward, 1965. – However, both perspectives overlap to a considerable extent in practice, which is probably inevitable, since they are not separated by water-tight bulkheads. (Burns and Stalker, 1961, and Woodward, 1965, even maintained that they are hard or impossible to distinguish, as the threads of the two have been interwoven.)

36 Robbins, 2000. In Part IV of his book, Robbins also takes up the influence of the organization at the macro level on its members, within his overarching definition of organizational behavior as "the systematic study of the actions and attitudes that people exhibit within organizations" (p. 2).

37 Nelson and Quick, 2000.

38 The authors define organizational behavior as "individual behavior and group dynamics in organizations" (op. cit.: 4). The authors note that the "study of organizational behavior is primarily concerned with the psychosocial, inter-personal, and behavioral dynamics in organizations. However, organizational variables that affect human behavior at work are also relevant to the study of organizational behavior. These organizational variables include jobs, the design of work, communication, performance appraisal, organisational design, and organizational structure." (Ibid.)

39 Senior, 1998. For the history of OD, see, for instance, Gottlieb and Sanzgiri, 1992. Burke, 1998, looks at OD in relation to current issues of re-engineering and downsizing, and also considers the impact of future challenges such as the diminishing of trust and culture clashes stemming from mergers and acquisitions.

40 See, for instance, Guerin, 1997. In the US, the sociotechnical ideas behind the autonomous work groups were rooted less in the Tavistock Institute than in social psychological and humanistic considerations. (Ibid.) See also the theme issue of *Human Relations*, 1997, on "Organizational Innovation and the Socio-technical Systems Tradition. Kolodny *et al.* (1996) refer to "sociotechnical systems theory" as "an emerging organizational paradigm", arguing that a paradigm takes about thirty years to reach full maturity.

41 Guest, 1987. For a broad presentation, see Beer *et al.*, 1985. Cf. also Kravetz, 1988; London, 1988; Morgan, 1988. Kerr and von Glinow, 1997, argue that HRM has not changed very much in the past forty years or so, but that in the future it will be required to take more into consideration the overarching objectives of companies. Ulrich, 1997, summarizes a number of additional aspects that will need to be dealt with by HRM, such as globalization, information strategy, a unified theory base, and organizational change. An interesting question for the future is also whether HRM will continue to be handled by special departments within companies, remain as a function but be spread over several departments, or even be outsourced (the latter development has already begun).

42 *SHRM at a glance* (1999).

43 Conway and McMackin, 1997/98.

44 Guest, 1997.

45 Burns and Stalker, 1961.

46 Woodward, 1965.

47 Lawrence and Lorsch, 1967; Pugh and Hickson, 1979; also see Chapter 4 in this book.

48 Miller and Friesen, 1984. The designation is "adaptive S_1B". In a replication of this study covering fifty-two other companies, Kets de Vries and Miller found largely the same pattern (ibid.).

49 Bordt, 1997; Mintzberg, 1983a, b; Sköldberg, 2001.

50 Cameron and Whetten, 1981.

51 Examples of the Idiographic method: hermeneutics and phenomenology.

52 O'Connor, 1999.

53 Taylor, 1986.

54 For reasons that will emerge later (see n. 66) we do not use the term Romantic Comedy.

55 Frye, 1973, pp. 181 ff.: 200 ff.

56 Op. cit.: 169.

57 Op. cit.: 172.

58 Op. cit.: 175 f.

59 Op. cit.:163–85.

60 Ibid.

61 Op. cit.: 200 ff.

62 Ibid.

63 Ibid.

64 Ibid. For an interpretation of this archetype in Jungian psychology, see Jung and Franz (1964, eds). Modern versions include the film *King Kong* about the girl and the giant gorilla; in popular romantic literature, the young, pure-hearted heroine who tames an intriguingly dangerous but domesticable hero (Frye: 200 ff.), e.g. the governess and the Scottish laird, the female traveller and the sheikh, etc., etc.

65 Particularly central in Oscar Wilde's *The Ghost of Canterville*, where the innocence, as is sometimes the case in such narratives (ibid.) applies to children.

66 In a Comic Romance, the Romance predominates, and in a Romantic Comedy, the Comedy. Here, thus, the former applies. An example of the latter – the

predominance of Comedy – is White's, 1985a, interpretation of Ranke's historiography.
67 Frye: 169.
68 Op. cit.: 182 ff.
69 Op. cit.: 201.
70 According to Landsberger, 1958.
71 Mayo, 1945.
72 Frye, 1973: 182. Cf. the leftist criticism for "cow sociology", n. 33, which pictorially targets the pastoral theme.

5 Comedy of the self-regulating system

1 White, 1985b: 212.
2 The following presentation is based in part on my account of holism in Månsson and Sköldberg, 1983.
3 " . . . the linguistic trope of metonymy, which is the favored trope of all *modern* scientific discourse (this is one of the crucial distinctions between modern and premodern sciences)." (White, 1985b: 131.)
4 We speak here of *dominating* trends of thought. Counter-currents, of course, appeared – for instance represented by rationalist philosophers such as Spinoza and Leibniz.
5 Althusser's (1970a, b) controversial thesis of a radical "break" with Hegel's dialectics between the young and the older Marx was later admitted by its originator as an attempt to provide the ideological basis of legitimacy for a new Stalinism (Kemp, 1981).
6 Spencer, 1966.
7 Wiener, 1948.
8 Shannon and Weaver, 1959.
9 See Checkland, 1981.
10 Parsons, 1951.
11 Ashby, 1960.
12 Prigogine and Stengers, 1984.
13 Wilber (ed.), 1982.
14 von Foerster, 1979.
15 These "refer to a family of more specific complex systems, with many genres of theoretical generative mechanisms: auto-catalysis, mutual causality, deviation amplifying feedback, self-referencing." (Contractor, 1998.)
16 Maturana and Varela, 1980. "Autopoietic" literally means self-creating. Roughly speaking, then, an autopoietic system is a system that (continually) (re-)creates – that is, maintains and transforms – itself as a unity, through the interaction between its internal components and its network of processes. An "Encyclopaedia Autopoetica" is being compiled by R. Whittaker, 1999. Application of autopoiesis to social systems: Luhmann, 1990.
17 If chaos and catastrophe theories are added to the list, these newer systems theories can be assigned to the umbrella concept "complexity sciences". These differ from the more stability-oriented general systems theory in "their emphasis on nonlinearities, unpredictability, and uncertainty". Also, their focus is on "systemic change", both discrete and continuous, something which makes them particularly suited for studying change and transformation in organizations (Mathews *et al.*, 1999). A special issue of *Organization Science*, 1999, 10/3, was dedicated to the "application of complexity theory to organization science". For a monograph, using models from catastrophe theory to build a theory of change and transformation between organizational types, see Sköldberg, 2001.

18 Carley, 1997; Eve *et al.*, 1997; Goldstein, 1994; Senge, 1990; Stacey, 1996; Warnecke, 1993; Wheatley, 1992.
19 von Glasersfeld, 1995.
20 Cilliers, 1998; Contractor, 1998; Spender, 1999.
21 This concerns currents of ideas. Naturally it does not prevent two currents from being united in one and the same individual. Norbert Wiener, for example, in addition to his interest in servo-mechanisms, was also influenced by biologists who studied neurophysiological control mechanisms (Checkland, 1981).
22 For a book focusing on organisms (the subject is the well-being of organizations), see Churchman (ed.), 1989.
23 Bunge, 1979.
24 See Sztompka, 1974: 52 ff.
25 Hegel, 1952, 1807.
26 Bertalanffy, 1968.
27 On the other hand, a structure can be defined as a number of interrelated elements. From this we conclude that a system is a special type of structure: that type which is furnished with an environment, and in which the relations between the elements consist of interactions.
28 Bunge, 1979.
29 Ibid.
30 Bertalanffy, 1968.
31 Bunge, 1979.
32 Cf. Rapoport, 1969.
33 Green and Welsh, 1988, provide a conceptual analysis of control in cybernetic terms, with links to resource dependence theory. To maintain their cybernetic interpretation, which only applies to the internal environment, they operate away external control in its various forms (vertical integration, fusion, diversification, joint ventures, etc.) by designating these as "dependence restructuring". Via this plastic surgery they already by definition exclude external control. A more natural way out would be, as we have done here, to accept control as a two-sided phenomenon, where the cybernetic aspect is the one, internal side of the matter, and the external forms referred to account for the other side.
34 Parsons, 1961: 327. For a modern proponent of the Functionalist method (which he seems to regard as almost a matter of course), see Luhmannn, 1995. His Functionalism moves far beyond Parsons' towards de-Metaphorization, in that even the actors have disappeared, and been substituted by interactions as the system's constituent elements.
35 Harris, 1980, p. 165. This Synecdochic style of thought of the systems theorists eventually had interesting consequences for their conception of man. Cf. the following quotation from Braverman, 1985: 58, taken from an article by K. J. W. Kraik in the *British Journal of Psychiatry*, vol. XXXVIII:
 " . . . as an element in a control system, a man may be regarded as a chain consisting of the following items: (1) sensory devices . . . (2) a computing system which responds . . . on the basis of previous experience . . . (3) an amplifying system – the motor-nerve endings and muscles . . . (4) mechanical linkages . . . whereby the muscular work produces externally observable effects."
36 Merton, 1959.
37 Selznick, 1949; Gouldner, 1954; Blau, 1955.
38 Crozier, 1964.
39 See, for example, Merton, 1959, for a discussion.
40 Ibid.
41 An expression coined by Lawrence and Lorsch, 1967, meaning conditioned by/dependent on (certain circumstances). (Fiedler, 1964, had previously used the term "contingency" for his model of leadership.)

42 Attempts to apply systems theory all the way in organizational research (e.g. Katz and Kahn, 1966) have been less influential. For a discussion of the reasons for this and suggestions for future applications, see Ashmos and Huber, 1987.

43 Burns and Stalker, 1961.

44 Op. cit.: 119 ff.

45 Criticism has been directed at the terms mechanistic and organic (originally organismic) management systems on the grounds that they were modelled on Durkheim's mechanical and organic solidarity (see Chapter 3 above, n. 113), and simply given inverted meanings. However, both these terms had been used long previously, without inversion of meaning at the two poles. In fact they appear in Samuel Taylor Coleridge's eloquent defence of Shakespeare from certain classicist critics in 1811. Burns and Stalker's concepts are more probably modelled on this:
   "The true ground of the mistake, as has been well remarked by a continental critic, lies in the confounding *mechanical* regularity with *organic* form. The form is mechanic when on any given material we impress a predetermined form, not necessarily arising out of the properties of the material, as when to a mass of wet clay we give whatever shape we wish it to retain when hardened. The organic form, on the other hand, is innate; it shapes as it develops itself from within, and the fullness of its development is one and the same with the perfection of its outward form." (Coleridge, 1930/1811. Italics added. – The distinction is of German origin; the continental critic referred to by Coleridge is the German literary historian, Schlegel, who adopted this terminology in his Lecture XII on Shakespeare, published in 1809.)

46 Lawrence and Lorsch, 1967. Burns and Stalker do not use the term in their book, except casually in a chapter heading (1961: 52), "Uncertainty and the Quest for Markets in the Post-War Period".

47 Frye, 1973: 163–86.

48 Below, we interpret uncertainty in terms of difficulties faced by organizations in their interpretation of symbols.

49 Ibid. Interestingly enough, interpretive uncertainty ("ambivalence") is a characteristic feature precisely of Comedy (Frye, 1973).

50 Ibid.

51 Frye, 1973: 168 f.

52 Burns and Stalker, 1961: 12 f.

53 Op. cit.: 10.

54 Op. cit.: 258. Italics K.S.

55 Op. cit.: 119. Italics K.S.

56 Op. cit.: 107.

57 "And that's all there is to natural selection: in the competition for resources, the variability in the population means that some organisms will be better equipped to survive – and thus to reproduce, to leave offspring to the next generation. On the average, the more fit will tend to leave more offspring" (Eldredge, 1986: 35; cf. Mayr, 1982). *Thus?*

58 Hannan and Freeman, 1977b. A possible counter-argument might be that organizational *forms* reproduce; for this reason the analogy with development biology and natural selection still holds, and there is a way out of the logical circle. But first, the concept of organizational form, on which population ecology rests, is notoriously vague in definition. Second, it is less than clear just how these incorporeal beings, organizational forms, would "reproduce", not to say how they would be able to do so in any way similar to that of biological flesh-and-blood organisms.

59 Geertz, 1973.

60 The current has still not run dry in the 1980s and 1990s. See, for example, Barker and Mone, 1998; DeWitt, 1993; Gillen and Carroll, 1985; Goffee and Scase,

1985; House, 1991; Zanzi, 1987; Parthasarthy and Prakash, 1993: all articles revolving around the mechanistic/organic distinction. Countless other books or articles include these categories as part of their design, or as an issue to discuss. Eccles, 1992, argues that many "new" organizational fashions, such as networks, flat organizations, post-Taylorism, post-Fordism, etc., are in reality only new names for the classical organic type of organization. They are used for rhetorical purposes in order to provide an aura of novelty to phenomena that have been known for decades (even since the 1930s, Eccles suggests). In fact, descriptions of the postmodern organization are often strikingly close to those of the classical organic organization (cf., for instance, Daft, 1998).

61 Jauch and Kraft, 1986.
62 Milliken, 1987.
63 This applies to so-called intensional definitions. Extensional definitions enumerate the phenomena which fall under the definition. See, for example, Sartori, 1984. For analysis in terms of set theory, see Bunge, 1974; Weingartner, 1982.
64 Bunge, 1974; Popper, 1981; Suppe (ed.), 1977.
65 Weick, 1979.
66 March and Olsen, 1976; Kandel, 1986: Chapter 3.1.
67 Cf. Hegel's, 1967/1812, dialectical logic on the difference between qualitative and reflexive determinations.
68 Woodward, 1965: 14.
69 Op. cit.: 11.
70 Op. cit.: 14.
71 Op. cit.: 14 ff.
72 Op. cit.: 18 ff.
73 Op. cit.: 23 ff.
74 Op. cit.: 25 ff. First-line supervision was defined as "the first level of authority spending more than 50 percent of the time on supervisory duties" (p. 26).
75 Op. cit.: 30.
76 Op. cit.: 30 ff. " . . . neither size nor type of industry seemed to be the variable on which organizational differences depended . . . " (p. 31).
77 Ibid.
78 Op. cit.: 33.
79 To be exact, the *very* first number of classes was eleven; two of these were hybrids.
80 Op. cit.: 38 f.
81 Op. cit.: 40 ff.
82 The terms "linear" and "curvilinear" as used here and henceforth are inappropriate on this level of measurement, but have been used in the literature. For reasons of convenience, we retain the same inadequate usage. The term "technological complexity" employed in the present text is a slight modification of Woodward's own "technical complexity".
83 Cf. below the Aston school's findings on the significance of size for structure.
84 Op. cit.: 32 f.
85 Op. cit.: 33.
86 Ibid.
87 Ibid.
88 Ibid. (Scientific Management techniques are clearly being referred to here.)
89 Op. cit.: 60 ff.
90 Op. cit.: 69. Adapted – cf. n. 78 above.
91 Generally less than ten, often less than five; in several cells only one.
92 The boundary between unit and mass production is fluid. As we remember, Woodward reduced the number of categories to three by merging cases from an

original list of nine. The latter included a category containing firms with different types of "batch" production. In reducing the number of categories Woodward allocated – as we have seen – some of these firms to unit production and others to mass production. The criterion Woodward offers for this is the distinction between "production of small batches to customers' orders" and "production of large batches".

Obviously the drawing of the boundary is delicate, as there are two different criteria which do not necessarily agree: size of batch and customer's order. Moreover, the concept of "customers' orders" is of course also fluid – from the situation where the customers decide everything to the one where they only determine some detail. Consequently, this leads to a considerable degree of uncertainty over whether batch firms should end up in the unit or the mass production category. Twenty-one companies belong in this transitional category. Given the very small number of cases in each cell, there is a great risk for a biased result. Suppose, for instance, that the two "below average" firms in unit production that were classed as 41–50 in control span might just as well have been allocated to mass production. Even this would have overturned the whole result.

93 Ibid.
94 Op. cit.: 71.
95 Op. cit.: 250 ff.
96 Ibid.
97 Op. cit.: 247.
98 Frye, 1973. In imaginative literature: the clever chambermaid in numerous plays; the servant Jeeves in P. G. Wodehouse.
99 Research after Woodward on the technological imperative has provided hard-to-interpret and contradictory findings, among other things depending on differences in study design, in the form of sampling, operationalizations, etc. Even surveys of this research have produced contradictory interpretations. A favourable picture of the state of research for Woodward and the technological imperative is, for example, given by Fry, 1982. However, the opposite, critical judgement is predominant; see, for example, Donaldson, 1976; Gerwin, 1981. The same view is held by Collins and Hull, 1986, but they point to an exception to the rule: later research of American, Japanese and British origin has consistently shown a *curvilinear relationship between production technology and span of control*. According to Collins and Hull, who also undertake an empirical investigation of their own, this is a spurious relationship; variations in span of control can instead be explained from size and task complexity.
100 Pugh and Hickson, 1979.
101 Among other important assisting characters in later contingency theory literature can be mentioned diversification, public/private ownership, and democracy (Donaldson, 1985); strategy, age, local labour market, union coverage, industry complexity, and munificence (Huselid and Rau, 1997).
102 Miller and Friesen, 1984.
103 See, for example, Child, 1972b; Khandwalla, 1974; Blau *et al.*, 1976; Reimann, 1977, 1980.
104 Child, 1972a.
105 Cyert and March, 1963.
106 So-called "enactment of the environment", Weick, 1979; first edition 1969.
107 Cyert and March, 1963.
108 In a statistical investigation, Donaldson, 1987, found strategic choice in only 4.7 per cent of the cases; the rest consisted of different kinds of contingency. However, such a Scientistic analysis is not very appropriate for testing Child's Romantic vision, which is based on the understanding of meanings, not statistical analysis.

109 Benson, 1977; Zeitz, 1980. Moreover, Child, 1972a: 6, himself touched in passing on the idea of interaction.
110 See, for example, Pfeffer and Salancik, 1978.
111 Weick, 1979.
112 Weick, 1982: 404.
113 Frye, 1973: 185 f., 202 f.
114 Op. cit.: 185.
115 Ibid.
116 Cyert and March, 1963.
117 Cohen, March and Olsen, 1972; 1976: 25. For a good summary of these theoretical formations see Enderud, 1977. For a recent application, also suggesting a measure of degree of anarchy, see Takahashi, 1997.
118 Weick, 1976.
119 Scott, 1987: 20 ff. The problem with the distinction between rational and natural systems is that the former are by definition said to focus on "relatively specific goals"; the latter, by contrast, on "survival" (op. cit.: 22 f). But survival is certainly also a goal, and the most specific one we have: there is nothing undetermined between life and death. By the artificial forcing of all organizational dramas into the Comic frame, difficulties arise in the drawing of boundaries *within* this drama.
　　The problem with Scott's open systems, on the other hand, is that they are defined in terms of "coalitions" which negotiate with each other (ibid.). But the open systems perspective also encompasses contingency theory which, on Scott's own account, has not the slightest to do with negotiating coalitions (pp. 87 ff.). Thus, the open systems category places under one hat organizations functioning according to both contingency and coalition patterns, but they are not both covered by Scott's definition of open systems. Our poetic logic gives a clue to the explanation. The dualistic genre of Comedy cannot be reduced to the disintegrating genre: the former contrasts a deficient with a desirable state, the latter portrays the Comic society's incipient collapse. It is probably in order to solve this problem with open systems that Scott's extended typology (comprising four types) has come into being, as we shall shortly discuss; in this typology, contingency and coalitions, dualistic and disintegrating genres, are in fact differentiated.
120 Op. cit.: 97 ff.
121 In an anthology on organizational change Weick, 1982: 375, associates Scott's open systems with his own loosely coupled systems, which he regards as a distinguishing feature of the former. More precisely, as we have seen, this applies to Scott's open natural systems. This inexactitude has led to a certain confusion in the book's concluding remarks where Kahn, 1982: 414, asserts that the association in question applies to "natural systems" and that he is not in agreement with this.
122 Scott, ibid; op. cit.: 262. The remaining dramas within Scott's type IV are also played as a Romantic reform of the normal, dualistic Comedy, albeit of the somewhat different type we presented just before the disintegrating genre: Pfeffer and Salancik's resource dependence perspective, Benson's dialectical interaction, both partially inspired by Child (op. cit., pp. 105 ff.). Instead of driving Comedy to the verge of disintegration, these *mix* it into Romantic Comedy. The difference can be compared with changing the wavelength of a colour so that it is close to being transformed into another, or combining two colours in one pattern.
123 Moreover, Scott's type IV serves as a general remainder category; in it are also stowed miscellaneous representatives of wholly diverging styles of thought, e.g. Silverman's, 1970, actor's frame of reference, and Goffman's, 1975, frame analysis, both with a phenomenological background. These pronounced Metaphorical authors are essentially alien to "systems" in any form, be they natural,

open or anything else. The actor's frame of reference is as such a sustained polemic against systems theories; and in Goffman's book, the word "system" is not even included in its index. This is one of several signs that Scott's framework of analysis is too restrictive. (Another is that Child's "strategic choice" has no real place within it, reasonably enough, considering that his organizational drama was pure Romance – inspired, among other things, by Silverman's Metaphorical style of thought.)

124 For such typologies, see, for example, Scott, 1987: 93 ff.

125 Mintzberg, 1973.

126 Mintzberg, 1979, 1983b.

127 See, for example, Williamson, 1975; Ouchi, 1981.

128 March and Olsen (eds), 1976.

129 Mintzberg, 1983a.

130 Op. cit.: 343.

131 Starbuck, 1965.

132 His seventh and final type, Political arena, appears in the conflict-filled transition between the other types; or also in organizations on the verge of collapse. We shall not consider this general transitional type in any further detail.

133 Mintzberg, 1984: 68 f.

134 Frye, 1973: 45, 180, 229.

135 Mintzberg, 1984: 86.

136 Miller and Friesen, 1984.

137 Factor analysis is a statistical technique that aims at eliciting hidden, underlying, and common properties of a number of variables or the cases to which these are linked. Most commonly, the technique is applied to variables; then it is called R factor analysis. Conversely, Q factor analysis, which Miller utilized, focuses on the cases, and seeks to bring out clusters of cases which lie close to each other in the values of the different variables.

138 McKelvey, 1975.

139 Sköldberg, 2001.

140 Functional explanation is a more general concept than *functionalism,* a systems-oriented school which emerged in the social sciences after the Second World War, and which we have discussed earlier in this chapter. Even though all functionalists subscribe to a Functional mode of explanation, not all supporters of a Functional mode of explanation are functionalists. "Functional" is also a more general term than White's, 1985a, corresponding "Organicist" mode of explanation. This usage, like the employment of "Scientistic" rather than White's "Mechanistic", has the advantage of avoiding confusion with Burns and Stalker's theory of mechanistic and organic management systems.

141 Examples of the Functional method: cybernetics, general systems theory, (structural-)functionalism, structuralism.

142 White, 1985a: 34.

143 For a linking between open systems theory and the notion of emergent change, see Wilson, 1992, writing from a Comic perspective, against a Tragic conception of (rational, planned) change.

144 Chester Barnard's influential book *The Functions of The Executive,* 1938, was a forerunner.

145 Donaldson, 1985. The system is defined more specifically as the organizational structure (or equivalently), not the entire organization, which justifies technology ending up outside (ibid.). – We recall that the assistant character in the Hawthorne studies also came from "outside"; there it consisted in the research team itself.

146 As its name suggests this also applies to the theory of planning cultures (Sköldberg, 2001).

6 Satire: the contrary culture

1 White, 1985b: 213.

2 For historical accounts of the cultural approach, see Alvesson and Berg, 1988; Barley, Meyer and Gash, 1988.

3 Meyer and Rowan, 1977: 361.

4 Alvesson and Berg, 1992; Barley *et al.*, 1988. Independently of each other, both these teams of authors have compiled statistics on published writings in the field, and have arrived at quite similar results (see Figure 1.2 in Alvesson and Berg; Figure 2 in Barley *et al.*).

5 Barley *et al.*, 1988.

6 See, for instance, Bierama, 1996; Boyce, 1996; Casey, 1999; Chia, 1997; Hendry, 1999; Rowlinson and Procter, 1999. These are all academic texts, yet the cultural vogue goes well beyond the academic fence: "Although relatively new as a concept in organizational behavior, administrative theory, and institutional change, organizational culture is widely referenced in academic literature, business journals, and popular magazines" (Stupak, 1998). Hawkins (1997) argues that the cultural perspective on organizations is still in a phase of expansion since the 1980s, and has not yet reached a phase of consolidation.

7 Barley, Meyer and Gash, 1988. The rapid development has led to a boom in "cultural engineering" – a phrase coined by P.-O. Berg to refer to the striving, often more or less consultancy-focused by nature, to utilize the cultural approach for practical ends. See Frost *et al.*, eds, 1985, Part 2, "Can Organizational Culture be Managed?" See also the report of proceedings from the major SCOS conference held in Montreal in 1986 (SCOS Proceedings, 1986). Cf. Alvesson and Berg, 1992. According to Barley *et al*, 1988, development over the 1980s took place in parallel among practitioners and academics, the values of the former even tending to predominate over those of the latter. As to current practical applications, any search on the Internet reveals countless sites where consultants advertise about culture and change, culture and effectiveness, culture and performance, culture as managerial control, culture and TQM, etc. The interest extends to non-profit and non-private organizations as well. An example among many: *Public Administration and Management: An Interactive Journal* devoted two issues (3/2, 3) in 1998 to papers from "Two Part Symposium on Organizational Culture: Theory, Practice, and Cases".

8 A dialectical view on organizational culture has also been suggested in Alvesson and Melin, 1987, and in Meyerson and Martin, 1987. As mentioned in the Preface, the dialectical ideas of this chapter are based on an article from the journal *Ledelse og Erhvers økonomi* (Sköldberg, 1987), originally published as a research report in 1984 (FE-publication 1984: 66, Department of Business Administration, Umeå university). From a postmodern perspective, Nodoushani, 1996, argues for a discourse on organizational cultures that "celebrates ambiguities and multiplicity of conflicting views due to the logic of difference", thus moving beyond the traditional conception of the (strong) culture as a kind of visionary grand narrative.

9 Shukman, 1981: 327.

10 Conceptions of culture as a set of variables to measure and/or as a subsystem (see, for example, Pennings and Gresov, 1986) express, on the other hand, a Scientist and/or Functional method, emerging under the attraction of positivism and systems theory respectively. (According to Barley *et al.*, 1988, the theorists of the cultural approach tend to be influenced by the practitioners' Functional methods.)

11 Geertz, 1973: 14. Italics added.

12 Op. cit.: 11.
13 Op. cit.: 10 ff. At least in the form of hermeneutics and phenomenology, less so as regards cognitivist methods, i.e. methods which seek to capture culture by formalizing the knowledge contained in single individuals. Geertz is half approving of an actor-orientation (i.e. taking the "actor's point of view", p. 14); according to him, it stops midway by not systematizing the knowledge of separate indiuals into a coherent interpretation of the culture.
14 Ibid.
15 Op. cit.: 11 f.
16 Op. cit.: 15. Italics, Geertz.
17 Op. cit.: 17 f.
18 Jelinek *et al.*, 1983; Smircich 1983a.
19 Laudan, 1977: 49 f.
20 Deal and Kennedy, 1982: 4.
21 Ibid.
22 Wittgenstein, 1953.
23 Wiener, 1948.
24 Bertalanffy, 1968.
25 Westerlund and Sjöstrand, 1979.
26 For the role of "absence" in concept formation, see Eco, 1972.
27 The "actor's frame of reference" of the 1970s (Silverman, 1970) was a movement in opposition to the roboticism of the prevailing systems approach. It never really achieved a breakthrough, probably because it proceeded from a Metaphoric reduction to the level of the individual, which was out of tune with its time.
28 Sköldberg, 2001.
29 Geertz, 1973; Lévi-Strauss, 1963.
30 White, 1985a.
31 Berg *et al.*, 1984.
32 See n. 27 above.
33 Explicit in, for example, Pondy and Mitroff, 1979; Broms and Gahmberg, 1983; Berg *et al.*, 1984.
34 Jones *et al.*, 1988 (eds), passim.
35 Wells, 1988. The leaders' underwear was hoisted up the flag pole at regular intervals. Buildings and other large or conspicuous objects were constantly garlanded in toilet paper – a form of entertainment which took on "epidemic proportions". A camp song was composed: "Shit, fuck, hell, damn, son of a bitch, I don't give a flying crap." Etc., etc.
36 Characteristically enough, on that occasion, the guides denied having anything to do with the scouts' movement; the true culture was not to be revealed to the uninitiated.
37 Wilson, 1988.
38 Christensen, 1988.
39 These cultural orientations, like the functionalist classics of Malinowski and Radcliffe-Brown, constitute transitional forms from the systems approach: hybrids where the concept of culture still does not appear in independent form, as it does, for example, in Geertz.
40 Smircich, 1983a.
41 Gregory, 1983; Riley, 1983.
42 Deal and Kennedy, 1982; Peters and Waterman, 1982.
43 Smircich, 1983a.
44 E.g. Pfeffer, 1981.
45 See, for example, Feldman, 1986.
46 Berger and Luckmann, 1966.

47 These are of course ideal types, where homogeneity and heterogeneity are at the extreme ends of the continuum. In practice, situations tend to be more nuanced, so that unity cultures would be classified as those where homogeneity strongly prevails and in mosaic cultures those where heterogeneity predominates; some elements of heterogeneity will appear in the first case and of homogeneity in the second. For instance, Beitz and Hook (1998) studied three organizational sub-cultures within the US Army and found some overlapping features (rites, rituals, etc.), but more non-overlapping characteristics. In the present terminology, this would be labelled a mosaic culture, since the differences strongly dominate over the similarities between the subcultures.

48 In Berg *et al.*, 1984.

49 Månsson and Sköldberg, 1983.

50 E.g. Beitz and Hook, 1998; Gregory, 1983; Riley, 1983.

51 Cf. Sköldberg, 2001, for planning cultures; Berg *et al.*, 1984, for technocultures.

52 Cf., for example, Douglas and Johnson (eds), 1977.

53 For such "structures with dominance", see Althusser, 1970a, b.

54 Deal and Kennedy, 1982: 21.

55 Eoyang, 1983: 113.

56 Dandridge, 1983: 72 f.

57 Naturally this is an idealization. In the real world every sender of symbolic meaning is also a receiver. Here, we freeze reality's complex, dialectical processes to study them simplified, microscopically. – Postmodernism, of course, decries any such "postal metaphor" of communicated meaning, However, if nothing is communicated, except meaningless signs, one wonders why postmodernists themselves take so much trouble to convey their own (meaningless) plays with signs to others: by publishing and participating in conferences, for example. (Conversely, intertextuality itself – that truly *fundamental* notion of post-modernism – seems rather haunted by delivery services, busy around the clock transmitting text fragments to other texts.) Cf. Alvesson and Sköldberg, 2000.

58 Månsson and Sköldberg, 1980a.

59 Månsson and Sköldberg, 1983.

60 Of course (see n. 57), postmodernists deny that such a balance ever exists, and even that there is such a transmission process of meaning, which is Ironically denounced as a "postal metaphor". Yet, it can be doubted whether the post-modernists' own recommendation for a substitute – the onanistic metaphor of "dissemination" – is so much the better (on this, see Alvesson and Sköldberg, 2000).

61 Cf., however, Morgan, Frost and Pondy, 1983: 12 ff.; but characteristically, the authors devote relatively little space to this aspect of organizational symbolism, compared with other aspects.

62 Against this concept, especially used by the modern hermeneutician Ricoeur, 1984a, his pupil, the postmodernist Derrida, 1982, has objected that it relies on the concept of context. That is, even if there are several meanings to a word, we can always ascertain its true meaning by checking the context. But, says Derrida, context is always undecidable, hence also meaning. Instead, the Nietzsche-inspired Derrida has launched the familiar notion of *"dissemination"* (cf. n. 60), in which it is impossible to retrieve any context-bound meaning. Dissemination ruptures all contexts. This, however, seems to be a somewhat extreme attitude. After all, it is difficult to see why there may not be contexts that are difficult to ascertain, or even impossible, but also contexts that are easy to read and relatively stable. Which of these possibilities prevails in the actual case cannot, of course, be established by a philosophical *a priori*.

63 Månsson and Sköldberg, 1980b.

64 Adapted from Arbnor *et al.*, 1980.

65 Evered, 1983.
66 Cf., however, Eoyang, 1983.
67 Smircich, 1983b: 61 f.
68 Deal and Kennedy, 1982: 27 f.
69 Stern, 1988.
70 Cf. Kant's, 1969/1787, *Critique of Pure Reason,* for such contradictions.
71 Smith and Simmons, 1983.
72 Bachtin, 1968: 199 ff. See, for example, in Rabelais' *Pantagruel:*
   "King Anarchus' uncrowning is pictured in a similar carnivalesque spirit. After having defeated Anarchus, Pantagruel turns him over to Panurge; the latter first of all dresses the former king in a strange clownish costume and then sends him out as a vendor of greensauce, the lowest step in the social hierarchy. . . . True, Panurge does not beat him but weds him to a grumpy old hag who abuses and thrashes him." (op. cit.: 199).
73 Lévi-Strauss, 1963, 1976.
74 Smircich, 1983a.
75 Abravanel, 1983.
76 Jönsson and Lundin, 1977. This is also the position taken by Sorel, 1999/1908.
77 Abravanel 1983: 286.
78 Hegel, 1967/1812.
79 Logical paradoxes and ambivalence are typical of Satire (given the sense we have put into the word) as a narrative form: on this, see Bachtin, 1968. He, however, rejects the term, on the grounds that it has a purely destructive meaning, while we do not place any such restriction on it – the quixotic Satire, for example, has many constructive features.
80 Månsson and Sköldberg, 1980a.
81 Cf. also Berg, 1979.
82 Cf. Smircich, 1983b.
83 A Satirical theme: see Bachtin, 1968.
84 Cf. Bloch, 1980. Many drastic examples of events in such a "time between times" are given by Duerr, 1985, and also by Bachtin, 1968.
85 Bachtin, 1968.
86 Månsson and Sköldberg, 1983.
87 Sköldberg, 1983; Hardy, 1994.
88 Pfeffer, 1981; Jones, 1983; Wilkins and Ouchi, 1983.
89 Pfeffer, 1981.
90 Cf., for instance, Beitz and Hook, 1998, who in their study of the US Army found that senior leaders played an important role in shaping its organizational culture(s). Barkdoll, 1998, found that organizational members, and especially leaders, try – sometimes successfully – to shape their organizational culture to match their personal preferences.
91 Månsson and Sköldberg, 1983.
92 Smircich 1983b: 57.
93 Kets de Vries, 1980.
94 Kets de Vries and Miller, 1985, initiated research on this, and Kets de Vries has continued to investigate this problematic. Much more research is needed here.
95 For a strong empirical relationship between these two phenomena, see Srole, 1956.
96 Geertz, 1973.
97 Ibid; White, 1985a – Textile metaphors also appear, as do chromatic and meteorological ones: instead of spirit, one speaks of the texture or fabric into which the events are woven; of the colour in which they bathe; of the clouds by which they are covered. *The choice of the specific metaphor is thus not as important as what the metaphors have in common – the style.*

 98 Op. cit.: 18.
 99 Examples of the Contextual method: post-positivism in a broad sense (Kuhn, Feyerabend, etc.), postmodernism (Derrida etc.).
100 Frye, 1973: 223.
101 Frye, 1973; White, 1985a.
102 Specially emphasized by Ricoeur, 1984b: 166 (referring to Frye).
103 White, 1985a.
104 Geertz, 1973.
105 After the hero in Cervantes' novel.
106 A case in point: the exceptionally successful advocates of the cultural perspective, Peters and Waterman, 1982. To the same genre as the cultural perspective – quixotic Satire – belong a number of related organizational dramas: on climate (Ashforth, 1985), myth-waves (Jönsson and Lundin, 1977), irrational, dominant ideologies (Starbuck, 1983; Brunsson, 1985) and aesthetics (Ramirez, 1988).
107 Frye, 1973. – For example, against a rational (classical or systems-oriented) view of myths as created either by conscious deliberation, or by pressure from the environment, or both, other possibilities may well be considered. Myths originally generated by chance can, for instance, become dominant through "autocatalytic" snowball effects (Lundin and Sköldberg, 1986). This model fits excellently within an irrational, Satirical organizational drama.
108 The first of the two fronts is dominating, for it is there that the opposition is strongest. The latter turns up, for example, in the method of organizational change, "cultural engineering", which wishes to succeed various psychodynamic sciences of salvation, and function as an invigorating "in drug" for tired executives. See note 7 above, and for the method's relative ineffectiveness, Alvesson and Berg, 1992. To the extent that the method is ineffective, this has been attributed to the sluggish nature of cultural change. The debate on this has to some extent been polarized between advocates of "instant cultures" and sceptics who regard cultures as intrinsically deep, historical phenomena. My own view is more differentiated, and suggests that cultures vary with respect to rapidity of change, as do layers *within* each culture (see Sköldberg, 2001, for a discussion). Yet, this front is weaker, for the culture perspective on organizations can be linked, for instance to Human Resource Management (and even more generally to Organizational Behaviour). In this case we may have a case of Romantic Irony – an idealistic drama, centred on liberating the individual, which founders on the Irony of organizational reality, in that the management's "big happy family" concept is met with overt or covert derision from the side of the employees.
109 Frye, 1973. Interestingly enough, this led Sculley, a man of practical action, to characterize the cultural perspective as static, conservative, and instead to recommend more contrarieties within organizations if they were to preserve of their vitality and creativity (Sculley, 1987). Sculley rightly pointed out that the cultural perspective is Japan-inspired, and emphasizes that it has not been shown that the Japanese organizational form, with unity in the forefront, can promote creativity; the Japanese economic successes have in fact, to a not insignificant extent, been based on the skilful and cheap exploitation of product licences assigned by American corporations.
110 Frye, 1973.

7 Da capo: organizational performance

 1 Campbell, 1977; Hannan and Freeman, 1977a; Kahn, 1977.
 2 Bluedorn, 1980: 485.
 3 Up until the turn of the last century efficiency and effectiveness were virtually

synonymous concepts. The current distinction in meaning was introduced as a result of the influence of the engineering concept of efficiency on the field of economics (Simon, 1957a). Cf. Barnard, 1938.

4 See, for example, Drucker, 1974: 75.
5 This is also the economists' definition of "efficiency" (Samuelson, 1964; Stigler 1949).
6 Etzioni, 1964.
7 Mintzberg, 1983a: 263.
8 Iacocca, 1984: 100 ff.
9 Friedman, 1953: 22.
10 Marx, 1961/1867.
11 Cyert and March, 1963.
12 Mintzberg, 1983a.
13 Iacocca, 1984: 187.
14 C.f. also Govindarajan, 1986, for market growth and profitability as the ends of a "build-harvest" continuum.
15 DeLamarter, 1986.
16 ABCNEWS.com, 6 November 1999.
17 Sculley, 1987: 18 ff.
18 Sculley, 1987: 17 ff.
19 Op. cit.: 25.
20 Reported in the Swedish newspaper *Svenska Dagbladet*, 2 September 1999.
21 Control and power have been strongly emphasized as goals by Perrow, 1981, as against the transaction cost analysts' focus on efficiency.
22 Pfeffer and Salancik, 1978.
23 Bluedorn, 1980
24 Selznick, 1957: 135 f. See also Ramirez, 1988: 319–41, 433 ff.
25 Sculley, 1987: 356 f.
26 Sculley, 1987: 213.
27 Ibid.
28 Interview with Steve Jobs, CNN 21 July 1999.
29 Iacocca, 1984: 102 f. Iacocca does not comment on the obvious racist overtones (assuming the quotation is correct) of the penultimate sentence.
30 See also section 7.4 below.
31 Daft, 1998: 63.
32 Quinn and Rohrbaugh, 1983.
33 Daft, 1998: 106. Adapted from Y. K. Shetty, "New Look at Corporate Goals," *California Management Review,* 22/2 (1979): 71–9.
34 One problem that has been discussed is what happens to performance, interpreted as degree of goal achievement, in a company with more than one goal. Does it not become multi-dimensional instead of one-dimensional, and must we not then abandon the idea of a *single* measure of performance (see Westerlund and Sjöstrand, 1975, for a discussion)? The problem can be split into sub-problems. First, we have the case where different subunits/members of the organization have different and conflicting goals. In this case, the so-called *multiple-constituency* (Connolly *et al.*, 1980; Martin, 1980), performance can be specified only *relative* to each individual group and goal. (Another form of relative performance arises when an *outsider* – evaluator, consultant, researcher – investigates performance relative to the goals he/she sets up). In the second case, we have various goals, but these are embraced more or less homogeneously by the entire organization. Then the different goals can be assigned weights according to their relative importance. (The distinct goal dimensions are thereby collapsed into indifference classes in accordance with ascribed value.) A common objection

to such a way of proceeding is that assignment of importance is unstable over time (see, for example, Mintzberg, 1983a, with references). But in the first place, uncertainty probably occurs in all phenomena that are assigned measures in social science (Galtung, 1977). Second, the instability is relative not absolute; in other words, it depends on the time period considered. Third, there is no instability when the goals have been ascribed by some outside evaluator. A complement to the above is to conceive the various goals as *constraints* on each other (Simon, 1964). – Mintzberg, 1983a, refers to the constraint model as a substitute not a complement; however, we have to ask whether his critique just referred to (concerning possible instability) might not also affect the constraint levels in question.

35 For a third alternative to input performance and outlook performance, see the discussion on *business performance* by the strategy researchers, Venkatram and Ramanujam, 1986. This concept encompasses both financial assessment (not just oriented towards accounting, i.e. input performance, but also linked to markets) and operative evaluation, concerning market shares, product quality, marketing performance, etc. Business performance is therefore a grey zone which extends over adjacent parts of both input performance and outlook performance. The article is informative with respect to various measures of business performance. – The authors further distinguish between indicators obtained from primary sources, i.e. the company itself, and secondary sources outside the company, i.e. business journals and magazines, etc.

36 See, for example, Ouchi, 1980.

37 See, for example, Ijiri, 1967; Hendriksen, 1982; Dawes 1999.

38 Hall, 1980. (For subjective vs. objective measures of *input* performance, see Dawes, 1999.)

39 Mahoney and Weitzel, 1969.

40 Cf. Ashby, 1956.

41 Mahoney and Weitzel, 1969.

42 Steers, 1975.

43 A similar list of mixed groceries, but containing thirty variables, is presented by Campbell, 1970.

44 For an extensive discussion of measures of performance in the Romantic style, focusing on "Human Resource Activities", see Steffy and Maurer, 1988.

45 See Pennings and Goodman, 1977, for a discussion.

46 See Sköldberg, 2001.

47 There are a number of pitfalls for the unwary in the analysis of goals, such as the difference between operative and official goals (e.g. Daft, 1998), real and declared goals, conscious and unconscious (subconscious, repressed) goals, and stereotypical goals (goals which agree with a stereotyped norm, without being adapted to the organization) (Westerlund and Sjöstrand, 1979). These can best be characterized as general problems of interpretation in the human sciences, and thus concern methodological issues that are not restricted to the problematic of goals. More specifically, they concern the issue of source criticism (on this, see Alvesson and Sköldberg, 2000). Source-critical and other general social-scientific interpretive praxis should therefore be utilized to solve these problems.

The problem of goals that fluctuate over time, and the goal-means hierarchy, where a goal at one level in the hierarchy is a means for the next, higher goal, however, are more specific. Fluctuating goals can be associated with organizations with specific power constellations (Mintzberg, 1983a). It is true that this renders it difficult or infeasible to measure performance over time, at least in terms of the organization's own goals. But, first, this instability only occurs in special types of organizations. Second, even here outside analysts can set up a (normative) goal and evaluate performance in relation to this. In the goal-means hierarchy, a goal at one level is quite rightly a means for the next higher, etc. Here, above all, the level to which the measure refers must be clearly defined, otherwise confusion will be inevitable.

A further argument commonly directed against analysis in terms of goals is that only individuals have goals, not organizations. This argument appears to rest on philosophical-metaphysical suppositions of a special kind – so-called reductionism – and the acceptance or non-acceptance of it is therefore mostly a matter of personal opinion and taste. A further tricky issue is that not all organizations have goals. (For an extensive discussion and typology of goal-driven and goal-less organizations, see Sköldberg, 2001.) In such cases, outside analysts can conduct evaluations of performance in relation to the normative goals they set up.

48 There are two schools of thought concerning what we have termed outlook performance. One of these maintains that such performance refers to goal achievement (Molnar and Rogers, 1976; Pennings and Goodman, 1977); the other that it has to do with resource acquisition (Yuchtman and Seashore, 1967). Bluedorn has constructed a synthesis, according to which performance in terms of resource acquisition also consists in (and can be reduced to) goal achievement – namely of the special kinds of goals that consist in resource acquisition. From a wider perspective it is subordinated under the goal of survival (Bluedorn, 1980). Both these points of Bluedorn agree well with what we have just argued in the previous section.

49 Simon, 1957a: 182f, argues on the basis of an opportunity cost reasoning that input performance does not have to be cost-oriented. He admits however (op. cit.: 179f) that even if his concept of efficiency has a "common denominator" on the cost side, it suffers from a lack of a "common numerator . . . the problem still remains of comparing the values which are attained". Even though there is no logical necessity to interpret efficiency as cost performance, the tendency in reality points very strongly in this direction, since decisions are usually made around measurable quantities, something which Simon himself admits in another context in his book. The revenue side of performance is notoriously hard to measure, in contrast to the cost side. Cf. Mintzberg, 1983a. The Swedish newspaper *Svenska Dagbladet* (23 October 1999) reported an interesting story from Norway of a fight between a company top management oriented towards cost performance and a local manager of a melting plant who tried to implement a policy of general profitability, in the more genuine output/input sense. Despite his successes in raising the profitability of the plant, his policy was resisted by the top management. After a prolonged and stubborn fight, the local manager – a Swedish immigrant in Norway – lost out, and had to quit his job and move from the country.

50 Frye, 1973: 186–206.

51 See, for instance, *Performance Appraisal* (1999). According to Pfeffer, 1997, human resources measurement systems risk contaminating HRM with short-sighted ideas of (cost) efficiency, otherwise mostly associated with accounting and finance.

52 Hurst, 1997.

53 Frye, 1973: 181 ff.

54 For discussion, theoretical interpretation, and literature references, see Sköldberg, 2001.

55 On Henry Ford I's crisis as an entrepreneur, see Kets de Vries, 1980.

56 Cf. Jönsson and Lundin's, 1977, "myth waves".

57 Iacocca, 1984.

58 Cf. Alvesson and Sköldberg, 2000, especially Chapters 3 and 7.
59 Sculley, 1987.
60 Love, 1986.
61 Ibid.
62 The standardized, organizational rule apparatus depicted in Chapter 3 in the section on Weber constitutes the machinery at workplace level in the individual restaurants, which guarantees the overall fulfilment of QSC. It should be observed that higher levels in the McDonald's organization are not characterized by such a bureaucratic structure. On the contrary boundaries of competence are, for example, fluid, and no formal organizational chart exists. (Ibid.)
63 Ibid.
64 Op. cit.: 265.
65 Mainstream economists of the neoclassic school are not at all disturbed by empirical refutations of their profit maximizing axiom. Their standard reply is that they do not aim at describing reality, they are just building models. The reduction of all goals to input performance is compared to the idealizations of theoretical physics where, for instance, friction is disregarded in the law of falling bodies. The problem is only that the analogy fails, because the other performance goals are not as marginal compared to input performance as is friction to the force of gravitation. In fact, the (mainstream, neoclassical) economists manage to reduce away the very dimensions of reality which are necessary to explain it. Some economists add in an instrumentalist, Friedmannian spirit that the models do not have to correspond to reality, if only they are useful for predicting events in reality. Since the models of economists have proven notoriously useless for predicting economic reality, this argument fails too. Hence we may safely draw the conclusion that the profit maximizing axiom of mainstream neoclassical economists is not an axiom at all, but a dogma, serving to underpin a theoretical edifice which lacks contact with reality and only survives due to its extraordinary rhetoric power of Metonymy.
66 Except for the case where goals are non-existent, unclear etc. (Cf. Sköldberg, 2001.)
67 For a discussion of similar "Icarus paradoxes", cf. Miller, 1990.
68 Quinn and Rohrbaugh, 1983.

References

ABCNEWS.com, 6 November, 1999. <http://abcnews.go.com/sections/tech/DailyNews/msdojii991105.html> (6 November 1999).

Abrahamsson, Bengt (1986) *Varför finns organisationer? Kollektiv handling, yttre krafter och inre logik [Why are there organizations? Collective Action, External Forces, and Internal Logic]*. Stockholm: Norstedts.

Abravanel, H. (1983) "Mediatory Myths in the Service of Organizational Ideology". In L. R. Pondy, P. J. Frost, G. Morgan and T. C. Dandridge (eds) *Organizational Symbolism*. Greenwich: Jai Press.

Agre, P. E. (1995) "From High Tech to Human Tech: Empowerment, Measurement, and Social Studies of Computing", *Computer Supported Cooperative Work,* 3/2: 167–95.

Aitken, H. G. J. (1960) *Taylorism at Watertown Arsenal. Scientific Management in Action 1908–1915*. Cambridge, MA: Harvard University Press.

Akin, G. and Palmer, I. (2000) "Putting Metaphors to Work for Change in Organizations". *Organizational Dynamics*, 28/3: 67–77.

Allcorn, S. (1997) "The Search for the Organizational Solution to the Industrial Revolution." CSOC (Center for the Study of Organizational Change. University of Missouri-Columbia). Paper presented at the Fall Colloquium on Organizational Psychodynamics, September 19–21.

Althusser, L. (1970a) *For Marx*. New York: Vintage.

Althusser, L. and Balibar, É. (1970b) *Reading Capital*. London: NLB.

Alvesson, M. (1993) *Cultural Perspectives on Organizations*. Cambridge: Cambridge University Press.

Alvesson, M. and Berg, P.-O. (1992) *Corporate Culture and Organizational Symbolism*. Berlin/New York: de Gruyter.

Alvesson, M. and Deetz, S. (1996) "Critical Theory and Postmodernism Approaches to Organizational Studies". In S. R. Clegg, C. Hardy and W. R. Nord (eds), *Handbook of Organization Studies*. London: Sage.

Alvesson, M. and Melin, L. (1987) "Major Discrepancies in Organizational Culture". Paper presented at the SCOS International Conference on the Symbolics of Corporate Artifacts i Milano.

Alvesson, M. and Sköldberg, K. (2000) *Reflexive Methodology. New Vistas for Qualitative Research*. London: Sage.

Apter, David E. (1966) *The Politics of Modernization*. Chicago: University of Chicago Press.

Arbnor, I., Borglund, S.-E. and Liljedahl, T. (1980) *Osynligt ockuperad. [Invisibly occupied]*. Malmö: Liber.

Aristoteles (1922) *Organon.* Band II. Topik. Leipzig: Felix Meiner.

Aristotle (1954) *Rhetoric and Poetics.* New York: Random House.

Ashby, W. R. (1956) *An Introduction to Cybernetics.* London: Chapman.

—— (1960) *Design for a Brain.* New York: Wiley.

Ashforth, B. E. (1985) "Climate Formation: Issues and Extensions". *The Academy of Management Review,* 10: 837–47.

Ashmos, D. P. and Huber, G. P. (1987) "The Systems Paradigm in Organization Theory: Correcting the Record and Suggesting the Future". *Academy of Management Review,* 12: 607–21.

Astley, W. G. (1985) "Administrative Science as Socially Constructed Truth". *Administrative Science Quarterly,* 30: 497–513.

Astley, W. G. and van de Ven, Andrew H. (1983) "Central Perspectives and Debates in Organization Theory". *Administrative Science Quarterly,* 28: 245–73.

Auerbach, E. (1974) *Mimesis. The Representation of Reality in Western Literature.* Princeton, NJ: Princeton University Press.

Bachrach, P. and Baratz, M. S. (1963) "Decisions and Nondecisions: An Analytical Framework". *American Political Science Review,* 57: 632–42.

—— (1970) *Power and Poverty: Theory and Practice.* New York: Oxford University Press.

Bachtin, M. (1968) *Rabelais and his World.* Cambridge, MA: MIT Press.

Barkdoll, G. L. (1998) "Individual Personality And Organizational Culture Or 'Let's Change This Place So I Feel More Comfortable', " *Public Administration and Management: An Interactive Journal,* 3/2. <http://www.pamij.com/barkdoll.html>

Barker, V. L. III and Mone, M. A. (1998) "The Mechanistic Structure Shift and Strategic Reorientation in Declining Firms Attempting Turnarounds". *Human Relations,* 51/10: 1227–57.

Barley, S. R., Meyer, G. W, and Gash, D. C. (1988) "Cultures of Culture: Academics, Practitioners and the Pragmatics of Normative Control". *Administrative Science Quarterly,* 33: 24–60.

Barnard, C. I. (1938) *The Functions of the Executive.* Cambridge, MA: Harvard University Press.

Bass, B. M. (1985) *Leadership and Performance Beyond Expectations.* New York: Free Press.

Beer, M., Spector, B., Lawrence, P. R., Quinn Mills, D. and Walton, R. E. (1985) *Human Resource Management: A General Managers Perspective.* Glencoe, IL: Free Press.

Beetham, David (1987) "Mosca, Pareto and Weber: A Historical Comparison". In W. J. Mommsen and J. Osterhammel (eds) *Max Weber and his Contemporaries.* London: Allen and Unwin.

Beitz, C. A. Jr. and Hook, J. R. (1998) "The Culture Of Military Organizations: A Participant-Observer Case Study Of Cultural Diversity". *Public Administration and Management: An Interactive Journal,* 3/3. <http://www.pamij.com/beitz.html> (31 October 1999).

Bennis, W. G. (1971) "The Coming Death of Bureaucracy". In H. E. Frank (ed.) *Organization Structuring.* London: McGraw-Hill.

—— (1974) "Conversation: An Interview with Warren Bennis". *Organization Dynamics,* 2: 50–66.

Benson, J. K. (1977) "Organizations: A Dialectial View". *Administrative Science Quarterly,* 22: 1–21.

—— (ed.) (1977) *Organizational Analysis: Critique and Innovation.* Beverly Hills, CA: Sage.

Berg, P.-O. (1979) *Emotional Structures in Organizations*. Diss. Lund: Studentlitteratur.
—— et al. (1984) "Organisationssymbolism och företagskultur". [Organisational symbolism and corporate culture.] Research programme at the Department of business administration, Lund University. Research report.

Berger, P. L. and Luckmann, T. (1966) *The Social Construction of Reality. A Treatise in the Sociology of Knowledge*. New York: Doubleday.

Berggren, Christian and Kjellström, S.-Å. (1981) *Verkstadsrationalisering och arbetsorganisation*. Malmö: Liber.

Bernstein, R. J. (1983) *Beyond Objectivism and Relativism*. Oxford: Basil Blackwell.

Bertalanffy, L. von (1968) *General System Theory*. New York: George Braziller.

Bidwell, C. E. and Kasarda, J. D. (1985) *The Organization and its Ecosystem. A Theory of Structuring in Organizations*. Greenwich, CT: Jai Press.

Bierema, L. L. (1996) "How Executive Women Learn Corporate Culture". *Human Resource Development Quarterly*, 7/2: 145–64.

Blau, P. M. (1955) *The Dynamics of Bureaucracy*. Chicago: University of Chicago Press.

Blau, P. M., McHugh Falbe, C., McKinley, W. and Tracy, P. K. (1976) "Technology and Organization in Manufacturing". *Administrative Science Quarterly*, 21: 20–40.

Bloch, M. (1980) "Ritual Symbolism and the Nonrepresentation of Society". In M. LeCron Foster and S. H. Brandes (eds) *Symbol as Sense. New Approaches to the Analysis of Meaning*: 93–102. New York: Academic Press.

Bluedorn, A. C. (1980) "Cutting the Gordian Knot: A Critique of the Effectiveness Tradition in Organizational Research". *Sociology and Social Research*, 64: 477–496.

Bokland, K. (1981) "On the Spatial and Cultural Characteristics of Courtly Romance". In P. V. Zima (ed.) *Semiotics and Dialectics. Ideology and Text*: 387–444. Amsterdam: John Benjamin BV.

Bordt, R. L. (1997) *The Structure of Women's Nonprofit Organizations*. Bloomington: Indiana University Press.

Bourdieu, P. and Wacquant, L. J. D. (1992) *An Invitation to Reflexive Sociology*. Cambridge: Polity Press.

Boyce, M. E. (1996) "Organizational Story and Storytelling: A Critical Review". *Journal of Organizational Change Management*, 9/5: 5–26.

Bramel, D. and Friend, R. (1981) "Hawthorne, The Myth of the Docile Worker, and Class Bias in Psychology". *American Psychologist*, 36: 867–78.

Braverman, H. (1974) *Labor and Monopoly Capital: The Degradation of Work in the Twentieth Century*. New York: Monthly Review Press.

Breeze, J. D. (1985) "Harvest from the Archives: The Search for Fayol and Carlioz". *Journal of Management*, 11: 43–54.

Brodie, M. B. (1967) *Fayol on Administration*. London: Lyon, Grant and Green.

Broms, H. and Gahmberg, H. (1983) "Communication to Self in Organizations and Cultures". *Administrative Science Quarterly*, 28: 482–95.

Brown, R. H. (1977) *A Poetic for Sociology*. Cambridge: Cambridge University Press.

Brumbaugh, R. S. (1984) *Unreality and Time*. Albany: State University of New York Press.

Bruner, J. (1986) *Actual Minds, Possible Worlds*. Cambridge, MA: Harvard University Press.

Brunsson, N. (1985) *The Irrational Organization*. Chichester: Wiley.

Brunsson, N. and Jönsson, S. (1979) *Beslut och handling [Decision and Action]*. Stockholm: Liber.

Buchanan, D. A. and Huczynski, Andrzej, A. (1985) *Organizational Behavior*. Englewood Cliffs, NJ: Prentice-Hall.

Bunge, M. (1974) *Treatise on Basic Philosophy. Vol 1. Semantics I: Sense and Reference*. Boston: Reidel.

—— (1979) *Treatise on Basic Philosophy. Vol 4. Ontology II: A World of Systems*. Dordrecht: Reidel.

Burke, K. (1969) *A Grammar of Motives*. Berkeley: University of California Press.

Burke, W. W. (1998) "The New Agenda for Organization Development". *Organizational Dynamics*, 26/1: 7–20.

Burns, J. M. (1978) *Leadership*. New York: Harper and Row.

Burns, T. and Stalker, G. M. (1961) *The Management of Innovation*. London: Tavistock.

Burrell, G. and Morgan, G. (1979) *Sociological Paradigms and Organisational Analysis*. London: Heinemann.

Cameron, K. S. and Whetten, D. A. (1981) "Perceptions of Organizational Effectiveness over Organizational Life Cycles". *Administrative Science Quarterly*, 26: 525–44.

Campbell, J. P. (1970) *Managerial Behavior, Performance, and Effectiveness*. New York: McGraw-Hill.

—— (1977) "On the Nature of Organizational Effectiveness". In J. M. Pennings and P. S. Goodman (eds) *New Perspectives on Organizational Effectiveness*. San Francisco: Jossey-Bass.

Cannella, A. A. Jr. and Paetzold, R. L. (1994) "Pfeffer's Barriers to the Advance of Organizational Science: A Rejoinder". *Academy of Management Review*, 19/2: 331–41.

Carey, A. (1967) "The Hawthorne Studies: A Radical Criticism". *American Sociological Review*, 32: 403–16.

Carley, K. (1997) "Organizations and constraint-based adaptation". In R. A. Eve, S. Horsfall, and M. E. Lee (eds) *Chaos, Complexity, and Sociology*. Thousand Oaks, CA: Sage.

Casey, C. (1999) " 'Come, join our family': Discipline and Integration in Corporate Organizational Culture". *Human Relations*, 52/2: 155–278.

Carlson, S. (1951) *Exexutive Behavior: A Study of the Work Load and the Working Methods of Managing Directors*. Stockholm: Strömbergs.

Carroll, S. J. and Gillen, D. J. (1987) "Are the Classical Management Functions Useful in Describing Managerial Work?" *The Academy of Management Review*, 12: 38–51.

Checkland, P. B. (1981) *Systems Thinking, Systems Practice*. Chichester: Wiley.

Chia, R. (1997) "Essai: Thirty Years On: From Organizational Structures to the Organization of Thought". *Organization Studies*, 18/4: 685–707.

Child, J. (1972a) "Organizational Structure, Environment, and Performance: The Role of Strategic Choice". *Sociology*, 6: 1–22.

—— (1972b) "Organization Structure and Strategies of Control: A Replication of the Aston Study". *Administrative Science Quarterly*, 17: 163–77.

Christensen, D. (1988) "Mirror, Mission, and Management: Reflections on Folklore and Culture in a Health Care Organization". In Michael Owen Jones, Michael Dane Moore and Richard Christopher Snyder (eds) *Inside Organizations. Understanding the Human Dimension*. Newbury Park, CA: Sage.

Churchman, G. W. (ed.) (1989) *The Well-being of Organizations*. Salinas, CA: Intersystems Publications.

Cilliers, P. (1998) *Complexity and Postmodernism*. London: Routledge

Clarkson, G. P. E (1963) "A Model of Trust Investment Behavior". In R. M. Cyert and J. M. March (eds) *A Behavioral Theory of the Firm*. Englewood Cliffs, NJ: Prentice-Hall.

Clegg, S. R. (1990) *Modern Organizations: Organization Studies in the Postmodern World*. London and Newbury Park, CA: Sage.

Clegg, S. R. and Dunkerley, D. (1980) *Critical Issues in Organizations*. London: Routledge and Kegan Paul.

CNN (1999), interview with Steve Jobs, 21 July.

Coenen, H. G. (1988) "Literarische Rhetorik". *Rhetorik*, 7: 43–62.

Cohen, M. D., March, J. G. and Olsen, J. P. (1972) "A Garbage Can Model of Organizational Choice." *Administrative Science Quarterly*, 17: 1–25.

—— (1976) "People, Problems, Solutions, and the Ambiguity of Relevance". In J. G. March and J. P. Olsen (eds) *Ambiguity and Choice in Organizations*. Bergen: Universitetsforlaget.

Coleridge, S. T. (1930/1808) *Coleridge's Shakespearean Criticism*. Cambridge, MA: Harvard University Press.

Collins, P. D. and Hull, F. (1986) "Technology and Span of Control. Woodward Revisited". *Journal of Management Studies*, 23: 143–64.

Conger, J. A. and Kanungo, R. N. (1987) "Toward a Behavioral Theory of Charismatic Leadership in Organizational Settings". *The Academy of Management Review* **12**: 637–47.

Connolly, T., Conlon, E. J. and Deutsch, S. J. (1980) "Organizational Effectiveness: A Multiple-Constituency Approach". *The Academy of Management Review*, 5: 211–17.

Contractor, N. S. (1998) "Self-organizing systems research in the Social Sciences: Reconciling the metaphors and the Models". Paper presented at a joint session of the Organizational Communication Division and Information Systems Division at the 48th Annual Conference of the International Communication Association, July 8, Jerusalem, Israel. <http://www.tec.spcomm.uiuc.edu/nosh/icasost/nc.html> (12 July 1999).

Conway, E. and McMackin, J. (1997/98) "Developing a Culture for Innovation: What is the Role of the HR System?" *DCUBS Research Papers* 1997–1998, No. 32. <http://www.dcu.ie/business/research_papers/no32.html> (14 October 1999).

Cooper, R. (1993/1990) "Organization/disorganization". In J. Hassard and D. Pym (eds) *The Theory and Philosophy of Organizations. Critical Issues and New Perspectives*. London: Routledge.

Crozier, M. (1964) *The Bureaucratic Phenomenon*. Chicago: University of Chicago Press.

Cyert, R. M. and March, J. M. (1963) *A Behavioral Theory of the Firm*. Englewood Cliffs, NJ: Prentice-Hall.

Czarniawska, B. (1997) *Narrating the Organization*. Chicago: University of Chicago Press.

—— (1999) *Writing Management. Organization Theory as a Literary Genre*. Oxford: Oxford University Press.

Daft, R. L. (1998) *Organization Theory and Design* (6th edn). Cincinnati, OH: South Western College Publishing (1986, 2nd edn).

Dahrendorf, R. (1987) "Max Weber and Modern Social Science". In W. J. Mommsen and J. Osterhammel (eds) *Max Weber and his Contemporaries*. London: Allen and Unwin.

Damblement, G. (1988) "Rhetorik und Textanalyse in französichen Sprachraum". *Rhetorik*, 7: 109–32.

Dandridge, T. C. (1983) "Symbol's Function and Use". In L. R. Pondy, P. J. Frost, G. Morgan and T. C. Dandridge (eds) *Organizational Symbolism*. Greenwich, CT: Jai Press.

Davies, K. (1984) "MTM-X: The Best Thing Since . . . ?" *Work Study*, 33: June, 10–14.

Davies, P. C. W. and Brown, Julian (eds) (1988) *Superstrings. A Theory of Everything?* Cambridge: Cambridge University Press.

Dawes, J. (1999) "The Relationship between Subjective and Objective Company Performance Measures in Market Orientation Research: Further Empirical Evidence". *Marketing Bulletin*, 10: 65–75.

Deal, T. E. and Kennedy, A. A. (1982) *Corporate Cultures: The Rites and Rituals of Corporate Life.* Reading, MA: Addison-Wesley.

DeLamarter, R. T. (1986) *Big Blue. IBM's Use and Disuse of Power.* New York: Dodd.

Deleuze, G. (1986) "Active and Reactive". In D. B. Allison (ed.) *The New Nietzsche.* Cambridge, MA: MIT Press.

Derrida, J. (1973/1967) *Speech and Phenomena.* Evanston: Northwestern University Press.

—— (1976/1967) *Of Grammatology.* Baltimore, MD: Johns Hopkins University Press.

—— (1982/1972) *Margins of Philosophy.* Chicago: University of Chicago Press.

Descartes, R. (1986/1637) *Discourse on Method and the Meditations.* Harmondsworth: Penguin.

Dessler, G. (1986) *Organization Theory: Integrating Structure and Behavior.* Englewood Cliffs, NJ: Prentice-Hall.

DeWitt, R.-L. (1993) "The Structural Consequences of Downsizing". *Organization Science*, 4/1: 30–40.

Donaldson, L. (1976) "Woodward, Technology, Organization Structure and Productivity: A Critique of the Universal Generalization". *Journal of Management Studies*, 13: 255–73.

—— (1985) *In Defense of Organization Theory: A Reply to the Critics.* Cambridge: Cambridge University Press.

—— (1987) "Strategy and Structural Adjustment to Regain Fit and Performance: In Defence of Contingency Theory". *Journal of Management Studies*, 24/1: 1–24.

Dormann, C. and Zapf, D. (1999) *Job Satisfaction.* <http://www.rz.uni-frankfurt.de/FB/fb05/psychologie/Abteil/ABO/2/2.5.e.htm> (2 October 2000).

Douglas, J. D. and Johnson, J. M. (1977, eds) *Existential Sociology.* Cambridge: Cambridge University Press.

Drucker, P. F. (1974) *Management: Tasks, Responsibilities, Practices.* New York: Harper and Row.

—— (1999) "Management's New Paradigms". <http://4bizness.com/toppage1.htm> (2 August 1999).

Duerr, H. P. (1985) *Dreamtime. Concerning the Boundary between Wilderness and Civilization.* Oxford: Basil Blackwell.

Durkheim, É. (1949/1893) *The Division of Labor in Society.* Glencoe, IL: Free Press.

Eccles, R. (1992) *Beyond the Hype.* Cambridge, MA: Harvard Business School Press.

Eco, U. (1972) *La structure absente. Introduction à la recherche sémiologique.* Paris: Mercure de France.

—— (1985) *Semiotics and the Philosophy of Language.* London: Macmillan.

Eden, R. (1987) "Weber and Nietzsche: Questioning the Liberation of Social Science from Historicism". In W. J. Mommsen and J. Osterhammel (eds) *Max Weber and his Contemporaries.* London: Allen and Unwin.

Edwards, R. (1979) *Contested Terrain. The Transformation of the Workplace in the Twentieth Century.* New York: Basic Books.

Eldridge, N. (1986) *Time Frames. The Rethinking of Darwinian Evolution and the Theory of Punctuated Equilibria.* New York: Simon and Schuster.

Eliade, M. (1974a) *The Myth of the Eternal Return or, Cosmos and History.* New York: Princeton University Press.

—— (1974b) *Shamanism. Archaic Techniques of Ecstasy.* New York: Princeton University Press.

—— (1982) *A History of Religious Ideas. 2. From Gautama Buddha to the Triumph of Christianity.* Chicago: University of Chicago Press.

Enderud, H. G. (1977) *Four Faces of Leadership in an Academic Organization.* København: Universitetsførlaget.

Eoyang, C. (1983) "Symbolic Transformation of Belief Systems". In L. R. Pondy, P. J. Frost, G. Morgan and T. C. Dandridge (eds) *Organizational Symbolism.* Greenwich, CT: Jai Press.

Etzioni, A. (1964) *Modern Organizations.* Englewood Cliffs, NJ: Prentice-Hall.

Eve, R., Horsfall, S. and Lee, M. E. (eds) (1997) *Chaos, Complexity, and Sociology.* Thousand Oaks, CA: Sage.

Evered, R. (1983) "The Language of Organizations: The Case of The Navy". In L. R. Pondy, P. J. Frost, G. Morgan and T. C. Dandridge (eds) *Organizational Symbolism.* Greenwich, CT: Jai Press.

Fayol, H. (1917) *Administration industrielle et générale.* Paris: Dunod. (First published in 1916, in Bulletin de Industrie Minérale, 3rd vol.)

—— (1949) *General and Industrial Management* (trans. C. Storrs), London: Pitman.

—— (1988) *General and Industrial Management* (revised by I. Gray), London: Pitman. (First published in 1984 by IEEE.)

Feldman, S. P. (1986) "Management in Context: An Essay on the Relevance of Culture in the Understanding Of Organizational Change". *Academy of Organizational Review*, 23: 587–608.

Feyerabend, P. (1975) *Against Method.* London: New Left Books.

—— (1985) *Problems of Empiricism.* Vol. 2. London: Cambridge University Press.

—— (1988) *Farewell to Reason.* London: Verso.

Fiedler, F. E. (1964) "A Contingency Model of Leadership Effectiveness". In L. Berkowitz (ed.) *Advances in Experimental Social Psychology.* Vol. 1. New York: Academic Press.

Fisher, W. R. (1987) *Human Communication as Narration: Towards a Philosophy of Reason, Value and Action.* Columbia, SC: University of South Carolina Press.

Foerster, H. von (1979) "Cybernetics of Cybernetics". In K. Krippendorff (ed.) *Communication and Control in Society.* New York: Gordon and Breach.

Foucault, M. (1973) *Madness and Civilization. A History of Insanity in the Age of Reason.* New York: Vintage/Random House.

—— (1979) *Discipline and Punish. The Birth of the Prison.* Harmondsworth: Penguin.

Friedman, M. (1953) "The Methodology of Positive Economics". In M. Friedman, *Essays in Positive Economics.* Chicago: University of Chicago Press.

Frost, P. J., Moore, L. F., Louis, M. R., Lundberg, C. C. and Martin, J. (eds) (1985)

Organization Culture. Part 2, "Can Organizational Culture be Managed?" Beverly Hill, CA: Sage.

Fry, L. W. (1982) "Technology-Structure Research: Three Critical Issues". *Academy of Management Journal*, 25: 532–52.

Frye, N. (1973/1957) *The Anatomy of Criticism: Four Essays.* Princeton, NJ: Princeton University Press.

Gabriel, Y. (2000) *Storytelling in Organizations. Facts, Fictions, and Fantasies.* Oxford: Oxford University Press.

Gagliardi, P. (1996) "Exploring the Aesthetic Side of Organizational Life", In S. Clegg, C. Hardy and W. R. Nord (eds), *Handbook of Organization Studies*, London: Sage.

Galtung, J. (1977) *Methodology and Ideology. Theory and Method of Research.* Vol. I. Copenhagen: Christian Ejlers.

Geertz, C. (1973) *The Interpretation of Cultures.* New York: Basic Books.

Gergen, K. J. (1999) "Organizational Science in a Postmodern Context". Draft copy for *Journal of Behavioral Science.* <http://www.swarthmore.edu/SocSci/kgergen1/text10.html> (31 October 1999).

Gerwin, D. (1981) "Relationships between Structure and Technology". In P. C. Nystrom and W. H. Starbuck (eds) *Handbook of Organization Design.* Vol. 2. London: Oxford University Press.

Gilbreth, F. B. and Gilbreth, L. (1916) *Fatigue Study.* New York: Sturgis and Walton.

Gillen, D. J. and Carroll, S. J. (1985) "Relationship of Managerial Ability to Unit Effectiveness in More Organic versus More Mechanistic Departments". *Journal of Management Studies*, 22: 668–76.

Glasersfeld, E. von (1995) *Radical Constructivism: A Way of Knowing and Learning.* London: The Falmer Press.

Glueck, W. F. (1974) "Decision Making: Organization Choice". *Personal Psychology*, 27: 77–93.

Goffee, R. and Scase, R. (1985) "Proprietorial Control in Family Firms: Some Functions of 'Quasi-Organic' Management Systems". *Journal of Management Studies*, 22: 53–68.

Goffman, E. (1975) *Frame Analysis.* Harmondsworth: Penguin.

Goldstein, J. (1994) *The Unshackled Organization: Facing the Challenge of Unpredictability Through Spontaneous Reorganization.* Portland, OR: Productivity Press.

Gottlieb, J. Z. and Sanzgiri, J. (1992) "Philosophic and Pragmatic Influences on the Practice of Organization Development, 1950–2000". *Organizational Dynamics,* 21/2, 57–70.

Gouldner, A. W. (1954) *Patterns of Industrial Bureaucracy.* Glencoe, IL.: Free Press.

—— (1959) "Organizational Analysis". In R. K. Merton (ed.) *Sociology Today*. New York: Basic Books.

Govindarajan, V. (1986) "Decentralization, Strategy, and Effectiveness of Strategic Business Units in Multibusiness Organizations". *Academy of Management Review*, 11: 844–56.

Grant, A. (1983) *Against the Clock. Work Study and Incentive Schemes.* London: Pluto Press.

Green, S. P. and Welsh, M. A. (1988) "Cybernetics and Dependence: Reframing the Control Concept". *The Academy of Management Review*, 13: 287–301.

Gregory, K. L. (1983) "Native-View Paradigms: Multiple Cultures and Culture Conflicts in Organizations". *Administrative Science Quarterly*, 28: 359–76.

Grof, S. (1985) *Beyond the Brain. Birth, Death, and Transcendence in Psychotherapy.* New York: State University of New York Press.

Guerin, M. L. (1997) "Teamwork at Barton Company: A Psychodynamic Perspective". Paper presented at the 1997 Symposium of the International Society for the Psychoanalytic Study of Organizations. <http://www.sba.oakland.edu/ispso/html/1997Guer.htm> (4 October 2000).

Guest, D. E. (1987) "Human Resource Management and Industrial Relations". *Journal of Management Studies*, 24: 503–22.

—— (1997) "Human Resource Management and Performance: A Review and research agenda". *The International Journal of Human Resource Management*, 8/3, 263–76.

Guillén, M. F. (1997) "Scientific Management's Lost Aesthetic: Architecture, Organization, and the Taylorized Beauty of the Mechanical". *Administrative Science Quarterly*, 42: 682–715.

Gulick, L. and Urwick L. (eds) (1972) *Papers on the Science of Administration.* Clifton, NJ: A. M. Kelly.

Haber, S. (1973) *Efficiency and Uplift. Scientific Management in the Progressive Era 1890–1920.* Chicago: University of Chicago Press.

Hall, R. H. (1963) "The Concept of Bureaucracy: An Empirical Assessment". *American Journal of Sociology*, 69: 32–40.

—— (1968) "Professionalization and Bureaucratization". *American Sociological Review*, 33: 92–104.

—— (1980) "An Ineffective Effectiveness Study and Some Suggestions for Further Research". *Sociological Quarterly*, 21: 119–34.

Handy, C. (1976) *Understanding Organisations.* Harmondsworth: Penguin.

Hannan, M. T. and Freeman, J. H. (1977a) "Obstacles to Comparative Studies". In J. M. Pennings, and P. S. Goodman (eds) *New Perspectives on Organizational Effectiveness.* San Francisco: Jossey-Bass.

—— (1977b) "The Population Ecology of Organizations". *American Journal of Sociology*, 82: 929–64.

Hanson, N. R. (1958) *Patterns of Discovery. An Inquiry into the Foundations of Science.* Cambridge: Cambridge University Press.

Hardy, C. (1994) *Managing Strategic Action. Mobilizing Change.* London: Sage.

Harris, C. C. (1980) *Fundamental Concepts and the Sociological Enterprise.* London: Croom Helm.

Hassard, J. (1993/1990) "An Alternative to Paradigm Incommensurability in Organization Theory". In J. Hassard and D. Pym (eds) *The Theory and Philosophy of Organizations. Critical Issues and New Perspectives.* London: Routledge.

Hassard, J. and Pym, D. (eds) (1993/1990) *The Theory and Philosophy of Organizations. Critical Issues and New Perspectives* London: Routledge.

Hawkins, P. (1997) "Organizational Culture: Sailing Between Evangelism and Complexity". *Human Relations*, 50/4: 417–40.

Hegel, G. W. F. (1952/1807) *Phänomenologie des Geistes.* Hamburg: Felix Meiner.

—— (1967/1812) *Wissenschaft der Logik.* 1–2. Hamburg: Felix Meiner.

—— (1971/1840) *Vorlesungen über die Geschichte der Philosophie. III.* Frankfurt am Main: Suhrkamp.

Heidegger, M. (1962/1927) *Being and Time.* Oxford: Blackwell.

—— (1982) *On the Way to Language.* New York: Harper and Row.

—— (1986) "Who is Nietzsche's Zarathustra?" In D. B. Allison (ed.) *The New Nietzsche*. Cambridge, MA: The MIT Press.

Hendriksen, E. S. (1982) *Accounting Theory*. Homewood, IL: Richard D. Irwin.

Hendry, J. (1999) "Cultural Theory and Contemporary Management Organization". *Human Relations*, 52/5: 557–77.

Hickson, D. J., Butler, R. J., Cray, D., Mallory, G. R. and Wilson, D. C. (1986) *Top Decisions: Strategic Decision-Making in Organizations*. San Francisco: Jossey-Bass.

Hofstede, G. (1986) "Editorial: The Usefulness of the 'Organizational Culture' Concept". *Journal of Management Studies:* 253–7.

Honour, H. and Fleming, J. (1991) *A World History of Art*. London: Macmillan.

House, R. J. (1991) "Distribution and Exercise of Power in Mechanistic and Organic Organizations". In H. L. Tosi (ed.) *Organizational Structure, Individual Differences and Management Processes*. Greenwich, CT: Jai Press.

Hunsaker, P. L. and Cook, C. W. (1986) *Managing Organizational Behavior*. Reading, MA: Addison-Wesley.

Hurst, D. (1997) "Expanding the parameters of Organizational Effectiveness". <http://www.fadmin.unb.ca/asb/paper33.htm> (23 October 1999).

Huselid, M.A. and Rau, B. L. (1997) "The Determinants of High Performance Work Systems: Cross-Sectional and Longitudinal Analyses". *Academy of Management Annual Meetings*, Human Resources Management Division.

Iacocca, L. (1984) *Iacocca. An Autobiography*. Toronto: Bantam Books.

Ijiri, Y. (1967) *The Foundations of Accounting Measurement: A Mathematical, Economic, and Behavioral Enquiry*. Englewood Cliffs, NJ: Prentice-Hall.

Introduction to Work Study (1978) Geneva: International Labour Office.

Jacques, E. (1951) *The Changing Culture of a Factory*. London: Tavistock.

Jauch, L. R. and Kraft, K. L. (1986) "Strategic Management of Uncertainty". *The Academy of Management Review*, 11: 777–800.

Jeffcut, P. (1993) "From Interpretation to Representation". In J. Hassard and M. Parker (eds) *Postmodernism in Organisations*. London: Sage.

Jelinek, M., Smircich, L. and Hirsch, P. (1983) "Introduction: A Code of Many Colors". *Administrative Science Quarterly*, 28: 331–8.

Jencks, C. (1984) *The Language of Post-Modern Architecture*. London: Academy Editions.

Jones, G. R. (1983) "Transaction Costs, Property Rights, and Organizational Culture: An Exchange Perspective". *Administrative Science Quarterly*, 28: 454–67.

Jones, M. O., Moore, M. D. and Snyder, R. C. (eds) (1988) *Inside Organizations. Understanding the Human Dimension*. Newbury Park, CA: Sage.

Jones, O. (2000) "Scientific Management, Culture and Control: A First-hand Account of Taylorism in practice". *Human Relations*, 53/5: 631–54.

Jönsson, S. A. and Lundin, R. A. (1977) "Myths and Wishful Thinking as Management Tools". In P. C. Nystrom and W. H. Starbuck (eds) *Prescriptive Models of Organizations*. New York: North-Holland.

Jung, C. G. and Franz, M.L. (eds) (1964) *Man and his Symbols*. New York: Doubleday.

Kahn, R. L. (1977) "Organizational Effectiveness: An Overview." In P. S. Goodman and J. M. Pennings (eds) *New Perspectives on Organizational Effectiveness*. San Francisco: Jossey-Bass.

—— (1982) "Conclusion: Critical Themes in the Study of Change". In P. S. Goodman *et al.*, *Change in Organizations. New Perspectives on Theory, Research, and Practice*. San Francisco: Jossey-Bass.

Kallinikos, J. (1996) *Technology and Society. Interdisciplinary Studies in Formal Organization.* Munich: Accedo.

Kandel, A. (1986) *Fuzzy Mathematical Techniques with Applications.* Reading, MA: Addison Wesley.

Kant, I. (1969/1787) *Critique of Pure Reason.* London: Dent.

Kanter, R. M. and Brinkerhoff, D. (1981) "Organizational Performance: Recent Developments in Measurement". *Annual Review in Sociology*, 7: 321–49.

Käsler, D. (1988) *Max Weber. An Introduction to his Life and Work.* Cambridge: Polity Press.

Katz, D. and Kahn, R. L. (1966) *The Social Psychology of Organizations.* New York: Wiley.

Kaufmann, W. (1974) *Nietzsche. Philosopher, Psychologist, Antichrist.* Princeton, NJ: Princeton University Press.

Kelly, J. E. (1982) *Scientific Management, Job Redesign and Work Performance.* London. Academic Press.

Kemp, P. (1981) *Marxismen i Frankrike. Apropå de "nya filosoferna" och marxismens kris [Marxism in France. A Propos the "New Philosophers" and the Crisis of Marxism].* Stockholm: Liber.

Kerr, S. and Glinow, M. A. von (1997) "The Future of HR: Plus Ça Change, Plus C'est La Même Chose". *Human Resource Management,* 36/1: 115–19.

Kets de Vries, M. F. R. (1980) *Organizational Paradoxes.* London: Tavistock Publications.

Kets de Vries, M. F. R. and Miller, D. (1985) *The Neurotic Organization.* San Francisco: Jossey-Bass.

Khandwalla, P. (1974) "Mass Output Orientation of Operations Technology and Organization Structure". *Administrative Science Quarterly*, 19: 74–97.

Kieser, A. (1997) "Rhetoric and Myth in Management Fashion." *Organization*, 4/2: 49–74.

Kolodny, H., Liu, M., Stymne, B. and Denis, H. (1996) "Technology and the Emerging Organizational Paradigm". *Human Relations*, 49/12: 1457–87.

Kotter, J. (1982) *The General Managers.* New York: Free Press.

Kravetz, D. J. (1988) *The Human Resource Revolution. Implementing Progressive Management Practices for Bottom-Line Success.* San Francisco: Jossey-Bass.

Krupp, S. (1961) *Patterns in Organizational Analysis.* New York: Holt, Rinehart and Winston.

Kuhn, T. S. (1970) *The Structure of Scientific Revolutions* (2nd edn). Chicago: University of Chicago Press.

Kuhnert, K. W. and Lewis, P. (1987) "Transactional and Transformative Leadership: A Constructive/Developmental Analysis". *The Academy of Management Review,* 12: 648–57.

Lakoff, G. and Johnson, M. (1980) *Metaphors We Live By.* Chicago: University of Chicago Press.

Landsberger, H. (1958) *Hawthorne Revisited.* Ithaca, NY: Cornell University Press.

Laudan, L. (1977) *Progress and its Problems. Towards a Theory of Scientific Growth.* London: Routledge.

Lawrence, P. R. (1981) "Organization and Environment Perspective. The Harvard Environment Research Program". In Andrew H. Van de Ven and William F. Joyce (eds) *Perspectives on Organization Design and Behavior.* New York: Wiley.

Lawrence, P. R. and Lorsch, J. W. (1967) *Organization and Environment.* Boston: Harvard University Press.

254   References

Lévi-Strauss, C. (1963) *Structural Anthropology.* New York: Basic Books.
—— (1976) *Structural Anthropology.* Vol. II. New York: Basic Books.
Lincoln, Y. S. and Guba, E. G. (1985) *Naturalistic Inquiry.* Beverly Hills, CA: Sage.
Lingis, A. (1986) "The Will to Power". In D. B. Allison (ed.) *The New Nietzsche.* Cambridge, MA: MIT Press.
London, M. (1988) *Change Agents. New Roles and Innovation Strategies for Human Resource Professionals.* San Francisco: Jossey-Bass.
Louis, M. R. (1987) "Top Decisions: Strategic Decision-Making in Organizations". Review. *Administrative Science Quarterly,* 32: 627–9.
Love, J. F. (1986) *McDonald's: Behind the Arches.* Toronto: Bantam Books.
Luhmann, N. (1990) "The Autopoiesis of Social Systems". In N. Luhmann, *Essays on Self-reference.* New York: Columbia University Press.
—— (1995) *Social Systems.* Stanford, CA: Stanford University Press.
Lundin, R. A. and Sköldberg, K. (1986) *A Bootstrap Theory of Power.* Umeå universitet: FE-publikation.
Lupton, T. (1971) *Management and the Social Sciences.* Harmondsworth: Penguin.
Luthans, F. (1988) "Successful vs. Effective Real Managers". *Academy of Management Executive,* 2/2: 127–32.
Lyotard, J.-F. (1986) *The Post-Modern Condition: A Report on Knowledge.* Manchester: Manchester University Press.
McCloskey, D. (1990) *If You're So Smart. The Narrative of Economic Expertise.* Chicago: University of Chicago Press.
McGregor, D. (1960) *The Human Side of Enterprise.* New York: McGraw-Hill.
MacIntyre, A. (1990/1981) *After Virtue.* London: Duckworth.
McKelvey, B. (1975) "Guidelines for the Empirical Classification of Organizations". *Administrative Science Quarterly,* 20: 509–25.
MacRae, D. (1979) *Weber.* London: Fontana.
Mahoney, T. A. and Weitzel, W. (1969) "Managerial Models of Organizational Effectiveness". *Administrative Science Quarterly,* 14: 357–65.
Månsson, B. and Sköldberg, K. (1980a) *Vision och verklighet. Enhetsstyrelserna i den nya högskolan [Vision and reality. The University and College Boards in the New Higher Education units].* UHÄ-report 1980: 13.
—— (1980b) *Vision och verklighet. Bilder från institutionsnivån i den nya högskolan. [Vision and reality. Pictures from the Departmental Level in the New Higher Education Units].* UHÄ-report 1980: 19.
—— (1983) *Symboliska organisationsmönster [Symbolic Organizational Patterns].* Dissertation. Department of Business Administration. Umeå University.
March, J. G. (1981) "Footnotes to Change". *Administrative Science Quarterly,* 26: 563–77.
March, J. G. and Olsen, J. P. (eds) (1976) *Ambiguity and Choice in Organizations.* Bergen – Oslo – Tromsø: Universitetsforlaget.
March, J. G. and Simon, Herbert A. (1959) *Organizations.* New York: Wiley.
Martin, P. Y. (1980) "Multiple Constituencies, Differential Power, and the Question of Effectiveness in Human Social Organizations". *Journal of Sociology and Social Welfare,* 7: 801–16.
Marx, K. (1961/1867) *Das Kapital. Kritik der Politischen Ökonomie. Erster Band. Buch I. Der Produktionsprozess des Kapitals.* Berlin: Dietz.
—— (1967) *Grundrisse. Texte zu Methode und Praxis. III. Der Mensch in Arbeit und Kooperation.* (Aus den Grundrissen der Kritik der politischen Ökonomie, 1857/58.) Hamburg: Rowohlt.

Marx, K. and Engels, F. (2000/1848) *The Communist Manifesto*. Avalon Project. From the English ed. of 1888, ed. by F. Engels. Transcr. by A. Lutins with assistance from J. Tarzia. <http://www.yale.edu/lawweb/avalon/mancont.htm> (10 November 2000).

—— (1968) *The German Ideology*. Parts I and III. New York: International Publishers.

Masterman, M. (1972) "The Nature of a Paradigm". In Imre Lakatos and Alan Musgrave (eds) *Criticism and the Growth of Knowledge*. London: Cambridge University Press.

Mathews, K. M., White, M. C. and Long, R. G. (1999) "Why Study the Complexity Sciences in the Social Sciences?" *Human Relations,* 52/4: 439–62.

Maturana, H. and Varela, F. (1980) *Autopoiesis and Cognition*. Dordrecht: D. Reidel.

Mayo, E. (1945) *The Social Problems of an Industrial Civilization*. Boston: Harvard University Press.

Mayr, E. (1982) *The Growth of Biological Thought. Diversity, Evolution, and Inheritance*. Cambridge, MA: Harvard University Press.

Mayr, O. (1986) *Authority, Liberty, and Automatic Machinery in Early Modern Europe*. Baltimore: Johns Hopkins University Press.

Merton, R. K. (1959) *Social Theory and Social Structure*. Revised and enlarged edition. Glencoe, IL: Free Press.

Meyer, J. W. and Rowan, B. (1977) "Institutionalized Organizations: Formal Structure as Myth and Ceremony". *American Journal of Sociology*, 83: 340–363.

Meyerson, D. and Martin, J. (1987) "Cultural Change: An Integration of Three Different Views." *Journal of Management Studies*, 24: 623–48.

Miller, D. (1990) *The Icarus Paradox. How Exceptional Companies Bring about their own Downfall: New Lessons in the Dynamics of Corporate Success, Decline, and Renewal*. New York: HarperBusiness.

Miller, D. and Friesen, P. H. (in collaboration with H. Mintzberg) (1984) *Organizations: A Quantum View*. Englewood Cliffs, NJ: Prentice-Hall.

Milliken, F. J. (1987) "Three Types of Perceived Uncertainty about the Environment: State, Effect, and Response Uncertainty". *Academy of Management Review*, 12: 133–43.

Mintzberg, H. (1973) "Strategy Making in Three Modes". *California Management Review*, 24: 44–53.

—— (1979) *The Structuring of Organizations*. Englewood Cliffs, NJ: Prentice-Hall.

—— (1980) *The Nature of Managerial Work*. Englewood Cliffs, NJ: Prentice-Hall.

—— (1983a) *Power in and around Organizations*. Englewood Cliffs, NJ: Prentice-Hall.

—— (1983b) *Structure in Fives*. Englewood Cliffs, NJ: Prentice-Hall.

—— (1984) "A Typology of Organizational Structure". In D. Miller and P. H. Friesen (in collaboration with H. Mintzberg), *Organizations. A Quantum View*. Englewood Cliffs, NJ: Prentice-Hall.

Misumi, J. and Peterson, M. F. (1985) "The Performance-Maintenance (PM) Theory of Leadership: Review of a Japanese Research Program". *Administrative Science Quarterly*, 30: 198–223.

Mitzman, A. (1985) *The Iron Cage. An Historical Interpretation of Max Weber*. New Brunswick, NJ: Transaction Books.

Molnar, J. J. and Rogers, D. L. (1976) "Organizational Effectiveness: An Empirical Comparison of the Goal and System Resource Approach". *Sociological Quarterly*, 17: 401–13.

Mommsen, W. J. (1974) *The Age of Bureaucracy. Perspectives on the Political Sociology of Max Weber*. Oxford: Basil Blackwell.

—— (1987) "Introduction". In W. J. Mommsen and J. Osterhammel (eds) *Max Weber and his Contemporaries*. London: Allen and Unwin.

Mooney, J. D. and Reiley, A. C. (1939) *The Principles of Organization*. New York: Harper.

Morgan, G. (1983) "More on Metaphor: Why We Cannot Control Tropes in Administrative Science". *Administrative Science Quarterly*, 28: 601–7.

Morgan, G. (1986) *Images of Organization*. London: Sage.

—— (1988) *Riding the Waves of Change*. San Francisco: Jossey-Bass.

Morgan, G., Frost, P. J. and Pondy, L. R. (1983) "Organizational Symbolism". In L. R. Pondy, P. J. Frost, G. Morgan and T. C. Dandridge (eds) *Organizational Symbolism*. Greenwich, CT: Jai Press.

Murti, T. R. V. (1980) *The Central Philosophy of Buddhism. A Study of the Madhyamika System*. London: Mandala Books.

Myrdal, G. (1990) *The Political Element in the Development of Economic Theory*. New Brunswick, NJ: Transaction Books.

Nagel, E. (1961) *The Structure of Science*. London: Routledge and Kegan Paul.

Nelson, D. (1980) *Frederick W. Taylor and the Rise of Scientific Management*. Madison: University of Wisconsin Press.

Nelson, D. L. and Quick, J. C. (2000) *Organizational Behavior. Foundations, Realities, and Challenges* (3rd edn). Cincinnati, OH: Thomson Learning.

Nietzsche, F. (1966) *Beyond Good and Evil. Prelude to a Philosophy of the Future*. New York: Vintage Books.

—— (1969) *On the Genealogy of Morals and Ecce Homo*. (ed. W. Kaufmann). New York: Vintage Books.

Nodoushani, O. (1996) "The Problems and Prospects of Post-modern Management Discourse". *Management Learning*, 27/3: 359–81.

O'Connor, E. S. (1999) "The Politics of Management Thought: A Case Study of the Harvard Business School and the Human Relations School". *Academy of Management Review*, 24/9: 117–31.

Ogden, C. K. and Richards, I. A. (1956) *The Meaning of Meaning: A Study of the Influence of Language upon Thought and of the Science of Symbolism*. New York: Harcourt Brace.

Organ, D. (1977) "A Reappraisal and Reinterpretation of the Satisfaction Causes Performance Hypothesis". *Academy of Management Review*, 2: 46–53.

Organization Science (1999), 10/3. "Special Issue: Application of Complexity Theory to Organization Science".

Ouchi, W. G. (1980) "Markets, Bureaucracies, and Clans". *Administrative Science Quarterly*, 25: 129–41.

—— (1981) *Theory Z: How American Business Can Meet the Japanese Challenge*. Reading, MA: Addison-Wesley.

Pareto, W. (1963) *The Mind and Society. A Treatise on General Sociology*. New York: Dover Publications.

Parsons, T. (1947) "Introduction". In M. Weber, *The Theory of Social and Economic Organizations*. Glencoe, IL: Free Press.

—— (1951) *The Social System*. New York: Free Press.

—— (1961) "The Point of View of the Author". In M. Black (ed.) *The Social Theories of Talcott Parsons. A Critical Examination*. Englewood Cliffs, NJ: Prentice-Hall.

Parthasarthy, R. and Prakash S. S. (1993) "Relating Strategy and Structure to Flexible

Automation: A Test of Fit and Performance Implications". *Strategic Management Journal*, 14/7: 529–549.

Pennings, J. M. and Goodman, P. S. (1977) "Toward a Workable Framework". In J. M. Pennings and P. S. Goodman (eds) *New Perspectives on Organizational Effectiveness.* San Francisco: Jossey-Bass.

Pennings, J. M. and Gresov, C. G. (1986) "Technoeconomic and Structural Correlatives of Organizational Culture. An Integrative Framework". *Organization Studies*, 7: 317–34.

Pepper, S. C. (1966) *World Hypotheses: A Study in Evidence.* Berkeley: University of California Press.

Performance Appraisal: Practice, Problems and Issues. Summary (1999) OECD report (PUMA)<http://www.oecd.org/puma/mgmtres/hrm/pubs/per93/summary.htm> (23 October 1999).

Perrow, C. (1981) "Markets, Hierarchies, and Hegemony". In A. Van de Ven and W. F. Joyce (eds) *Perspectives on Organization Design and Behavior.* New York: Wiley.

—— (1986) *Complex Organizations: A Critical Essay.* New York: Random House.

—— (1994) "Pfeffer slips!" *Academy of Management Review*, 19/2: 191–4.

Peters, T. J. and Waterman, R. H. (1982) *In Search of Excellence.* New York: Harper and Row.

Pettigrew, A. (1979) "On Studying Organizational Cultures". *Administrative Science Quarterly*, 24: 570–81.

Pfeffer, J. (1981) *Power in Organizations.* Marshfield, MA: Pitman.

—— (1993) "Barriers to the Advance of Organizational Science: Paradigm Development as a Dependent Variable". *Academy of Management Review*, 18/4: 599–620.

—— (1997) "Pitfalls on the Road to Measurement: The Dangerous Liaison of Human Resources sith the Ideas of Accounting and Finance". *Human Resource Management,* 36/3: 357–65.

Pfeffer, J. and Salancik, G. R. (1978) *The External Control of Organizations: A Resource Dependence Perspective.* New York: Harper and Row.

Pondy, L. R. (1983) "The Role of Metaphors and Myths in Organization". In L. R. Pondy, P. J. Frost, G. Morgan and T. Dandridge (eds) *Organizational Symbolism: Monographs in Organizational and Industrial Relations,* Vol. 1. Greenwich, CT: Jai Press.

Pondy, L. R. and Mitroff, I. I. (1979) "Beyond Open System Models of Organizations". In B. M. Staw (ed.) *Research in Organizational Behavior.* Vol I. Greenwich, CT: Jai Press.

Popper, K. R. (1981) *Conjectures and Refutations. The Growth Of Scientific Knowledge.* London: Routledge and Kegan Paul.

Porter, L. W. and Lawler, E. E. (1968) *Managerial Attitudes and Performance.* Homewood, IL: Richard D. Irwin.

Prigogine, I. and Stengers, I. (1984) *Order out of Chaos.* New York: Bantam.

Pugh, D. S. and Hickson, D. J. (1979) *Organizational Structure in Context.* Westmead, Farnborough, Hants: Saxon House.

Quinn, R. E. and Rohrbaugh, J. (1983) "A Spatial Model of Effectiveness Criteria: Toward a Competing Values Approach to Organizational Analysis". *Management Science,* 29: 363–77.

Radnitzky, G. (1968) *Contemporary Schools of Meta-Science.* Göteborg: Akademiförlaget.

Rajchman, J. and West, C. (eds) (1985) *Post-Analytic Philosophy.* New York: Columbia University Press.

Ramirez, R. (1988) *Towards an Aesthetic Theory of Social Organization.* Dissertation. (facsimile). Ann Arbor: UMI Dissertation Information Service.

Rapoport, A. (1969) "Mathematical Aspects of General Systems Analysis". In J. A. Litterer (ed.) *Organizations: Systems, Control and Adaptation.* Vol II. New York: Wiley.

Reimann, R. C. (1977) "Dimensions of Organizational Technology and Structure". *Human Relations*, 30: 545–66.

—— (1980) "Organization Structure and Technology in Manufacturing System Versus Workflow Level Perspectives". *Academy of Management Journal*, 23: 61–77.

Ricoeur, P. (1984a) *Hermeneutics and the Human Sciences.* Cambridge: Cambridge University Press.

—— (1984b) *Time and Narrative.* Vol 1. Chicago: University of Chicago Press.

—— (1985) *Time and Narrative.* Vol 2. Chicago: University of Chicago Press.

—— (1988) *Time and Narrative.* Vol 3. Chicago: University of Chicago Press.

Riley, P. (1983) "A Structurationist Account of Political Cultures". *Administrative Science Quarterly*, 28: 414–27.

Robbins, S. P. (2000) *Essentials of Organizational Behavior* (6th edn). Upper Saddle River, NJ: Prentice-Hall.

Roethlisberger, F. J. (1941) *Management and Morale.* Cambridge, MA: Harvard University Press.

Roethlisberger, F. J. and Dickson, William J. (1943) *Management and the Worker.* Cambridge, MA: Harvard University Press.

Rowlinson, M. and Procter S. (1999) "Organizational Culture and Business History". *Organization Studies*, 20/3: 369–96.

Russell, B. (1975) *History of Western Philosophy and its Connection with Political and Social Circumstances from the Earliest Time to the Present Day.* London: Allen and Unwin.

Samuelson, P. A. (1964) *Economics.* New York: McGraw-Hill.

Sartori, G. (1984) "Guidelines for Conceptual Analysis". In G. Sartori (ed.) *Social Science Concepts: A Systematic Analysis.* Beverly Hills, CA: Sage Publications.

Schluchter, W. (1981) *The Rise of Western Capitalism. Max Weber's Developmental History.* Berkeley: University of California Press.

SCOS Proceedings (1986) The International Conference on Organization Symbolism and Corporate Culture. On the theme: Cultural Engineering: The Evidence for and Against. Vol 1–2. Montreal, 25–27 June.

Scott, W. R. (1987) *Organizations. Rational, Natural, and Open Systems* (2nd edn). Englewood Cliffs, NJ: Prentice-Hall.

Sculley, J. (1987) *Odyssey. From Pepsi to Apple.* London: Collins.

Selznick, P. (1949) *TVA and the Grass Roots.* Berkeley: University of California Press.

—— (1957) *Leadership in Administration.* New York: Harper and Row.

Senge, P. (1990) *The Fifth Discipline: The Art and Practice of the Learning Organization.* New York: Doubleday Currency.

Senior, B. (1997) *Organizational Change.* Pitman: London.

Shannon, C. E. and Weaver, W. (1959) *The Mathematical Theory of Communication.* Urbana, IL: University of Illinois Press.

Shepard, J. (1971) "On Alex Carey's Radical Criticism of the Hawthorne Studies". *Academy of Management Journal*, 14: 23–31.

SHRM at a glance (1999) <http://www.shrm.org/press/history.html> (14 October 1999).

Shukman, A. (1981) "The Dialectics of Change: Culture, Codes, and the Individual". In P. V. Zima (ed.) *Semiotics and Dialectics. Ideology and the Text*. Amsterdam: John Benjamin BV.

Siegel, H. (1987) *Relativism Refuted. A Critique of Contemporary Epistemological Relativism*. Dordrecht: Reidel

Silverman, D. (1970) *The Theory of Organizations: A Sociological Framework*. London: Heinemann.

Simon, H. A. (1957a) *Administrative Behavior: A Study of Decision-Making Processes in Administrative Organization*. (2nd edn, with new Intro.) New York: Macmillan. (1st edn 1947. Prel. version 1945.)

—— (1957b) *Leadership in Administration*. Evanston, IL: Row, Peterson.

—— (1964) "On the Concept of Organizational Goal". *Administrative Science Quarterly*, 9: 1–22.

—— (1988) "Making Management Decisions: The Role of Intuition and Emotion". *The Academy of Management Executive*, 1: 57–64.

Sköldberg, K. (1984) *Maktens mekanismer. En diskussion om klassiska och icke-klassiska maktbegrepp och -strategier i organisationsanalys [The Mechanisms of Power. A Discussion of Classical and Non-classical Concepts and Strategies of Power in Organizational Analysis]*. FE-report, 1984: 61. Department of Business Administration. Umeå University.

—— (1986) "Organizational Change as Displacement of Problems". *Scandinavian Journal of Management Studies*, 2: 231–50.

—— (1987) "Den motsatta kulturen." *Ledelse og Erhvervsøkonomi*, 1: 11–25.

—— (1991) *Reformer på vridscen. Organisationsförändringar i kommun och landsting [Reforms on a Revolving Stage. Organizational Change in Local Government]*. Lund: Studentlitteratur.

—— (1994) "Tales of Change. Public Administration Reform and Narrative Mode". *Organization Science*, 5/2: 219–38.

—— (2001) *Tracks and Frames. The Economy of Symbolic Forms in Organizations*. London: Elsevier.

Smircich, L. (1983a) "Concepts of Culture and Organizational Analysis". *Administrative Science Quarterly*, 28: 339–58.

—— (1983b) "Organizations as Shared Meanings". In L. R. Pondy, P. J. Frost, G. Morgan and T. C. Dandridge (eds) *Organizational Symbolism*. Greenwich, CT: Jai Press.

Smith, K. K. and Simmons, V. M. (1983) "A Rumpelstitskin Organization: Metaphors on Metaphors in Field Research". *Administrative Science Quarterly*, 28: 377–92.

Soelberg, P. (1966) "Unprogrammed Decision Making". In *Papers and Proceedings*, 26th Annual Meeting: 3–16.

Sorel, G. (1999/1908) *Reflections on Violence* (ed. by J. Jennings). Cambridge: Cambridge University Press

Spencer, H. (1966) *The Study of Sociology*. Ann Arbor: University of Michigan Press.

Spender, J.-C. (1999) "Pluralist Epistemology and the Knowledge-Based Theory of the Firm". <http://iris.nyit.edu/~spender/text/Plurorg326.htm> (2 August 1999).

Srole, L. (1956) "Social Integration and Certain Corollaries: Eunomia and Anomia". *American Sociological Review*, 21: 709–16.

Stacey, R. D. (1996) *Complexity and Creativity in Organizations.* San Francisco: Berrett-Koehler.

Starbuck, W. H. (1965) "Organizational Growth and Development". In J. G. March (ed.) *Handbook of Organizations.* Chicago: Rand McNally.

—— (1983) "Organizations as Action Generators." *American Sociological Review,* 48/1: 3–27.

Staw, B. M., Sandelands, L. E. and Dutton, J. E. (1981) "Threat-rigidity effects in Organizational Behavior: A Multilevel Analysis." *Administrative Science Quarterly,* 26: 501–24.

Steers, R. M. (1975) "Problems in the Measurement of Organizational Effectiveness". *Administrative Science Quarterly,* 20: 546–58.

Steffy, B. D. and Grimes, A. J. (1986) "A Critical Theory of Organization Science". *Academy of Management Review,* 11: 322–36.

Steffy, B. D. and Maurer, Steven D. (1988) "Conceptualizing and Measuring the Economic Effectiveness of Human Resource Activities". *Academy of Management Review,* 13: 271–86.

Stern, F. (ed.) (1970) *The Varieties of History from Voltaire to the Present.* London: Macmillan.

Stern, S. (1988) "Symbolic Representation of Organizational Identity: The Role of Emblem at the Garrett Corporation". In M. O. Jones, M. D. Moore and R. C. Snyder (eds) *Inside Organizations. Understanding the Human Dimension.* Newbury Park, CA: Sage.

Stigler, G. J. (1949) *The Theory of Price.* London: Macmillan.

Storing, H. J. (1962) "The Science of Administration: H. A. Simon". In H. J. Storing (ed.) *Essays on the Scientific Study of Politics.* New York: Holt, Rinehart and Winston.

Strati, A. (1999) *Organization and Aesthetics,* London: Sage.

Stupak, R. J. (1998) "Symposium on Organizational Culture: Theory, Practice, and Cases". *Public Administration and Management: An Interactive Journal,* 3/3. <http://www.pamij.com/stupintro2.html> (31 October 1999).

Stymne, B. (1970) *Values and Processes. A Systems Study of Effectiveness in Three Organizations.* Diss. Lund: Studentlitteratur.

Sugarman, B. (1999) "Notes Towards a Closer Collaboration Between Organization Theory, Learning Organizations and Organizational Learning in the Search for a New Paradigm". *The Society for Organizational Learning.* <http://www.sol-ne.org/res/kr/Sugarman.html#part2_classical> (31 October 1999).

Suppe, F. (ed.) (1977) *The Structure of Scientific Theories.* Urbana: University of Illinois Press.

Svenska Dagbladet (23 October 1999).

Sztompka, P. (1974) *System and Function. Toward a Theory of Society.* New York: Academic Press.

Takahashi, N. (1997) "A Single Garbage Can Model and the Degree of Anarchy in Japanese Firms". *Human Relations,* 50/1: 417–40.

Taylor, C. (1986) *Hegel.* Stockholm: Symposion.

Taylor, F. W. (1947) *Scientific Management.* New York: Harper.

—— (1947a) "Shop Management". In F. W. Taylor, *Scientific Management.* New York: Harper.

—— (1947b) "Principles of Scientific Management". In F. W. Taylor, *Scientific Management.* New York: Harper.

—— (1947c) "Testimony before the Special House Committee". In F. W. Taylor, *Scientific Management*. New York: Harper.

Thompson, J. D. (1967) *Organisations in Action*. New York: McGraw-Hill.

Thompson, J. D. and Tuden, A. (1963) "Strategies, Structures, and Processes of Organizational Decision". In J. D. Thompson, P. B. Hammond, R. W. Hawkes, B. H. Junker and A Tuden (eds) *Comparative Studies in Administration*. Pittsburg: University of Pittsburg Press.

Toennies, F. (1957) *Community and Society*. East Lansing, MI: Michigan State University Press.

Toulmin, S. (1977) *Human Understanding*. Princeton, NJ: Princeton University Press.

Turner, B. (1971) *Exploring the Industrial Subculture*. London: Macmillan.

Turner, B. S. (1992) *Max Weber: From History to Modernity*. London: Routledge.

"Two Part Symposium on on Organizational Culture: Theory, Practice, and Cases". (1998) *Public Administration and Management: An Interactive Journal* 3/2,3. <http://www.pamij.com/> (29 October 1999).

Udy, S. H., Jr. (1959) "'Bureaucracy' and 'Rationality' in Weber's Organization Theory". *American Sociological Review*, 24: 791–5.

Ulrich, D. (1997) "HR of the Future: Conclusions and Observations". *Human Resource Management,* 36/1: 175–9.

Venkatraman, N. and Ramanujam, V. (1986) "Measurement of Business Performance in Strategy Research: A Comparison of Approaches". *Academy of Management Review*, 11: 801–14.

Vico, G. (1963/1744) *The New Science*. Ithaca, NY: Cornell University Press.

Warnecke, H. J. (1993) *The Fractal Company: A Revolution in Corporate Culture*. Berlin: Springer.

Weber, M. (1975) *Max Weber: A Biography*. New York: Wiley.

—— (1947) *The Theory of Social and Economic Organization* (ed. by T. Parsons; trans. by A. M. Henderson and T. Parsons). New York: Oxford University Press.

—— (1968) *Economy and Society: An Outline of Interpretive Sociology* (ed. by G. Roth and C. Wittich; trans. by E. Fischoff) Vols 1–3. New York: Bedminster Press.

—— (1972) *Wirtschaft und Gesellschaft. Grundriss der Verstehenden Soziologie*. Tübingen: J. C. B. Mohr.

—— (1951/1922) *Gesammelte Aufsätze zur Wissenschaftslehre*. Tübingen: J. C. B. Mohr.

—— (1948) *From Max Weber: Essays in Sociology*. (ed. H. H. Girth and C. W. Mills.) London: Routledge and Kegan Paul.

Weick, K. E. (1976) "Educational Organizations as Loosely-Coupled Systems". *Administrative Science Quarterly*, 1976, 21: 1–19.

—— (1979) *The Social Psychology of Organizing* (2nd edn). Reading, MA: Addison-Wesley.

—— (1982) "Management of Organizational Change Among Loosely Coupled Elements". In P. E. Goodman *et al.*, *Change in Organizations. New Perspectives on Theory, Research, and Practice*: 375–408. San Francisco: Jossey-Bass.

Weingartner, P. (1982) "A New Theory of Intension". In J. Agassi and R. S. Cohen, (eds) *Scientific Philosophy Today*. Dordrecht: Reidel.

Weiss, R. M. (1983) "Weber on Bureaucracy: Management Consultant or Political Theorist?" *Academy of Management Review*, 8: 242–8.

Wells, P. A. (1988) "The Paradox of Functional Dysfunction in a Girl-Scout Camp: Implications of Cultural Diversity for Achieving Organizational Goals". In M. O.

Jones, M. D. Moore and R. Christopher Snyder (eds) *Inside Organizations. Understanding the Human Dimension*. Newbury Park, CA: Sage.

Westerlund, G. and Sjöstrand, S. E. (1979) *Organizational Myths*. New York: Harper and Row.

Wheatley, M. J. (1992) *Leadership and the New Science: Learning about Organization from an Orderly Universe*. San Francisco: Berrett-Koehler.

White, H. (1985a) *Metahistory: The Historical Imagination in Nineteenth-Century Europe*. Baltimore: Johns Hopkins University Press.

—— (1985b) *Tropics of Discourse. Essays in Cultural Criticism*. Baltimore: Johns Hopkins University Press.

Whittaker, R. (1999) *Encyclopaedia Autopoetica. An Annotated Lexical Compendium on Autopoiesis and Enaction.* <http://www.informatik.umu.se/~rwhit/EAIntro.html> (12 July 1999).

Wiener, N. (1948) *Cybernetics or Control and Communication in the Animal and the Machine.* Cambridge, MA: Technology Press.

Wilber, K. (ed.) (1982) *The Holographic Paradigm and Other Paradoxes*. Boulder, CO: Shambala Publications.

Wilkins, A. L. and Ouchi, W. G. (1983) "Efficient Cultures: Exploring the Relationship Between Culture and Organizational Performance". *Administrative Science Quarterly*, 28: 468–81.

Williamson, O. E. (1975) *Markets and Hierarchies: Analysis and Antitrust Implications*. New York: Free Press.

—— (1985) *The Economic Institutions of Capitalism: Firms, Markets, Relational Contracting*. New York: Free Press.

Wilson, D. C. (1992) *A Strategy of Change*. New York: Routledge.

Wilson, W. A. (1988) "Dealing with Organizational Stress: Lessons from the Folklore of Mormon Missionaries". In M. O. Jones, M. D. Moore and R. Christopher Snyder (eds) *Inside Organizations. Understanding the Human Dimension*. Newbury Park, CA: Sage.

Wittgenstein, L. (1953) *Philosophical Investigations*. London: Blackwell.

Wood, D. (1988) "Nietzsche's Transvaluation of Time". In *Exceedingly Nietzsche. Aspects of Contemporary Nietzsche-Interpretation*. London: Routledge.

Woodward, J. (1965) *Industrial Organization: Theory and Practice*. New York: Oxford University Press.

Worthy, J. C. (1950) "Organizational Structure and Employee Morale". *American Sociological Review*, 15: 169–79.

Wright, G. H. von (1971) *Explanation and Understanding*. Ithaca, NY: Cornell University Press.

Young, R. M. (1990) "Scientism in the History of Management Theory". *Science as Culture*, 8: 118–43.

Yuchtman, E., and Seashore, S. E. (1967) "A System Resources Approach to Organizational Effectiveness". *American Sociological Review*, 32: 891–903.

Zanzi, A. (1987) "How Organic is Your Organization? Determinants of Organic/Mechanistic Tendencies in a Public Accounting Firm". *Journal of Management Studies*, 24: 125–42.

Zeitz, G. (1980) "Interorganizational Dialectics". *Administrative Science Quarterly*, 25: 72–88.

Subject index

Name index

Abravanel, H. 170
Aristotle 38, 117–18, 206
Ashby, W. R. 120
Aston school 10, 85, 108, 137–8, 149

Bakunin, M. 69–70, 218n97
Barnard, C. 78, 81, 83, 89
Beethoven, L. van 178
Bergson, H. 119
Bertalanffy, L. von 119, 120, 121
Blau, P. M. 122, 147
Bluedorn, A. C. 181
Bonnier, A. 201
Bordt, R. L. 108
Boulding, K. 120
Bourdieu, P. 30
Bower, M. 157
Brinkerhoff, D. 182
Brumbaugh, R. S. 32
Bunge, M. 121
Burns, T. 153; Comedy 116, 117, 137;
  contingency theory 123–31, 137, 141;
  innovation study 85, 108;
  mechanistic/organic organizations
  132, 136, 150; organizational drama
  10; poetics 147–8

Cameron, K. S. 85, 108
Cannon, W. B. 119
Child, J. 10, 138–9, 149
Copernicus, N. 118
Crozier, M. 122–3, 147
Cyert, R. M. 10, 85, 140, 149, 185

Dandridge, T. C. 164
Deal, T. E. 154, 157, 159, 164, 168–9
Derrida, J. 13, 26, 31, 33
Descartes, R. 56

Dessler, G. 15
Dickson, W. J. 90, 106, 112, 114, 115,
  129
Driesch, H. A. E. 119
Drucker, P. 54–5
Durkheim, É. 99, 119

Enderud, H. G. 85
Engels, F. 34
Eoyang, C. 164
Evered, R. 167

Fayol, H. 17; administration 8, 39;
  concrete organizations 86–7;
  machine metaphor 22; Scientism 9;
  top management 55–61; translations
  216n47, n48; unity of command 52
Feyerabend, P. 20–1, v
Ford, E. 174
Ford, H. 174, 184–5, 200, 202
Ford, H. II 200, 201
Foucault, M. 3
Fowles, J. 177
Freud, S. 128
Friedman, M. 185
Friesen, P. H. 85, 108, 144, 145
Frye, N. 50, 140, xiv

Galileo G. 118
Geertz, C. 129, 155–6, 157, 178
Gerard, R. 120
Gilbreth, F. B. 92, 93, 215–16n32
Gouldner, A. W. 122, 147
Gregory, K. L. 159
Gulick, L. 61

Hadrian, Emperor 24
Handy, C. 153